Guide to

Firewalls and Network Security: with Intrusion Detection and VPNs

Greg Holden

THOMSON
COURSE TECHNOLOGY

Australia • Canada • Mexico • Singapore • Spain • United Kingdom • United States

THOMSON

COURSE TECHNOLOGY

Guide to Firewalls and Network Security: with Intrusion Detection and VPNs

By Greg Holden

Senior Editor:
William Pitkin III

Senior Product Manager:
Laura Hildebrand

Production Editor:
Brooke Booth

Development Editor:
Jill Batistick

Technical Reviewers:
Eileen Vidrine, Dave DiFabio,
Rob Andrews, Gary Sparks,
Jeffrey Monts

Quality Assurance Manager:
John Bosco

MQA Project Leader:
Nicole Ashton

Associate Product Manager:
Tim Gleeson

Editorial Assistant:
Nick Lombardi

Marketing Manager:
Jason Sakos

Text Designer:
GEX Publishing Services

Compositor:
GEX Publishing Services

Cover Design:
Julie Malone

BRIEF

Contents

TABLE OF

Contents

CHAPTER THREE
Firewall Configuration Strategies   61

CHAPTER FOUR
Packet Filtering   101

CHAPTER FIVE
Working with Proxy Servers and Application-Level Firewalls   135

CHAPTER EIGHT
Choosing a Bastion Host   **243**

CHAPTER NINE
Setting Up a Virtual Private Network   **277**

Introduction

This book is intended to provide an introduction to firewalls and other network security components that can work together to create an in-depth defensive perimeter around a Local Area Network (LAN). Firewalls are among the best-known security tools in use today, and they are growing in popularity among the general public as well as Information Technology professionals. However, firewalls work most effectively when they are backed by a security policy and when they work in consort with anti-virus software, intrusion detection systems, and other tools.

Accordingly, this book examines firewalls in context with the other elements needed for effective perimeter security as well as security within a network. These include packet filtering, authentication, proxy servers, encryption, bastion hosts, virtual private networks (VPNs), log file maintenance, and intrusion detection systems.

Where Should You Start?

This book is not intended to be read in sequence, from beginning to end. The first three chapters, however, do provide you with a solid introduction to firewalls and where they fit in a network security program, so it's highly recommended that you start with them. The chapters are as follows:

Chapter 1, "Firewall Planning and Design," provides you with an overview of the different kinds of firewalls and their primary functions, so you can choose the right one to meet your needs.

Chapter 2, "Developing a Security Policy," helps you coordinate the goals of a firewall with the goals of an organization's overall security policy. You also learn how to work with administration in a step-by-step way to make sure your security policy works. **Chapter 3**, "Firewall Configuration Strategies," introduces you to the different approaches you can take to locating one or more firewalls on your network perimeter and coordinating them to work with other components such as DMZs, routers, and VPNs.

The next several chapters discuss specific topics important to firewalls and network security. You are encouraged to read the chapters that have the most immediate interest to you rather than feeling you have to read them in a linear fashion. **Chapter 4**, "Packet

Filtering," explores the first, and in some ways, the most fundamental activities of firewalls. Both stateless and stateful packet filtering are examined, as well as the establishment of a packet filtering rule base for common protocols such as ICMP, TCP, and UDP. **Chapter 5**, "Working with Proxy Servers and Application-Level Firewalls," discusses how proxy servers work to shield individual hosts on the internal network by acting on their behalf. **Chapter 6**, "Authenticating Users," describes why firewalls do authentication and how they are able to identify authorized individuals through user, client, and session authentication, as well as through centralized authentication systems and one-time password systems. **Chapter 7**, "Encryption and Firewalls," focuses on the role encryption plays in firewall architecture, and the establishment of a Public Key Infrastructure (PKI) for a network. **Chapter 8**, "Choosing a Bastion Host," explains how to secure the host computers that run firewall or intrusion detection software or that provide public services on the DMZ.

The book's last three chapters delve into more advanced topics and focus on a survey of popular firewall and VPN options. **Chapter 9**, "Setting Up a Virtual Private Network," discusses the establishment of VPNs, which provide corporations with a cost-effective means for conducting secure communications over the public Internet. Because VPNs use encryption and authentication, it's a good idea to read Chapters 6 and 7 before you get to this chapter. **Chapter 10**, "Building Your Own Firewall," teaches you about the two categories of firewalls and explains how desktop and enterprise firewalls work. **Chapter 11**, "Ongoing Administration," talks about the various periodic maintenance tasks you need to perform when administering a firewall, including log file rotation and examination. It also delves into the integration of anti-virus and intrusion detection systems with firewalls.

Readers are also encouraged to investigate the many pointers to online and printed sources of additional information that are cited throughout this book.

Features

To aid you in fully understanding networking concepts, there are many features in this book designed to improve its pedagogical value.

- **Chapter Objectives:** Each chapter in this book begins with a detailed list of the concepts to be mastered within that chapter. This list provides you with a quick reference to the contents of that chapter, as well as a useful study aid.

- **Illustrations, Tables, and Screenshots:** Numerous illustrations of networking configurations aid you in the visualization of common firewall setups and architectures. In addition, many tables provide details and comparisons using both practical and theoretical information. Some tables provide specific examples of packet filtering rules you can use to build a firewall rule base. Because most campus laboratories use Microsoft operating systems, we use their products for screen shots and Hands-on Projects for this book.

- **Chapter Summaries**: Each chapter's text is followed by a summary of the concepts it has introduced. These summaries provide a helpful way to recap and revisit the ideas covered in each chapter.

- **Key Terms**: Following the Chapter Summary, a list of new networking terms and their definitions encourages proper understanding of the chapter's key concepts and provides a useful reference.

- **Review Questions**: End-of-chapter assessment begins with a set of review questions that reinforce the ideas introduced in each chapter. These questions ensure that you have mastered the concepts.

- **Hands-on Projects**: Although it is important to understand the theory behind networking technology, nothing can improve upon real-world experience. With the exceptions of those chapters that are purely theoretical, each chapter provides a series of exercises aimed at providing students with hands-on implementation experience.

- **Case Projects**: Finally, each chapter closes with a section that proposes certain firewall and security-related situations. You are asked to evaluate the situation and decide upon the course of action to be taken to remedy the problems described. This valuable tool will help you to sharpen decision-making and troubleshooting skills—important aspects of firewall and security systems administration.

Text and Graphic Conventions

Wherever appropriate, additional information and exercises have been added to this book to help you better understand what is being discussed in the chapter. Icons throughout the text alert you to additional materials. The icons used in this textbook are described below.

Notes present additional helpful material related to the subject being described.

Tips highlight suggestions on ways to attack problems you may encounter in a real-world situation. As an experienced network administrator, the author has practical experience with how networks work in real business situations.

Hands-on Project icons precede each hands-on activity in this book.

Case Project icons are located at the end of each chapter. They mark more involved, scenario-based projects. In this extensive case example, you are asked to independently implement what you have learned.

Endmatter

In addition to its core materials, this book includes several appendices.

- **Appendix A**: **Security Resources:** This appendix provides suggestions of places you can go online to find the latest security-related information. You get descriptions of well-known and highly regarded Web sites that provide background information on network security as well as virus alerts, port scanners that can test your existing security configuration, and places where you can go to obtain certifications that can help you find employment in a network security field.

- **Glossary:** This is a complete compendium of all of the acronyms and technical terms used in this book, with definitions.

Instructor's Materials

The following supplemental materials are available when this book is used in a classroom setting. All of the supplements available with this book are provided to the instructor on a single CD-ROM.

Electronic Instructor's Manual. The Instructor's Manual that accompanies this textbook includes additional instructional material to assist in class preparation, including suggestions for classroom activities, discussion topics, and additional projects.

Solution Files. The Solution Files include answers to all end-of-chapter materials, including the Review Questions, and when applicable, Hands-on Projects, and Case Projects.

ExamView®. This textbook is accompanied by ExamView, a powerful testing software package that allows instructors to create and administer printed, computer (LAN-based), and Internet exams. ExamView includes hundreds of questions that correspond to the topics covered in this text, enabling students to generate detailed study guides that include page references for further review. The computer-based and Internet testing components allow students to take exams at their computers, and also save the instructor time by grading each exam automatically.

PowerPoint presentations. This book comes with Microsoft PowerPoint slides for each chapter. These are included as a teaching aid for classroom presentation, to make available to students on the network for chapter review, or to be printed for classroom distribution. Instructors, please feel at liberty to add your own slides for additional topics you introduce to the class.

Figure Files. All of the figures in the book are reproduced on the Instructor's Resource CD in bit-mapped format. Similar to the PowerPoint presentations, these are included as a teaching aid for classroom presentation, to make available to students for review, or to be printed for classroom distribution.

Coping with Change on the Web

Sooner or later, all the specific Web-based resources mentioned throughout the rest of this book will go stale or be replaced by newer information. In some cases, the URLs you find here may lead you to their replacements; in other cases, the URLs will lead nowhere, leaving you with the dreaded 404 error message, "File not found."

When that happens, please don't give up! There's always a way to find what you want on the Web, if you're willing to invest some time and energy. To begin with, most large or complex Web sites offer a search engine. As long as you can get to the site itself, you can use this tool to help you find what you need.

Don't be afraid to use general search tools like *http://www.google.com*, *http://www.hotbot.com*, or *http://www.excite.com* to find related information. Although certain standards bodies may offer the most precise and specific information about their standards online, there are plenty of third-party sources of information, training, and assistance in this area as well. The bottom line is: if you can't find something where the book says it lives, start looking around. It's got to be around there, somewhere!

Visit our World Wide Web Site

Additional materials designed especially for you might be available for your course on the World Wide Web. Go to *www.course.com* and search for this book title periodically for more details.

Acknowledgments

I would like to thank the team at Course Technology for the opportunity to write this book on a topic of such value and interest. This team includes but is not limited to Laura Hildebrand, Product Manager, Brooke Booth, Production Editor, and the excellent work of the copy editors and quality assurance folks. Thanks also to Jill Batistick, Development Editor, for her always-excellent edits, her words of encouragement, and her periodic reminders that kept me on track. I would also like to thank the reviewers, who guided me with excellent and helpful feedback on each chapter. I would also like to thank Mark Ciampa, who is a great author, for helping us make changes to the book in the final stages of production. A special thanks goes to my best friend Ann Lindner and to my daughters Lucy and Zosia, whose patience and support made this project successful.

Read This Before You Begin

This book contains more than 70 hands-on projects, many of which require you to install and use different security-related software programs. You need to have access to a computer that is connected to the Internet and that can run those programs. The suggested hardware and software requirements are described below.

Hardware Requirements

Your computer's CPU should be at least a Pentium II and running at 300MHz or faster. To run Web browsers, word processing programs, and other applications at the same time, you should have at least 192MB of RAM (ideally, 256MB or more of RAM) and a minimum of 75MB of available hard disk space.

Software Requirements

Most of the projects in this book can be completed using a computer that runs Windows 2000 or XP or Red Hat Linux 7.3 or later.

Many of the programs used for the Hands-on Projects require you to download and install software. At the very least, your computer should be equipped with a Web browser and the archiving utility WinZip (available at *www.winzip.com*). You'll also need a word processing program or text editor to record answers from the Hands-on Projects. An e-mail application such as Outlook Express or Netscape Messenger is used in several of the projects as well.

Special Requirements

In this book, you will find references to Check Point NG. If you have the software, note that you will need to have a minimum of 128 MB of RAM on your system to run it. Note also that Check Point NG is designed to run on Windows 2000; it will run with limited functionality on Windows XP.

Free Downloadable Software Is Required in the Following Chapters:

Chapter 3:

- Sygate Personal Firewall, *www.sygate.com*

Chapter 4:

- Tiny Personal Firewall, *www.tinysoftware.com*

Chapter 5:

- NetProxy, *www.grok.co.uk*
- SOCKS, *www.socks.nec.com*

Chapter 7:

- PGP (Pretty Good Privacy), *http://web.mit.edu/network/pgp.html*

Chapter 8:

- NetScan Tools 4, *www.netscantools.com*
- IP Sentry, *www.ipsentry.com*

Chapter 9:

- Symantec Enterprise Virtual Private Network 7.0, *www.symantec.com/downloads*

Chapter 10:

- ZoneAlarm Pro, *www.zonelabs.com*

 In Chapter 10, you learn about Linksys (*www.linksys.com*), which offers a wide variety of routers, hubs, wireless access points, firewalls, and other hardware. The image of the Linksys product in the chapter is courtesy of Linksys.

1

FIREWALL PLANNING AND DESIGN

> **After reading this chapter and completing the exercises, you will be able to:**
> ♦ Understand the misconceptions about firewalls
> ♦ Realize that a firewall is dependent on an effective security policy
> ♦ Understand what a firewall does
> ♦ Describe the types of firewall protection
> ♦ Understand the limitations of firewalls
> ♦ Determine the best hardware and software selections for your firewall

Network security comprises a continually evolving set of technologies, especially in regard to networks that connect to the Internet for communications or commerce. One of the most important recent developments in network security is the central role that firewalls have assumed. Due to high-profile hacker and terrorist attacks and the proliferation of **viruses** and other invasive software, firewalls have become a fundamental security tool. They are now a required rather than an optional part of virtually every network as well as of many individual computers.

No security system can ensure with absolute certainty that all of its information will be protected all of the time. But firewalls—used in conjunction with security policies, developed in accord with the needs of the businesses they protect, and maintained and upgraded on a regular basis—are one of the most effective security tools a network administrator can deploy.

This chapter gives you the big-picture view of the issues involved in planning and designing firewalls. First, you get a "Firewalls 101" introduction to what a firewall is *not* so that you can begin to get a clearer idea of what it actually is. Then you learn about security policies and the **rules** and procedures that govern how a firewall works. You then learn about types of firewall protection, the limitations of firewalls, and how hardware is used to create firewalls. The chapter finishes with evaluations of firewall software packages.

Throughout this book the term "firewall" is used in the singular. However, this doesn't necessarily refer to a single **router**, computer, VPN gateway, or software program. Any individual firewall program is actually a combination of multiple software and hardware components.

Throughout this chapter, we assume that you have a working knowledge of TCP/IP and the basics of network infrastructures. We also assume you have a working knowledge of IP addressing and the domain system and are familiar with the Internet and Web-based software. If, after reading this chapter, you find that you're a bit rusty on the basics of TCP/IP or other aspects of network infrastructure, please visit *www.course.com* to find resources to refresh your skills.

MISCONCEPTIONS ABOUT FIREWALLS

Most people have heard of the term "firewall," but not in connection with the Internet. They may have heard their auto mechanic mention the fireproof barrier between the engine of a car and the interior, or perhaps they're thinking about a brick wall or other fire-proof structure. These firewalls are intended to keep even the smallest amount of a single kind of dangerous substance—specifically, fire—from passing from one side to the other.

Even some business managers who've heard of a firewall in relation to Internet security have the notion that it's designed to prevent all hackers, viruses, and would-be intruders from entering a computer or computer network. Their notion is not true, however; firewalls are simply designed to enable authorized traffic to pass through and to block unauthorized traffic (as shown in Figure 1-1).

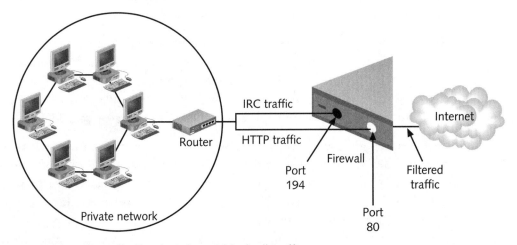

Figure 1-1   Firewalls filter but do not block all traffic

1

Some managers who are familiar with firewalls may also think that once you deploy the firewall, you only need to let it operate on its own. The fact is that all firewalls aren't perfect. They work best when they are part of a multi-pronged approach to network security called **Defense in Depth (DiD)**. Firewalls also need constant maintenance to keep up with the latest security threats.

 DiD encompasses a **security policy**, the firewall, intrusion detection software, virus scanners, and encryption. **Encryption** is the process of encoding information by using a mathematical formula called an algorithm to render it unreadable; the unreadable information subsequently is decoded, using the same algorithm, so the recipient can read it. You'll learn more about DiD as you progress through this book.

What Is a Security Policy?

DiD begins with an effective security policy, which is a set of rules and procedures developed by management in conjunction with security professionals. An effective security policy tells employees and business partners what constitutes acceptable and unacceptable use of the network, what resources need to be protected, and how the company will respond to breaches of security. The policy contains a number of component parts, including the following:

- A list of physical, logical, and network assets to be protected
- Specifications on how communications across the firewall will be **audited** (i.e., reviewed), through log files, for instance
- An Acceptable Use Policy that tells employees what constitutes acceptable use of company resources
- A statement describing the organization's overall approach toward security and how it impacts the firewall

 You learn more about security policies in Chapter 2.

What Is a Firewall?

Firewalls come in many forms, and it's difficult to come up with a single definition that covers all possible network configurations. In general, though, a **firewall** is hardware or software (or a combination of hardware and software) that monitors the transmission of **packets** of digital information that attempt to pass through the perimeter of a **network**.

Firewalls perform two basic security functions:

- *Packet filtering:* The firewall determines whether to allow or deny the passage of packets of digital information, based on security policy rules that have been established by the network administrator.

- *Application proxy gateways:* They provide network services to users inside the firewall while shielding individual **host** computers. This is done by breaking the IP flow (which is the traffic into and out of the network) between the network being protected and the network outside.

Firewalls can be complex, but if you make an effort to thoroughly understand only these two functions, you'll make a lot of progress toward being able to choose the right firewall and configure it to protect a computer or network.

An Analogy: Security Guard Sam

A firewall is like a security guard at a checkpoint. Suppose your name is Sam and you have taken a job as a security guard at a big, modern office tower. Thousands of people pass into and out of the building's security checkpoint every day. (For security reasons, there's only *one* security checkpoint.) "How do I know who's an authorized employee and who's an intruder?" you think, scratching your head. Luckily, the security department has set up rules that enable you to make decisions about who gets in and who does not:

- All personnel must enter and leave through Entrance 1 and no other.

- Staff who are wearing a green ID card can go through the checkpoint without signing in.

- Individuals who are wearing blue ID cards must sign in when entering and sign out when leaving.

- Everyone must pass through the metal detector and surrender knives or other potentially harmful devices.

- If someone passes through the checkpoint without being checked, push the red security button to alert the response team.

Similarly, a firewall performs the same types of functions as a security checkpoint—plus a few advanced gimmicks that a real-life security guard would never handle, like filtering unacceptable content or **caching** data (storing it on disk). In fact, the security rules listed for Sam have an equivalent in the digital realm of the firewall:

- Entry and exit points (called ports) are specified for different types of content. (Web page content typically travels through port 80, for instance.)

- Information that meets specified security criteria (such as an IP address) is allowed to pass, while other data is filtered—it can't pass through freely.

- Many firewalls include software that function as a sort of electronic metal detector, scanning for viruses and repairing infected files before they invade the network.

- Firewalls can be configured to send out alert messages if viruses are detected and to notify staff of break-ins.

Firewalls Provide Security Features

As firewalls become more widely used, their manufacturers compete more fiercely to make their products stand out from the competition. To make their products more attractive, some companies add a number of advanced security functions, such as the following:

- Logging unauthorized (as well as authorized) accesses both into and out of a network

- Providing a **virtual private network (VPN)** link to another network

- Authenticating users who provide usernames and passwords so that they can be identified and given access to the services they need

- Shielding hosts inside the network so that hackers cannot identify them and use them as staging areas for sustained attacks

- Caching data so that files that are repeatedly requested can be called from cache to reduce server load and improve Web-site performance

- Filtering content that is considered inappropriate, such as video streams, or dangerous, such as executable mail attachments

Firewalls Provide Protection for Individual Users

For a single home user who regularly surfs the Web, uses e-mail, and does Instant Messaging, a firewall's primary job is to keep viruses from infecting files and prevent **Trojan horses** from entering the system through hidden, often secret, openings called **back doors**. Norton Internet Security, for instance, comes with an anti-virus program that alerts users when an e-mail attachment or file containing a known virus is found (as shown in Figure 1-2).

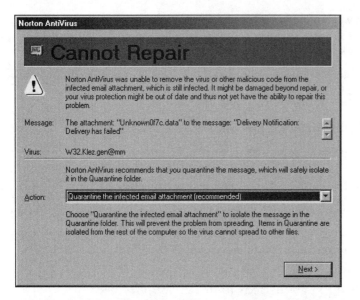

Figure 1-2   Some firewalls contain virus detection software

Firewalls Provide Perimeter Security for Networks

A firewall is often said to provide "perimeter security" because it sits on the outer bound-ary, or perimeter, of a network (as shown in Figure 1-3). The **network boundary** is the point at which one network connects to another.

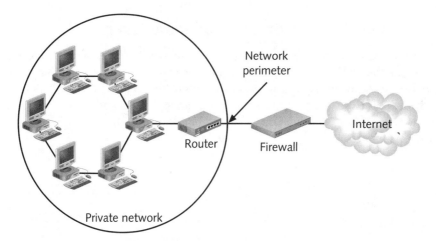

Figure 1-3   A firewall stands as a checkpoint on the perimeter of the network being protected

If you have an **extranet**, an extended network that combines two or more LANs, the location of the "perimeter" of a network becomes unclear. If you maintain a VPN with

1

a supplier or business partner, the VPN should have its own perimeter firewall because your network boundary technically extends to the end of the VPN. To be really secure, you should install a firewall on the partner's VPN host (as shown in Figure 1-4). For more about VPNs, see Chapter 9.

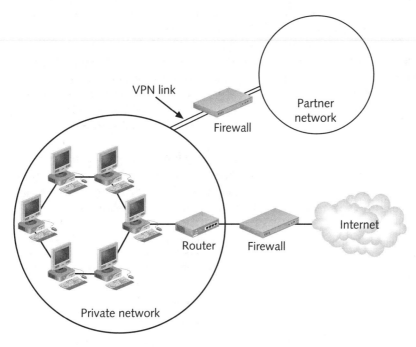

Figure 1-4   A VPN should have its own perimeter firewall

Locating the firewall at the perimeter has one obvious benefit: it enables you to set up a checkpoint where you can block "bad things" like viruses and infected e-mail messages before they get inside. However, it has less obvious benefits, too. A perimeter firewall enables you to log passing traffic, protecting the whole network at one time. If an attack does occur, having a security **subnet** at the perimeter—especially one that includes a firewall—can minimize the damage.

 Firewalls can protect networks both large and small. Personal firewall programs such as BlackICE Defender, Tiny Personal Firewall, or ZoneAlarm are used with increasing frequency to protect a single computer.

From the standpoint of a professional network administrator or security expert, you also need to become familiar with firewalls that function as checkpoints, protecting large companies or other organizations from hackers and thieves. The firewall is positioned at the border of the network, providing security for all the computers within it, so each individual workstation need not provide its own security.

Firewalls Consist of Multiple Components

A firewall isn't just a single piece of software. It can contain many components, including a packet filter, a proxy server, an **authentication** system, and software that performs **Network Address Translation (NAT)**. Some firewalls can encrypt traffic, and some help establish VPNs. Some firewalls (such as those made by Cisco Systems) come packaged in a hardware device that also functions as a router.

Firewalls themselves are part of multiple-component security setups. The most effective protection systems in use by large corporate networks employ not just one but two or more firewalls. They combine the firewalls with routers and other components to create a secure mini-network called a **demilitarized zone (DMZ)** that is positioned between the internal network and the outside world.

Many firewalls make use of a **bastion host**, a machine that has no unnecessary services— only the bare essentials. A network that needs to connect to the Internet might have a bastion host and a **service network** (another term for DMZ). Together, they are the only part of the organization exposed to the Internet. Figure 1-5 shows such a configuration.

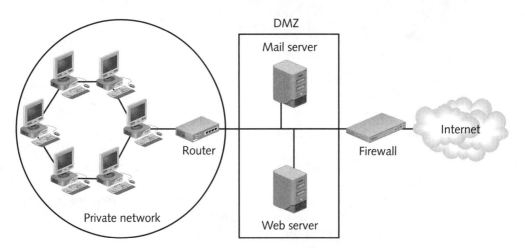

Figure 1-5   More than one firewall can be used to create a secure network called a DMZ

You learn more about bastion hosts in Chapter 8 and more about DMZs in Chapter 3.

Firewalls Confront Many Threats and Perform Many Security Tasks

To understand the specific activities of a firewall, you need to have a general idea of the range of possible threats against which you need to protect your network. You also need to know the security tasks that the firewall can perform. This section discusses multiple examples of each.

Restricting Access from Outside the Network

The most obvious goal of a firewall is to restrict which packets of information can enter the network. To do so, a firewall examines each packet and determines whether it meets the necessary "authorized" criteria. The criteria might be protocols or **IP addresses** on an "approved" list. Anything not on the list would then be excluded. Such packet filtering is discussed in more detail later in this chapter.

A firewall that does packet filtering (and virtually all do) addresses the tendency of hackers to open an attack by scanning for network addresses and open ports. (A **port** is a virtual gateway on a computer through which a particular type of data is allowed to pass. Each port is assigned a number between 0 and 65,535.) Initially, a hacker uses special software to scan a series of addresses, attempting to connect to a computer on each one. If any computer answers, it gives the hacker a target. Any gateway or router acting as a packet filter on your network or in your firewall should be configured to reject connection requests from computers that aren't on your network.

Hackers who identify a computer on a network do port scanning to determine what services it is running. Open, unused ports are one of the biggest vulnerabilities that firewalls need to guard against. A firewall can be set up to block services that you don't want outsiders to access, such as print and file sharing through an open port.

 Packets, by themselves, do not necessarily launch attacks against a network. They may be sent by a hacker in an attempt to do snooping. Hackers hope to identify specific computers to attack and hopefully find out something about the organization being targeted. They look for IP addresses of computers within a **Local Area Network (LAN)**, DNS requests to a computer, NetBIOS updates that might point to a vulnerable host on a network, or other information.

The SANS Institute provides a regularly updated list of the biggest security problems online. You can view "The Twenty Most Critical Internet Security Vulnerabilities" list at *www.sans.org/top20.htm*.

Any computer that's connected to the Internet (or that uses TCP/IP to communicate) needs to communicate using the Web, e-mail, newsgroups, chat, or other services. Each of those services could provide a way to intrude into the local system.

As you probably know from your study of basic networking and TCP/IP, a port number combined with a computer's IP address constitutes a network connection called a **socket**. Software that is commonly used by hackers attempts to identify sockets that respond to connection requests. The sockets that respond can be targeted to see if they have been left open or have security vulnerabilities that can be exploited. Some examples include the following: **Simple Mail Transport Protocol (SMTP)** listens on port 25; **Post Office Protocol, version 3 (POP3)** listens for incoming e-mail on port 110, and **Hypertext Transport Protocol (HTTP)** Web services use port 80. HTTP, in fact, is among the most commonly exploited services.

To get an idea how many connections you have open, go to any Windows-based computer that's connected to the Internet and run the built-in network application netstat.exe, which monitors network connections. Follow these general steps:

1. Click **Start**, point to **Programs**, point to **Accessories**, and then click **Command Prompt** to open a command prompt window.

2. Type **netstat –an**. (Note that if you launch netstat.exe and type netstat –an5, you'll refresh the display every five seconds. Periodically refreshing the display enables you to track connections as new services are launched or stopped.)

3. Press **Enter** to view command prompt information such as that shown in Figure 1-6.

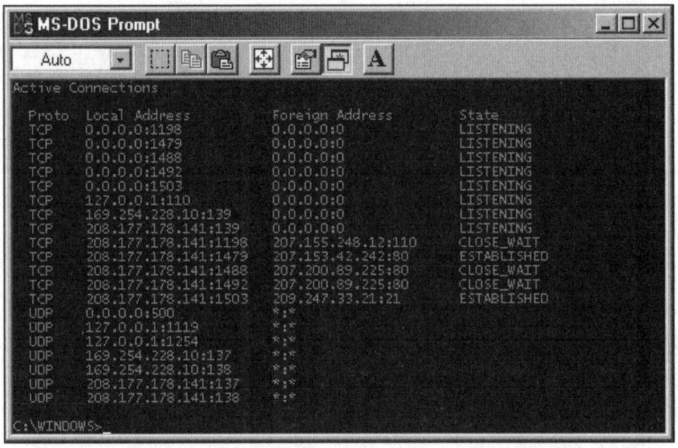

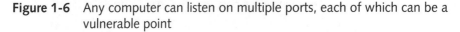

Figure 1-6   Any computer can listen on multiple ports, each of which can be a vulnerable point

As you can see, you might have one or more services **listening** on ports that you don't even use.

 If you are working at a Windows XP computer, you can determine which program is listening on a given port by typing netstat -o. The resulting information will allow you to turn off the service, which will close the port.

Restricting Unauthorized Access from Inside the Network

In some ways, it's relatively easy to protect a network from the Internet but more difficult to protect it from an *inside* attack. Whether they are disgruntled, dishonest, or just ignorant of the proper security procedures, employees can be a major source of trouble. Be aware of the following possibilities:

- Staff who bring floppy disks in to the office that contain virus-infected files
- Staff who access their office computers from home using remote access software that bypasses the perimeter firewall

- **Social engineering**, one of the most insidious network attacks, in which a hacker obtains confidential information by contacting employees and deceiving them into giving up passwords, IP addresses, server names, and so on.

- Poorly trained firewall administrators; the better the instructions, the more effective the firewall. A firewall, for instance, can be configured to filter out certain IP packets, but it might get confused if those packets come in fragments.

- Employees who receive e-mail messages with executable attachments, perhaps the most common internal danger: if the employee attempts to download the attachment, it begins executing. The program might spread itself to other computers using the recipient's e-mail address book. It might begin to damage files on the host machine or undertake any number of harmful activities.

Firewalls can help prevent some, but not all, of these internal threats. You can configure a firewall to recognize packets or to prevent access to protected files from internal as well as external hosts. Note, however, that remote access and social engineering attacks can be prevented only by raising awareness and training about security procedures.

Giving Clients Limited Access to External Hosts

Along with restricting unauthorized traffic from entering the network from the outside, firewalls can selectively permit traffic to go from inside the network to the Internet or other network. In other words, the firewall can act as a **proxy server**, which is software that makes high-level application connections on behalf of internal hosts and other machines. A single firewall product can provide both outbound packet filtering (shown in Figure 1-7) and proxy services.

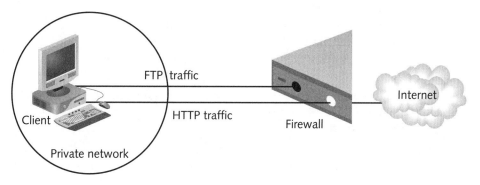

Figure 1-7 Outbound IP packet filtering

Application proxies will also help to restrict users inside your company who might want to gain unrestricted access to the Internet. Some technically sophisticated users might be able to circumvent the security systems you set up. They might, for instance, dial into the office using remote access, thus opening a security hole. They might use a remote access program like gotomypc.com, which provides them with client software they install on both their home and work computers. The software is configured so that every 15 or 20 seconds the work computer sends out a query "Does anyone want to connect to me?" (The target port used is TCP port 80, the commonly used HTTP port.) Such traffic may well go through the firewall unchecked and present an obvious security risk.

Protecting Critical Resources

Firewalls control access and monitor the transmission of data into and out of the network. They also protect resources within the network—both human and informational.

Attacks on critical resources are becoming all too common: **Worms** are one type of attack. They "worm" their way into a computer in an e-mail attachment or a downloaded file, where they then replicate themselves. They are only slightly different from viruses, which also worm their way into a computer but then do much more destructive behavior than just replication. Trojan horses are similar to viruses; they contain malicious code that is hidden inside supposedly harmless programs. **Distributed Denial of Service (DDoS)** attacks are just as harmful. They are caused when a hacker floods a server with requests, shutting down the server and making Web sites and networks that depend on that server unreachable.

Protecting Against Hacking

Hacking, in general, is the practice of infiltrating computers or networks to steal data, cause harm, or simply claim credit for getting inside. Credit card number theft is perhaps the most harmful result of a hacker attack to individuals. Such attacks can also have tangible impact on a larger organization, including the following:

- *Loss of data:* Many organizations now use the Internet to run their business. They calculate payroll online, they publish health insurance information, they maintain staff directories, and they may even keep their books online. Such personnel and financial information is among a company's most valuable assets and, if lost, can have a big impact on its bottom line.

- *Loss of time:* The time spent recovering files, rebuilding servers, and otherwise dealing with security breaches can be extensive, far outweighing the time spent preventing trouble.

- *Staff resources:* In response to a security incident, many staff may need to take time away from their regular business activities to recover data.

- *Confidentiality:* A growing number of companies use the Internet to sell their goods and services. They store customer data that needs to be kept private, such as contact information and credit card numbers. Yet, hack attacks have occurred in which such information has been uncovered and even published online.

Note that the more advanced firewalls, like Check Point FireWall-1, can be configured to send out notices as soon as an intrusion is detected. Early notification can reduce the amount of data lost as well as staff time spent in dealing with the incident. You learn more about CheckPoint FireWall-1 later in this chapter.

Providing Centralization

A firewall centralizes security for the organization it protects. It simplifies the security-related activities of the network administrator, someone who typically has many other responsibilities to handle. Having a firewall on the perimeter of a network gives the network administrator a single location from which to set up security policies and monitor traffic into and out of the company.

 As stated earlier, firewalls might not be in a single location. In addition, note that the more elaborate security setups—even those that use a single perimeter location—incorporate more than one firewall. Multiple-firewall DMZs are discussed in Chapter 3.

Enabling Documentation

Every firewall should be set up to provide information to the network administrator in the form of **log files**. These log files record attempted break-ins as well as more mundane events like legitimate file accesses, unsuccessful connection attempts, and the like. Looking through log files is tedious, but the goal is to identify any weak points in the security system so they can be strengthened.

Another goal of providing documentation is to identify intruders so that they can be apprehended in case theft or damage actually occurs. The regular reviewing and analyzing of the log file data they accumulate is what makes firewalls effective because methods of attack change all the time. The firewall rules must be evaluated and adjusted to account for new viruses and other threats.

Providing for Authentication

If you are an experienced user of the Internet, you are probably familiar with authentication—the process of logging in to a server with a username and a password to access protected information. Only users who have previously registered their username and password in a database are recognized by the server and allowed to enter.

The authentication process can also make use of encryption to protect the usernames and passwords transmitted from client to server (or client to firewall). However, encryption isn't as safe as it seems, at least where firewalls are concerned. Encrypted authentication can actually make a firewall *less* secure than it would be otherwise. Employees who work at home and who authenticate themselves through the firewall can make themselves targets for hackers who see a way to get into the network. If the authentication process has bugs, it can open a hole in the firewall too.

 Authentication should be used in firewalls with caution, but it can work; see Chapter 6 for more information.

Contributing to a VPN

A firewall is an ideal endpoint for VPN, which connects two companies' networks over the Internet. A VPN is one of the safest ways to exchange information online. You find out more about VPNs in Chapter 9.

TYPES OF FIREWALL PROTECTION

Firewalls provide network security in many different ways. We discuss multilayer firewall protection first so that you get an overview of the different network levels at which firewalls work. After the overview, we discuss the following specific firewall functions: packet filtering (both stateful and stateless), NAT, and application proxy gateways.

Multilayer Firewall Protection

Firewalls work at many different levels of the seven-layer OSI networking model, which is one reason why they're so effective. Table 1-1 gives some examples of firewall functions and the corresponding layers at which they operate.

Table 1-1   Network layers and firewalls

Layer Number	OSI Reference Model Layer	Firewall Technology
1	Application	Application-level gateway
2	Presentation	Encryption
3	Session	SOCKS proxy server
4	Transport	Packet filtering
5	Network	NAT
6	Physical	N/A
7	Data Link	N/A

Packet Filtering

Packet filtering is a key function of any firewall. In fact, packet filters were one of the first types of firewalls. Packet filters are an effective element in any perimeter security setup. In addition, they have the advantage of not taking up **bandwidth**, or the capacity of network cables to convey information, the way proxy servers do.

What are packets, and how do they work? A packet (which is sometimes called a **datagram**) contains two types of information:

- The **header**, which contains general information about the size of the packet, the protocol that was used to send it, and the IP address of both the source computer and its destination

- The data, which is the information you view and use; it's the text of an e-mail message, the contents of a Web page, and so on

1

Packet filters use packet headers to decide whether to block the packet or allow it to pass through a firewall. Of course, hackers know about packet filters and often attempt to put false information in the headers about their source IP address. This is called **IP spoofing**, and it's one way in which hackers try to sneak a packet into a network by making it seem legitimate.

Sometimes, hackers uncover a real IP address within a network. They then place the legitimate address in the header of a harmful file to make it look as though the file is coming from another computer within the organization. Your job, as firewall administrator, would be to configure the firewall to deny all packets that arrive from outside but with a source IP address that seems to be coming from *within* the network.

Stateless Packet Filtering Firewalls

Stateless inspection, also called **stateless packet filtering**, occurs when a firewall inspects packet headers without paying attention to the state of the connection between the server and client computer. A firewall that conducts stateless packet filtering will simply block a packet based on the information in the header.

All packet filters are not created equal. The differences in how they do their filtering can be a factor in your choice of firewall. They are mentioned here briefly and in more detail in Chapter 4.

Stateful Packet Filtering Firewalls

Stateful inspection, also called **stateful packet filtering**, examines the data contained in a packet, and a memory of the state of the connection between client and server is kept in disk cache. Stateful is superior to stateless inspection because it pays attention to the data payload of a packet; it can detect and drop those that can overload the server, such as malformed e-mail attachments.

Stateful inspection will also block packets that are sent by a host that is not actually connected to the server. Here's an example of how stateful inspection works. Suppose you have set up a firewall for a company and an employee attempts to connect to the Web site for the White House. When the employee's request packet arrives at the stateful firewall, the following events occur:

1. The firewall first checks a list of active connections called a "state table" to see if an active connection exists.

2. Because a connection does not yet exist, the firewall then checks its list of rules (called a **rulebase**). Assume that users inside the network are allowed to access the Internet on TCP port 80 and are allowed to access any host on the Internet. The packet would be allowed to go on its way—after making an entry to the state table recording that the connection was attempted.

3. At the White House server, when the packet is received (after probably passing through one or more firewalls), a reply packet would be generated and returned to the source company's firewall.

4. At our originating firewall, the state table is checked, and the inbound packet's header is inspected. The header conveys the following information:

- *Source IP: www.whitehouse.gov*
- *Source port:* 80
- *Destination IP:* the originating user's computer address
- *Protocol:* TCP

5. Because there's nothing suspicious about this packet, the firewall would send it to the computer that made the request.

Now, suppose a very different scenario. A hacker at IP address *hack.yourcomputer.net* tries to access your system through port 80. The packet header contains the following:

- *Source IP: hack.yourcomputer.net*
- *Source port:* 80
- *Destination IP:* The address of a computer on your system that the hacker has previously uncovered through address or port scanning
- *Destination port:* 2400

The firewall's stateful packet inspector first checks its state table to see if such a request matches a previous entry. Because no such entry exists, the firewall then consults its rulebase. Because the only rule specified is that only internal users can connect to port 80, the packet would be blocked.

 Packets are like packages that are received at the postal service. The postal employees use address information to sort the packages into the appropriate routes. If packages don't have a critical bit of information—a return address or street address—it is "blocked" from delivery.

Packet Filtering Rules

Packet filtering depends on the establishment of rules. Some of the most general rules include the following:

- Any outbound packet must have a source address that is in your internal network.
- Any outbound packet must not have a destination address that is in your internal network.
- Any inbound packet must not have a source address that is in your internal network.
- Any inbound packet must have a destination address that is in your internal network.
- Any packet that enters or leaves your network must have a source or destination address that falls within the range of addresses in your network. Your

network may use (but does not have to use) private addresses or addresses listed in RFC1918 reserved space. These include 10.x.x.x/8, 172.16.x.x/12, or 192.168.x.x/16, and the loopback network 127.0.0.0/8.

Filter rules can affect the transmission of packets. These rules include the use of the following:

- **Internet Control Message Protocol (ICMP):** IP, by itself, has no way of letting the host that originated a request know whether a packet was received at its destination in its entirety. It can, however, use ICMP to report any errors that occurred in the transmission. Utilities like Ping and Traceroute use ICMP. The danger is that ICMP packets can be filled with false information that can trick your hosts into redirecting or stopping communications.

- **User Datagram Protocol (UDP):** This protocol is similar to TCP in that it handles the addressing of a message. UDP breaks a message into numbered segments so that it can be transmitted. UDP then reassembles it when it reaches the destination computer. Unlike TCP, UDP is connectionless: it simply sends segments of messages without performing error checking or waiting for an acknowledgment that the message has been received. Such a protocol is useful for video and audio broadcasts on the Internet. TCP and UDP are often mentioned together in discussions of firewalls because both transmit data through ports and thus open up vulnerabilities. It's useful to set up rules to block UDP traffic on ports 21 and below and to block traffic on ports that control hardware such as keyboards, hubs, and routers; see Chapter 2 for more information.

- *TCP filtering:* These rules are similar to UDP rules. You should block packets that use ports below 20, and you can block incoming Telnet connections on port 23.

- *IP filtering:* These rules control the overall flow of IP traffic through your network. If you have identified a computer or network that you want to block from accessing your company's network, you would specify Source IP or Destination IP rule criteria.

 Packet filtering has limitations. Filtering does not hide the IP addresses of the hosts that are on the network inside the filter. The IP addresses are contained in the outbound traffic, which makes it easy for hackers to target individual hosts behind the filter to attack them. They don't check to make sure the protocols inside packets are legitimate either. Packet filtering can limit addresses based only on the source IP address listed in the packet's header. This makes it subject to IP spoofing. Packet filters alone are no longer adequate for performing firewall functions on their own.

Larger organizations use multiple packet filters in a DMZ perimeter security setup. They might use a router that functions as a **static packet filter**, a stateful packet filter that has been set up in a bastion host, and firewall software (as shown in Figure 1-8).

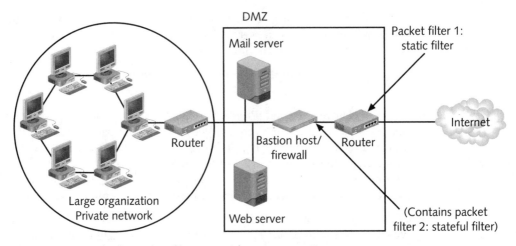

Figure 1-8   Multiple packet filters provide extra security

NAT

Each computer on the network is assigned an IP address. If that address is static, it's relatively easy for a hacker to find it and gain access to the computer more than once. With a static, reliable IP address, a hacker can use a computer as a staging area for launching long, sustained attacks.

NAT makes up for one shortcoming of packet filters. It is used to hide the TCP/IP information of hosts in the network being protected. Hiding the TCP/IP information is important because it prevents hackers from getting the address of an actual host on your internal network; thus, they are unable to send a malformed packet or virus-laden message to that machine.

NAT functions as a network-level proxy; it acts as a single host that makes requests on behalf of all the internal hosts on the network. NAT hides the identity of the hosts from anyone outside the network by converting the IP addresses of internal hosts to the IP address of the firewall. To someone on the Internet or other outside network, it seems like all information is coming from a single computer. (This is sometimes called IP masquerading.)

Thus, thanks to NAT, the computers on the protected network can be made to *look* to the outside world like they have the same public IP address as the computer that's running NAT. In reality, the individual machines can be assigned IP addresses in a private address range—for example, 10.0.0.1, 10.0.0.2, 10.0.0.3, and so on. When the NAT-equipped firewall receives a request from one of these computers, it replaces the real IP address with its own. The remote computer outside the network that receives the request gets a packet whose header includes a source IP address of, say, 24.33.9.0, not 10.0.0.3 (as shown in Figure 1-9).

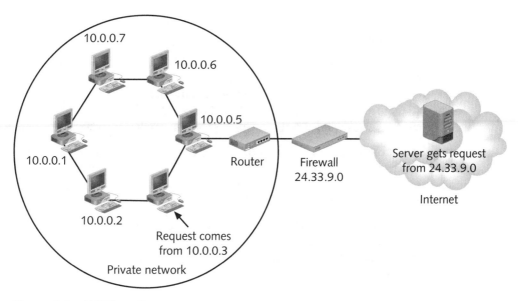

Figure 1-9   NAT in action

 Along with the RFC1918 private address spaces mentioned in the "Packet-Filtering Rules" section of this chapter, NAT can also work with the Automatic Private IP Addressing (APIPA) range 169.254.0.0/16. This address range is private and can't be routed on the Internet.

NAT is also built into Linux and many UNIX operating systems. In Windows 2000/98/Me/XP, the simpler form of NAT is part of Internet Connection Sharing (ICS). The other feature, Routing and Remote Access, gives you more control. However, you should avoid enabling NAT using both ICS and Routing and Remote Access—you're essentially telling Windows to route the same IP address to two different addresses. Pick one or the other feature, not both.

 Hands-On Project 1-7 shows you how to enable ICS on a Windows workstation.

Application Layer Gateways

Another type of firewall protection is the **application layer gateway**, also known as a proxy server. This type of gateway works at the Application layer, the top layer of the OSI model of network communications.

Application layer gateways can control the way applications inside the network access the outside world by setting up proxy services. This service acts as a substitute (i.e., as a proxy) for the client, making requests for Web pages or sending and receiving e-mail on behalf of individual users who are thus shielded from directly connecting with the Internet. This shielding minimizes the effect of viruses, worms, Trojan horses, and the like.

An application layer gateway provides you with one especially valuable security benefit. In contrast to a packet filter, which decides whether to allow or deny a request based on the information contained in the packet header, the gateway understands the contents of the requested data. It can be configured to allow or deny (both of which are actions that can be taken as a result of filtering) specific content, such as viruses and executables.

Such content filtering is only one of the complex tasks that enable application layer gateways to accomplish security tasks that go far beyond blocking specified IP addresses. A complete overview of firewalls and what they can do wouldn't be complete without mentioning these security techniques:

- *Load balancing:* If the big office building described in the beginning of this chapter has two secure entrances, the number of people having to pass through each can be reduced substantially. In the same way, large organizations commonly install more than one firewall so each can divide the traffic load between them.

- *IP address mapping:* (You might also see this called address vectoring or static IP mapping.) This is a type of NAT in which a static IP address assigned by an ISP is mapped to the private IP address of a computer on the local network. The benefit of this to an internal network is to shield actual internal IP addresses from the prying eyes of unauthorized external clients.

- *Filtering content:* An application proxy server can be set up to filter on some detailed criteria. You can block files that have a certain file name or part of a file name, a keyword, an e-mail attachment, or content type.

- *URL filtering:* This can be used to block a site's **Domain Name System (DNS)** name, such as *www.criminalactivity.com*.

Most of these application-level security techniques are discussed in more detail in Chapter 5.

LIMITATIONS OF FIREWALLS

Firewalls can do a lot, but they can't be expected to do it all. Firewalls should not be the only form of protection for a network. They should be part of an overall security plan (as shown in Chapter 2) and should be used in conjunction with other forms of protection, including ID cards, passwords, and employee rules of conduct. For instance, even the most elaborate firewall can't protect against an employee who brings a floppy disk to work containing files that have been infected with a virus, or employees who use a host inside the firewall to gain unauthorized access to sensitive information.

EVALUATING FIREWALL PACKAGES

If you become a security specialist or network administrator whose responsibilities include security for your organization, you'll be called upon to evaluate the different kinds of firewall software and hardware packages and recommend the best choice for your company's needs.

Firewalls come in many varieties. They all do the core functions: filtering, proxying, and logging. Some of the expensive packages add "bells and whistles" like caching and address translation. However, don't let price rule your decision. Some freeware products like PGP let you do many of the same things as, say, Microsoft's Internet Security and Acceleration Server.

This section shows how the basic strategies and concepts governing firewalls are implemented in a range of software and hardware combinations you are likely to encounter in the workplace. Having this overview should help you choose your own package when the time comes. The discussion is divided into two sections: hardware and software.

Firewall Hardware

Some firewall options are hardware options. Routers are essential parts of any network. Many routers can be configured to do packet filtering and perform other functions. Some routers are part of full-featured firewall appliances that place the firewall inside a hardened bastion host that you add to the perimeter of your network.

Routers

Many routers come equipped with packet-filtering capabilities built into them. Others come with full-fledged firewalls. The Linksys EtherFast Cable/DSL router comes with NAT functions that enable it to act as a firewall. Other Linksys routers enable users to set up VPNs and other gateways. Competitive pricing makes these products suitable for both home and business use.

Appliances

Vendors use this term to describe their expensive firewall products, but don't be intimidated. A firewall appliance performs the same basic tasks you learned about in the first half of this chapter: packet filtering, application-level gateways, and logging. The vendor might package the firewall inside a hardened bastion host, thus saving you the trouble of installing it yourself.

Some hardware firewalls not only have a low profile and sleek design but also provide you with two advantages over software-only products:

- If the operating system of one of your network's hosts is plagued by bugs or is simply slow, its problems don't affect the firewall because the firewall appliance is self-contained.

- If the firewall software needs to be patched or updated, installation is generally easy. Some hardware firewalls, such as the Cisco PIX line, have no moving parts and have a lower failure rate than other firewalls.

Software-Only Packages

Software-only packages are the kinds of firewalls that people think consist solely of firewall software. This software can be combined with various hardware devices to make an extra-secure DMZ. This section of the chapter gives an overview of the most popular software packages.

Free Firewall Tools on the Internet

Most of the free firewall software on the Internet, such as the packet filter IPChains and TIS Firewall Toolkit, also run on a free operating system, such as Linux, The Berkeley Software Design variety of UNIX (BSD), or DOS.

Free firewall programs aren't perfect. Their logging capabilities aren't as robust as some commercial products, they can be difficult to configure, and they usually don't include a way to monitor the firewall in real-time. Nonetheless, they have a place in networking because of their convenience, simplicity, and unbeatable price.

Note the following products:

- *Pretty Good Privacy (PGP):* PGP is a program that's highly regarded for providing e-mail and disk encryption. Created by Phil Zimmerman and originally released for free on the Internet, a commercial version of PGP has also been developed by Network Associates. Although the commercial version of PGP is available through the NAI Web site, the freeware version is still available through MIT at *http://web.mit.edu/network/pgp.html*. The latest versions of PGP work with Windows 95/98/NT/2000, Macintosh, AIX/HP-UX/Linux, and Solaris. PGP is noteworthy not only for its ability to encrypt files but for its firewall and VPN functions. The fact that it's available for free makes it a good test program, and it will be used in exercises throughout this book.

- *Netfilter:* Netfilter is the firewall software that comes with the Linux 2.4 kernel and is a powerful (and freely available) solution for stateless and stateful packet filtering, NAT, and packet processing. Netfilter doesn't have all the features of commercial programs such as VPN, but it does one thing very well: logging. Netfilter records copious information about the traffic that passes through it, but that information is well organized and easy to review.

Personal/Small Business Firewalls

Most well-known personal firewall products are considered "lightweight" in terms of firewall protection. Some work with multiple protocols, whereas most guard only against IP threats. Some programs don't do outbound connection blocking, while others do. Some, like BlackICE Defender, are inconvenient to configure because the program doesn't work on a "configure-as-you-compute" basis. Rather, you set a general security level (such as Cautious, Nervous, and Paranoid), and the software adjusts its security settings accordingly. Other programs, such as ZoneAlarm, let you establish rules as needed; whenever an application such as a Web browser or FTP program attempts to access the Internet, the program prompts you to establish a rule.

Personal firewall products work by locating themselves between the Ethernet adapter driver of the machine on which they are installed and the TCP/IP stack, where they inspect traffic going between the driver and the stack. They include programs such as Norton Internet Security, ZoneAlarm, BlackICE Defender, and Symantec Personal Firewall.

Enterprise Firewall Systems

If it's bells and whistles you're looking for, turn to these full-featured, powerful firewall packages:

- *Check Point FireWall-1:* FireWall-1, by Check Point Software Technologies Ltd., is considered by many security experts to be the product of choice when it comes to software firewalls. The product is notable for being among the first to use stateful packet inspection to monitor network traffic.

  FireWall-1 includes a full array of security tools, including authentication, virus checking (through a third-party application that is integrated into the FireWall package), intrusion detection, and packet filtering. FireWall-1 is the only firewall that is compliant with the OPSEC security standard. It's an especially good choice for large networks. A **high availability** feature enables a corporate network to run two parallel installations of FireWall-1 in tandem. If one firewall goes down, the other remains functioning, keeping the network connected and maintaining current connections, thus making it especially good for large-scale networks.

  FireWall-1's software engine has been incorporated into a number of firewall appliances. FireWall-1 also comes in several variations, including a wireless model and a VPN-1 version for VPNs (though the standard version of FireWall-1 includes VPN capabilities as well).

- *Cisco PIX:* PIX is not a single product but a name given to a series of secure, self-contained hardware devices that contain full-featured firewalls. The line ranges from the PIX 535, which is able to handle up to 500,000 concurrent connections, to the PIX 501 for home office environments.

  The Cisco PIX firewalls are notable for competitive pricing, extensive online documentation, and highly regarded customer support. Cisco's firewall products have been available for several years and are reliable and feature-rich, including high availability, an intrusion detection system, and protection against DoS attacks.

- *Microsoft Internet Security & Acceleration Server:* Internet Security & Acceleration Server (ISA) 2000 is an application-level firewall from Microsoft Corporation. ISA 2000 features includes authentication through integration with Active Directory, virus scanning (through integrated third-party products), data-aware filtering capabilities, and IP packet-filtering functionality. ISA also supports the Cache Array Routing Protocol (CARP) so that the product can be scaled to fit larger traffic requirements.

- *NAI Gauntlet:* Gauntlet is one of the longest-established firewall products available today. It is a flexible product, supporting application proxies, packet filtering, and the ability to adjust the speed of the firewall as needed. Gauntlet is integrated by McAfee's anti-virus software.

CHAPTER SUMMARY

- This chapter covers the basics of firewalls and what they do. The author assumes that you have a working knowledge of TCP/IP and network infrastructures. Some knowledge of IP addressing and DNS is also assumed. The author also assumes that you are familiar with the Internet and have at least a casual end-user's knowledge about Web browsers and other client software.

- The chapter begins with examinations of what firewalls are and what they are not. An analogy is made to the security checkpoint of a modern office building. This introductory analogy makes you aware of the need for rules and the need to let traffic pass through the gateway as well as the need to block unauthorized traffic.

- The text then examines where firewalls fit in network topology. Strictly speaking, they can be located anywhere on a network, and multiple firewalls can be placed in more than one location. However, the most common location is at the point where an internal network connects to the Internet or another external network such as a corporate extranet. If a company operates a VPN that links it to another company's network, the perimeter is extended to the entry point to that partner company network.

- The text then discusses the many different kinds of firewall components that make up a security perimeter for a large-scale organization. These include not only the firewall hardware and/or software itself, but a bastion host and Web server, mail server, and other computers that together compose a service network. Other routers that provide static and stateful packet filtering can be used.

- Next is a discussion of the primary security tasks that firewalls perform—in other words, the things they do that make a network more secure. Packet filtering is discussed first because that was the original function of early firewalls. Then NAT and application proxy gateways are examined, followed by brief mentions of authentication and VPNs. Examination of these features is combined with discussion of the kinds of tactics hackers use and that firewalls need to defend against. These include port and network address scanning, social engineering and other kinds of outright deception, IP spoofing, and DoS attacks.

❏ The importance of establishing rules by which the firewall operates comes next in the course of a discussion of static and stateful packet inspection. (Rules are discussed in more detail in Chapters 2 and 4.) Application-layer gateways are then discussed.

❏ Finally, some pointers on how to evaluate different firewall packages are given, along with a brief description of a few of the major firewall packages. This is by no means a comprehensive examination of all firewall products on the market, only a comparison of how firewall appliances differ from software solutions and the kinds of features the expensive commercial programs can give you compared with free or low-cost software options.

KEY TERMS

application layer gateway — A fundamental activity of firewalls. Proxy services are provided to hosts inside the network to shield them from the outside. The proxy receives requests from a host and forwards them to their destination on behalf of the host.

audit — A review of a system's operation to evaluate its performance.

authentication — The process of identifying that individuals are who they claim to be. This is usually accomplished using a username and password.

back door — A way into a system (or network) that is not the usual or typical way. A "back door" is usually a secret or hidden way leading into the system (or network).

bandwidth — The amount of data that can be transmitted over a network in a fixed amount of time. Bandwidth for digital transmission is usually expressed in bits per second (bps) or bytes per second. Bandwidth for analog transmission is usually expressed in cycles per second, or Hertz (Hz).

bastion host — A gateway between an internal (private) network and an external (public) network. Bastion hosts typically have all unnecessary services disabled to reduce the chance of exploitation.

caching — The process of storing data in a part of a hard disk called a cache so that it can be retrieved later on. Files that are requested repeatedly can be called up from the disk cache, thus relieving the load on a Web server.

datagram — *See* packet.

Defense in Depth (DiD) — A term used to describe a multilayered approach to network security. Rather than relying on a single security mechanism, DiD makes use of several security components that work together.

demilitarized zone (DMZ) — A secure network located at the perimeter of another network that combines firewalls with bastion hosts, proxy servers, and other components to provide an extra level of security for the network being protected.

Distributed Denial of Service (DDoS) attacks — Many compromised systems attack a single target. This causes a denial of service to users who would regularly use the targeted system. DDoS attacks flood the target system with incoming messages and essentially forces it to shut down, thereby denying service to the system to legitimate users.

Domain Name System (DNS) — The system that enables Internet domain names to stand as aliases for IP addresses. The lists of DNS addresses are maintained by official registrars and mapped by DNS servers that are used by ISPs.

encryption — The process of rendering data unreadable by processing it through an algorithm so that intruders cannot read it if intercepted.

extranet — An internal network that uses Internet technology (an intranet) and that is made partially accessible to authorized outsiders. Usually, the authorized users are business partners, such as suppliers. Extranets join two or more LANs and are often joined by a VPN; they are a popular means for business partners to exchange information quickly and reliably.

firewall — Hardware or software that monitors and records the transmission of data into and out of a network and that permits packets to pass based on rules.

header — The part of a packet that contains general information, such as the protocol and the source and destination IP addresses.

high availability — The ability of some software or hardware firewalls to run 24 hours a day, seven days a week, 365 days per year. Often, this level of uptime is achieved by running two devices in parallel so that if one fails, the other can take over seamlessly.

host — Any hardware device (not just a desktop computer) that can access the Internet and communicate via a network; it also has an IP address.

Hypertext Transport Protocol (HTTP) — The set of standards used to transmit data on the World Wide Web.

Internet Control Message Protocol (ICMP) — A protocol that handles error reporting and provides status information and limited control for Internet Protocol (IP).

IP address — A number that identifies a machine that is connected to the Internet and sends or receives information in the form of packets. The newest version of Internet Protocol, IPv6, provides for 128-bit IP addresses.

IP spoofing — An attempt by a hacker to put a false IP source address into a packet header to make it seem legitimate and sneak it past the firewall.

listening — In computer systems, this generally is a term used for TCP or UDP ports. The ports on a system have the ability to listen to the network to see if traffic coming into the system is intended for that particular port.

Local Area Network (LAN) — Two or more computers that are connected (either physically or by wireless communications) so that they can share files and communicate. Networked computers that are part of a LAN are usually in the same building or in physical proximity to one another.

log file — Keeps a record of specific actions that occur on a computer or network.

network — One or more computers connected and able to share information.

Network Address Translation (NAT) — Offers a form of protection to internal (private) networks. An internal network can be configured with an IP address range that is not routable on the external (public) network. For internal users to communicate on the external network, a NAT device translates the user's private IP address to a public IP address.

network boundary — The point at which one network stops and another network begins.

packet — Discrete chunks of digital information that are transmitted over the network.

packet filtering — A fundamental activity of firewalls. (The first firewalls were packet filters.) The firewall determines whether to allow or deny the passage of a packet of digital information based on the IP address or IP header information.

port — A virtual pathway through which data can pass. Each TCP/IP protocol is assigned its own port so that it won't interfere with other types of information.

Post Office Protocol, version 3 (POP3) — Protocol used to retrieve and organize mail from an e-mail server.

proxy server — A server that sits between a client and a server (usually between a client and a web server). It intercepts all requests from the client to the Web server to see if it can fulfill the requests itself. If not, it forwards the request to the real server.

router — A device that connects and directs traffic between networks.

rulebase — A set of rules that has been set up on a firewall and that tells the firewall how to treat inbound and outbound communications.

rules — Statements that tell a firewall which packets to allow and which to deny based on the packet's source IP address, protocol, or other characteristics.

security policy — A set of rules and objectives for protecting an organization's stores of information as well as the privacy of its employees. A good security policy clearly states the priorities for firewalls and other security components and helps determine how they are to be deployed.

service network — *See* demilitarized zone (DMZ).

Simple Mail Transport Protocol (SMTP) Used to send mail between servers.

social engineering — A hacker obtains confidential information by contacting employees and deceiving them into giving up passwords, IP addresses, server names, and so on.

socket — A protocol used to establish TCP/IP network connections; a standard identifier that represents an established connection.

stateful inspection — The examination of the data contained in a packet; memory of the state of the connection between the client and the server is kept in disk cache.

stateful packet filtering — *See* stateful inspection.

stateless inspection — Occurs when a firewall inspects packet headers without paying attention to the state of the connection between the server and client computer.

stateless packet filtering — *See* stateless inspection.

static packet filter — When data arrives at an interface, static packet filters either allow or deny it based on information in the packet header only.

subnet — A collection of network devices that share a common network ID.

Trojan horse — A destructive program that acts as an innocent program until it is activated. Trojan horses have varying levels of destructive capabilities.

User Datagram Protocol (UDP) — A connectionless protocol, UDP is primarily used for broadcasting messages over a network.

virtual private network (VPN) — Is a network between two hosts over a public network. These hosts use encryption and other security mechanisms to create a virtual tunnel. This helps to ensure that only authorized users can access the network and that the data cannot be intercepted.

viruses — A script or code that is placed on a machine without the knowledge of the machine's owner. The virus could be destructive, replicate itself, or perform any number of other malicious actions.

worms — Programs or algorithms that replicate themselves over a computer network and that are usually malicious in action or intent. These actions can include using up the computer's resources or shutting down the system.

REVIEW QUESTIONS

1. Why is it important that a firewall provide a centralized security checkpoint for a network?

2. Which of the following are important activities of a firewall?
   a. permitting
   b. restricting
   c. logging
   d. greeting visitors

3. The first kinds of firewalls were _____.
   a. routers
   b. proxy servers
   c. logging utilities
   d. packet filters

4. Why is packet filtering alone inadequate for security purposes? (Choose all that apply.)
   a. Filtering does not monitor for legitimate protocols.
   b. Filtering does not screen out unauthorized IP addresses.
   c. Filtering limits addresses based solely on the destination IP address in the header.
   d. Filtering does not conceal host IP addresses inside the filter.

5. When does packet filtering give you an advantage over other security methods, such as proxy services?
   a. when encryption is available to conceal passwords
   b. when bandwidth demands on the company's Web server are high
   c. when you need to conceal IP addresses inside the network
   d. when available bandwidth is not a concern

1

6. Most large corporate networks deploy multiple instances of what perimeter security features? (Choose all that apply.)

   a. packet filters

   b. service networks

   c. firewalls

   d. DNS servers

7. When a request from a user is received by a firewall, what can the firewall do? (Choose all that apply.)

   a. authenticate

   b. filter

   c. log

   d. cache

8. Most of the requests to a Web site go to which TCP port?

   a. 21

   b. 25

   c. 80

   d. 1028

9. What can TCP do that UDP cannot do?

   a. verify that all packets have been sent

   b. verify that all packets are received

   c. filter packets

   d. translate IP addresses

10. How do you allow FTP traffic to go through your firewall?

   a. Configure the firewall so that it recognizes all FTP traffic and lets it through.

   b. Configure the firewall so that FTP data traffic uses only port 20 and no other port.

   c. Configure the firewall so that FTP goes through any port.

   d. You cannot do this.

11. A computer connected to a network can make use of up to how many available ports?

   a. 1024

   b. 65,535

   c. There is no limit.

   d. This depends on the number of connectors in the back of the machine.

12. Name three benefits of locating your firewall on the perimeter of a network.

13. Hackers initially try to find what network resource?

    a. contact information for individual staff members

    b. open ports on your network

    c. the IP address of a computer to target

    d. the protocols used on your network

14. Which firewall is OPSEC compliant?

    a. Microsoft ISA

    b. FireWall-1

    c. Cisco PIX

    d. NAI Gauntlet

15. Name two reasons why a hardware firewall solution is a good choice compared with software-only solutions.

16. Check Point FireWall-1 was the first firewall to perform what security function?

    a. NAT

    b. stateful packet inspection

    c. high availability

    d. static packet inspection

17. Which of the following is a connectionless protocol?

    a. TCP

    b. ICMP

    c. UDP

    d. IP

18. For what kinds of communications is a connectionless protocol useful? (Choose all that apply.)

    a. video broadcasts

    b. FTP file transfers

    c. audio broadcasts

    d. Internet Relay Chat

19. At what network layer does SOCKS operate?

20. Which of the following is true about proxy servers?

    a. They can add latency to network communications.

    b. They shield internal users from those outside the network.

    c. They translate internal IP addresses for external ones.

    d. They are positioned between the internal and external networks.

HANDS-ON PROJECTS

Project 1-1: View Active Connections

The Netstat application is useful when you need to isolate problems with a computer's Internet or local network connection. You can use it not only to show active network connections but also for statistics related to a specific protocol, such as TCP, UDP, IP, or ICMP.

> To do this project, you will need a computer running Windows 2000 or XP that is configured with TCP/IP on a network with other properly configured TCP/IP computers.

1. If your computer is not powered up, power it up now.
2. Click **Start**, point to **Programs** (or **All Programs** on Windows XP), point to **Accessories**, and then click **Command Prompt** to open a Command Prompt window.
3. To begin, type **netstat**.
4. Press **Enter** to view the computer's current active connections.
5. Type **netstat −a**.
6. Press **Enter** to view not only the currently established connections but also the ports on which your computer is listening for new connections.
7. Type **netstat −p TCP** and press **Enter** to view information about TCP connections.
8. Type **netstat −p UDP** and press **Enter** to view information about UDP connections.
9. To get a summary of all of Netstat's switches, type **netstat /?** and press **Enter**.
10. Type **exit** and press **Enter** to close the window.

Project 1-2: Search for a Numbered Request for Comment (RFC) Document

When you need to assign private IP addresses, it's important to choose the right numbers. The ultimate source for IP addresses is RFC document 1918, which is maintained by the Internet Engineering Task Force (IETF), a group dedicated to providing standardized solutions to the technical problems of running the Internet. Follow these steps to locate an RFC document when you know the RFC number.

1. If your computer is not powered up, power it up now.
2. When the Log on to Windows dialog box opens, in the User Name text box, type **administrator**.
3. In the Password text box, type **password**. (If this does not work, ask your instructor for the password.)

4. Double-click the **Internet Explorer** icon on the desktop to start your browser.

5. In the Address box, type **www.ietf.org**.

6. Press **Enter**. The home page of the Internet Engineering Task Force will appear in the browser window.

7. On the IETF home page, click the **RFC Pages** link. The IETF RFC Page appears.

8. On the IETF RFC Page under IETF repository retrieval, type **1918** in the text box for the RFC number.

9. Click **go**. Record the title of the document in a lab book or word-processing file. Click the **back arrow** on the toolbar of the Internet Explorer window to return to the IETF RFC page.

10. On the IETF RFC page, type **791** in the box for the RFC number.

11. Click **go**. A very old and very important document related to the development of the Internet appears. Record the title in a lab book or word-processing document.

12. Scroll down the RFC 791 document to section 3.1 to view some important information about packets. Record the information in a lab book or word-processing document.

13. Exit the site and close your browser.

Project 1-3: Use Whois To Learn About an Individual

This chapter discussed how easy it is to find vulnerabilities in a system. To illustrate the amount of ready information available online to hackers who are willing to put out only minimal effort, do your own Whois search. Whois is a service that looks up the information submitted by an individual upon registering a domain name. Whois is accessible from many ISPs, including VeriSign, which is illustrated in the steps that follow:

1. If your computer is not powered up, power it up now.

2. When the Log on to Windows dialog box opens, type **administrator** in the User Name text box.

3. In the Password text box, type **password**. (If this does not work, ask your instructor for the password.)

4. Double-click the **Internet Explorer** icon on the desktop to start your browser.

5. In the Address box, type **www.netsol.com/cgi-bin/whois/whois**. The WHOIS VeriSign page appears.

6. In the Search Our WHOIS Records text box, enter the name of your own school or university, such as **myuniversity.edu**.

7. Click **GO!**. A Search Results page appears containing the registration information for the site.

8. Scroll down the page and copy the name server addresses for your school into your lab book or a word-processing document.

9. Exit the site and close your browser.

Project 1-4: Do Your Own Manual "Port Scanning" at the Internet Assigned Numbers Authority (IANA) Web Site

Any networked computer has access to as many as 65,535 ports through which it can exchange information. When configuring firewalls, it's often important to record port numbers on which you want to block traffic. Certain port numbers are frequently used by hackers, and you should be aware of what they are. You can research these and many other ports online at the IANA Web site.

1. If your computer is not powered up, power it up now.

2. When the Log on to Windows dialog box opens, type **administrator** in the User Name text box.

3. In the Password text box, type **password**. (If this does not work, ask your instructor for the password.)

4. Double-click the **Internet Explorer** icon on the desktop to start your browser.

5. In the Address box, type **www.iana.org/assignments/port-numbers**.

6. Press **Enter**. The PORT NUMBERS document appears.

7. Write down port numbers that are considered Well Known Ports, which are Registered Ports, Dynamic Ports and/or Private Ports, in a lab book or a word-processing document.

8. Scroll down the page. Find which port number is assigned to Whois, which is presented in the list as Who Is. Because the list is very long, you can save time by clicking **Edit** and choosing **Find (on This Page)**.

9. In the Find What text box in the Find dialog box, type **Who Is**, and then click **Find Next**.

10. Repeat Steps 8 and 9 to look up the port numbers used by other common applications that need to be monitored by a firewall. These applications include HTTP, FTP, SMTP, POP3, Telnet, and DNS. Write down the answers in a lab book or word-processing document.

11. Exit the site and close your browser.

Project 1-5: Determine Your Computer's IP Address

Every computer that is connected to the Internet is assigned an IP address. Often the address is dynamically generated; that is, it changes from session to session. With some DSL connections and many T-1 or other connections, a static IP address is obtained. To determine the IP address of one of the computers to which you have access, follow these steps:

1. If your computer is not powered up, power it up now.

2. Click **Start**, point to **Programs** (or **All Programs** on Windows XP), point to **Accessories**, and then click **Command Prompt** to open a Command Prompt window.

3. To begin, type **ipconfig**.

4. Press **Enter**. The display that comes up will show you your IP Address. This will be four numbers separated by periods. In some cases you might have several addresses. The IP address assigned to your Ethernet adapter is the external address.

5. Write down the address in a lab book or word-processing document.

6. Type **exit** and press **Enter** to close the command prompt window.

Project 1-6: Run a Vulnerability Test on Your Computer

To get an idea of just how vulnerable your computer is to hackers, go to one of the sites that give run a security test on your machine. If your lab computer is already equipped with a firewall, so much the better. Even if it is not firewall-equipped as yet, you can still get an idea of the kinds of sensitive information you need to protect. Follow these steps:

1. If your computer is not powered up, power it up now.

2. When the Log on to Windows dialog box appears, in the User Name text box, type **administrator**.

3. In the Password text box, type **password**. (If this does not work, ask your instructor for the password.)

4. Double-click the **Internet Explorer** icon on the desktop to start your browser.

5. In the Address box, type **www.securityspace.com/smysecure/index.html**.

6. Press **Enter**. The Security Space Security Audits page will appear in the browser window.

7. In order to run a free security scan on your workstation, you need to register with the site's owner, Security Space. Registration is free, however. Scroll down the page to the How to Order/Run Audit section. Under New User, enter your e-mail address, and a user name and password of your own choosing. Deselect the two check boxes asking if you want to receive e-mail notifications from this site, and then click **Register**. A Member Services page appears, telling you your registration has been accepted and directing you to check your e-mail.

8. Open the program you usually use to receive e-mail. Retrieve the e-mail message with the subject line Member Services Registration Request and click the link included in the e-mail message. A Member Services Web page appears stating that your registration has been confirmed.

9. In the Registered User section of the same Member Services page, enter the UserID and password you just created, and then click **Login**.

10. The Security Space Member Services page appears. Click the link **Security Audits**.

11. Scroll down the page and click **No Risk Audit**. Click the **Run Audit** button. In the Web page that appears, choose **No Risk Audit** from the Audit Type drop-down list.

12. Click **Begin Audit**. A Web page appears stating that the test is either being run or is in a queue behind other tests. Check your e-mail periodically for a message entitled Security Audit Alert. Open the message and click on the link supplied in the body of the message. A Web page appears with a detailed report about any vulnerabilities found on your system.

Project 1-7: Enable Internet Connection Sharing

Internet Connection Sharing (ICS) is a simple NAT tool that is a built-in feature on Windows XP or 2000. Follow these steps to enable ICS on a Windows XP or 2000 workstation that is not configured to use a static IP address. If your workstation has a static IP address, skip this project.

1. Open your current network connection: In Windows XP, click **Start**, and then click **Control Panel**. Click **Network and Internet Connections**. Click **Network Connections**. (In Windows 2000, click **Start,** point to **Settings**, and choose **Control Panel**.) Double-click **Network and Dial-up Connections**.

2. In Windows XP, click your Internet connection to select it. Then, click the arrow next to **Network Tasks**, and then click **Change settings of this connection**. In Windows 2000, right-click the connection and choose Properties from the popup menu.

3. The Properties dialog box for the Internet connection opens. In Windows XP, click the **Advanced** tab. In Windows 2000, click the **Sharing** tab. If you do not have a Sharing tab on your current connection, create a new connection.

4. In Windows XP, check the box next to **Allow other network users to connect through this computer's Internet connection**. In Windows 2000, check the box next to **Enable Internet Connection Sharing for this computer**.

5. Click **OK**. Windows automatically changes the IP address of your local area network adapter to 192.168.0.1 with a subnet mask of 255.255.255.0. Computers on your network are allocated IP addresses in the range of 192.168.0.1 to 192.168.0.255.

CASE PROJECTS

Case 1-1: Making a Case for a Firewall

You are assigned by upper management to purchase a firewall and hardware, but first you have to prepare a report that 1) describes your organization's network, 2) lists three primary goals of a firewall, and 3) compares two different firewall packages that seem to be good options. Prepare the report based on your classroom's network.

Case 1-2: Locating the Network Perimeter

Create a diagram of your classroom's network. Be sure to determine where the network connects with the larger network—your school's network or the Internet. Indicate on the diagram where a firewall would go by drawing a miniature brick wall.

2

DEVELOPING A SECURITY POLICY

After reading this chapter and completing the exercises, you will be able to:

♦ Understand why a security policy is an important part of a firewall implementation

♦ Determine the goals of your firewall and incorporate them into a security policy

♦ Follow the seven steps to building a security policy

♦ Account for situations the firewall can't handle

♦ Define responses to security violations

♦ Work with adminstration to make your security policy work

An effective firewall starts with a well-defined security policy. In this chapter, you examine what a security policy is, why security policies are important, and how to set goals that govern how a firewall is configured to protect a network. You follow seven steps to building a security policy. You learn how to define responses to attacks and other intrusions. Finally, you get some directions on a subject that's often overlooked: guiding your security policy through corporate bureaucracy to gain management support and, ultimately, to achieve your organization's security policy goals.

WHAT IS A SECURITY POLICY?

Every organization with a computer network that is connected to outside networks such as the Internet needs to have a **security policy**. In the business world, a security policy tells employees and business partners what constitutes acceptable and unacceptable use of the network, what resources need to be protected, and how the company will respond to breaches of security.

An effective firewall depends on a clearly defined and comprehensive security policy. In fact, you might say that it's a good rule, when designing security systems, to *start with the policy, not the firewall*. In other words, instead of purchasing and installing one or more firewalls and then developing a policy around them (which many companies do), an organization should first identify what needs to be protected and develop a policy that addresses that protection in a comprehensive way, and then install a firewall as part of that policy. This chapter focuses on a particular type of policy: one that is used in the corporate and business world to protect network resources.

 If you are setting up a firewall to protect a single computer at home or to protect a small network of one or two computers, you don't need a full-fledged security policy. The material in this chapter assumes you are studying to become a network administrator or a security specialist in a mid- (20 to 100 employees) to large-scale (greater than 100 employees) organization, where a security policy is of great importance.

A security policy can cover a wide range of topics, from acceptable use to virtual private networks (VPNs). A single statement may prove insufficient to encompass all of a large organization's security needs. Many companies choose to compose a series of short statements, each on a specific topic; they are less intimidating to employees and easier to present on the company's Web site. For example, the University of Toronto's Computing and Networking Services (CNS) department publishes its security policy on their Web site in a series of short, hyperlinked statements, as shown in Figure 2-1.

When presenting your own security policy, be sure to include some of the essential information that is shown in Figure 2-1: the date the policy was last updated, the name of the office that developed the policies, a clear list of policy topics, and an equal emphasis on positive points (access to information) and negative points (unacceptable policies) for a well-balanced presentation.

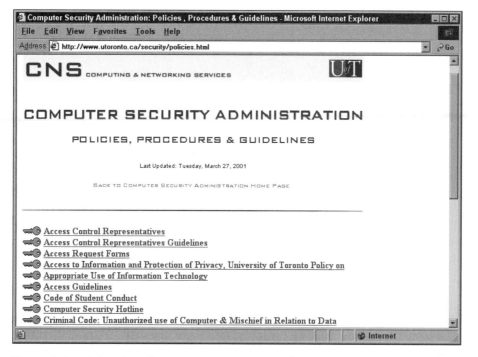

Figure 2-1   University of Toronto CNS security policies

WHY IS A SECURITY POLICY IMPORTANT?

You might wonder why you, a network administrator or security professional-in-training, need to concern yourself with the development of a corporate security policy in the first place. After all, administrative policies don't involve (at least directly) things like cables and routers and IP addresses. They probably seem like matters best left to management.

If you overlook the importance of setting such policies, however, you'll hamper the implementation of the firewall you are charged with designing and maintaining. The design of the firewall depends on the resources to be protected and the risks to those resources, both of which are spelled out in the security policy. As an essential component of a fully functional firewall, a security policy should be in place (or at least approved in draft form) before you begin to design your organization's firewall.

If the administrators of an organization for which you work are able to develop a clear policy, it makes your job easier because the security policy defines what you need to do when you configure a firewall for the organization. In addition, the policy tells you what kinds of intrusion detection and auditing systems you need to set up and covers you in case end users complain about certain aspects of the firewall.

Another reason the security policy associated with a firewall is so important is the impact it has on the organization that implements it. All users behind the firewall—as well as those who connect to the network—must conform to the security policy remotely. Their cooperation minimizes the impact of a "hack attack" or other unauthorized intrusion. The impact can be enormous and carry the following costs:

- *Staff time:* Employee resources have to be directed toward patching the security holes and preventing future attacks.

- *Data loss:* Sensitive customer and financial information can be compromised, which can impact the company's ability to generate revenue in the future.

- *Productivity:* When staff are recovering files and patching holes, they aren't pursuing the business of the organization. Salespeople can't take orders, and technicians cannot manage the system. A serious incident can put the network down for days at a time.

Employees need to have a clear idea of what the policy is and conform to it. If they don't accept the policy, they are likely to find ways around the security measures you have labored to put in place and open up the very holes you are trying to prevent.

SETTING GOALS FOR AN EFFECTIVE SECURITY POLICY

All security policies need to reflect the needs of the organization, taking into account critical assets to be protected and clearly identifying the goals to be accomplished. To be truly effective, such a policy needs to do the following:

- Describe a clear vision for a secure networked computing environment

- Be flexible enough to adapt to changes in the organization

- Be consistently communicated and implemented throughout the organization

- Spell out how employees can and cannot use the Internet—whether they can use FTP or telnet, for instance, or whether they can exchange personal e-mail or instant message from their office computers

- Define what constitutes appropriate and inappropriate behavior on the part of both employees and managers as it pertains to privacy and security (such as how to maintain password privacy or access the company network remotely)

The SANS Institute, a well-respected security organization, defines a "policy" as "a document that outlines specific requirements or rules that must be met. In the information/network security realm, policies are usually point-specific, covering a single area." (See *www.sans.org/newlook/resources/policies/policies.htm* for more information.) Related to a policy are standards, which are collections of system-specific requirements that all users must meet, and guidelines, which are sets of suggestions for best practices.

Some examples might clarify the differences between policies, standards, and guidelines. A policy that covers intrusion response would outline specific rules and regulations to follow in case a network intrusion is detected. A standard that describes how to prepare a Linux workstation for placement on a DMZ would list a set of system-specific or procedural requirements to follow to place the workstation on an external network. Guidelines for protecting passwords would spell out where and how passwords can and cannot be stored.

THE SEVEN STEPS TO BUILDING A SECURITY POLICY

Now that you have an overview of what a security policy is and why it is important, you can walk through the seven steps to building a security policy.

Developing a Policy Team

Don't be the only one who is responsible for preparing a security policy, even if you are the only one in the company who knows anything about firewalls and Internet security. You are more likely to get your policy approved by assembling a policy development team. Such a group should include the following:

- A senior administrator
- A member of the legal staff
- A representative from rank-and-file employees
- A member of the IT department
- An editor or writer who can structure and present the policy coherently

You should also identify the person who will be the official policy interpreter. This person communicates the recommendations to the staff and management. A general rule of thumb is that the policy team should contain five to ten people.

Determining the Organization's Overall Approach to Security

A good security policy should reflect the company's overall stance or *slant* toward security. As stated in Chapter 1, a firewall is a tool (or set of tools acting in combination) that enforces an access control/security policy between two networks. For a firewall to work, the organization that sets up the firewall has to determine the overall approach toward access control. That overall approach can take many forms, but, in general, it boils down to one of two primary activities:

- *Restrictive:* The primary emphasis is restricting traffic between the two networks to only a few authorized activities.
- *Permissive:* The primary emphasis calls for traffic to flow freely between the two networks except for communications using specified ports, services, or computers.

These two categories are pretty general in scope, however. When preparing a security policy for a real-world company, you need to be as specific as possible. Consider categorizing your approach according to one of several well-known (and more specific) security stances:

- *Open:* An organization that is aware of the need for security but that wants to make network resources open to end users and outsiders still needs to perform basic functions such as scanning security logs, installing operating system patches, keeping passwords secret, and scanning for viruses. The primary emphasis is on making resources available; an example would be a university library catalog system.

- *Optimistic:* An organization that takes an optimistic approach to security follows the basic procedures of the "open" organization but shows a higher degree of concern for potential problems. If you develop a policy that follows such an approach, install a stateless packet filter—one that receives and reviews packets of digital information at the perimeter of the network and either allows them to pass or blocks them based on IP address, port number, or other factors. The packet filter could be configured to let most packets pass but to block traffic from troublesome or questionable IP addresses or deny access to specific database servers on the internal network. A stateless filter would process packets without regard to the state of the connection. It might allow packets to pass through even though a connection does not currently exist between the host and destination computers.

- *Cautious:* A cautious security policy would specify basic packet filtering at the network perimeter but with a more strict approach. To follow this approach, you need to specify in the security policy that all packets will be blocked by default. The only traffic that will be allowed through the packet filter or firewall is traffic that meets stringent rules. In this case, a stateful packet filter should be used. This filter first verifies that the external host has actually established a connection with a host on the internal network. Stateful filters guard against letting mangled or fragmented packets into the network that could initiate denial-of-service or other attacks.

- *Strict:* A policy that advocates strict control over network security emphasizes breaking the connection between the private network and external networks. If you want to follow this approach, advocate application-layer gateways that would handle all traffic between internal and external hosts. The application-level gateway would allow only basic Web and e-mail traffic.

- *Paranoid:* A paranoid approach completely disconnects the internal network from the Internet. This approach is used by the U.S. government to protect its sensitive networks. You need to supply employees with a pool of workstations where they can access the Internet, but that pool would be completely separate from the internal network. The Internet-based workstations should be protected by a stateful packet filter as well.

In addition, many organizations have as a primary goal the need to audit and log traffic passing through the firewall. This gives companies information about who is trying to access them from outside, as well as data on how employees are using the Internet.

The policy you develop will determine which approach (restrictive or permissive) you want to emphasize or whether you want to give equal weight to both. The policy will also help you identify the kinds of traffic you want to block and specific types of traffic you want to permit. Without such a policy, even the most elaborate firewall system in the world can still be compromised.

Identifying the Assets To Be Protected

A good security policy lists in detail the resources owned by the company that need to be protected by the firewall. By formally stating that the company owns its computers, servers, and files stored on the network, it gains the right to search those devices in case a security incident occurs. A company's assets fall into the general categories described in the following sections.

You should create a master list of resources in your network. Include the names of all printers, scanners, computers, monitors, modems, routers, laptops, and other equipment; the serial numbers, if applicable; the offices where the items can be found; and the names of the current users. Because it can be easy to miss smaller items, such as palm devices or cell phone adapters, e-mail all employees and ask them to list all the equipment that they have in the office. You can then check these lists against your master list to see if anything has been overlooked.

The following sections provide more suggestions of what to catalog and how to keep track of everything.

Physical Assets

Your company's physical computing assets—the actual hardware devices that keep data flowing throughout the network—are the most obvious objects that need to be identified. List servers, routers, cables, workstation PCs, printers, and all other pieces of hardware owned by the company. Make a topology map that shows how the devices are connected, along with an IP allocation register.

You should pay special attention to the bastion host, which is the computer that sits at the periphery of your network and contains your firewall software. For more about bastion hosts, see Chapter 8.

Logical Assets

Logical assets are what most people think of when they think about a firewall. These assets are the digital information that can be viewed and misused by hackers or other "bad people." This information includes not only word processing, spreadsheet, Web page, and other documents but also e-mail messages, records of instant messaging conversations, and the log files that are compiled by the firewall. It also includes personnel, customer, and financial information that your company needs to protect.

Network Assets

Network assets comprise the routers, cables, bastion hosts, servers, and firewall hardware and software that enable those within your organization to communicate with one another and other computers on the Internet. Examine your network and take into account existing security mechanisms (routers with access lists, or **Intrusion Detection Systems [IDS]**) that you might already have in place.

System Assets

System assets refer to the software that runs your system—not so much the physical computers and routers and wires, but the server software and other applications that make information accessible to authorized users.

In listing physical, logical, network, and system assets, it is often helpful to assign a value to each object. The value can be an arbitrary number; what's important is to rank resources in order of importance so that you can focus your security efforts on the most critical resources first.

The team that helps you prepare your security policy will probably determine that data is more important than the digital devices on which they are stored. A possible set of values associated with a set of assets is presented in Table 2-1. The numbers shown are somewhat arbitrary and based on the author's own experience; you should derive your own rankings with the cooperation of your own organization's higher management:

Table 2-1   Resources to be protected

Resource	Order of Importance (1 to 100, with 100 most critical)
Financial data	100
Customer files	96
Job records and databases	92
Company archives	85
Employee files	82
E-mail messages	80
Computers, printers, and related hardware	78
Servers	75
Cabling	72
Routers	70

Determining What Should Be Audited for Security

The security policy you develop should also specify how communications across the firewall will be audited. **Auditing** is the process of recording which computers are accessing a network and what resources are being accessed. It also includes recording the information in a log file.

You should specify what types of communications (e-mail, FTP, Web) should be recorded. You should also state how long they will be stored (for a few days, a week, or a month, depending on how much storage space you have). Be up-front with your users about whether the audited communications will be used to investigate unauthorized use of the network.

Tripwire, a program that is available for both Unix and Windows, specializes in auditing system resources. It can prepare detailed reports on the state of one or more workstations' operating system and available applications. The program can be configured to run regular "integrity checks" (such as the one shown in Figure 2-2) and report on any changes to the system. A report of any changes found can either be e-mailed to the network administrator or written to a log file.

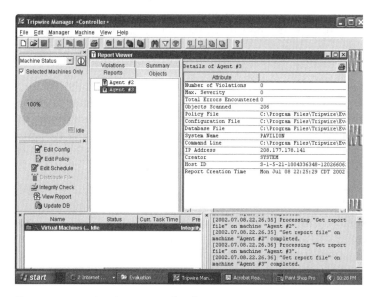

Figure 2-2   Tripwire can audit changes to system resources

A firewall log can audit a variety of security events. Note the information in the log for Norton Internet Security, which is shown in Figure 2-3. You can audit both successful and unsuccessful events, such as unsuccessful logon attempts. Repeated attempts to log on may indicate an attempt by an unauthorized individual to access the network.

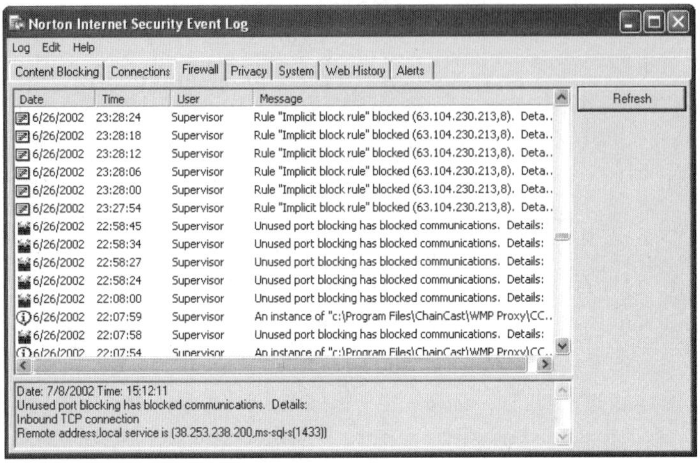

Figure 2-3 Norton Internet Security's audit event log

Auditing security events is an important part of a security policy. Your policy can spec-ify whether you want to audit unsuccessful attempts by external clients to access your network; you can also identify critical objects and audit those individuals who access them (you can also audit who attempts to access them and fails). In either case, you need to specify, in your security policy, the extent to which your firewall will audit general network access and individual object access.

Auditing Log Files

This is the most obvious type of auditing. The network administrator reads and analyzes log files to see who is accessing the network from the Internet. All connection attempts that were rejected by the firewall should be recorded in the hope of identifying possi-ble intruders or vulnerable points in the system.

Windows 2000 includes a Security log that can track when someone attempts and fails to log on to a file or folder. If you enable the logging of access failures, you can view whether users are attempting to gain access to files for which they do not have authorization to access. Figure 2-4 shows how to set up the logging of such events in Windows 2000's Local Security Settings. See Hands-on Project 2-5 for step-by-step instructions on how to acti-vate access failure logging.

Auditing Object Access

Through auditing, the firewall not only tells a company who is trying to break into the system or run malicious code there, but also who is accessing the Internet from inside the company. Often, security breaches come not from hackers in another country but from an employee in one office trying to access files in another office.

You can activate security auditing for individual folders in Windows 2000, as long as the disk that contains the folder is formatted in NTFS. Hands-on Project 2-6 shows how to activate auditing for an individual folder.

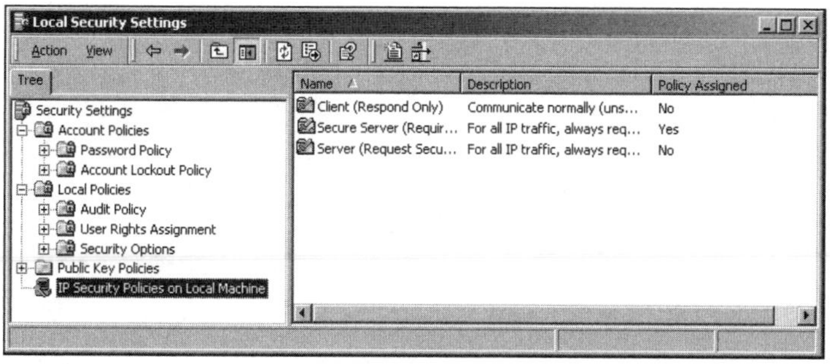

2

Figure 2-4   Windows 2000 Local Security Settings

In the case of an internal intranet protected by a firewall, such internal auditing can tell the administrator who is trying to access the protected information from elsewhere in the company. A security policy should spell out which logical resources are to be protected from unauthorized employees and the consequences of such intrusions.

Identifying Security Risks

Be specific about the kinds of attacks the firewall needs to guard against. These may include:

- Denial of service attacks

- Disclosure of information due to fraud

- Unauthorized access

Detailed descriptions can help you to determine appropriate security measures to guard against such attacks.

> The SANS Institute's Short Primer for Developing Security Policies (*www.sans.org/newlook/resources/policies/Policy_Primer.pdf*) goes into more detail about the kinds of security risks you need to account for in your own security policy.

Defining Acceptable Use

Every security policy must have an acceptable use policy. It defines acceptable computing and communications practices on the part of employees and business partners. Aspects of an acceptable use policy include:

- *E-mail:* Can the employees use corporate e-mail accounts for personal use? Can they exchange personal e-mail through a Web-based e-mail gateway? Should they encrypt and/or digitally sign e-mail messages?

- *News:* What constitutes acceptable newsgroup postings? Are cross-postings acceptable? Are attachments permitted?

The following is a sample acceptable use policy:

"Users shall not attempt to send or receive personal e-mail through the company gateway unless they use a personal account on a Web-based site. They may not use e-mail software with their own accounts through the gateway. No mailing lists other than the company newsletter will be distributed through the office gateway."

Providing for Remote Access

A large organization often includes staff who work at home, freelancers, and employees in remote offices. They all need remote access. In addition, Application Service Providers (ASPs) often need to access the company extranet and possibly access sensitive data. Last, business partners who are eager to process transactions online may need to connect through a VPN.

A security policy will address concerns surrounding such access by spelling out what protocols are acceptable. It will also determine the use of Telnet or **Secure Shell (SSH)** access to the internal network from the Internet and describe the use of cable modem, VPN, and DSL connections to access the internal network through the firewall. Remote users should be required to have a firewall on their computer to prevent intrusions into your network when they access files on it. (If a word-processing file is infected with a virus and a user transmits the file to your network by e-mail, it could potentially infect one of your network's computers.)

The following is an example of a remote access section of a security policy:

"Remote access to the company network is only permitted to individuals who have been issued passwords and usernames and can thus authenticate themselves. Passwords and usernames must not be handed out. Users with dial-up modems must use PPP with one of the company numbers to access the modem pool. Routers used to access the company network via ISDN must use the Password Authentication Protocol (PAP) or the Challenge Handshake Authentication Protocol (CHAP)."

 Within your network, or between your own company and partner companies you work with regularly, everyday communications may be secured adequately through firewalls and passwords. However, some resources are critical and need an enhanced level of protection. For instance, some businesses let trusted partners view their inventory and even place orders and schedule deliveries through the Internet. Other companies that have offices in multiple locations and that need to exchange sensitive information about payroll or health insurance might need extra-secure protection as well.

If you are on a Windows 2000 or XP network or another type of network that supports it, you can enable and use **IP Security (IPSec)** to protect communications. A security policy can address the specifications of IPSec between certain companies or computers. Keep in mind that the higher the security level you choose, the greater the negative effect on network performance. For more about IPSec, see Chapter 7.

ACCOUNTING FOR WHAT THE FIREWALL CANNOT DO

Many organizations rely solely on firewalls for their security. They think the more firewalls they add, the better off their security will be. They create a **firewall sandwich** at the perimeter of a network. Then, two or more (perhaps dozens) of firewalls are placed outside the local network, and they are enclosed by two **load balancing switches**. They then leave the multiple-firewall configuration alone, thinking that they're safe.

Note, however, that even the preceding setup can be compromised in different ways. Here are some actions that can breach even the most elaborate firewall setup:

- The flooding of the network with more traffic than the firewalls can handle, which is a **brute force attack** that causes the firewall(s) to crash
- The sending of an encrypted e-mail message to someone within the network with a virus attached to the message; the encrypted message will pass through the firewall and the virus can then infect the system
- Employees who give out remote access numbers so that unauthorized users can access the company network
- Employees who give out passwords

Firewalls are an important part of a network security scheme, but they aren't everything. An overarching security policy that sets policies for e-mail, passwords, and giving out inside information and that supplements the policy with firewalls is much more effective.

OTHER SECURITY POLICY TOPICS

Security policies can be as detailed as you wish, as long as you don't make them so long and unwieldy that you lose the attention of the very coworkers whose cooperation you need. Here are some suggestions for other security-related topics you might cover in a security policy:

- Passwords
- Encryption
- Restrictions on removable media
- ASPs
- Acceptable users
- Secure use of office-owned laptop computers
- Wireless security
- Use of VPNs
- Key policy (how you manage your private and public keys)

Defining Responses to Security Violations

It's important to use the security policy to define how you will respond to security break-ins. You may want to fill out a form specially intended to record what happens during a break-in. You can find incident response forms such as the one shown in Figure 2-5 at the SANS Institute's Web site to aid you in gathering information. You may also want to define disciplinary action to be pursued if employees access the Internet improperly.

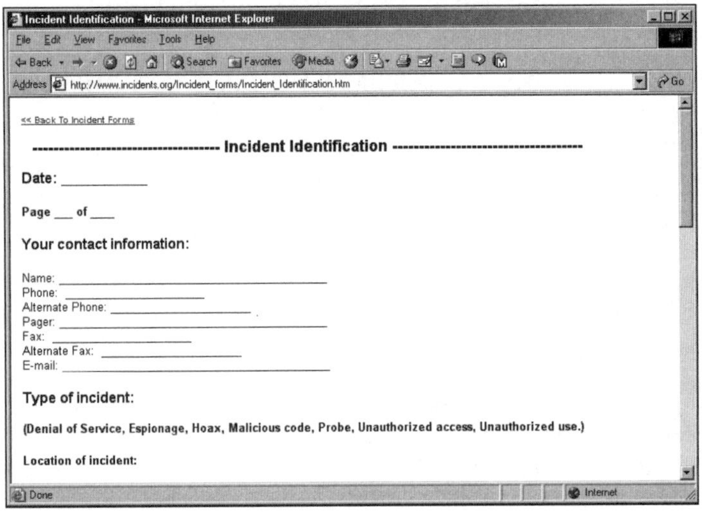
Incident Identification - Microsoft Internet Explorer

http://www.incidents.org/Incident_forms/Incident_Identification.htm

<< Back To Incident Forms

---------- Incident Identification ----------

Date: ____________

Page ___ **of** ___

Your contact information:

Name: ____________
Phone: ____________
Alternate Phone: ____________
Pager: ____________
Fax: ____________
Alternate Fax: ____________
E-mail: ____________

Type of incident:

(Denial of Service, Espionage, Hoax, Malicious code, Probe, Unauthorized access, Unauthorized use.)

Location of incident:

Figure 2-5 Sample incident response form

The Incident.org Web site also includes an Incident Survey form and an Incident Containment form, which provides a record of how a virus or other intrusion was contained, and the SANS Institute Web site includes an extensive Intrusion Detection FAQ (*www.sans.org/newlook/resources/IDFAQ/ID_FAQ.htm*). In addition, be sure to visit the CERT Coordination Center, part of Carnegie-Mellon University, which publishes a wide range of security-related news, alerts, and papers. In particular, learn more about their Incident, Detection, and Response (IDAR) Project at *www.cert.org/idar*.

Be sure to identify not only the primary individual to be contacted in case of intrusion but two or three backups as well, in case the first person is unavailable—or if a response team needs to be assembled in the event of a serious attack.

Overcoming Administrative Obstacles

Often, the hardest part of installing a firewall is not working with the hardware or software or interpreting log files, but justifying to those around you the restrictions you want to impose or, conversely, convincing a very security-conscious organization why it is sufficiently safe to access the Internet in the first place.

The development of a security policy typically only takes one to two weeks, in this author's experience. That's the easy part. However, after you have determined the items to be protected and the general security approach, the policy needs to be reviewed. The review and approval process can take anywhere from several weeks to several months, depending on the size of the company and number of approvals. Participants might benefit from seeing a timeline of the stages involved in developing a policy, as illustrated in Figure 2-6.

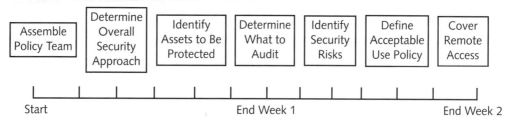

Figure 2-6   Security policy development timeline

The two-week period for developing a policy is by no means a hard and fast rule. It might be a goal to shoot for, but don't be dismayed if things take longer due to the need to set up meetings, hold discussions, get approvals, and participate in other bureaucratic processes.

Educating Employees

Keep in mind that for a security policy to work, the people who use it have to accept it and use it on a daily basis. Yet, security policies aren't something that workers are likely to welcome. Their priority is to get access to the information they need to complete their assigned tasks. Don't make the policy so strict and hard to comply with that staff will rebel and find ways around the system. Nonetheless, you may still encounter resistance, which is natural in any policy that affects the organization as a whole. [The staff may not like having rules imposed upon them, particularly security policies that may affect the speed with which they get work done.]

A **Security User Awareness program** can help employees understand and accept the organization's security strategy. This is something you'll have to manage on an ongoing basis—not just during the period when the security policy is being implemented. Some organizations give workers a security briefing that includes a security handbook tailored to their industry or site. Alternatively, you can also simply advise workers of what is expected of them and the consequences (both personally and for the corporation) for failure to abide by the policies. You can also review critical policies with users, go over each area of the agreement, and solicit questions.

Many organizations print out a set of acceptable use policies and require employees to read and sign them before they are issued system accounts or ID cards.

After policies have been distributed to employees, they should be made available on the local network, either on a Web page or in a database file, so that new hires can review them when they join the staff or at any time thereafter.

 Don't forget to date each policy when it is approved, and note when something is revised. If you are responsible for security in your organization, it may fall to you to distribute announcements of new security policies by broadcast e-mails to the staff as a whole.

Presenting and Reviewing the Process

Don't make reports too long. To make your report easier for management to digest, keep it short and concise—five pages or less in length, if possible. Give people one or two weeks to respond after the policy statement is issued. The policy development process is thus an ongoing one. You may also need to provide refresher courses or issue security updates as changes are made.

Amending the Security Policy

A security policy isn't written in stone. It should change when the organization makes substantial changes in its hardware configuration or when the firewall is reconfigured in response to security breaches. Any changes made to the firewall should be amended in the security policy.

CHAPTER SUMMARY

- ❑ Security policies are used in mid- to large-scale organizations rather than small home networks. A security policy should describe the organization's general approach to security and how the firewall is to implement that approach. It describes how communications through the network gateway are to be audited and how log files are to be used in case of intrusions.

- ❑ A successful firewall policy outlines specific goals of the firewall and reflects the company's overall stance or *slant* toward security. It takes into account critical assets that need to be protected. It also spells out how employees can and cannot use the Internet.

- ❑ The development of an effective security policy includes seven well-defined steps: develop a policy team; define an organization's overall security approach; identify assets to be protected; determine what security events should be audited; identify the security risks you want to combat; define acceptable use; and provide remote access to the network.

- ❑ A security policy can describe VPN and remote access as well as responses to security breaches. For situations where a higher-than-normal level of security is needed, the use of IPSec can be specified in the security policy.

❐ Finally, to succeed, a security policy must be developed with the cooperation and approval of management as well as the participation and acceptance of rank-and-file employees. You learned steps that you can take to make acceptance of a security policy possible.

Key Terms

auditing — The process of recording which computers are accessing a network and what resources are being accessed and recording the information in a file.

brute force attack — A way of breaching a firewall-protected network by flooding it with so much traffic that the firewalls crash and cease to function, thus letting traffic pass through.

firewall sandwich — A combination of two firewalls enclosed by two load balancing switches.

Intrusion Detection System (IDS) — Hardware or software that is designed to detect unauthorized access to network resources.

IP Security (IPSec) — A set of security standards developed by the IETF and for the next version of IP—Ipv6—as an optional extension to IP4. It is included in Windows 2000 and XP as well as many routers sold by Cisco Systems Inc. IPSec enables devices to connect in a secure manner. First, host and destination computers authenticate one another. Then data is transmitted using encryption.

load balancing switch — A hardware device that routes requests for information to the best Web server or cache available on a network, based on best response time and lightest load for the requested content.

Secure Shell (SSH) — A Unix-based protocol that enables secure access to a remote computer through a command interface.

security policy — A set of organization-level rules governing acceptable use of computing resources, security practices, and operational procedures.

Security User Awareness program — A program that instructs employees on an organization's overall security policy.

Review Questions

1. Which of the following describes an approach to security in which all packets will be blocked by default?

   a. optimistic

   b. cautious

   c. strict

   d. paranoid

2. Which of the following networking rules should be conveyed to employees? (Choose all that apply.)

   a. Use a password you can remember easily.

   b. Choose a password from an approved pool of suggestions.

   c. Pick a password that only you know.

   d. Use both characters and numerals in your password.

3. Which of the following describes aspects of a policy as opposed to a standard or a guide? (Choose all that apply.)

   a. makes suggestions without specifying alternatives

   b. outlines specific requirements or rules

   c. covers a single area

   d. a collection of requirements that must be met by everyone

4. What is the name for the part of the security policy that spells out how employees dial into the office network to access files?

   a. acceptable use policy

   b. remote access policy

   c. encryption policy

   d. audit policy

5. Explain what it means to "Start with the policy, not the firewall."

6. Why would you want to change a security policy?

   a. when you hire new employees

   b. when your equipment needs change significantly

   c. when you change your firewall configuration

   d. when staff requests that a change be made

7. What amount of time should you expect to spend on the security policy development process?

8. It's important for security specialists to remember that rank-and-file employees' primary concern is _____.

   a. keeping their address, phone number, and other personal information private

   b. getting access to the information they need

   c. making sure viruses don't damage their files

   d. protecting job files and customer records from theft

9. Why would you specify the use of IPSec in a security policy?

2

10. Which of the following is an essential component of a security policy? (Choose all that apply.)

    a. date of the most recent update

    b. list of policy topics

    c. emphasis on both positive and negative points

    d. all of the above

11. Why does a good security policy make your job easier?

12. A policy that describes how to respond to intrusions would include what specific types of information?

    a. IP addresses to be blocked

    b. who will be in charge in case of attack

    c. rules and regulations to follow in case of intrusion

    d. none of the above

13. A "cautious" approach to network security would spell out which approach to packet filtering?

    a. All packets will be allowed by default.

    b. All packets will be blocked by default.

    c. Static or stateful packet filtering should be used.

    d. Telnet connections are allowed.

14. How could you ensure that a far-flung and mobile student population knows their university's security policies? (Choose all that apply.)

    a. publish the security policy on the Web

    b. send out a broadcast e-mail to all students, informing them of the policy

    c. hold a special orientation session educating students about the policies

    d. print out the policies and require all students to read, sign, and return an acceptable use agreement

15. Your university has two campuses, 50 miles apart. Most communications between the campus do not need to be secure. However, some, like grade reports and admissions files, do require an extra level of security. How would you set up a policy that provides for extra-secure communications on an as-needed basis? Be as specific as possible.

16. When should a security policy be changed?

17. Which of the following is a reason to audit network communications?

    a. to track who makes purchases online

    b. to track the most popular pages on the company's Web site

    c. to investigate unauthorized accesses to the network

    d. to log excessive personal e-mail usage

18. You are hired by a company that employs a number of freelance transcriptionists who work at home. They need to access the network remotely so they can submit timesheets online and send the company transcriptions of medical tests that need to be confidential. What would you include in the remote access portion of the security policy for this company?

19. Explain what a Security User Awareness program is and how it can be implemented.

20. Explain what can happen if a security policy is too strict.

HANDS-ON PROJECTS

Project 2-1: Locate and Fill Out an Incident Identification Form

You don't have to start from scratch when it comes to creating security policies. In fact, if you are hired to handle security at a company, when it comes time to discuss the development of a security policy you can produce a template and show it to management so they get an idea of what's required.

1. If your computer is not powered up, power it up now.

2. When the Log on to Windows dialog box opens, type your user name in the User Name text box. (If the Log on to Windows dialog box does not appear, click **Start**, click **Log Off**, and then log on with your username and password.)

3. In the Password text box, type the password your instructor has given you.

4. Press **Enter**.

5. When the desktop appears, double-click the **Internet Explorer** icon button to start your browser.

6. In the Address box, type **http://www.incidents.org/Incident_forms**. The Incident Handling Forms page of the Incidents.org Web site opens.

7. When the Incident Handling Forms page appears, click **Incident Identification**.

8. Print out the sample Incident Identification page. Fill it out as though there has been an unauthorized access in your school lab. Save the page so you can in turn it in later to your instructor.

9. Close your browser.

Project 2-2: Draw Up a List of Resources To Be Protected

Refer to Table 2-1 of this chapter. Draw up a checklist of the resources in your own computer lab that need to be monitored; rank them in order of importance. Follow these steps in your own lab to get practice for similar situations in the corporate world later on.

1. On a piece of paper or in a word-processing document, create a three-column table. In the first column, write down or type the names of the servers, workstations, printers, hubs, and other hardware devices in your computer lab.

2. At the head of the second column, write or type **Model Number**.

3. At the head of the third column, write or type **Serial Number**.

4. Fill in the table for the hardware devices in your lab.

5. Turn the list in to your instructor. Did you forget any equipment, and did you account for everything?

Project 2-3: Enable IPSec on a Windows 2000 Workstation

 You need access to a computer running Windows 2000 Professional or Server for this project.

You need to use IPSec for an extra-secure level of communication between computers. To start using IPSec for communications between machines running Windows 2000 or XP, you need to enable IPSec and then configure the IPSec policy through local or group policy security settings for each Windows machine that needs the heightened security. IPSec is an important protocol that is widely used to encrypt communications between computers in a VPN. The first step in setting up such a connection is to enable IPSec on both computers, as you will do in this project.

1. If your computer is not powered up, power it up now.

2. When the Log on to Windows dialog box opens, enter your user name in the User Name text box.

3. In the Password text box, type the password you have been assigned.

4. Press **Enter**.

5. When the desktop appears, click **Start**, point to **Settings**, click **Network and Dial-Up Connections**, and double-click **Local Area Connection**.

6. Click **Properties**.

7. In the Local Area Connection Properties dialog box, click **Internet Protocol (TCP/IP)**, and then click **Properties**.

8. In the Internet Protocol (TCP/IP) Properties dialog box, click **Advanced**.

9. In the Advanced TCP/IP Settings dialog box, click the **Options** tab.

10. In the **Optional settings** box of the Options tab, click **IP security**, and then click the **Properties** button.

11. In the IP security dialog box, click the **Use this IP security policy** radio button, and then choose one of the three security policy options in the list box (Client, Secure Server, or Server). Click **Client** if your workstation will function as the client in a VPN connection with a server that is also running IPSec. Click **Server** if your workstation will function as the VPN server, and click **Secure Server** if you plan to use encryption and authentication as part of the VPN connection.

12. Click **OK** to close the IP Security dialog box.

13. Click **OK** to close all the other open dialog boxes in succession and return to the Windows desktop.

Project 2-4: Make a Topology Map

The topology of a computer network is a study of how different nodes in that network are connected to each other and how they communicate. A network topology drawing can be a valuable tool in selling and promoting a security policy both to managers and to rank-and-file employees. By showing how many nodes there are and indicating all the different ways in which information flows through the network, you can impress readers and gain value for the approach to security you are advocating. Draw a topology map of your own computer lab by following these steps:

1. Draw a map of your lab that shows where the windows are located and that includes the tables or desks on which computer workstations and other network devices sit.

2. Determine how the workstations in your lab connect to one another. Is there a central server to which all the workstations connect (in other words, does the network have a star topology)? Or are the machines connected in a chain, without a central server (in other words, a bus topology)?

3. If your network has a central server, draw it first, and then draw the workstations connected to it. If not, draw the workstations in a diagram that indicates how they are connected.

4. Go to each workstation in your lab and determine its IP address by doing the following: Click **Start**, point to **Programs**, point to **Accessories**, and click **Command Prompt**. At the command prompt, type **ipconfig**, and then press **Enter**. The IP address is listed along with the subnet mask, default gateway, and other information.

5. Label each node in the network with its corresponding IP address. Turn the map in to your instructor.

Project 2-5: Activate Windows 2000 Logon Auditing

Auditing policies are part of many security policies. To understand which policies you can audit, you should view the types of policies that can be tracked by Windows 2000, and then enable logging for a specific type of policy that can indicate intrusion attempts.

1. Click **Start**, point to **Settings**, and click **Control Panel**.

2. In the Control Panel dialog box, double-click **Administrative Tools**.

3. In the Administrative Tools dialog box, double-click **Local Security Policy**.

4. In the Local Security Policy Management Console, double-click the **Local Policies** folder, and then double-click the **Audit Policy** folder.

5. In the right pane of the Management Console, double-click **Audit account logon events**.

6. In the Local Security Policy Setting dialog box, check the **Success** and **Failure** check boxes, and then click **OK**.

7. Close the Local Security Policy Management Console.

8. Log off Windows 2000 Professional and then log back on so you can see the effect of the new audit policy you enabled.

9. Click **Start**, point to **Settings**, and click **Control Panel**.

10. Double-click **Administrative Tools**.

11. Double-click **Event Viewer**.

12. In the left pane of the Event Viewer, click **Security Log**.

13. View any events in the security log by double-clicking each event. Click the **Success Audit event** that was created when you just logged on.

14. Log off and log on to Windows 2000 again—but this time with an incorrect password. Then log on with your correct password and check the security log.

15. How many events were created by your two logon attempts?

Project 2-6: Activate Object Access Auditing

As part of a security policy you create, you can specify that certain folders or other objects be restricted as far as who can access them. The following project will help you to understand what kinds of auditing specifications you can impose on a folder or other object. This type of auditing will work only on NTFS-formatted drives. Skip this project if you do not have access to a workstation with an NTFS-formatted drive.

1. Click **Start**, point to **Settings**, and click **Control Panel**.

2. In the Control Panel dialog box, double-click **Administrative Tools**.

3. In the Administrative Tools dialog box, double-click **Local Security Policy**.

4. Double-click the **Local Policies** folder, and then double-click the **Audit Policy** folder.

5. In the right pane of the Management Console, double-click **Audit object access**.

6. In the Local Security Policy Setting dialog box, check the **Success** and **Failure** check boxes, and then click **OK**.

7. Close the Local Security Policy Management Console. Next, you need to select the folder for which you want to track access.

8. Open Windows Explorer and select a drive that is formatted for NTFS. Your instructor can tell you which drive to select.

9. Create a new folder under the root of the drive, and name it **Secure-info**.

10. Right-click the **Secure-info** folder, and then click **Properties** from the context menu.

11. Click the **Security** tab, and then click the **Advanced** button.

12. Click the **Auditing** tab, and then click the **Add** button.

13. In the Select User, Computer, or Group dialog box, click **Authenticated Users**, and then click **OK**.

14. In the Auditing Entry for Secure-info dialog box, under the Successful column, check the **List Folder/Read Data** check box, and then click **OK**.

15. Click **OK** to close all open dialog boxes and return to Windows Explorer.

16. Double-click the **Secure-info** folder.

17. Open the Event Viewer.

18. Click **Security Log**.

19. How many events did simply opening the Secure-info folder create?

CASE PROJECTS

Case 2-1: Develop a Response Plan

Your firewall software sends you an "urgent" e-mail message notifying you that your company's customer database has been accessed by an unauthorized user. You are nervous and can't remember what to do, so you turn to the security policy. What should your policy tell you to do in response?

Case 2-2: Create a Security Policy Team

You work in a small university with about 3000 students and 350 administrative staff. The university has a president, vice-president, provosts, and various departments (public relations, legal, admissions, human relations, student affairs, human relations, housing, accounting, and so on). You are assigned to assemble a security policy development team. Draw up a list of the essential participants.

Case 2-3: Develop a Security Policy for Your Computer

You live in a dorm room with two roommates. You share one personal computer that has a high-speed "always-on" connection to the Internet. You continually have animated discussions regarding who is to use the computer and when. It is not unusual for one user to download another's e-mail by mistake and read it because the previous user didn't log off the machine. Apply what you've learned about security policies in this chapter to your own situation. What policies would you come up with for your own shared computer, and how would you implement them? Report to your instructor on the policy you developed.

Case 2-4: Justify a Security Policy

You are installing a firewall and intrusion detection system for a small company. You suggest drawing up a security policy, but management doesn't understand why one is needed. You are told, "All our employees are responsible, honest people." You need to make a case for a security policy. Explain why a security policy is important in relation to a firewall, why even honest employees can breach a firewall, and what can happen as a result of a security breach.

3

FIREWALL CONFIGURATION STRATEGIES

> **After reading this chapter and completing the exercises, you will be able to:**
> ♦ Set up firewall rules that reflect an organization's overall security approach
> ♦ Understand the goals that underlie a firewall's configuration
> ♦ Identify and implement different firewall configuration strategies
> ♦ Employ methods of adding functionality to your firewall

In this chapter, you learn how to design perimeter security for a network that integrates firewalls with a variety of other software and hardware components. Firewalls aren't intended to do just one thing or to block just one type of threat. By using one or more firewalls in conjunction with routers, gateways, hubs, and switches, you can block many common attacks while permitting hosts inside the network to access the Internet.

The main objective in this chapter is to give you an overview of the kinds of approaches you can use so you can put them together in specific situations. This chapter begins with a review of the kinds of rules and restrictions that influence how you configure a security perimeter. Then, you are presented with a variety of security configurations that either perform firewall functions or that use firewalls to create protected areas.

ESTABLISHING RULES AND RESTRICTIONS FOR YOUR FIREWALL

After you have set a security policy as described in Chapter 2, you can begin to implement the strategies that policy specifies. One way is "train" your firewall by setting rules. Rules can give the firewall specific criteria on which to make decisions on whether to allow packets through or drop them.

The firewall rules and the definitions you set up tell the firewall what types of traffic to let in and out of your network. All firewalls have a rules file; it is the most important configuration file on your firewall.

 An important question to ask your firewall vendor is whether you will need to reboot the firewall every time you make a change to the rules file. If you are shopping for a carrier-class firewall, this is a must. If you are in the market for a SOHO firewall, an occasional firewall reboot will probably not impact you too much.

In the sections that follow, you learn about general approaches to follow when setting up a set of rules for a firewall. You learn about the role of the rules file in a firewall's operation. Then you learn about rules for firewalls that are designed to be primarily restrictive in operation versus those that are designed to enable connectivity. Once you understand the different options, you can create specific rules that determine how the firewall actually behaves.

The Role of the Rules File

The specific **packet-filtering** rules that you set up for a firewall actually implement the security approach specified in your security policy. A restrictive approach will be reflected in a set of rules that blocks all access by default, then permits only specific types of traffic to pass through. A connectivity-based approach will have fewer rules because its primary orientation is to let all traffic through and then block specific types of traffic.

The rules that you establish not only block traffic coming from outside your network, but they enable traffic to get outside the network from individual hosts. Rules that permit traffic to your DNS server, for instance, are essential if your internal users are going to access other computers on the Internet using domain name resolution.

Finally, the rules are important because they establish an order that the firewall should follow. Firewalls should process rules in top-to-bottom order, so the first rules should cover the most basic types of traffic, such as ICMP messages that computers use to establish basic communications. Rules are usually processed in the same order to avoid confusion about which is most important.

Restrictive Firewalls

If the primary goal of your planned firewall is to block unauthorized access, the emphasis needs to be on restricting rather than enabling connectivity. In such a "Deny-All" approach, the firewall will block *everything* by default and only specifically allow those services you need on a case-by-case basis. Deny-All and other primarily restrictive approaches are described in Table 3-1.

3

Table 3-1 Restrictive Firewall Approaches

Approach	What It Does	Advantage	Disadvantage
Deny-All	Blocks all packets except those specifically to be allowed	More secure; requires fewer rules	May result in user complaints
In Order (sometimes called "first fit")	Processes firewall rules in top-to-bottom order	Good security	Incorrect order can cause chaos
Best Fit	The firewall determines the order in which the rules are processed—usually it starts with the most specific rules and goes to the most general	Easy to manage; reduces risk of operator error	Lack of control

If you decide to first restrict all transmissions through the gateway except a specific set of services, you are following the concept of "**least privilege**." This refers to the practice of designing operational aspects of a system to operate with a minimum amount of system privilege. Least privilege reduces the authorization level at which various actions are performed and decreases the chance that a process or user with high privileges will perform unauthorized activity, resulting in a security breach.

There are other ways in which you can implement the overall approaches described in an organization's security policy. You can carry out specific elements of the policy in the firewall by following strategies such as these:

- Spell out services that employees cannot use. On the firewall, you can block services such as FTP or Telnet. You can use authentication to enable such services to be used only by a network administrator.

- Use and maintain passwords. Enable authentication on the firewall so users can only surf the Web or use e-mail after they successfully authenticate themselves—this forces employees to keep track of passwords and to remember them.

- Follow an "open" approach to security. Set the firewall to allow all traffic to pass through by default, but block specific Web sites or specific services as needed.

- Follow an "optimistic" approach to security. Set up a stateful packet filter configured to let most packets pass but to block traffic from troublesome or questionable IP addresses, or deny access to specific database servers on the internal network.

- Follow a "cautious" approach to security. Set up a stateful instead of (or in addition to) a stateless packet filter.

- Follow a "strict" approach to security. Set up application proxy gateways that forward requests on behalf of internal users.

- Follow a "paranoid" approach to security. Set up one or more packet filters to protect a pool of workstations set aside to allow access to the Web and e-mail only and that are not connected to the internal network, which has no connection at all to any external networks.

Connectivity-Based Firewalls

If the primary orientation of your firewall is permissive—that is, permitting connectivity through the gateway—this places a burden on you in your role as security administrator to educate your coworkers on how to use the network responsibly. Most employees don't want to put the company at risk. However, at the same time, they want to access data and be productive. It's your job to help them understand how to get their work done in a secure manner.

Table 3-2 lists the advantages and disadvantages of whether your firewall should enforce a restrictive policy or one that emphasizes connectivity.

Table 3-2   Connectivity-based Firewall Approaches

Approach	What It Does	Advantage	Disadvantage
Allow-All	Allows all packets to pass through except those specifically identified to be blocked	Easy to implement	Provides minimal security; requires complex rules
Port 80/ Except Video	Allows Web surfing without restrictions, except for video files	Lets users surf Web	Opens network to Web vulnerabilities

In almost all instances, this is not an either/or question. Most firewalls are partly restrictive and partly connective. Your job is to strike a balance between the two.

The order in which rules are set can be critical. Another feature to find out about is if the firewall supports automatic order-independent rules. The rules on a firewall need to be in a very specific order or they will not work properly. Some firewalls have the ability to order the rules automatically. This feature can be both good and bad, so you will want to make sure that if it exists, you have the capability to turn it on and off. The algorithms and code used to make the order-independent rule-setting decisions need to be completely bug free, or using this feature could open up security holes on your network. In a perfect technical world, automatic order-independent rule setting is a great feature because if you have a lot of firewall rules, it can help you understand how to order the rules properly. However, there is no substitute for human knowledge in setting up your firewall rules.

FIREWALL CONFIGURATION STRATEGIES: THE 10,000-FOOT OVERVIEW

No two firewalls are exactly alike. The requirements for an online trading company's firewall differ from that of a mail-order catalog, which differ from a law firm's Web site, and so on. When you are configuring a firewall for an organization, you need to set it up so that it meets certain criteria. It needs to be scalable so it can grow with the network it protects. It needs to take into account the communication needs of individual employees, who see Web surfing and e-mail as must-haves to be productive. Because TCP/IP is the protocol of choice for internal networks these days as well as the Internet itself, the firewall also needs to deal with the IP address needs of the organization—to do IP forwarding or Network Address Translation (NAT), for instance.

Scalability

A firewall needs to adapt to the changing needs of the organization whose network it protects. Hopefully, one of those changes will be the growth of the company itself. More business coming in from the Internet and more staff on board may mean more firewall resources. Be sure to provide for the firewall's growth by recommending a periodic review and upgrading software and hardware as needed.

Productivity

One of the challenges of implementing a firewall is the speed with which staff are able to communicate and exchange data. The stronger and more elaborate your firewall, the slower those data transmissions are likely to be. Productivity is definitely a concern if you use a proxy server, which tends to slow down communications between users inside the company who are trying to access the Internet.

Two important features of the firewall are the processing and memory resources available to the **bastion host**. A bastion host, though it may not be the only hardware component in a firewall architecture, is of central importance to the operation of the firewall software that it hosts. If the host machine runs too slowly or doesn't have enough memory to handle the large number of packet-filtering decisions, proxy service requests, and other traffic, the productivity of the entire organization can be adversely affected. That's because the bastion host resides on the perimeter of the network and, unless other bastion hosts and firewalls have been set up to provide the network with load balancing, the bastion host is the only gateway through which inbound and outbound traffic can pass.

A bastion host, then, is not just a computer that has been specially hardened and that runs the firewall, proxy server, or other software. It also needs to have sufficient processor speed and memory to handle all of the network's present traffic and increased traffic as the network grows. Scalability and security are important not only to the firewall but to its bastion host machine as well.

Memory, however, is critical to firewall performance and the productivity of the individual users that the firewall protects. Your bastion host needs sufficient RAM to support every instance of every program necessary to service the load placed on the machine. Otherwise, the host starts to do memory swapping and productivity goes down.

A **critical resource** is defined as a software- or hardware-related item that is indispensable to the operation of a device or program. Table 3-3 lists critical resources for a firewall's successful operation. Restricting the items in the second column of the table will conserve critical resources.

Table 3-3   Critical Resources for Firewall Services

Critical Resource	Service To Be Restricted
Disk I/O	E-mail
Disk I/O	News
Bastion Host OS Performance	IP Routing
Bastion Host OS Performance	Web Cache
Bastion Host OS Performance	Web

Dealing with IP Address Issues

The more complex a network becomes, the more IP-addressing complications arise. It's important to plan out the installation, including IP addressing, before you start purchasing or installing firewalls.

Both a Demilitarized Zone (DMZ) and a service network need IP addresses. If your service network needs to be privately rather than publicly accessible, which DNS will its component systems use? You can ask your ISP for more addresses if they are available. If not, you may need to do NAT and convert the internal network to private addressing.

However, when you mix public and private addresses, this brings up more questions. How will your Web server and DNS servers communicate? If the Web server uses a public IP address that is stored in your external DNS server and the local subnet uses private addressing, communications may fail. You can solve the problem by switching to public addresses on the private network or by binding two IP addresses—one public and one private—to each network. Be sure to figure out such problems beforehand rather than encountering them after you've purchased and installed your hardware.

IP forwarding enables a packet to get from one network's OSI stack of interfaces to another. Most operating systems are set up to perform IP forwarding. Many operating systems perform IP forwarding, as do routers. Proxy servers that handle the movement of data from one external network to another perform the same function; however, if a proxy server is working, IP forwarding should be disabled on routers and other devices that lie between the networks. It's better to let the proxy server do the forwarding because it's the security device —having routers do the IP forwarding will defeat the purpose of using the proxy and make communications less secure.

 The need for advance planning applies not only to firewalls but to servers and other hardware. There may be specific aspects of your design that influence your hardware selection. For example, suppose you want your firewall to include a proxy server function. You have to make sure you have the hardware to support a proxy server that provides services for the Web, e-mail, FTP, chat, instant messaging, and other means of network communication. Assess the hardware that will host the firewall or proxy server. If you expect the firewall to experience high traffic volumes—for instance, if you run a busy e-commerce Web server—you may be better off avoiding a proxy server and sticking with packet filters, which don't require as much memory and processor speed. Proxy servers quickly consume memory and processor time, so if you plan to run them, buy a machine that has as much of these resources as you can afford.

DIFFERENT FIREWALL CONFIGURATION STRATEGIES YOU CAN USE

After you have set up a security policy as described in Chapter 2 and determined the overall rules you want the firewall to follow, you can start designing your firewall architecture to be a practical implementation of your desired policy. This section describes a variety of different firewall configurations; they are described in Table 3-4.

Table 3-4   Different Firewall Configurations

Name	Description
Screening router	Packet-filtering router sits between client computers and the Internet.
Dual-homed host	A client computer that is connected to the Internet hosts firewall software.
Screened host	A host dedicated to security functions hosts the firewall software.
Two routers with one firewall	Routers are positioned on the external and internal interfaces of the firewall and perform packet filtering.
DMZ screened subnet	A network of publicly accessible servers (the DMZ) is connected to the firewall but is outside the internal network being protected.
Multi-firewall DMZ	A DMZ is enclosed by two firewalls for added security.
Reverse firewalls	A firewall that monitors outbound rather than inbound traffic.
Specialty firewalls	Firewalls designed to protect specific types of communications, such as e-mail.

Firewalls can and do get complex in large organizations that have multiple networks and VPNs that connect them to branch offices and partners. To understand those architectures, you first need to understand the simple firewall setups you might use yourself for home or small office use.

First, you need to settle on the general approaches you are going to try and establish rules for them. Then, you deploy your firewall(s), router(s), VPN tunnel(s), and other tools in a way that will implement the rules.

Table 3-5 presents a few suggestions about the different kinds of security components you can use to defend against common attacks.

Table 3-5   Firewall Threats and Defenses

Threat	Defense
SYN flooding	Cisco PIX Firewall has a Flood Defender that can cut such attacks short.
Port scanning	Review your firewall logs and block access from "bad" IP addresses.
Viruses	Make sure virus protection software is incorporated into your firewall hardware or software.
Harmful e-mail attachments	Use software that scans Port 25 for SMTP traffic, such as MailGuard, which comes with the Cisco PIX Firewall.

Once you understanding a simple firewall's components, as described in the following sections, you'll have a foundation that will help when you get to the more sophisticated **network topologies**.

In this chapter, not only the single software program that is called a firewall is discussed, or a hardware appliance that is sold as a firewall, but also all of the hardware and software that goes into creating a firewall architecture. That includes routers, firewall software, bastion hosts, VPN devices, and the like. In reality, a firewall is made up of multiple hardware and/or software entities. The diagrams in this chapter may show routers, firewalls, and servers as separate entities, but don't take this as the only way a configuration can be made. In fact, a firewall may include a router and proxy server, and they may all be contained within a single bastion host.

Screening Router

One of the simplest types of protection is a router that sits between the client computer(s) and the Internet and that is set up to do packet filtering. Such a **screening router** filters traffic to individual computers within the internal network. You should only choose this very simple, minimally secure setup in a situation such as a subnet within a network that is already protected by a firewall.

A router has two interfaces: the **external interface** is the one that connects to the outside network. The **internal interface** connects to the internal network that's being protected (see Figure 3-1). Each interface has its own unique IP address.

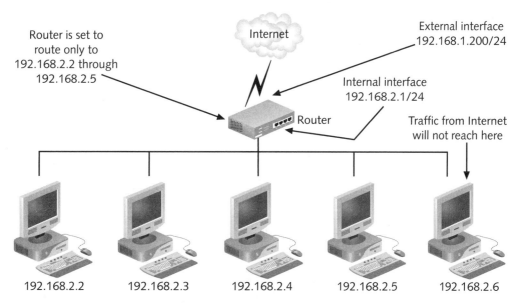

Figure 3-1   Screening router functioning as packet filter

The primary function of a router is to perform IP forwarding: it forwards packets from one network to another one. It determines where packets should go through an interface and which should be blocked based on a set of rules called an **access control list (ACL)** or simply access list.

As you learned in Chapter 1, some routers do static packet filtering: they allow traffic to pass through whether a connection has been established or not. This allows a hacker to format the packet header to make it look like there is a connection and thus sneak a packet through. Other more sophisticated routers perform **stateful packet filtering**: the device first verifies whether data from a host within the network being protected has gone outbound to the host making the request. Only if data has gone outbound will the device allow traffic to pass inbound (see Figure 3-2).

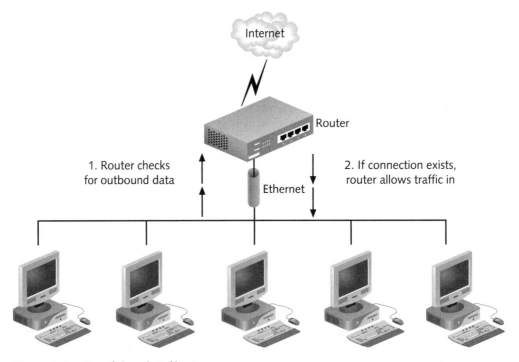

Figure 3-2   Stateful packet filtering

 An even simpler network security measure doesn't involve the installation of routers or any other hardware. The individual or small business depends on an Internet Service Provider (ISP) to provide firewall functions. Usually those functions involve packet filtering to filter traffic into and out of the client's network. The ISP may also provide proxy services or NAT. Not all ISPs provide such service, however, and not all can guarantee protection against all viruses or Trojan horses.

Dual-Homed Host

Another security setup, one that is used by scores of individuals with personal computers connected to the Internet, is a **dual-homed host** equipped with a firewall. Dual-homed host is a fancy-sounding term for a computer that has two network interfaces (and correspondingly, two network interface cards). Typically, one interface card is assigned to the Internet and the other to a local area network. By default, the host's ability to forward IP packets from one network to the other is completely disabled. Rules are then established by the end user to enable traffic to flow through the firewall as needed. You might choose this setup in situations such as securing a single standalone workstation and securing a small home network.

As an added defense, the computer is equipped with firewall software that works between the operating system and the network interface card that connects it to the Internet. Such a system is good for casual use by one computer or a small home network. It can be set up to do packet filtering, like the packet-filtering router mentioned in the previous section.

Note that a dual-homed host has obvious limitations from the standpoint of business security. The firewall depends on the same computer system that is used for day-to-day communications, so any problems with the host machine weaken the firewall. Although the firewall can do packet filtering, it may be able to do little or no logging so you can track break-in attempts. The big disadvantage is that the host serves as a single point of entry to the organization. Although it's true that having a single "checkpoint" is usually a good thing, there is a downside: having a simple checkpoint means that a hacker has only one layer of protection to break through to infiltrate the local network that needs to be protected. Thus, Defense in Depth proves to be even more important with this firewall architecture. On the other hand, if the layers of protection at that single checkpoint are configured correctly, a hacker's attempts to infiltrate the network will usually be repulsed successfully.

Screened Host

A screened host is sometimes also called a dual-homed gateway or bastion host. A bastion host is a screened host, but one that been hardened through the addition of all available security patches and service packs. In addition, the bastion host has had all but the necessary services and TCP and UDP ports disabled, and all of its security-related events are extensively logged. A screened host setup is similar to the dual-homed host, but the big difference is that the host is dedicated to performing security functions. A router is often added between the screened host and the Internet to do IP packet filtering. You might choose this setup in situations such as perimeter security at the edge of a corporate network, for instance.

The screened host still needs to have two network connections, as shown in Figure 3-3.

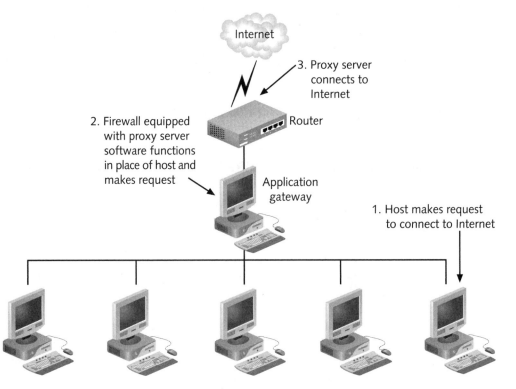

Figure 3-3   Screened host security configuration

A common enhancement is to have the screened host function as an application gateway or proxy server. The only network services that are allowed to pass through the proxy server are those for which proxy applications are already available.

 The difference between a screened host and a bastion host is in the degree of security. Both sit exposed on the perimeter of the network rather than behind the firewall.

Two Routers, One Firewall

A common configuration is to put a router on either side of the screened host that serves as a firewall. The router positioned on the outside can perform initial, static packet filtering. The router positioned just inside the network can route traffic to the appropriate computers in the LAN being protected. You might choose this setup in situations where you truly need Defense in Depth, such as a government office network or a financial institution.

The interior router can do stateful packet filtering (a subject covered in more detail later in this chapter). (See Figure 3-4.) Alternatively, the firewall itself might be equipped with a stateful packet filter, in which case a second interior router might not be needed at all. Having another router present adds another layer of protection between the LAN and the outside network.

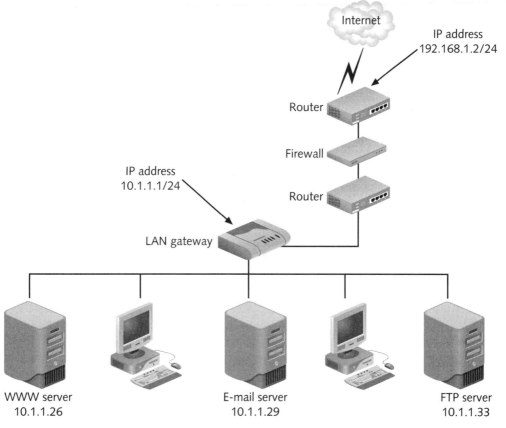

Figure 3-4 Two routers surround the firewall

 Multiple routers inside the firewall can be used to direct traffic to subnets within a large organization.

DMZ Screened Subnet

As stated, a DMZ is a network that sits outside the internal network but that is connected to the firewall and that provides publicly available servers, such as Web servers, and a host-and-router combination is the combination of a single workstation (the host) with a router that directs traffic to it and the other machines on the network. What is the key difference between a DMZ and a host-and-router combination? You create a **screened subnet** by adding servers that permit public services like a Web or FTP site and combining them to the firewall's subnet (see Figure 3-5). You might choose this setup when you need to provide services that are accessible to the public, such as an FTP server, Web server, or e-mail server.

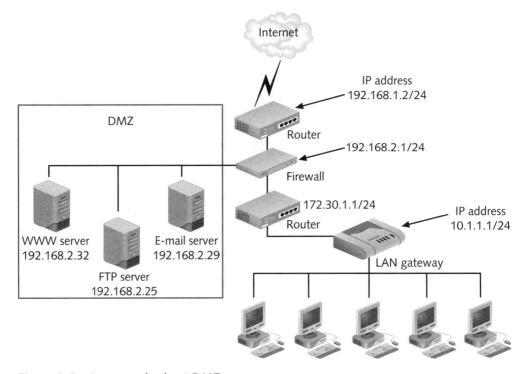

Figure 3-5   A screened subnet DMZ

The firewall in a DMZ screened subnet setup is sometimes described as a **three-pronged firewall** (sometimes also called a tri-homed firewall). The firewall connects to three separate networks and thus requires a separate network interface card for each. The three networks are as follows:

- The external network—the Internet or a branch office
- The DMZ screened subnet
- The LAN being protected

The subnet that's attached to the firewall and contained in the DMZ is sometimes called a **service network** or **perimeter network** by those who dislike the military connotations of the term DMZ. The service network contains all of the systems that

3

an organization wishes to be accessible to and from the Internet. The contents of a service network vary according to an organization's needs; the most common systems are described in the following sections.

Three-pronged firewalls that use only a single firewall have advantages and disadvantages, which are summarized as follows:

- Simplification. Three-pronged firewall setups that only use a single device only need one set of rules to be configured.

- Complexity. Although only one set of rules needs to be configured, those rules can be complex and lengthy because they need to control both inbound and outbound traffic.

- Lower cost. Only one firewall to license is less expensive than two or more.

- Vulnerability. The firewall and DMZ provide a single point of protection that, if breached, open the entire local network and DMZ to the hacker.

- Performance: The firewall and DMZ can become a bottleneck slowing down traffic for the entire network.

As a general rule, if your company is able to afford the cost and complexity of managing two firewalls, the three-pronged network will be better protected with a multi-firewall setup.

Service Networks That Contain Web and Mail Servers

The service network usually includes one or more bastion hosts on which the systems have been installed. They enable the organization's employees to access the Internet or other branch offices. The most common systems are those that provide Web and e-mail access.

If your organization runs a Web or FTP server or needs to give employees access to others on the Internet via e-mail, putting the public servers in the DMZ gives you a measure of protection. However, when you give individuals access to the outside world through the DMZ servers, you open up a way for hackers to connect to your network through the firewall. For this reason, many companies provide an extra level of security for their exposed public servers by adding a second firewall, as described in "Multiple Firewall DMZs" later in this chapter.

Another advantage of putting your company's Web server in the exposed subnet is that it makes the server better equipped to handle heavy traffic. Consider a Web server that gets as many as 20,000 hits per minute. If the server is behind the firewall, that amount of traffic could crash or at least seriously slow down the firewall, as well as the other traffic that needs to pass through it. If the server is outside the protected network but in the DMZ, the firewall's performance won't be compromised. To protect the local network, inbound connectivity from the Web server should be blocked, and accesses should be closely logged.

Service Networks That Contain DNS Servers

For organizations that need subnets and have branch offices and many different networks, DNS service is essential, and a DNS server can also be included in the screened subnet that's protected by the firewall. You have a couple of alternatives for how to arrange DNS. One alternative is to split the DNS servers so that one is on the external DMZ and the other on the internal network. This enables you to control what information is accessible to external users. The DNS server in the DMZ needs only list a limited number of public IP addresses, while the internal DNS server can hold the IP addresses for the protected network.

Another option is to locate both the internal and external DNS gateways in the DMZ. All requests from external users would go to the external DNS gateway, which would, again, not hold any internal DNS names or IP addresses. Those would be on the internal DNS gateway, which would only receive requests from internal users because the firewall would be configured to route only internal requests to that gateway.

Service Networks That Contain Tunneling Servers

Large organizations with branch offices or partnerships with other companies commonly need to set up Virtual Private Network (VPN) connections. In a VPN connection, the two organizations set up a **tunnel** connecting their respective LANs. This tunnel is a secure, encrypted connection that joins two individual computers or two networks.

A three-pronged, or tri-homed, firewall is a firewall that has three interfaces—one to the internal network, one to the DMZ, and one to the Internet—and is used to create separate zones for these three networks. When you set up a three-pronged firewall, you have the option of locating the **tunnel server** (which is a server that creates a secure tunnel connection, along with a tunnel client) in the DMZ and then doing authentication with a RADIUS server located in the private network. Configuring the network in this way is advantageous for financial reasons as well as reasons of simplicity. You only have to purchase a license for a single firewall, and you only have to configure and maintain a single firewall. (See the section on VPNs later in this chapter, as well as the section "Two Firewalls, Two DMZs.")

 As an alternative to using a tunnel server, you can encrypt data on the host computer and send it to a client that has encryption software installed. See Chapter 7 for more on encryption.

Multiple-Firewall DMZs

Firewall security is a tradeoff between enabling access from the protected network to the Internet, while providing the maximum security possible to the private network. For many large corporations, two or more firewalls is a necessity rather than a luxury. They develop security policies that mandate the use of more than one firewall to protect the LAN from the Internet. The added security offsets any slowdown in performance that two firewalls will bring to the network. End users may have to wait a few seconds before connecting to a Web site or downloading a file, but the added security makes it worthwhile. You will find this configuration used in business scenarios such as high-budget corporate networks that need to make information available to the public through a service network but that put a premium on protecting their Web sites and other public information as well as the information on the internal network.

The most effective Defense in Depth is achieved through the implementation of multiple firewalls. The following sections describe different ways in which two or more firewalls can be used to protect not only an internal network but one DMZ, two DMZs, and branch offices that need to connect to the main office's internal network. In addition, multiple firewalls can help you achieve load distribution that can keep heavy traffic flowing smoothly through the gateway.

Two Firewalls, One DMZ

One of the more common corporate firewall configurations is shown in Figure 3-6. The DMZ is enclosed by two firewalls. This arrangement is sometimes called a **tri-homed firewall**.

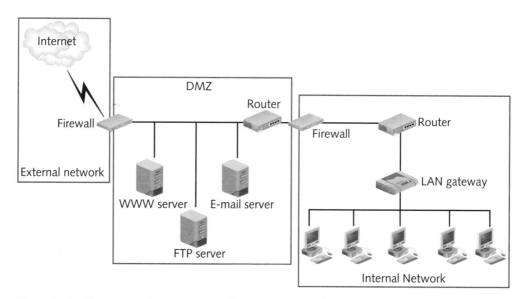

Figure 3-6 Two firewalls enclose the DMZ to protect the internal network

 The term *tri-homed firewall* is also used to refer to any single firewall that connects to three interfaces: the internal network it's protecting, the service network, and the Internet.

You can set up a three-pronged network with a DMZ using two (or even more) firewalls for a number of different reasons:

- One firewall can control traffic between the DMZ and the Internet, while the other can control traffic between the protected LAN and the DMZ.

- The second firewall can serve as a **failover firewall**. It provides a backup that can be configured to switch on if the first one fails, thus providing uninterrupted service for the organization.

 The Cisco PIX series of hardware firewalls supports **stateful failovers**. The failover firewall keeps a copy of the connection states that are in the primary firewall so that, if the primary firewall goes down, the failover unit keeps ongoing connections alive.

One of the advantages of setting up a DMZ with two firewalls is that you can control where traffic goes in the three networks you're dealing with: the external network that's outside the DMZ, the external network that's within the DMZ, and the internal network that's behind the DMZ. You can identify certain protocols such as outbound HTTP Port 80 that should go to the external network within the DMZ, while allowing other protocols to pass through to the internal network.

 Each of the three networks in the tri-homed firewall configuration can have its own security settings, which gives you even more control over what passes through to—and out of—the internal network.

Many issues become more complicated when you work with two firewalls. They must be configured to work in tandem. The way they do NAT becomes more complex too. Some services that are incompatible with NAT, like Kerberos or IPSec, must be behind the firewall rather than in the DMZ. The other applications within the firewall need to support NAT as well.

In a two-firewall configuration, the firewall that interfaces with the Internet is typically configured so that only specific types of traffic can enter the DMZ from the Internet. The firewall that interfaces with the internal network controls which traffic passes between the DMZ and the internal network.

Two Firewalls, Two DMZs

A company that commits to using multiple firewalls makes its security setup more complex, but it gains flexibility as well. The company can set up separate DMZs for different parts of the organization. This is advantageous because it helps balance the traffic load between parts of the organization. Figure 3-7 shows a firewall setup in which two firewalls have separate DMZs attached to them.

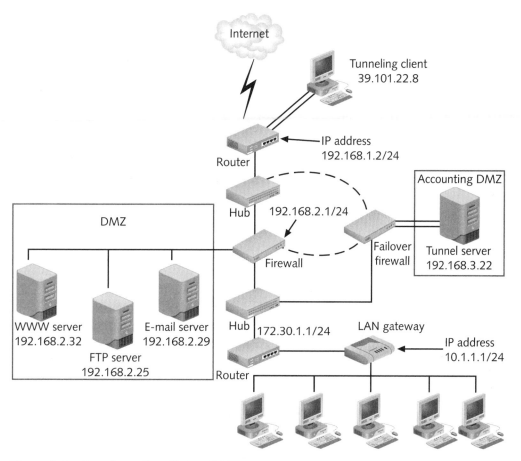

Figure 3-7 Two firewalls with two DMZs

 In Figure 3-7, the second firewall is designated as the failover firewall, but the second firewall in a two-firewall configuration doesn't necessarily need to be a "failover" device. If you do want a failover firewall, both it and the primary firewall need to be exactly the same model or at least compatible so you can configure them for seamless operation in case the primary device fails.

In Figure 3-7, the hub allows the external router to connect to both of the firewalls. Each of the firewalls has a separate DMZ connected to it. One of the DMZs contains publicly accessible servers for Web, e-mail, and DNS. The other contains a VPN tunnel server that holds files needed by the accounting office to maintain personnel and other records. The company may, for instance, work with a partner company whose own accounting department needs to securely trade data with the originating company's accounting department. Putting a tunnel server in the DMZ makes the server accessible to off-site workers that have a tunneling client but without giving them access to other servers in the internal LAN.

In addition, the two firewalls in Figure 3-7 are compatible models (they may, for example, both be Cisco PIX 500-series firewalls), so that the second firewall functions as a stateful failover firewall. Suppose the first firewall fails due to heavy traffic or some other cause. Without a second firewall, all connections currently in progress would simply grind to a halt until the problem is resolved, which could take a few minutes, several hours, or even more. In contrast, if a second stateful firewall is in place, data describing the state of the current connections would be held in memory by both firewalls. (Specifically, the Cisco PIX Failover Firewall uses **state update packets** to pass data about the state of current connections between the primary and failover firewalls.) That would enable the second firewall to take over when the first one fails without end users experiencing little to no interruption in service.

Multiple Firewalls to Protect Branch Offices

A multinational corporation that needs to share information among branch offices in far-flung locations can communicate securely using a single security policy that is implemented by multiple firewalls. The central office has its own centralized firewall, a firewall that directs traffic for branch offices and their own individual firewalls. The central office develops the security policy and deploys the policy through its centralized firewall with its associated rules on a dedicated **security workstation.** Each office has its own firewall (see Figure 3-8), but the central office can develop and control the security policy. The policy is then copied on to each of the other firewalls in the corporation.

Load Distribution through Layering of Firewalls

When multiple firewalls are deployed around the perimeter of a network, they can work together to balance the traffic load in and out of the network. In a large organization with many networks and subnets, it may be necessary to maximize network uptime and optimize performance by setting up layers of protection that include multiple firewalls. The DNS servers for the company can, as mentioned earlier, be split into separate databases to better control over what information reaches both the internal servers and those on the external screened subnet.

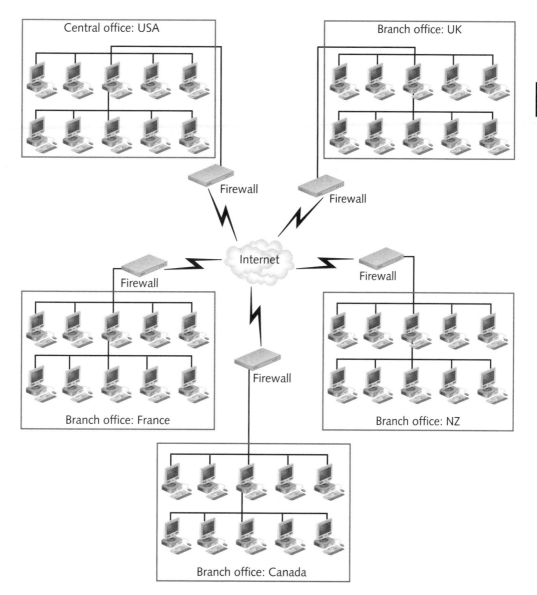

Figure 3-8   A multinational corporation can use multiple firewalls

Some of the other typical network components in a load-balanced network that uses multiple firewalls include the following:

- Inbound and outbound SMTP can be divided among two servers to better manage e-mail.

- Inbound and outbound HTTP can be split among two machines to distribute the Web traffic for an organization. This is particularly helpful for retail companies that get many inquiries, catalog visits, and (hopefully) purchases through their Web stores.

- A central server can be set up to log all systems; having all logging done on a single machine provides the network administrator with a single, central location from which to track down problems.

- A central server can also be designated to hold an **Intrusion Detection System (IDS)**, software that notifies the appropriate personnel when an event occurs.

One possible combination of such logical layers of network security is shown in Figure 3-9.

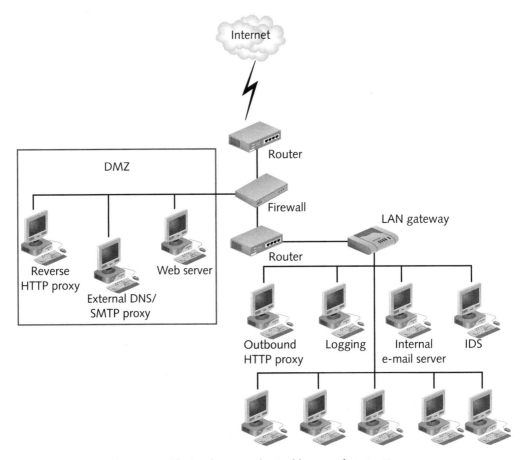

Figure 3-9 Distributing traffic load among logical layers of protection

Reverse Firewalls

Some forward-thinking companies have installed a **reverse firewall**, a device that monitors information going out of a network rather than trying to block what's coming in. In a Denial of Service attack, information will be flooding out of the network from the infected computer(s), thus overloading the network. A reverse firewall, such as the hardware device sold by Los Angeles-based company Cs3, inspects outgoing packets and tracks where they're coming from within the network. If a high number of "unexpected" packets is detected leaving the network, the firewall notifies the network administrator. Such functionality, in fact, could be part of any firewall, and could be programmed into a hardware or software firewall by a qualified engineer, alleviating the need to purchase a specialized reverse firewall.

Specialty Firewalls

Some firewalls are designed to protect specific types of network communications, and if your company is primarily concerned with e-mail or instant-messaging security, consider installing a specialty firewall like MailMarshal or WebMarshal by Marshal Software.

Both systems monitor and control a particular kind of content that passes into and out of a network. They can be configured to filter out pornographic content, junk e-mail, and malicious code. MailMarshal, for instance, unpacks and scans the content of each e-mail message before it reaches the recipient. This opens up obvious privacy issues that need to be balanced against an organization's need for protection—a tradeoff that applies to virtually all aspects of network security, not just e-mail messages. Other examples of specialty firewalls include the following:

- OpenReach, a maker of VPN software, includes a small-scale packet-filtering firewall designed to work only with its VPN.

- VocalData (*www.vocaldata.com*), a hardware manufacturer, sells VOISS Proxy Firewall (VF-1), which is designed to create a safe environment for IP voice communications over the Internet.

- Speedware Corporation (*www.speedware.com*) is just one example of a company that sells its own firewall software (Autobahn Application Firewall) that is designed to work specifically on computers that run Speedware business-reporting and analysis software platforms.

APPROACHES THAT ADD FUNCTIONALITY TO YOUR FIREWALL

While a few of the configurations depicted thus far might seem somewhat complex, network security setups can be incrementally more complex when specific functions are added. To keep the discussion simple, each function is discussed on its own. You should assume, though, that any or all of the following can be part of a perimeter security system that includes a firewall.

NAT

A router or firewall that performs NAT converts publicly accessible IP addresses to private ones and vice versa, thus shielding the IP addresses of computers on the protected network from those on the outside. The sequence of steps in a simple data transfer using NAT is shown in Figure 3-10.

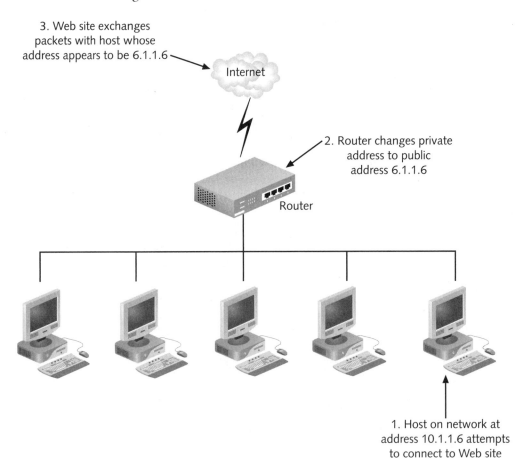

3. Web site exchanges packets with host whose address appears to be 6.1.1.6

Internet

2. Router changes private address to public address 6.1.1.6

Router

1. Host on network at address 10.1.1.6 attempts to connect to Web site

Figure 3-10   Network Address Translation

Encryption

A firewall or router that can do Secure Sockets Layer (SSL) or some other type of encryption takes a request, turns it into gibberish using a private key, and exchanges the public key with the recipient firewall or router. The recipient then decrypts the message and presents it to the end user in understandable form (see Figure 3-11).

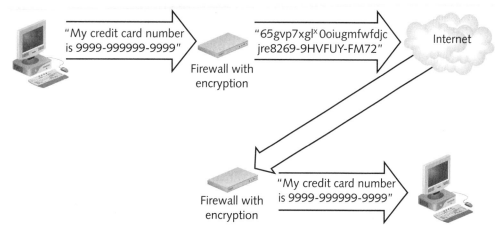

"My credit card number is 9999-999999-9999"

Firewall with encryption

"65gvp7xgl^x 0oiugmfwfdjc jre8269-9HVFUY-FM72"

Internet

Firewall with encryption

"My credit card number is 9999-999999-9999"

Figure 3-11   Routers or firewalls can encrypt messages for extra security

You don't have to use a router or firewall to do encryption, of course: it can also be done on the host using encryption software (see Chapter 7).

Application Proxies

An application proxy is software that acts on behalf of a host, receiving requests, rebuilding them completely from scratch, and forwarding them to the intended location as though the request originated with it (the proxy). It can be set up with either a dual-homed host or a screened host system. In a dual-homed host setup, the host that contains the firewall or proxy server software has two interfaces, one to the Internet and one to the internal network being protected (see Figure 3-12).

Because the dual-homed host lies between the internal LAN and the Internet, the hosts on the internal network never access the Internet directly. (At least, they shouldn't; some employees may get frustrated with the slower functioning of the proxy system and try to establish their own independent Internet connections, and you should be on the alert for this.) The proxy server software on the dual-homed host makes requests on their behalf and forwards packets from the Internet to them.

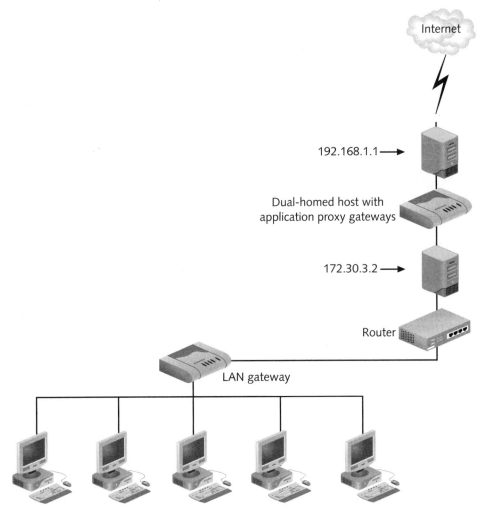

Figure 3-12   Application proxies on a dual-homed host

In a screened subnet system, the host that holds the proxy server software has a single network interface; packet filters on either side of the host filter out all traffic except that which is destined for the proxy server software.

Chapter 5 explores screened subnet and other types of application proxy configurations in more detail.

VPNs

Many companies use the Internet to provide them with a VPN that connects internal hosts with specific clients in other organizations. The advantage to a VPN over a conventional Internet-based connection is that VPN connections are encrypted and limited only to machines with specific IP addresses. The VPN gateway can go on a DMZ (see Figure 3-7 earlier in this chapter). On the other hand, the gateway can bypass the firewall and connect directly to the internal LAN, as shown in Figure 3-13.

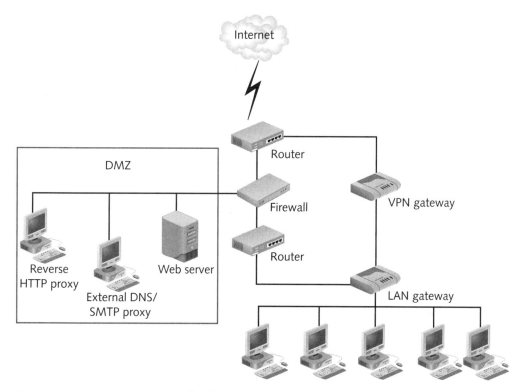

Figure 3-13   A VPN gateway that bypasses the firewall

 VPNs are discussed further in Chapter 9.

Intrusion Detection Systems

When it comes to installing software that detects possible intrusion attempts and notifies you of trouble, you have a couple of options for installing them. The Intrusion Detection System (IDS) can be installed in the external and/or the internal routers at the perimeter of a network (see Figure 3-14). IDS is also built into many popular software firewall packages, including Sidewinder by Secure Computing.

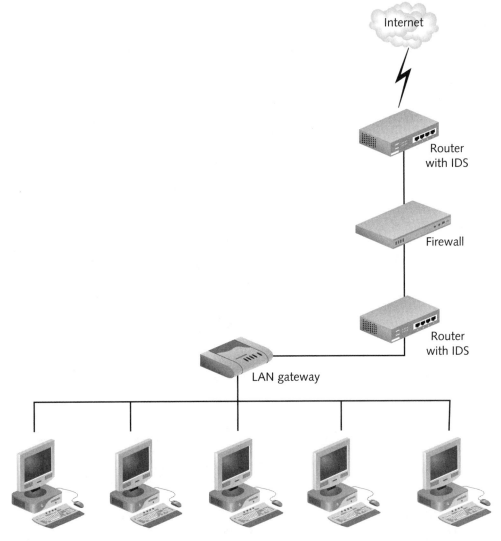

Figure 3-14   IDS systems integrated into perimeter routers

Why install IDS on both routers? An external router with IDS can notify you of intrusion attempts from the Internet. An internal router with IDS can notify you when a host on the internal network attempts to access the Internet through a suspicious port or using an unusual service, which may be a sign of a Trojan horse that has entered the system. An IDS might also be configured to look for a large number of TCP connection requests (SYN) to many different ports on a target machine, thus discovering if someone is attempting a TCP port scan. The IDS sends the alert so an administrator can either prevent it or cut the attack short before too much damage occurs.

The Cisco CIDS Intrusion Detection System works in a different way. It monitors the area between the firewall and the Internet. It can be configured to tell you when an attack on the firewall from the Internet occurs (see Figure 3-15).

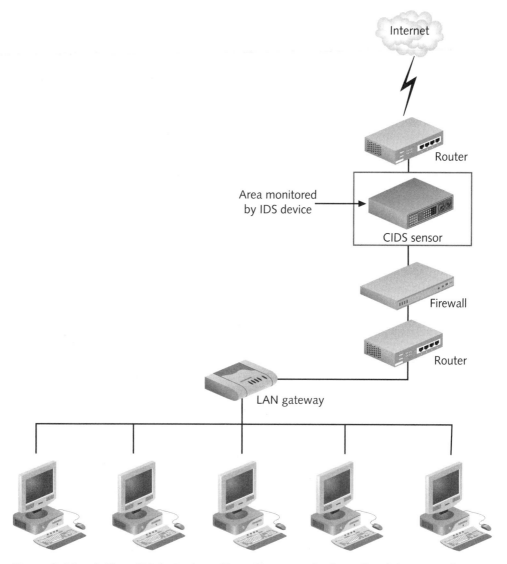

Figure 3-15   A Cisco IDS device is positioned between the firewall and the external router

CHAPTER SUMMARY

This chapter began with an overview of the kinds of rules you need to establish to give a firewall the criteria it needs to decide whether to allow packets through the gateway or drop them. You learned about the role a rules file plays in the firewall's operation: they establish the order that the firewall should follow, and they tell the firewall which packets should be blocked and which should be allowed. Approaches ranging from Deny-All to Allow-All were described, along with the advantages and disadvantages of each. Requirements included the need for scalability and the importance of enabling productivity of end users while maintaining adequate security.

Following this introductory material, the text presented an overview of firewall configuration strategies. You learned that a firewall needs to be scalable—it needs to be able to handle an increasing amount of traffic as the organization it protects grows. The firewall needs to enable workers to be productive by connecting to the Internet services they need. Finally, the firewall needs to deal with the IP address requirements of the organization.

The next section delved into specific firewall configurations, starting with simple router setups. A variety of DMZ configurations were described, ranging from simple ones that provide Web services to the public to more complex ones that include DNS servers and VPN tunnel servers on the DMZ. Next, some more complex real-world business configurations were discussed, including single- and multiple-DMZ setups, VPN gateways, and layered protection schemes. Reverse firewalls and specialty firewalls were also described.

In the final section, you learned about approaches that add functionality to any firewall and that should be part of any configuration. These include NAT, application proxies, and IDS. These can all be incorporated into a perimeter security area, but there should always be consideration of the need to balance security with employees' need to be productive and communicate using the Internet.

KEY TERMS

access control list (ACL) — Rules that are applied to router interfaces that determine what traffic should be allowed in or out of the interface.

bastion host — A specially hardened computer that hosts firewall software and that has all but the most essential services removed or disabled to optimize performance.

critical resource — A software- or hardware-related item that is indispensable to the operation of a device or program.

dual-homed host — A workstation that has both an internal interface and an external interface to the Internet.

external interface — The interface that connects a router to an external network such as the Internet.

3

failover firewall — A firewall that is designed to maintain connections in case a primary firewall stops working.

internal interface — The interface that connects a router to an internal network, such as a LAN, that it is protecting either on its own or with a firewall or other devices.

Intrusion Detection System (IDS) — A system that monitors traffic into and out of a network and automatically alerts personnel when suspicious traffic patterns occur, indicating a possible unauthorized intrusion attempt.

IP forwarding — A function that allows packets to be sent from one network interface to another. Many operating systems perform IP forwarding, as do routers.

least privilege — The practice of designing operational aspects of a system to work with a minimal amount of system privilege.

network topology — The structure of how the computers and other devices within them are connected to one another. For instance, in a network with a star topology, the computers, printers, and other hardware are connected in a star pattern to a central server. In a bus topology the computers and other devices are connected in a line.

packet filtering — A basic firewall function in which IP packet header information is screened and decisions to allow or drop the packet are based on rules in the firewall's rule base.

perimeter network — A screened subnet that connects to a firewall positioned at the perimeter of a protected network; same as screened subnet or DMZ.

reverse firewall — A firewall that has the primary responsibility of inspecting and monitoring traffic that leaves a local network rather than blocking incoming traffic. Such a firewall helps block Distributed Denial of Service (DDoS) attacks.

screened subnet — A network that is exposed to an external network, such as the Internet, but that is partially protected by a firewall.

screening router — A router that filters traffic passing between one network and another.

security workstation — A machine dedicated to holding security policies a firewall, and other security software, for a corporation.

service network — A screened subnet that contains an organization's publicly accessible servers, such as its Web server or e-mail server.

stateful failover — A situation in which a primary firewall stops functioning and a second firewall (the failover firewall) provides backup services by maintaining copies of the connection states that were in the primary firewall.

stateful packet filtering — A type of packet filtering in which a firewall checks a state table to make sure a connection has actually been established before checking its rule base to decide whether to allow or block a packet.

state update packets — Packets sent between primary and failover firewalls that contain information about the state of current network connections.

three-pronged firewall — A firewall that has three network interfaces connecting it to the external network, the DMZ, and the protected LAN.

tri-homed firewall — 1) A firewall that has interfaces with an internal protected network, a service network, and the Internet. 2) The use of two firewalls to set up three separate networks, the internal protected network; the external private network or service network, which includes Web and e-mail servers and other publicly accessible services; and the external network (the Internet or another branch network).

tunnel — A private network that uses a VPN client and VPN gateway to set up secure communications between two specific computers in different networks.

tunnel server — A computer that enables VPN clients to connect to it based on their IP addresses.

REVIEW QUESTIONS

1. What is the primary function of a router?

    a. static packet filtering

    b. stateful packet filtering

    c. blocking unauthorized access

    d. IP forwarding

2. What are the limitations of a single dual-homed computer that uses a software firewall installed on the same computer for its security?

3. Give three reasons why a set of packet-filtering rules is important to a firewall.

4. How would a firewall implement a "strict" approach to security?

    a. set up packet filtering rules

    b. specify a stateful packet filter

    c. require passwords to be used at all times

    d. use application proxy gateways

5. A specialty firewall can be installed to work with what kind of network feature and/or service?

6. The ability of a firewall to grow in capacity to meet the changing needs of the organization it protects is called what?

    a. newsgroups

    b. VPN

    c. telnet

    d. e-mail

7. What's the problem with letting the firewall process rules in top-to-bottom order?

   a. It may result in complaints from end users.

   b. Incorrect order can cause chaos.

   c. It can open a network to Web vulnerabilities.

   d. Incorrect order can reduce security.

8. What's the advantage of adding a second router between a firewall and the LAN it protects in addition to a router outside the firewall? (Choose all that apply.)

   a. It adds a layer of protection.

   b. It can do stateful packet filtering.

   c. It can direct traffic to the LAN.

   d. It can do load balancing.

9. Consider the following scenario: Your company operates a Web server and is promoting a new line of products. The server experiences a high number of visits from users on the Internet who want to place orders. Yet, the server needs to provide protection from viruses and harmful programs for users in the company; however, for business reasons you are instructed that commerce and revenue should take priority over security. Under these circumstances, the server should be positioned where?

   a. in the protected network for added security

   b. in the screened subnet

   c. in a DMZ protected by two firewalls

   d. It doesn't make any difference where the server is located.

10. In addition to an internal network, what other two networks have interfaces with a tri-homed firewall? (Choose all that apply.)

    a. external private network and Internet

    b. remote worker's home office and branch office

    c. service network and Internet

    d. accounting subnet and Internet

11. Proxy servers, routers, and operating systems are all designed to perform IP forwarding. If your security configuration includes a proxy server, why should IP forwarding be disabled on routers and other devices that lie between the networks?

12. The most important configuration file in a firewall is called the _____.

    a. access control list

    b. rules file

    c. protocol list

    d. authentication database

13. A "Deny-All" approach would work under what circumstances?

14. What is the concept of "least privilege?"

15. If a firewall is primarily permissive, this places a greater burden on the network administrator to perform what function?

    a. educate employees on responsible use

    b. educate employees on Internet software use

    c. establish packet-filtering rules

    d. set up proxy services

16. Which of the following is a problem that can arise as a result of a "Deny-All" policy?

    a. Complex rules are required.

    b. User complaints may result.

    c. It is difficult to implement.

    d. No one can surf the Web.

17. What is the primary difference between a screened host and a dual-homed gateway?

18. Name two enhancements that are added to a screened host machine.

19. Layers of protection add what benefits to a network? (Choose all that apply.)

    a. improved network performance

    b. better connections to partner companies

    c. maximum network uptime

    d. better Internet access

20. Why place two routers with IDS at the perimeter of the network rather than one?

    a. The second device serves as a backup in case the primary router fails.

    b. The more IDS systems you install, the faster you are notified.

    c. One router checks for external attack attempts, while the other checks for attempts to access the Internet from inside.

    d. The external router guards against attempts to access the Internet from inside, while the internal router monitors for attack attempts from the Internet.

21. How does a reverse firewall protect against DoS attacks?

HANDS-ON PROJECTS

Project 3-1: Draw a simple packet-filtering design

The following project gives you some experience designing a basic firewall setup by asking you to draw a simple network that is protected from the Internet by a single packet-filtering router doing stateful packet filtering. Although the configuration is simple, it can serve as the foundation for more complex designs.

1. Get a pencil and paper, or start a drawing program on your computer.
2. At the top of the drawing area, draw a large circle and label it "the Internet".
3. Draw a line leading from the circle to a packet-filtering router.
4. Identify the external and internal router interfaces.
5. Assign IP addresses to the interfaces and to the computers being protected.
6. Draw a line leading from the router to a group of computers on an internal network.
7. Draw a line joining the computers on the internal network to indicate that they are networked. Show one computer on the network that will not receive packets from the Internet.

Project 3-2: Drawing a DMZ

Now that you've drawn a simple network/router setup, you can draw a similar one that's a little more involved: a DMZ screened subnet connected to a firewall that has a router on either side of it.

1. Get a pencil and paper, or start a drawing program on your computer.
2. At the top of the drawing area, draw a large circle and label it "the Internet."
3. Draw a line leading from the circle to a packet-filtering router.
4. Draw a line leading from the Internet to a rectangle, and label this the firewall.
5. Draw a short line leading from the firewall to a second router.
6. Draw a line leading from the second router to a network of computers. Label this group of computers the "internal LAN."
7. Draw a line leading in another direction from the firewall to a DMZ. The DMZ should contain one or two computers. Label one computer a "Web server", the other an "FTP server." Label these computers (the ones in the DMZ) the "screened subnet."

Project 3-3: Failover Firewall Configuration

After the failure of a firewall and the interruption of all Internet connections for several hours, you have been directed to set up a second firewall that will provide interrupted service for the protected internal network. In addition, each firewall needs to have has its own DMZ with publicly accessible servers. What would you include in the configuration to permit data to travel from the Internet to both firewalls? What condition enables the second firewall to function as a failover device? Draw the configuration that would make this setup possible.

1. Repeat Steps 1 through 7 in Hands-On Project 3-2.

2. Draw a dashed line leading from the first router (the one between the Internet and the firewall) leading to the top of a rectangle. Label the rectangle "Failover Firewall."

3. Draw a dashed line leading from the bottom of the failover firewall to the other firewall in the drawing.

4. Draw a solid line leading from the bottom of the failover firewall to the second router (the one positioned between the original firewall and the internal LAN).

5. Draw a line leading from the side of the failover firewall to a second DMZ.

6. Draw two computers in the second DMZ and label this "Second DMZ".

Project 3-4: Use the Tracert Command To Trace Network Connections

As you have seen in this chapter, routers are an important part of any network connection. Routers can be placed both before and after a firewall, or between different areas of a network. How many routers lie between your own computer and the computer that holds your school's home page on the Web? You can find out by using the tracert command with any Windows computer.

1. On the Windows desktop, click **Start**, point to **Programs** (**All Programs** on XP), point to **Accessories**, and then click **Command Prompt**.

2. At the command prompt, type **Tracert *[site name or IP address]***, where *[site name or IP address]* is the site name or IP address you want to trace. For example, if your school's home page is at *www.uchicago.edu*, type **Tracert www.uchicago.edu**, and then press **Enter**.

3. A list of IP addresses appears. When the trace is complete, subsequent "hops" up to the default of 30 hops will appear with the message "Request timed out." How many lie between your computer and the school's home page? Make a note in your lab book or notebook.

4. Type **exit** and then press **Enter** to close the command prompt window.

Project 3-5: Enable RIP Listening

Routing Information Protocol (RIP) is one of the fundamental network protocols that enable packets to be forwarded from one location to another. Windows XP enables you to set up RIP listening to trace RIP v1 packet paths. You must be logged on to your Windows XP computer as an Administrator or a member of the Administrators group to perform this project. You'll also need the Windows XP installation disk available.

1. From the Windows XP desktop, click **Start**, and then click **Control Panel**,

2. In the Control Panel dialog box, double-click **Add or Remove Programs**.

3. In the Add or Remove Programs dialog box, click **Add/Remove Windows Components**.

4. In the Windows Components Wizard dialog box, click **Networking Services** (highlight the name, but do not click the check box), and then click **Details**.

5. In the Networking Services dialog box, check the **RIP Listener** check box, and then click **OK**.

6. You return to the Windows Components Wizard dialog box, where the box next to Networking Services is now checked. Click **Next**.

7. When prompted to do so, insert the Windows XP installation disk, then follow the rest of the steps presented in the wizard.

8. When installation is complete, click **Finish** to exit the wizard.

Project 3-6: Install Sygate Personal Firewall

For the following Hands-On Project and many of the other projects in this book, you'll use a free version of a commercial firewall program, Sygate Personal Firewall. This program prompts you whenever packets are sent into or out of your computer. You can use the firewall to monitor services and set up logs. You can use any Windows computer to install the program.

1. Open your Web browser. In the Address box, type **http://www.sygate.com** and press **Enter**.

2. Click **Sygate Personal Firewall** in the list on the right side of the page.

3. The Sygate Personal Firewall – Free Download & Product Information page appears. Scroll down the page and click the **Download Now!** button.

4. Under the heading Sygate Personal Firewall, click either **Download site #1** or **Download site #2**.

5. A Download page appears with a list of links to servers in different geographic locations. Click the link that's closest to your own location to download the software.

6. A File Download dialog box opens. Click **Open** to download the file and automatically begin installing it.

7. When the Installer program opens, follow the steps indicated to install Sygate personal firewall on your computer. Then, restart your computer as instructed.

8. When you restart your computer and the Registration dialog box opens, click **Register Later**. You are presented with a series of prompts asking you to set up rules for various types of network communications. Click **Yes** to enable such communications. Record the rules you set up in a lab book or a word-processing document.

9. As a courtesy to other users of this lab computer who might not need or want to use a firewall (or who might be confused by the alert messages), right-click the **Sygate Personal Firewall** icon in the System Tray, and then click **Exit Firewall** to stop the program from running. When the Warning dialog box opens, click **Yes**.

Project 3-7: Setting Up IPv6 Forwarding

Windows, Linux, and other operating systems are set up to perform IP forwarding; it's not normally a service you have to configure. However, because Windows XP supports a prerelease version of the new version of IP, IPv6, you have the chance to configure IP forwarding using this new protocol. (IPv6 was not approved at the time this was written, so you can't actually use it, but you can get some practice with it for research purposes.) This exercise assumes you have Sygate Personal Firewall installed on your computer as described in Hands-On Project 3-1.

1. On the Windows XP desktop, click **Start**, point to **Programs** (**All Programs** on XP), point to **Sygate Personal Firewall**, and then click **Sygate Personal Firewall** to start the software.

2. You may see a Registration dialog box asking you to register Sygate Personal Firewall. Consult with your instructor on whether to register the software now (in which case, you should click **Register Now**) or at a later time (in which case, you should click **Register Later**).

3. On the Windows XP desktop, click **Start**, point to **Programs** (**All Programs** on XP), point to **Accessories**, and then click **Command Prompt**.

4. At the command prompt, type **ipv6 install**, and then press **Enter**.

5. The "Installing..." message appears. After a short time, the "Succeeded." message appears. Sygate Personal Firewall immediately opens an alert dialog box. What does this dialog box say? Note the answer in a lab book or word-processing document.

6. Click **Yes** to close the Sygate Personal Firewall dialog box.

7. In the Command Prompt dialog box, type **ipv6 if**, and then press **Enter**. A list of details about your network interface—the interface index—is presented. How many interfaces are listed, and what are they called? Note the answers in a lab book or word-processing document. Also note which interface forwards and performs router discovery.

8. In the Command Prompt dialog box, type **ipv6 ifc *[InterfaceIndex]* forwards**, where *[InterfaceIndex]* is the index number of the interface you want to configure. If Interface 4 was listed in Step 7 as the interface that forwards, type **ipv6 ifc 4 forwards**. Press **Enter** to configure the interface.

9. Type **exit** and then press **Enter** to close the command prompt window.

Case Projects

Case 3-1: Firewall Rule-Processing Approaches

3

Consider a user named Ken who works as a work-study student in a university department protected by a firewall and is a member of the Work-Study user group in the Windows domain. Ken wants to access a Web site on the Internet from within the firewall. When Ken launches his Web browser and attempts to connect, the request is received by the firewall. The firewall has been configured with the rules pertaining to HTTP Web access shown in Table 3-6.

Table 3-6   Sample HTTP Firewall Rules

Rule	Port	Users	Action
1	80 (HTTP)	All	Allow
2	80 (HTTP)	Work-Study	Deny
3	80 (HTTP)	Ken	Allow

What happens to the request if the firewall processes its rules using a) In Order, b) Deny All, c) Allow All, and d) Best Fit?

Case 3-2: Develop Deny-All Rules

You are instructed to take a restrictive approach to firewall rules "as close to deny-all as is practically possible." However, staff needs to look at training videos online during regular business hours. People should be allowed to use the Web and to exchange e-mail at all times. However, access to multimedia should be prohibited at night. What rules would you set up for this?

Case 3-3: Design a Public Access and Private Security Plan

Sterling Silver Widgets, a manufacturer of luxury office supplies for high-powered executives, sells its products through a Web site that receives an average of a thousand visits per day. The company regularly receives shipments from Silver Supply Inc., a supplier that wants to access its own shipping and receiving information in the office network as well as transmit invoices to the Sterling Silver Widgets accounting department. Sterling Silver Widgets has had problems in the past with DoS attacks. Design a perimeter setup that includes stateful packet filtering, public Web server access, a firewall-protected internal, and VPN access to the accounting department server.

PACKET FILTERING

After reading this chapter and completing the exercises, you will be able to:

♦ Understand packets and packet filtering

♦ Understand the approaches to packet filtering

♦ Set specific filtering rules

To understand how firewalls work and how to configure them, you need to start working with their most fundamental components: **packet filters**. Packet filters either block or allow transmission of packets of information based on criteria such as port, IP address, and protocol.

Packet filters not only help you learn about firewalls but also provide a gateway to understanding TCP/IP network communications. To figure out how to control the movement of traffic through the network perimeter, it's a good idea to understand how packets are structured and what goes into packet headers. Accordingly, the first parts of this chapter examine packet header criteria that can be used to filter traffic. The rest of the chapter discusses approaches to packet filtering and provides examples of specific packet filter rules you can set up.

UNDERSTANDING PACKETS AND PACKET FILTERING

Think of a packet filter as acting like a ticket-taker in a multiplex movie theatre. The ticket-taker's first task is to admit only those with valid tickets, which are tickets for this day and not any other day. Having stripped off part of the ticket and handed the remainder back to the customer, the ticket-taker then provides directions on where to find the desired screen within the theater complex.

Similarly, the packet filter reviews the **header**, strips it off, and replaces it with a new header before sending it on its way to a specific location within the network. Some of the more common rules for packet filtering are as follows:

- Drop all inbound connections; allow only outbound connections on Ports 80 (HTTP), 25 (SMTP), and 21 (FTP).

- Eliminate packets bound for all ports that should not be available to the Internet, such as NetBIOS, but allow Internet-related traffic, such as SMTP, to pass.

- Filter out any ICMP redirect or echo (ping) messages that may be an indication that hackers are attempting to locate open ports or host IP addresses.

- Drop all packets that use the IP header **source routing** feature. In IP source routing, the originator of a packet can attempt to partially or completely control the path through the network to the destination. Source routing is widely considered a suspect activity from a security standpoint.

A good way to get started with packet filtering is by understanding what devices perform packet filtering and what is contained in the packets themselves. Then you can begin to appreciate why packet filtering is important in your own network.

Devices That Perform Packet Filtering

As you delve into network administration and security, you're likely to encounter a variety of hardware devices and software programs that do packet filtering. Here are a few examples:

- *Routers*: These are probably the most common packet filters.

- *Operating systems*: Some systems, like Windows and Linux, have built-in utilities that can do packet filtering on the TCP/IP stack of the server software. Linux has a kernel-level packet filter called IPchains; Windows has TCP/IP Filtering.

- *Software firewalls*: Most enterprise-level programs, such as Check Point FireWall-1, do packet filtering; Check Point's product specializes in stateful filtering, which is explained later in this chapter. Personal firewalls like ZoneAlarm and Sygate Personal Firewall do a less-sophisticated version called stateless packet filtering. This is also discussed later in the chapter.

A router can keep unauthorized traffic from entering the protected network altogether. If a software filter is the only kind of packet filter being used, this means that an intentionally mangled, spoofed, or otherwise harmful packet can reach a target machine before being detected. For that reason, many security experts caution against using only software packet filters.

Anatomy of a Packet

As you know from your previous studies, packets are part of Transport Control Protocol/Internet Protocol (TCP/IP), the collection of protocols that computers use to communicate with one another on the network and, increasingly, in local area networks (Windows 2000 and Windows XP use TCP/IP as the basis for file sharing and communications). TCP/IP provides for the transmission of **data** in small, manageable chunks called **packets**.

Each packet (also called a **datagram**) consists of two parts: the header and data. The header contains information that is normally only read by computers, such as where the packet is coming from and its destination. The data is the part that end users actually see—the body of an e-mail message or a Web page.

Understanding exactly what goes in a packet header is important because it can help you configure packet filters against possible attacks. Some firewall programs can give you a glimpse of the contents of a packet. When Sygate Personal Firewall detects a packet for which a rule has not been established, for instance, it presents you with an alert box asking whether it should allow the packet to pass. When you click on the Details button, you can view the header contents, as shown in Figure 4-1, to decide if anything is suspicious.

To find out more about headers and their contents, go to the original Internet Protocol specification at *www.ietf.org*, click RFC Pages, and search for RFC 791.

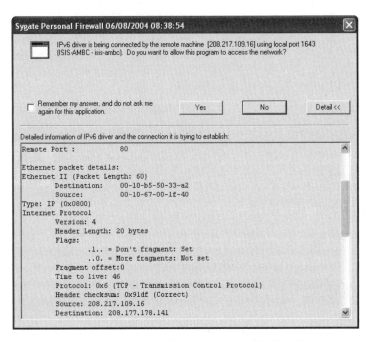

Figure 4-1   Some firewalls let you view packet header contents

The header of an IP packet is commonly illustrated according to the layers of information within it, as shown in Figure 4-2:

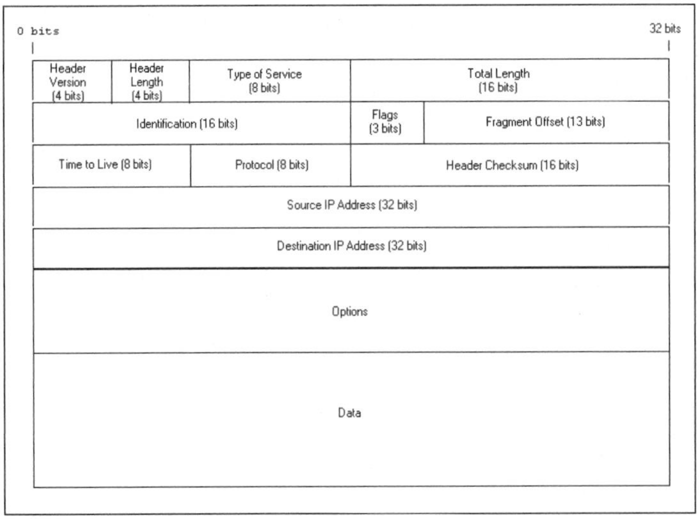

Figure 4-2   IP packet header information

Knowledge of the elements in the figure will help you configure packet filters. Each is discussed in the following list:

- *Version:* This identifies the version of IP that was used to generate the packet. At the time this was written, version 4 was still the most common. However, some ISPs have begun to deploy IPv6.

- *Internet Header Length:* This describes the length of the header in 32-bit words and is a 4-bit value. The default value is 20.

- *Type of Service:* This expresses the quality of service desired in the transmission of the packet through the network. Four options are available: minimize delay, maximize throughput, maximize reliability, and minimize cost. This field is of limited value, however, because most IP network setups don't enable an application to set the Type of Service value.

- *Total Length:* This 16-bit field gives the total length of the packet, to a maximum of 165,535 bytes.

- *Identification:* This 16-bit value aids in the division of the data stream into packets of information. The receiving computer (possibly a firewall) uses the identification number of each packet to reassemble in the correct order the packets that make up the data stream.

- *Flags:* This 3-bit value tells whether this packet is a **fragment** of a whole packet and, more specifically, whether it's the last fragment or whether more fragments are to follow.

- *Fragment Offset:* If the data received is a fragment, this value indicates where the fragment belongs in the sequence of fragments so that a packet can be reassembled.

- *Time to Live (TTL):* This 8-bit value identifies the maximum time the packet can remain in the system before it is dropped. Each router or device through which the packet passes reduces the TTL by a value of one. Having a TTL prevents a packet from getting caught in loops because it is undeliverable. When the value reaches zero, the packet is destroyed and an ICMP message is transmitted to the sender.

- *Protocol:* This identifies the IP protocol that was used in the data portion of the packet and should receive the data at its destination (for example, TCP, UDP, or ICMP).

- *Header Checksum:* This is a summing up of all of the 16-bit values in the packet header in a single value.

- *Source Address:* This is the address of the computer or device that sent the IP packet.

- *Destination Address:* This is the address of the computer or device that is to receive the IP packet.

4

- *Options:* Various elements can exist in this category. These include a Security field, which enables the sender to assign a classification level to the packet (such as Secret, Top Secret, and so on). They also include several source routing fields by which the sender of the packet can supply routing information that gateways can use to send the packet to its destination.

- *Data:* This is the part that the end user actually sees, such as the body of an e-mail message.

Also, some packets have an additional segmented section at the end that is either called a **trailer** or **footer** and that contains data that indicates the end of the packet. An error-checking procedure called a **Cyclical Redundancy Check (CRC)** might also be added.

A Quick Tutorial on Packet Filtering

Packet filtering is the procedure by which packet headers are inspected by a router or firewall to make a decision on whether to let the packet pass. The packet-filtering device evaluates the information in the header and compares the information to the rules that have been set up. If the information corresponds to one of the "Allow" rules, the packet is allowed to pass. On the other hand, if the information matches one of the "Deny" rules, the packet is dropped. Note that packet filters examine only the header of packets, in contrast to application proxies, which do their own kind of packet filtering by examining the data in the packet and then forwarding the packet to its destination on behalf of the originating host.

The Use of Rules

Note that although small-scale, software-only "personal" firewall programs are effective at protecting one computer, they can cause problems in a network situation. Often, they block traffic between networked computers unless rules are set up to enable communications. Thus, you need to set up an access list that includes all of the computers in your local network by name or IP address so communications can flow between them.

Norton Internet Security 2002's built-in firewall has an easy way to identify computers on the local network: it puts them in a list of machines in a trusted zone. The software can detect other networked machines that have IP addresses in one of the private ranges (10.0.0.1 and so on), or you can add IP addresses of networked machines yourself, as shown in Figure 4-3.

Other firewall programs require you to set up rules yourself. Typically, you start with a protocol such as ICMP, UDP, or HTTP. Your first rule may well be to block all traffic that uses that protocol on all ports. In subsequent rules, you identify types of communications you want to permit, based on time of day, port, IP address, or other criteria. Sygate Personal Firewall, for example, lets you identify hosts yourself and set up the filtering criteria that the program uses to block or allow packets (see Figure 4-4).

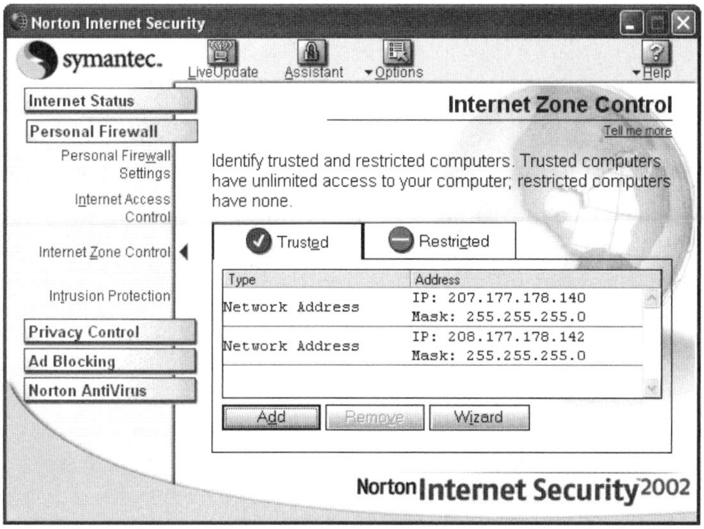

Figure 4-3   One simple filtering rule allows all traffic between "trusted" hosts

See Hands-On Project 4-1 for step-by-step instructions on how to set up simple rules that enable networked computers to communicate through a personal firewall program.

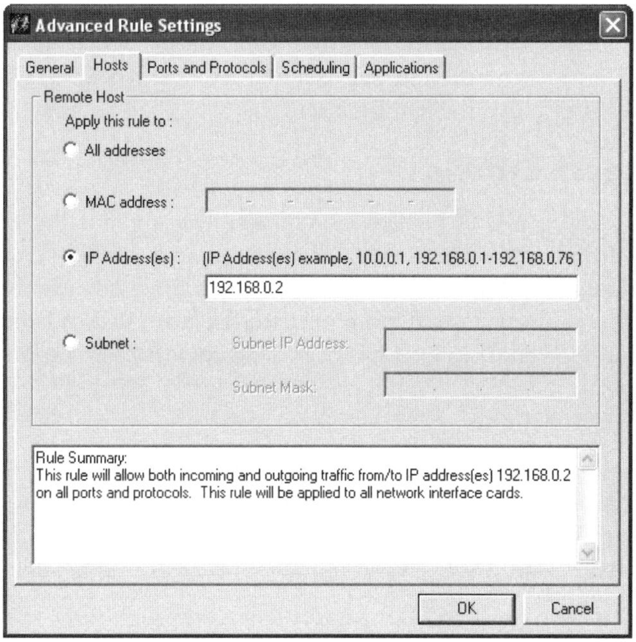

Figure 4-4   You can identify a host and set up packet filtering criteria for it

APPROACHES TO PACKET FILTERING

In the previous section, you got an overview about packet header fields that can be flagged when you establish packet filter rules. In the sections that follow, you learn about different approaches to filtering packets based on selected header contents. The simplest approach, stateless packet filtering (also called static packet filtering), reviews packet header content and makes decisions on whether to allow or drop the packets based on whether a connection has actually been established between an external host and an internal one. A more sophisticated and secure approach, stateful packet filtering, occurs when the filter maintains a record of the state of a connection and can thus make "intelligent" decisions on whether to allow traffic that is a genuine reply to an established connection. The last approach performs packet filtering based on the contents of the data part of a packet and the header.

We discuss each approach in turn.

Stateless Packet Filtering

It's easy to jump to the conclusion that **stateless packet filtering** is of no value at all because, unlike stateful packet filtering, it doesn't pay attention to the state of the connection when decisions are made about whether to block a packet. However, stateless packet filters are useful when you need to completely block traffic from a subnet or other network.

The following subsections examine the most common criteria that a stateless filter can be configured to use: IP header information, the TCP or UDP port number being used, the ICMP message type, and fragmentation flags such as ACK and SYN. The final section will address filtering suspicious inbound packets.

Filtering on IP Header Criteria

A stateless filter looks at each packet's header individually. It compares the header data against its **rule base** and forwards only those packets that match a rule. For instance, if the filter has been assigned a rule stating that all connections from outside the network are to be blocked and it receives a request from an external host, it drops the packet(s) associated with that request. As another example, if it has a rule that all incoming HTTP traffic needs to be routed to the public Web server at IP address 192.168.100.2, it sends any HTTP packets to 192.168.100.2.

A stateless filter has no means of remembering the packets that preceded it. Some years ago, when packet filters first appeared, this was an adequate level of security. It's inadequate now because hackers can do IP spoofing and insert false information into a packet header. For instance, a hacker can insert a false source IP address in a header.

Suppose you have set up a filter to allow TCP packets to pass through for a session with a client that has already been established. Such sessions make use of one or more identifiers called flags. Flags that identify the status of a session are found in the TCP header section of a packet. Figure 4-5 shows detailed packet information taken from the packet log of Sygate Personal Firewall. The upper part of the log shows attributes of the packet, such as source IP, destination IP, and so on. The TCP header information is shown in the box in the lower-left corner. The Flags section shows that the **Acknowledgement (ACK) flag** has been set, signifying that the destination computer has received the packets that were previously sent.

A hacker can craft a false TCP header that contains an ACK flag (and, presumably, a Trojan horse or other harmful software). The stateless packet filter would allow such a packet to pass through even though no connection has actually been established.

 IETF RFC 793 includes specifications for six control flags in a TCP header, and you should be aware of them when configuring packet filter rules for TCP: URG, Urgent; ACK, Acknowledgment; PSH, Push Function; RST, Reset the connection; SYN, Synchronize sequence numbers; and FIN, No more data from sender.

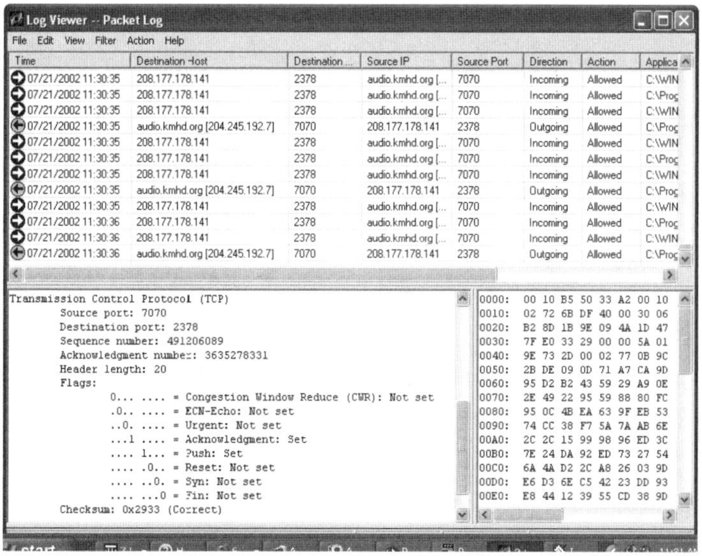

Figure 4-5   TCP flags in a packet header

One of the first IP header criteria you can filter on is the packet's source IP address. If someone tries to access your database server from IP address 62.10.100.6, however, it doesn't do any good to simply set up a single rule blocking all access from 62.10.100.6. If this is a hack attempt, the hacker will make another attempt from a different host. In addition, so many hackers will attempt to come at you from so many different addresses that it will be impossible to keep up with all of them. A much more effective approach is to allow only certain source IP addresses to access your resources. That is, denying all hosts except for a group of trusted IP addresses is the most effective security approach for a stateless packet filter.

You can use a stateless filter to block all access from "suspicious" networks or subnets.

You can also set up filter rules based on the destination or target IP address. The most obvious example is to enable external hosts to connect to your public servers in the DMZ but not to hosts in the internal LAN.

You can also go a step further and specify a protocol for the hosts to which you want to grant access. For instance, you could set up a rule that allows all external hosts to access your Web server at TCP Port 80 but that limits internal addresses to access TCP Port 23 (Telnet).

Table 4-1 shows the filtering rules that combine IP addresses and port numbers to control how hosts gain access to your internal network.

Table 4-1   Filtering by destination IP and port number

Protocol	Transport Protocol	Source IP	Source Port	Destination IP	Destination Port	Action
HTTP	TCP	Any	Any	192.168.0.1	80	Allow
HTTPS	TCP	Any	Any	192.168.0.1	443	Allow
Telnet	TCP	10.0.0.1/24	Any	192.168.0.5	223	Allow

Packets can also be filtered based on the IP protocol ID field in the header. The filter can use the data to allow or deny traffic of an entire type of service, including the following:

- TCP (Protocol number 6)

- UDP (Protocol number 17)

- IGMP (Protocol number 2)

- ICMP (Protocol number 1)

Internet Group Management Protocol (IGMP) enables a computer to identify its multicast group membership to routers so that it can receive a multicast (a broadcast of streaming media, newsletters, or other content) from another computer. You can find a complete list of protocol numbers at *www.iana.org/assignments/protocol-numbers*.

Most simple packet filters are unable to store a list of the allowed hosts that can access a particular protocol. They can only block or allow traffic for an entire designated protocol. Filtering by protocol might work if you can block all traffic of one protocol—all UDP traffic on a public FTP server, for instance. However, in most cases, the number of protocols is so low that it's not practical to completely block one of them.

The Options field in an IP header can be set by both hosts and routers. Options, though, are rarely used. Source routing, for instance, is not required by any protocol or ISP. Yet, source routing is a tempting tool to hackers, who only need to enter their own IP addresses in the destination to have the packet returned to them.

Filtering by TCP or UDP Port Number

Filtering by TCP or UDP port number is commonly called either port filtering or protocol filtering. Using TCP or UDP port numbers can help you filter a wide variety of information, including SMTP and POP e-mail messages, NetBIOS sessions, DNS requests, and Network News Transfer Protocol (NNTP) newsgroup sessions. For instance, you can filter out everything but TCP Port 80 for Web, TCP Port 25 for e-mail, and TCP Port 21 for FTP.

Filtering by ICMP Message Type

Internet Control Message Protocol (ICMP) functions as a sort of housekeeping protocol for TCP/IP, helping networks to cope with various communication problems. From a security standpoint, ICMP packets have a downside: they can be used by hackers to crash computers on your network. Because ICMP packets have no authentication method to verify the recipient of a packet, hackers can attempt man-in-the-middle attacks, in which they impersonate the intended recipient; they can also send packets that send the ICMP Redirect message type to direct traffic to a computer they control that is outside the protected network.

A firewall/packet filter must be able to determine, based on its message type, whether an ICMP packet should be allowed to pass. Some of the more common ICMP message types are shown in Table 4-2.

Table 4-2   ICMP message codes

ICMP Type	Name	Possible Cause
0	Echo reply	Normal response to a ping
3	Destination unreachable	Destination unreachable
3 code 6	Destination network unknown	Destination network unknown
3 code 7	Destination host unknown	Destination host unknown
4	Source quench	Router receiving too much traffic
5	Redirect	Faster route located
8	Echo request	Normal ping request
11	Time exceeded	Too many hops to destination
12	Parameter problem	There is a problem with a parameter

You'll find a complete list of ICMP message types at *www.iana.org/assignments/icmp-parameters*.

In one kind of network protocol attack that takes advantage of the ICMP Echo Request message type, a hacker floods a target computer with a constant stream of ICMP echo requests. The receiving machine is so busy fielding requests that it can't process any other network traffic. If the computer that goes down is one that provides important services such as DNS, the hacker can gain access to internal hosts. Then, an ICMP Redirect packet can be sent, pointing target computers to the hacker's computer where the hacker can attempt to access confidential information such as passwords.

Reviewing firewall logs can tell you if a large number of echo messages are being received. You can configure your firewall to drop ICMP packets that change network behavior (for example, that do ICMP Redirect) and that have come from sources outside your own network.

Filtering by Fragmentation Flags

Fragmentation of IP packets isn't bad in theory. Fragmentation was originally developed as a means of enabling large packets to pass through early routers that couldn't handle them due to frame size limitations. Routers were then able to divide packets into multiple fragments and send them along the network, where receiving routers would reassemble them in the correct order and pass them to their destination.

From a security standpoint, however, the difficulty with fragmentation is that because the TCP or UDP port number is provided only at the beginning of a packet, it will appear only in fragments numbered 0. Fragments numbered 1 or higher will simply be passed through the filter because they don't contain any port information. All a hacker has to do is modify the IP header to start all fragment numbers of a packet at 1 or higher. All fragments would go through the filter and be able to access internal resources.

To be on the safe side, you should configure the firewall/packet filter to drop all fragmented packets—especially because fragmentation is seldom if ever used due to improvements in routers. Alternatively, you could have the firewall reassemble fragmented packets and allow only complete packets to pass through.

Filtering by ACK Flag

A single bit of information in a TCP packet—the ACK bit or ACK flag—indicates whether a packet is requesting a connection or whether a connection has already been established. Packets requesting a connection have the ACK bit set to 0, whereas those that already have an ongoing connection have the ACK bit set to 1. The problem is that a hacker can insert a false ACK bit of 1 into a packet in an attempt to fool a host into thinking a connection is ongoing. You should configure the firewall to allow packets with the ACK bit set to 1 to access only the ports you specify and only in the direction you want.

Filtering Suspicious Inbound Packets

If a packet arrives at the firewall from the external network but containing an IP address that is inside the network, the firewall should send an alert message. In Figure 4-6, Tiny Personal Firewall has encountered a request from an external host to access the protected host's SQL server.

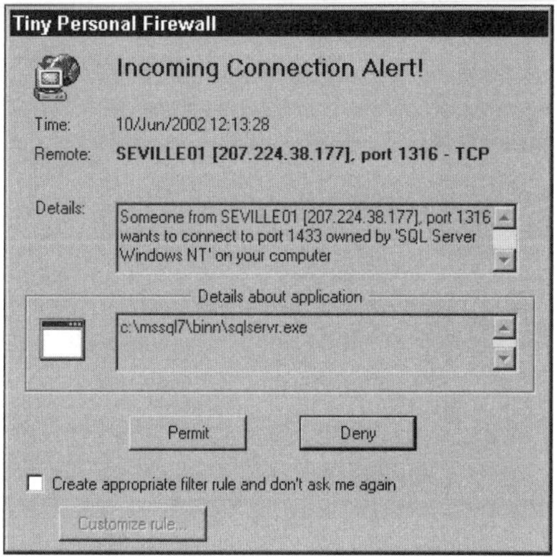

Figure 4-6   A firewall creates an alert when packets arrive for which no rule has been established

This firewall, like others, lets users graphically decide whether to permit or deny the packet in two types of instances:

- On a case-by-case basis
- Automatically, by setting up a rule to cover all future instances of such connection attempts

Most firewalls will give you the opportunity not only to set up a rule but also to customize it so that it works with all ports or all protocols, if you wish. If you receive an alert message like the one shown in Figure 4-6, click the Customize rule button at the bottom of the alert message window. You can then customize the rule to apply to specific ports or addresses, as shown in Figure 4-7.

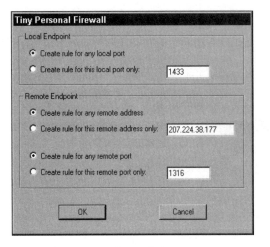

Figure 4-7   Most firewalls let you customize rules you establish

You can also set up other common rules for inbound packets:

- Dropping any inbound packets that have a source IP address that is within your internal network

- Dropping all inbound traffic that has the loopback address 127.0.0.1 as the source IP address

- Dropping traffic that has a source IP address that has not yet been allocated to any network, such as 0.x.x.x, 1.x.x.x, or 2.x.x.x

 You may encounter repeated alerts if you block packets individually rather than setting up rules for them that the firewall can handle automatically. However, it can also be enlightening to track how many connection attempts are made, what ports and services are being accessed, and where the attempts are originating—provided you have the time to review them.

Stateful Packet Filtering

Stateful inspection takes the concept of packet filtering a step further than stateless filtering. A stateful filter can do everything a stateless filter can but with one significant addition: the ability to maintain a record of the state of a connection. By "remembering" which packets are part of an active connection and which are not, the stateful filter can make "intelligent" decisions to allow traffic that is a true reply to an established connection and to deny traffic that represents "crafted" packets that contain false information.

 The more powerful enterprise firewalls such as those in the Cisco PIX series or Check Point FireWall-1 do stateful packet filtering. However, versions 1 and 2 of FireWall-1 did stateful filtering only on UDP. More recent versions handle UDP, TCP, and some ICMP packets.

In addition to a rule base, a stateful filter has a **state table**, which is a list of current connections. The packet filter compares the packet with the state table as well as the rule base. Entries that match criteria in both the state table and rule base are allowed to pass; all others are dropped. Figure 4-8 illustrates steps involved in processing a single request from a computer within your network to access the Web site *www.course.com*.

A stateful packet filter has to consult its state table and its rule base when a packet is encountered. However, it's worth noting that when the packet shown in Figure 4-8 arrives at the router, the state table is consulted but the rule base is not. It is not consulted because the rule base was consulted initially when the state table entry was created. It's also important to understand that a rule that lets a filter allow reply packets to pass does not have to be created. With a stateless filter, on the other hand, such a rule would be needed.

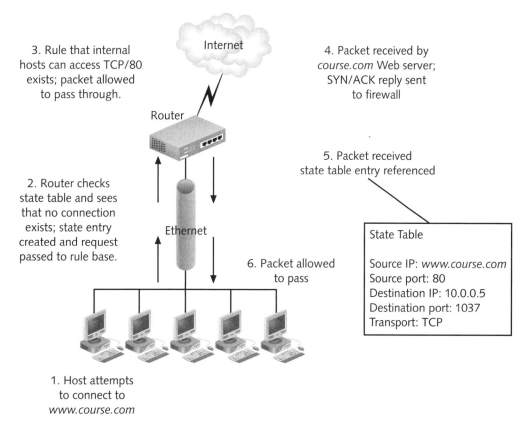

Figure 4-8   Stateful packet filtering

Stateful filters allow packets based on previously accepted packets. If a hacker tries to craft a packet with a false ACK bit set to1, the stateful filter would pass it to the rule base because no entry exists in the state table. The rule base should then drop the packet because the only rule needed is one that enables internal users to access TCP Port 80. There's no need to create a special rule for packets that have the ACK bit set to 1.

Assume that a stateful packet filter encounters a packet exchange that includes some of the flags that are part of a packet's TCP header information and that indicate whether a session is beginning or ending. These flags include RST (Reset, which tells a host to immediately terminate a connection) and FIN (Finished, which tells a host to gracefully end a connection). The firewall will assume that the session is finished and the entry will be deleted from the state table. Otherwise, if a session ends abnormally (if one system goes offline or a computer crashes), the filter will use a timer to remove state table entries. The timer can be set to remove entries as soon as 60 seconds or as late as several days after a session ends.

Even stateful packet filtering has limitations. It inspects only header information and doesn't verify the data part of a packet. It works by controlling the type of transport and the port number being used. If one of your servers is set up to listen for inbound communications on a nonstandard but well-known port, such as TCP/25 for SMTP, the filter might let in traffic that is bound for the well-known port but block traffic bound for other ports.

Filtering Based on Packet Contents

As mentioned, both stateless and stateful packet filters examine the header of a packet. Some traffic, such as ICMP traffic, uses packets that are hard to filter reliably. One fact that contributes to this problem is that ICMP packets don't always originate from the same source and destination IP addresses—if an unreachable message is created, ICMP packets might originate from an intermediary device instead. Because this message comes from a different source IP address than was recorded in the original state table entry, the message would be dropped by a stateful filter even though it's part of a legit-imate session.

To handle such cases, some stateful firewalls are able to examine the contents of packets as well as the headers for signs that they are legitimate. Such content filtering is some-times called stateful inspection. For example, active FTP might use a variety of different ports that are determined on the fly as a session is initiated. A stateless or stateful packet filter that supports active FTP must allow all traffic coming from TCP Port 20 as well as outbound traffic coming from ports above 1023. However, a stateful inspection looks at the data part of the FTP command packets and can determine which ports are to be used for this session—instead of opening all possible FTP ports, the packet filter opens ports as needed. After the session is done, the ports are again closed.

Note that two other types of firewall-related programs examine the contents of packets. One type is the proxy gateway. It looks at the data within a packet and decides which application should handle it. The other type is the specialty firewall, such as MailMarshal (*www.mailmarshall.com/*). It looks at the body of e-mail messages or Web pages for profanities or other content identified as "offensive." It then blocks the transmission of such information based on the presence of such terms. Such specialty firewalls are primarily designed to keep employees within an organization from visiting Web sites that are considered offensive and to keep them from sending or receiving inappropriate e-mail messages.

SETTING SPECIFIC PACKET FILTER RULES

4

After you have a general idea of how packet filtering works, it's time to establish the actual packet filter rules that control traffic to various resources. The following sections describe the types of rules you can set up to filter potentially harmful packets and the rules that you can set up to pass packets that you want to be passed through.

Packet Filter Rules That Cover Multiple Variations

The trick in coming up with packet filter rules is to account for all possible ports that a type of communication might use or for all variations within a particular protocol (for instance, passive and active FTP, or standard HTTP and secure HTTP). Some of this comes by trial and error. For instance, an employee complains that he or she can't communicate with someone using MSN Messenger, and you adjust the packet filter's rule base accordingly (after consulting the security policy, of course).

Consider the network shown in Figure 4-9, which will serve as a basis for the discussion in this section.

Figure 4-9 illustrates a typical LAN that is protected by a firewall and two routers. A DMZ connected to the firewall provides services that the public needs, such as a Web server, FTP server, and e-mail server. Accordingly, packet filter rules need to be set up to allow Web, FTP, e-mail, and other services, while blocking potentially harmful packets from getting to the internal LAN.

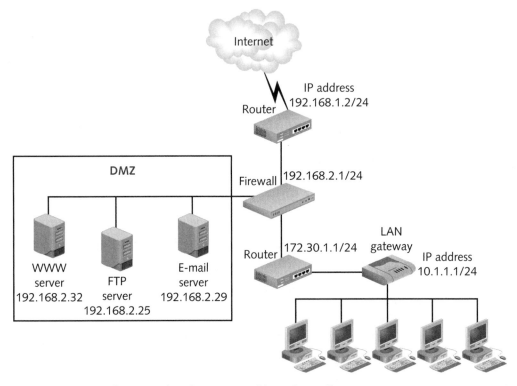

Figure 4-9   Sample network to be protected by a firewall

Packet Filter Rules That Cover ICMP

One of the first sets of rules you should establish covers ICMP, the protocol used to let you test network connectivity and make you aware of communications problems. ICMP rules are especially important because ICMP packets can be easily forged and used to redirect other communications.

Packet Filter Rules That Block Ping Packets

The most common command to use ICMP is Packet Internet Groper (commonly called ping). The command determines if a host is unreachable on the network. You send a packet to a host you're trying to reach, and the host responds with an ICMP response packet that tells you the host is "alive." Many hackers begin attacks by using ping to see whether a host is reachable by *them* as well. If all of your hosts respond to the ping command, you could be opening up your network to an attack.

To prevent hackers from using the ping command to identify some of your resources, you need to establish specific ICMP commands that cover common ICMP messages. Table 4-3 gives some rules that enable you to send and receive the ICMP packets you need while blocking those that open your internal hosts to intruders.

Table 4-3   ICMP packet filter rules

Rule	Protocol	Transport Protocol	Source IP	Destination IP	ICMP Message	Action
1	ICMP Inbound	ICMP	Any	Any	Source Quench	Allow
2	ICMP Outbound	ICMP	192.168.2.1/24	Any	Echo Request	Allow
3	ICMP Inbound	ICMP	Any	192.168.2.1/24	Echo Reply	Allow
4	ICMP Inbound	ICMP	Any	192.168.2.1/24	Destination Unreachable	Allow
5	ICMP Inbound	ICMP	Any	192.168.2.1/24	Service Unavailable	Allow
6	ICMP Inbound	ICMP	Any	192.168.2.1/24	Time to Live (TTL)	Allow
7	ICMP Inbound	ICMP	Any	192.168.2.1/24	Echo Request	Drop
8	ICMP Inbound	ICMP	Any	192.168.2.1/24	Redirect	Drop
9	ICMP Outbound	ICMP	192.168.2.1/24	Any	Echo Reply	Drop
10	ICMP Outbound	ICMP	192.168.2.1/24	Any	TTL Exceeded	Drop
11	ICMP Block	ICMP	Any	Any	All	Drop

4

The rules shown in Table 4-3 serve the following purposes:

- *Rule 1 (Source Quench)*: Lets external hosts tell your internal hosts if the network is saturated

- *Rule 2 (Echo Request)*: Gives your computers the ability to ping external computers

- *Rule 3 (Echo Reply)*: Enables your computers to receive ping replies from external hosts

- *Rule 4 (Destination Unreachable)*: Lets your hosts receive packets that an external resource is unreachable

- *Rule 5 (Service Unavailable)*: Lets your hosts receive packets that an external resource is unavailable

- *Rule 6 (Time to Live Exceeded)*: Lets your hosts know that an exterior resource is too many "hops" away

- *Rule 7 (Echo Request)*: Blocks ping packets that might be used to locate internal hosts

- *Rule 8 (Redirect)*: Prevents hackers or others from changing your **routing tables**

- *Rule 9 (Echo Reply)*: Prevents hackers from receiving replies to ping requests

- *Rule 10 (Time to Live Exceeded)*: Prevents hackers from determining the number of hops inside your network

- *Rule 11 (ICMP Block)*: After setting your rules, drops all other ICMP packets for extra security; that is, all ICMP packets not listed in the preceding rules will be dropped at the firewall

Packet Filter Rules That Enable Web Access

The first priority of employees in a protected network is (not surprisingly) to be able to surf the Web and exchange e-mail messages. The rules for accessing the Web need to cover both standard HTTP traffic on TCP Port 80 as well as Secure HTTP (HTTPS) traffic on TCP Port 443. The rules for the Internet-accessible Web server in our test network would look like those shown in Table 4-4. The rules in the table assume that the firewall uses a Deny-all policy. All packets are denied except for those that meet the rules listed in the rule base.

Table 4-4   HTTP access rules

Rule	Protocol	Transport Protocol	Source IP	Source Port	Destination IP	Destination Port	Action
12	HTTP Inbound	TCP	Any	Any	192.168.2.32	80	Allow
13	HTTPS Inbound	TCP	Any	Any	192.168.2.32	443	Allow
14	HTTP Outbound	TCP	192.168.1.2/24	Any	Any	80	Allow
15	HTTPS Outbound	TCP	192.168.2.32	Any	Any	443	Allow

Packet Filter Rules That Enable DNS

To connect to Web sites, the employees in our sample organization need to be able to resolve the **fully qualified domain names (FQDNs)** they enter, such as course.com, to their corresponding IP addresses using the Domain Name System (DNS). Internal users connect to external hosts using a DNS server located in the DMZ of the security perimeter. DNS uses either UDP Port 53 or TCP Port 53 for connection attempts. In addition, you need to set up rules that enable external clients to access computers in your own network using the same TCP and UDP ports, as shown in Table 4-5:

Table 4-5   Rules that enable DNS resolution

Rule	Protocol	Transport Protocol	Source IP	Source Port	Destination IP	Destination Port	Action
16	DNS Outbound	TCP	192.168.2.31	Any	Any	53	Allow
17	DNS Outbound	UDP	192.168.2.31	Any	Any	53	Allow
18	DNS Inbound	TCP	Any	Any	192.168.2.31	53	Allow
19	DNS Inbound	UDP	Any	Any	192.168.2.31	53	Allow

If your network uses DNS forwarding to an ISP's DNS server, you would enter the IP address of the ISP's DNS server as the destination IP and your own DNS server as the source IP. Some security administrators consider letting their company's DNS server communicate with any DNS server a security risk, and thus they direct all DNS traffic to a single DNS server operated by an ISP.

Packet Filter Rules That Enable FTP

As stated, FTP transactions can either be of the active or passive variety. The rules you set up for FTP need to support two separate connections: TCP Port 21, which is the FTP Control port, and TCP 20, which is the FTP Data port. If some clients in your network support active FTP, you can't specify a particular port because the client can establish a connection with the FTP server at any port above 1023. Instead, you specify the IP address of your FTP server, as shown in Table 4-6.

Table 4-6   Rules to enable active and passive FTP

Rule	Protocol	Transport Protocol	Source IP	Source Port	Destination IP	Destination Port	Action
20	FTP Control Inbound	TCP	Any	Any	192.168.1.25	21	Allow
21	FTP Data Inbound	TCP	192.168.1.25	20	Any	Any	Allow
22	FTP PASV	TCP	Any	Any	192.168.1.25	Any	Allow

Table 4-6   Rules to enable active and passive FTP (continued)

Rule	Protocol	Transport Protocol	Source IP	Source Port	Destination IP	Destination Port	Action
23	FTP Control Outbound	TCP	192.168.1.25	Any	Any	21	Allow
24	FTP Data Outbound	TCP	Any	20	192.168.1.25	Any	Allow

Some administrators prefer to drop incoming active FTP connections because of the danger of FTP port scanning. They allow only passive connections to go through.

Packet Filter Rules That Enable E-Mail

E-mail service is one of the most essential forms of communication in both personal and office environments. Yet, setting up firewall rules that permit the filtering of e-mail messages is not trivial. One reason is the variety of e-mail protocols that might be used:

- Post Office Protocol version 3 (POP3) and Internet E-mail Access Protocol version 4 (IMAP4) for inbound mail transport

- Simple Mail Transfer Protocol (SMTP) for outbound mail transport

- Lightweight Directory Access Protocol (LDAP) for looking up e-mail addresses

- HyperText Transport Protocol (HTTP) for Web-based mail service

To keep things simple, our sample configuration only uses POP3 and SMTP for inbound and outbound e-mail, respectively. However, SSL encryption is used for additional security. Some sample rules are found in Table 4-7.

Table 4-7   POP3 and SMTP e-mail rules

Rule	Protocol	Transport Protocol	Source IP	Source Port	Destination IP	Destination Port	Action
25	Outbound POP3	TCP	192.168.2.1/24	Any	Any	110	Allow
26	Outbound POP3/S	TCP	192.168.2.1/24	Any	Any	995	Allow
27	Inbound POP3	TCP	Any	Any	192.168.2.1/24	110	Allow
28	Inbound POP3/S	TCP	Any	Any	192.168.2.1/24	995	Allow
29	SMTP Outbound	TCP	192.168.2.29	Any	Any	25	Allow

Table 4-7   POP3 and SMTP e-mail rules (continued)

Rule	Protocol	Transport Protocol	Source IP	Source Port	Destination IP	Destination Port	Action
30	SMTP/S Outbound	TCP	192.168. 2.29	Any	Any	465	Allow
31	SMTP Inbound	TCP	Any	Any	192.168.2.29	25	Allow
32	SMTP/S Inbound	TCP	Any	Any	192.168.2.29	465	Allow

To set up your own configuration rules, you need to assess whether your organization needs to accept incoming e-mail messages at all, whether internal users can access mail services outside your company (such as Hotmail), and what e-mail clients are supported by your company. By identifying the e-mail clients your company will support, you can provide the highest level of security without blocking e-mail access.

Chapter Summary

- ◻ This chapter took a more in-depth look at one basic aspect of firewall security: packet filtering. Packet filtering was originally the only security activity performed by routers. Today, routers, operating systems, and firewalls all do some form of packet filtering.

- ◻ TCP/IP provides for transmission of data in manageable chunks called packets. Filtering such packets is a fundamental first line of security toward protecting a network. Each packet contains two parts: the header and data. The header is examined against a set of rules by packet filters. If some of the header information matches one of the rule criteria, the packet is allowed to pass; if not, the packet is dropped. Remember, the rules are examined in the order they were written. Typical rules include the direction of the packet (inbound or outbound, or both), the source and destination IP addresses and ports, and the protocol being used. Some filters also let you filter for the ACK bit in a TCP header.

- ◻ Packet filtering is important because it helps block attempts by hackers to locate hosts, sneak packets through by inserting false or "spoofed" information in the header, or possibly even crashing a computer by flooding it with ICMP echo requests.

- ◻ Stateful packet filtering is useful when you need to block traffic from an entire network or subnet. Stateful filtering is more efficient and effective: a firewall that does stateful filtering keeps a record in a state table whenever a request for connection is received. It only allows the replying packets to pass if their header information matches an entry that's already contained in the state table.

❏ When coming up with actual packet filter rules, you first need to think about ICMP packets, which result from ping commands, unsuccessful communications, and other incidents. Although the ping command is an important tool for diagnosing network connectivity problems, you have to develop well-defined rules for filtering ICMP packets to block ping attempts and redirect messages from hackers. Web access, e-mail, FTP, and DNS are among the other rules you need to set up.

❏ In general, it's good practice to use a firewall that follows a Deny-all policy: the firewall allows only packets that match specific filter rule criteria to pass, and it denies all other traffic.

KEY TERMS

ACK (Acknowledgement) flag — A part of a TCP header that tells a computer that sent a packet that the packet reached its destination.

Cyclical Redundancy Check (CRC) — An error-checking procedure performed in the trailer section of an IP packet.

data — The part of a packet that contains the information it is intending to send (such as the body of an e-mail message) and that is visible to the recipient—in contrast to the header of a packet, which is not visible to an end user.

datagram — Another term for a packet of digital information.

footer — A short section that tells a machine that the end of a packet has been reached.

fragment — An incomplete part of a packet that needs to be reassembled so that the packet can be processed.

fully qualified domain name (FQDN) — The complete DNS name of a computer, including the computer name, domain name, and domain name extension; example is *www.course.com*.

header — The part of a packet that contains IP source and destination addresses and other information. Routers and firewalls that do packet filtering make decisions on whether to allow the packet to pass by examining the header.

packet — A chunk of digital information that is sent along a network. Messages and files are broken into chunks by the Transmission Control Protocol (TCP). If they are sent to a host in a network that is protected by a firewall, the firewall has to reassemble them in the correct order.

packet filters — Block or allow transmission of packets of information based on criteria such as port, IP address, and protocol.

routing table — A list of network addresses and corresponding gateway IP addresses that a router uses to direct traffic.

rule base — The set of rules that a packet filter uses to decide whether to allow or deny traffic.

source routing — A group of values in the Options field of an IP packet header that supply routing instructions. Gateways can use such instructions to send the packet to its destination. However, such instructions can easily be misused by a hacker and are often blocked by packet filters or firewalls.

stateful inspection — The ability of some packet filters to examine the data portion of IP packets as well as headers and to allow only those packets that result from connections that have already been established.

stateless packet filtering — Packet filtering that determines whether to block or allow packets based on protocol type, IP address, port number, or other information, without regard to whether a connection has been established.

state table — A list of active connections maintained by a stateful packet filter. Such a filter allows only those packets that match the state table to pass through.

trailer — A short section that tells a machine that the end of a packet has been reached.

REVIEW QUESTIONS

1. A hacker can craft a false TCP _____ that contains an ACK flag.

2. What's the primary difference between the way routers treat packets and the way application proxies handle packets?

    a. Routers do IP forwarding and application proxies do not.

    b. Routers examine criteria within the packet and application proxies do not.

    c. Routers examine the header, whereas application proxies examine the data.

    d. Routers examine the data, whereas application proxies examine the header.

3. How do content-based filtering programs decide whether to allow packets into the protected network?

    a. They look for suspicious information contained in the header.

    b. They block traffic on SMTP Port 25.

    c. They only permit packets that have an active state with the server.

    d. They look for terms that have been identified as being "offensive."

4. Which of the following can be used to attack a network?

    a. source IP address

    b. source routing

    c. fragmentation

    d. all of the above

5. What tells a firewall how to reassemble a data stream that has been divided into packets?

   a. the source routing feature

   b. the number in the header's Identification field

   c. the destination IP address

   d. the Header Checksum field in the packet header

6. Why is it important to be familiar with the fields in an IP packet header?

7. What does stateful packet filtering do that stateless packet filtering does not do?

8. Which of the following is a function of an IP packet footer? (Choose all that apply.)

   a. error checking

   b. source routing

   c. designating an end of packet

   d. identifying packets to a gateway

9. Although it's true that stateless packet filters aren't as sophisticated as stateful ones, they are useful when you need to _____.

   a. filter packets individually

   b. filter packets without regard to connection state

   c. block an entire subnet

   d. block all traffic from a particular application

10. Which of the following is information that a hacker can insert into a TCP header to fool a stateless packet filter?

   a. source IP number

   b. ACK flag

   c. fragmentation flag

   d. protocol number

11. What is the most effective security approach for a stateless packet filter?

   a. deny all except specified hosts

   b. allow all except specified hosts

   c. allow access to only specified destination servers

   d. deny access to all destinations except specified servers

12. Why isn't it practical to filter by the protocol ID field in an IP header?

   a. There are too many protocols.

   b. There are no circumstances in which completely blocking one protocol would be practical.

   c. There are too few protocols.

   d. none of the above

13. How can ICMP packets be misused by a hacker to gain access to internal network resources? What weakness of ICMP packets enables such attacks?

14. How would you configure a firewall/packet filter to prevent ICMP attacks?

15. Which fragment numbers could be security risks because a packet filter might let them through?

   a. those numbered only 0 or higher

   b. those numbered only 1 or higher

   c. those numbered 0 or 1 only

   d. those numbered 2 through 10 only

16. What kinds of packets can cause problems for even a stateful packet filter?

   a. fragmented

   b. ICMP

   c. UDP

   d. TCP

17. State three reasons why internal clients need to be able to send outbound ICMP packets to hosts on the Internet.

18. Where should a packet be directed when it doesn't match any host in the interior LAN?

   a. It should be dropped.

   b. firewall

   c. default gateway

   d. loopback address

19. Which two ICMP messages are directly involved in blocking hack attempts? (Choose all that apply.)

   a. Inbound echo requests

   b. Inbound service unavailable

   c. Inbound Time to Live Exceeded

   d. Outbound echo replies

20. What is the difference between active and passive FTP that makes stateful packet filtering a good choice?

21. What is the purpose of blocking all ICMP packets after specifying a group of ICMP rules?

HANDS-ON PROJECTS

Project 4-1: Install and Configure Tiny Personal Firewall

Tiny Personal Firewall contains software that makes it easy for you to view and configure rules and perform other basic firewall functions. Like Sygate Personal Firewall, this program comes in both commercial versions and a free version. The following steps show you how to install the program and begin using it to set up some packet-filtering rules on a Windows 2000 or XP computer.

1. Double-click the **Internet Explorer** icon on your desktop to start the browser.

2. In the Address box, type **http://www.tinysoftware.com**, and then press **Enter**. (Note that the URL might default to a different address.) The home page of the Tiny Software, Inc. Web site appears.

3. Click the **Get It!** button. The Buy Standalone PC Security Products page appears.

4. Click the **Download/Support** link on the left side of the page. The Download and Support page opens.

5. Consult with your instructor as to what name and contact information to type when you fill out the short form near the bottom of the Support page. Click **Tiny Personal Firewall 2.0** on the drop-down list at the bottom of the page, and then click the **Continue to Download Page** button. The Files for Download page appears.

6. Click **Tiny Personal Firewall 2.0**. When the File Download dialog box opens, click **Save** to save this program to disk and select the location in which to save the file. Then click **Save** to begin downloading the file.

7. After the download is complete, double-click the **pf2.exe** file to start the installation. Click the **Next** button four times, accepting all defaults. When the install is finished, click the **Finish** button to restart your computer.

8. When you return to the Windows desktop, you'll see an alert dialog box asking if you want to accept NetBIOS packets from other computers in your "trusted network." Click **OK**.

9. Double-click the **Tiny Personal Firewall** icon in the Windows system tray. The Tiny Personal Firewall dialog box opens.

10. Click **Advanced**. The Firewall Configuration dialog box opens. You should set up a rule that enables other computers in your local network to communicate with you using the basic local networking protocols TCP, UDP, and ICMP.

11. Click **Filter Rules**, and then click **Add**. The Filter rules dialog box opens.

12. In the Description text box, type a description for this rule.

13. Leave the default selection, Any, chosen in the Protocol box. In the Direction box, click **Both directions** on the drop-down list.

14. In the Address type box, select the option that makes most sense for your network setup. If your network only has one other computer with a fixed address, click **Single address** and then type the address in the Host Address text box. If your network has IP addresses in the same range, such as 10.0.0.1/24, click **Network/Range**, and then type the appropriate addresses in the First Address and Last Address text boxes.

15. Make sure Always is selected under Rule valid and that the Permit radio button is selected. Click **OK**. The Filter Rules box closes and you return to the Firewall Configuration dialog box, where the new rule appears at the bottom of the list in the Filter Rules tab.

16. What appears under the Application column in Filter Rules pertaining to the new rule you just created? Double-click the rule's name to open the Filter Rules dialog box once again. Which option would you choose in Filter Rules to specify a particular application for this rule?

17. Click **OK** to close the Filter Rules, Firewall Configuration, and Tiny Personal Firewall dialog boxes and return to the Windows desktop.

Project 4-2: Set Up Windows Packet Filtering

Windows 2000 and XP have a variety of TCP/IP packet filtering that can be applied to a local area connection. This isn't a very sophisticated form of packet filtering, but it can prove useful if you have a specific port or protocol you want to block. The steps shown are for a Windows 2000 workstation. The steps for Windows XP are similar.

1. On the Windows 2000 desktop, click **Start**, point to **Settings**, point to **Network and Dial-up Connections**, and then click **Local Area Connection**. The Local Area Connection Status dialog box opens.

2. Click **Properties**. The Local Area Connection Properties dialog box opens.

3. Click **Internet Protocol (TCP/IP)**, and then click **Properties**. The Internet Protocol (TCP/IP) Properties dialog box opens.

4. Click **Advanced**.

5. In the Advanced TCP/IP Settings dialog box, click **Options**, click **TCP/IP filtering**, and then click **Properties**. The TCP/IP Filtering dialog box opens.

6. In the TCP/IP filtering dialog box, make sure the Enable TCP/IP Filtering (All adapters) check box is checked. Click the **Permit Only** radio button above TCP Ports. The TCP Ports option becomes active.

7. Click **Add**. The Add Filter dialog box opens.

8. In the TCP Port text box, type the DNS Port **53**, and then click **OK**.

9. Repeat the preceding three steps for the UDP Ports section. Use Port **53**.

10. Repeat Steps 6, 7, and 8 for the IP Protocols section. Enter protocol number **45** for Inter-Domain Routing Protocol.

11. Close all open windows.

Project 4-3: Start Up Routing and Remote Access Services

Routing and Remote Access Services (RRAS) is a Windows 2000 and XP service that functions as a software router and dial-up remote access server. This project assumes you have installed Tiny Personal Firewall as described in Hands-on Project 4-1 and that it is running on a Windows 2000 or XP workstation.

1. Click **Start**, point to **Settings**, and click **Control Panel**.

2. In the Control Panel window, double-click **Administrative Tools**.

3. In the Administrative Tools window, double-click **Services**.

4. In the Services console, double-click **Routing and Remote Access**.

5. In the Routing and Remote Access Properties dialog box, change the Startup type to **Manual**, and then click **Apply**. Stop the service by clicking **Stop**. After the Service status message reads Stopped, click **Start** to start it.

6. After a few seconds, Tiny Personal Firewall should send you an alert message with the heading Outgoing Connection Alert. In the Details box, you can read a message about Generic Host Process for Win32 Services wanting to send a UDP datagram. Click **Permit**.

7. Track how many alerts the firewall sends you. When each alert box appears, note the contents in a lab book or word-processing program. Then click **Permit** to close the alert box. How many packets does RRAS use when it is starting, and what ports does it use?

8. When the last alert box is closed and you return to the Routing and Remote Access Protocol dialog box, click **Cancel** to close the dialog box.

9. Close all open windows.

Project 4-4: View Packet Header Information

Usually, packet header information is not visible to end users. However, some firewall programs give you details about packets when they are encountered, and this gives you a glimpse into a packet's header.

 Before starting this project, make sure you have enabled IPv6 forwarding, as described in Hands-On Project 3-7.

1. Click **Start**, point to **Programs** (or **All Programs** on Windows XP), point to **Sygate Personal Firewall**, and click **Sygate Personal FirewallPro**. The program starts, and an alert dialog box opens, telling you that IPv6 wants to send a packet. (If the alert dialog box does not appear immediately, log off your computer and then log back on.)

2. Click **Detail**. The alert dialog box expands to show you detailed information about the attempted connection.

3. Scroll down and read the IP packet header information, which is presented under the heading Internet Protocol.

4. Scroll down further. What is at the bottom of the details? Note the answer in a lab book or word-processing document.

5. Click **Yes** to accept the packet and close the alert dialog box. The Sygate Personal Firewall window appears. Click the close box to close the window and return to the Windows desktop.

Project 4-5: Use Windows IPSec Packet Filtering

You can set up an IPSec filter to block or permit traffic without regard to encryption. This exercise gives you a chance to do some rudimentary packet filtering. For this exercise, you need a Windows XP workstation that has IPSec enabled.

1. Click **Start** and click **Control Panel**.

2. In the Control Panel window, double-click **Administrative Tools**.

3. In the Administrative Tools dialog box, double-click **Local Security Policy**.

4. In the Local Security Settings management console, click **IP Security Policies on Local Computer** in the left pane.

5. In the right pane, right-click **Secure Server (Require Security)**, and then click **Properties**.

6. If the Add Standalone Snap-in dialog box appears, click **Close**, and then click **OK** to close Add/Remove Snap-in.

7. In the Rules tab of the Secure Server (Require Security) Properties dialog box, make sure the check box next to **Use Add Wizard** is checked, and then click **Add**.

8. Click **Next** four times until you get to the screen in the Security Rule Wizard entitled "IP Filter List." (If you receive a dialog box stating that your computer is not a member of a domain, click **Yes** to continue.)

9. Click the **All IP Traffic** button, and then click **Add**.

10. For the purposes of this exercise, let's assume you want to enable Port 80 communications between your computer and one with the IP address 192.168.1.1. In the name text box, delete the default name **New IP Filter List** and replace it with **Project 4-5 Rule**.

11. In the Description text box, type **Enables IPSec secure communication with one computer**.

12. Uncheck the **Use Add Wizard** check box, and then click **Add**.

13. In the Filter Properties dialog box, leave My IP Address in the Source address box. Click the **Destination address** list arrow and click **A specific IP Address**. The IP address and Subnet mask boxes appear.

14. Type **192.168.1.1** in the IP address box, and then click the **Protocol** tab.

15. Click the **Select a protocol type** list arrow, and click **TCP** on the drop-down list.

16. Under Set the IP protocol port, click the **From this port** button, and type **80** in the text box beneath.

17. Click the **To this port** button, and type **80** in the text box beneath.

18. Click **OK**.

19. Because this is a very restrictive filtering policy with a fictitious computer, you should click **Cancel** to close Filter Properties and return to IP Filter List. If you were setting up actual security policies, you would click **Add in IP Filter List** and enter information for protocols and ports to be used by the computers in your local network.

20. Click **Cancel** to return to the Security Rule Wizard, click **Cancel**, and then click **Cancel** again to close the Secure Server (Require Security) Properties dialog box.

Project 4-6: View Your Local Network Routing Table

Every router or gateway makes use of a routing table—a list of IP addresses for the resources on the network as well as default gateways. If you're on a network and you have a Windows workstation, it's easy to view the routing table.

1. Log on to your Windows workstation.

2. Click **Start**, and then click **Run**.

3. Type **cmd** in the Open text box in the Run dialog box, and then press **Enter**.

4. In the Command Prompt window, type **netstat −r**, and then press **Enter**.

5. Review the list of destinations—particularly, the Network Destination column. What is the address of your network's default gateway? Write it in a lab book or word-processing document. Where else does this same IP address appear in the list?

6. Type **exit** and then press **Enter** to close the command prompt window and return to the Windows desktop.

CASE PROJECTS

Case 4-1: Design a Packet Filtering Solution

Your employer asks you to block traffic from the Web site *www.offensivecontent.com*, which a group of employees has been caught visiting. You open a command prompt window and type ping *www.offensivecontent.com* to determine the IP address of the site. After a few minutes, the IP address 197.34.5.56 comes back, but you get several messages stating that the request has timed out, and no packets are exchanged. Based on what you've read in this chapter, what does this tell you about the security measures at the *www.offensivecontent.com* Web site? What rule would you add to the rule base to block access to this site?

Case 4-2: Troubleshooting Local Network Connectivity

When you install a personal firewall, it doesn't work. You suddenly lose the ability to share files with other computers in your lab. You open a command prompt, ping your default gateway router, and get a successful response. You try to ping another computer on your network and get a series of "Request Timed Out" messages. You are sure the problem has to do with the firewall blocking communications with the supposedly "trusted" computer. What would you do to restore communications with the other local machine?

4

Case 4-3: Access Problems

Employees complain that it's taking longer than usual time to access the Web, receive e-mail messages, and otherwise communicate with external hosts. In reviewing your firewall logs, you notice a large number of ICMP echo requests coming from external host 63.10.100.4. You suspect an attempted ICMP flooding attack. How would you respond?

Case 4-4: Filtering Spam

Employees in your organization are complaining about the amount of spam e-mail messages they are receiving. You are asked to attempt to "filter out" such messages. Come up with two different ways to help reduce such messages.

5

WORKING WITH PROXY SERVERS AND APPLICATION-LEVEL FIREWALLS

After reading this chapter and completing the exercises, you will be able to:

♦ Understand proxy servers and how they work

♦ Understand the goals that you can set for a proxy server

♦ Make decisions regarding proxy server configurations

♦ Choose a proxy server and work with the SOCKS protocol

♦ Know the benefits of the most popular proxy-based firewall products

♦ Know the uses of the reverse proxy

♦ Understand when a proxy server isn't the correct choice

Proxy servers were originally developed as a way to speed up communications on the Web by storing a site's most popular pages in cache. Since then, they have developed into a formidable security solution. Proxies can conceal the end users in a network by working on their behalf. They can filter out undesirable Web sites, and they can block harmful content in much the same manner as packet filters. Today, most proxy servers function as firewalls at the boundary of a network, performing packet filtering, Network Address Translation (NAT), and other services.

This chapter gives you an overview of what proxy servers are and how they work. Next, you examine the goals of proxy servers as well as the vulnerabilities and other drawbacks they bring to a security setup. You then learn about the different kinds of proxy servers you can install. Finally, you compare and contrast proxy-based firewalls so that you can make an informed decision about the one that's right for you.

OVERVIEW OF PROXY SERVERS

The first thing you need to learn about **proxy servers** is that they go by many other names as well: **proxy services**, **application-level gateways**, or simply **application proxies**. These terms all refer to the same thing: software that can scan the data portion of an IP packet and act on it (in contrast to the packet filters you learned about in Chapter 4, which interpret only the header of an IP packet). The most common term—proxy server—is used throughout this chapter.

The Proxy Analogy

Previous chapters have used the analogy of a security guard named Sam in an office building to describe various firewall services. The guard can function like an application proxy, too. Suppose one of the higher managers calls Sam and asks him to buy a bunch of flowers from the flower store in the lobby of the building for a colleague's birthday. Sam dutifully purchases the flowers on the individual's behalf, and then wraps the flowers and puts a note on them stating they are from the manager (not Sam). He hands them to the elevator operator with instructions to take them to the top floor of the building and hand them to the receptionist on that floor. If Sam does all of these things (and possibly even logs the purchase in a list of such errands that he maintains), he will be functioning in much the same way as a proxy server. In other words, Sam is to the proxy server as the flowers are to the packets of information.

How Proxy Servers Work

Proxies function as a sort of software go-between, forwarding data between internal users and external hosts. They work by focusing on the port each service uses, screening all traffic into and out of each port and deciding whether to block or allow traffic based on rules set up by the proxy server administrator.

In a typical transaction, a proxy server intercepts a request from a computer on the internal network being protected and passes it along to a destination computer on the Internet. This might seem like a complex and time-consuming process, but it takes only a matter of seconds for the following steps to occur:

1. An internal host makes a request to access a Web site.

2. The request goes to the proxy server, which examines the header and data of the packet against rules configured by the firewall administrator.

3. The proxy server recreates the packet in its entirety, with a different source IP address.

4. The proxy server sends the packet to its destination; the packet appears to be coming from the proxy server, not the original end user who made the request.

5. The returned packet is sent to the proxy server, which inspects it again and compares it against its rule base.

6. The returned packet is rebuilt by the proxy server and sent to the originating computer; when received, the packet appears to have come from the external host, not the proxy server.

Figure 5-1 illustrates these steps.

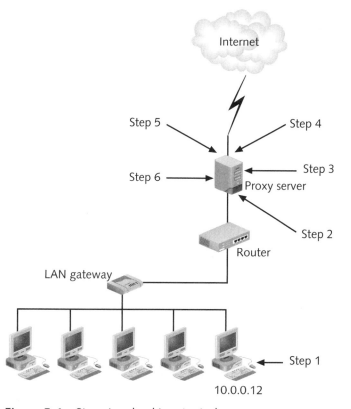

Figure 5-1   Steps involved in a typical proxy transaction

Naturally, it takes several seconds for the proxy server to inspect, compare, and rebuild information, which probably seems far longer than the usual Internet connection that occurs without a proxy. The main complaint about proxy servers is the time they add to communications. However, in return, they conceal clients, translate network addresses, and filter content, among other tasks.

How Proxy Servers Differ From Packet Filters

Ultimately, proxy servers and packet filters need to be used together in a firewall to provide multiple layers of security of different varieties. Both work at the Application layer, but they inspect different parts of IP packets and act on them in different ways.

It's useful to contrast proxies and packet filters so that you understand the different types of network security they provide:

- Because proxy servers scan the entire data part of IP packets, they create much more detailed log file listings than packet filters. For instance, packet filters log only header information, whereas proxy servers can log much more.

- If a packet matches one of the packet filter's rules, the filter simply allows the packet to pass through as is and go to the destination computer. On the other hand, a proxy server rebuilds the packet with new source IP information, which shields internal users from those on the outside.

- The use of a proxy server means that a server on the Internet and an internal host are never directly connected to one another. Because the proxy rebuilds all packets that pass between them, attacks that can start with mangled packet data never reach the internal host.

- Proxy servers are far more critical to network communications than packet filters are. If a packet filter fails to work for some reason, one possible result is that all packets might be allowed through to the internal network. If a proxy server **gateway** or firewall were to crash, all network communications would cease.

 Of course, if a failover firewall is in use, it would be able to keep network communications up and running while the primary device is being serviced. See "Two Firewalls, One DMZ" in Chapter 3 for more on failover configurations.

Sample Proxy Server Configurations

A proxy server needs to be positioned between the hosts in the internal LAN and the outside network to provide services on behalf of both internal and external users. A proxy server has two interfaces: one between itself and the external network, the other between itself and the internal network. The dual-interface nature of a proxy server suggests that a dual-homed host computer (which is a computer that has two separate network interfaces, one to the external Internet and one to the internal LAN) provides an ideal setup for hosting (see Figure 5-2).

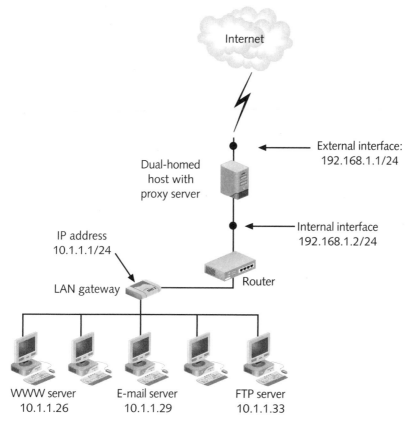

Figure 5-2   A proxy server/firewall on a dual-homed host

You can also configure a proxy server on a screened host and install routers that func-tion as packet filters on either side, as shown in Figure 5-3.

In Figure 5-3, the packet filter that has an interface on the Internet is configured so that external traffic is allowed to pass only if it is destined for a service provided on the proxy server, which sits on the protected side of the perimeter.

In Figure 5-3, it's important to note that although the screened host/proxy server has a direct interface on the Internet, you shouldn't really do this. In practice, it's far better to use a proxy server behind a firewall: the firewall should have an interface to the Internet and protect the proxy server behind it. The need for protection is critical because, if the proxy is compromised by a hacker, the hacker can make it look as though he or she is actually an internal client, and the results can be disastrous for the organization being protected. The only reason you should place a proxy server directly on the Internet is if the proxy is intended to serve as a **reverse proxy**. (See the "Reverse Proxy" section later in this chapter.)

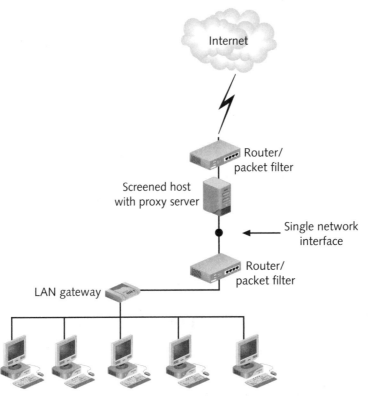

Figure 5-3   A proxy server/firewall on a screened host

 If you use proxy servers in conjunction with either stateful or stateless packet filters, make sure you disable IP forwarding on the packet servers; then, the proxy server will handle packet delivery from one network to another.

GOALS OF PROXY SERVERS

When you consider setting up a proxy system to protect a network, you should understand the goals that proxy systems can help you achieve. These goals—from concealing internal clients to redirecting URLs—are described in the following sections.

Concealing Internal Clients

Perhaps the most important benefit of using a proxy server is its ability to conceal internal clients from external clients who try to gain access to the internal network. Rather than connecting directly to internal hosts with IP addresses like 10.0.0.4, 10.0.0.5, and so on, external clients see the network as appearing to be a single machine—the one that hosts the proxy server software. The network appears as a single machine because only that single machine is seen by external hosts as relaying requests from the internal network (see Figure 5-4). This concealment is useful to you because if external users are never able to detect hosts on your internal network, they won't be able to initiate attacks against those hosts.

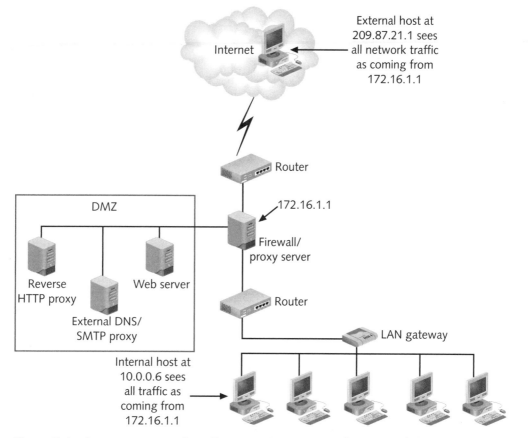

Figure 5-4   A proxy server makes all communication come from a single gateway

The type of concealment that proxy servers perform resembles NAT. However, proxy servers don't simply insert a new source IP into the headers of the packets they send out in response to a request. Rather, the proxy server receives requests as though it were the destination server. It then completely regenerates a new request, which is then sent to its destination.

 Because proxy servers route all client requests through a single gateway, they are commonly used to share Internet connections. Simple proxy servers such as WinGate (Windows) or Squid (Unix) are used frequently to provide Internet connection sharing in small office or home environments.

Blocking URLs

Network administrators and managers like the fact that they can block users from certain URLs. This feature is frequently used to keep employees from visiting Web sites that offer content that management regards as unsuitable. URLs can be specified as either IP addresses or DNS names.

In practice, blocking URLs is unreliable. The main reason is that URLs are typically blocked by proxy servers as full-text URLs. The simple proxy server NetProxy, for example, lets you enter the URLs of sites that you want to block from passing through the WWW proxy gateway (see Figure 5-5). However, if you have only entered the domain name of the site and the end users use the IP address that corresponds to the URL, they can still access the site.

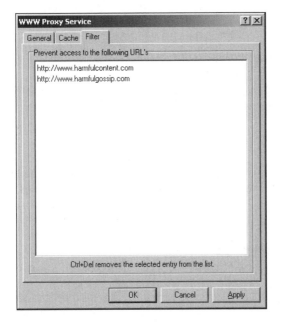

Figure 5-5   NetProxy lets you block URLs based on domain name

 If you want to keep employees from visiting certain Web sites, it's more effective to communicate this in a security policy rather than by simply blocking URLs, which change frequently as new sites come up and move from one location to another.

Blocking and Filtering Content

Proxy servers can be configured to scan the packet for content that can cause problems. The proxy can be set up to not only block but also to strip out Java applets or ActiveX controls if you don't want them to enter the internal network. In addition, you should certainly have the proxy delete executable files attached to e-mail messages.

 Instruct employees that anyone who wants to send them an executable program should pack it in a **Zip archive** or **StuffIt** file before e-mailing it. The benefit of this transmission method is protection: if the legitimate executable file passes through the proxy server as is, without being packed in an archive, it will be dropped because the proxy will see it as a potentially harmful file. If the file is packed, the recipient can decide whether to unzip the file.

Proxy servers, like packet filters, can filter out content based on rules that contain a variety of **parameters**, including time, IP address, and port number. Virtually all proxy server products capitalize on the ability to scan the payload of a packet and provide some sort of content-filtering system. Typically, this is used to block children (in a home environment) or employees (in a work environment) from viewing Web sites that are considered unauthorized or unsuitable.

E-Mail Proxy Protection

Casual users often assume that a proxy server exists primarily to protect users who are surfing the Web. However, a variety of other proxy servers can be used, including e-mail. Figure 5-6 shows a configuration that provides e-mail protection for a network with a proxy Simple Mail Transfer Protocol (SMTP) server.

In Figure 5-6, a Sendmail server has been placed in the DMZ where it receives e-mail from the Internet. It passes requests on to the real mail server, which is the Exchange server located on the internal network. Mail that originates on an internal host is sent from the Exchange server to the Sendmail server, which strips out the IP source address information when it rebuilds the packets and sends them on to the Internet. External e-mail users never interact directly with internal hosts, which is the great advantage of using this configuration.

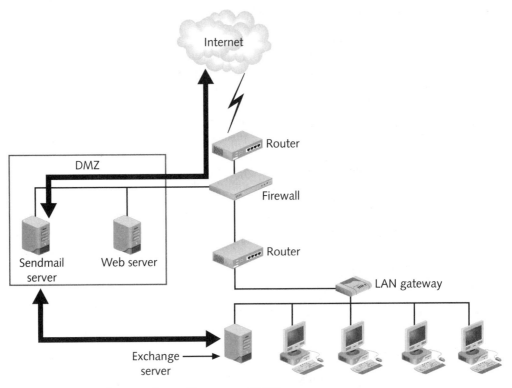

Figure 5-6 E-mail protection with a proxy SMTP server

Improving Performance

Although proxy servers can slow down some requests for information, they can also speed up access to documents that have been requested repeatedly. For instance, they can be configured to store Web pages in a disk **cache**. When someone requests the same Web page in the future, the proxy server can retrieve it from the cache. This relieves the load on the Web server, which doesn't have to serve up the same documents repeatedly.

 A reverse proxy—a proxy that monitors outbound traffic—also improves performance.

Ensuring Security

Log files, which maintain records of events such as logon attempts and accesses to files, might be tedious and time consuming to review, but they can serve many different functions when it comes to ensuring the effectiveness of a firewall:

- *Detect intrusions*: By reviewing the firewall logs in detail, you can determine whether an unauthorized user has accessed resources that should be protected.

- *Uncover weaknesses*: Log files can point to ports, machines, or other vulnerable computers through which hackers can gain entry. These entry points are known as **holes**.

- *Provide documentation*: If intrusions occur, log files can give you a record that indicates when the attack occurred and provide indications of the method that was used.

As stated, proxy servers provide complete log files. The fact that proxies require all communications to flow through a single gateway means you have a reliable checkpoint from which to monitor network activity. To keep log files from getting unwieldy and eating up an inordinate amount of disk space, you should log only the services and **events** you view as most critical. (Events you want to log should certainly include unauthorized connection attempts.)

NetProxy, like other proxy servers, lets you select services from a list for logging (see Figure 5-7). Note that the selection of applications and events you are going to log should be spelled out in your organization's security policy, as described in Chapter 2.

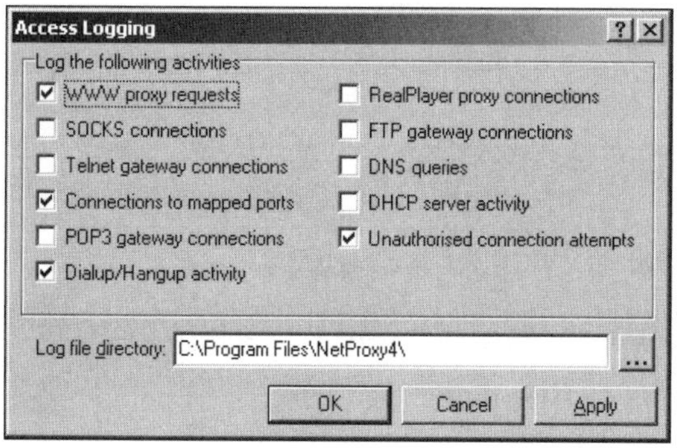

Access Logging	?|X
Log the following activities	
☑ WWW proxy requests	☐ RealPlayer proxy connections
☐ SOCKS connections	☐ FTP gateway connections
☐ Telnet gateway connections	☐ DNS queries
☑ Connections to mapped ports	☐ DHCP server activity
☐ POP3 gateway connections	☑ Unauthorised connection attempts
☑ Dialup/Hangup activity	

Log file directory: `C:\Program Files\NetProxy4\`   `...`

`OK`   `Cancel`   `Apply`

Figure 5-7   Select only the most critical services and events to log

Some proxy servers have an **alerting** feature: they can notify you if a possible attack is in progress. An example of a possible attack is an attempted connection at the external interface of the proxy server.

Providing User Authentication

If user authentication is used in combination with a proxy server, you enhance security even more. Look for a proxy server that does this; most products include the ability to prompt users who connect to the server for a username and password, which the server then checks against a database in your system.

 Authentication is discussed in more detail in Chapter 6.

Redirecting URLs

Some proxies can scan specific parts of the data part of an HTTP packet and redirect it to a specific location. The proxy can be configured to recognize two types of content (and perform **URL redirection** to send them to other locations):

- Files or directories requested by the client
- The host name with which the client wants to communicate

The second method, which involves scanning the Host field in the HTTP packet header, is the most popular. It enables you to direct clients to a different Web server based on the host being requested. Suppose you have a single machine with a static IP address that hosts half a dozen or more virtual Web servers within it. Requests for the host *www.widgets.org* can be directed to one server, requests for *www.knicknacks.org* can be directed to another, and so on.

Many Web servers, such as the popular freeware program Apache, have URL redirection built in, thus alleviating the need for a proxy server to do redirection.

PROXY SERVER CONFIGURATION CONSIDERATIONS

Proxy servers bring many security-related benefits, but they also require you to perform special tasks and to take some important concepts into consideration. These include scalability issues that affect the proxy server as the network grows, the need to configure each piece of client software that will use the proxy server, the need to have a separate proxy service available for each network protocol you will use, and the need to create packet filter rules. Besides that, proxy servers carry with them potential security vulnerabilities of which you need to be aware, such as the creation of a single point of failure for the network.

We discuss each in turn.

Providing for Scalability

As the number of users on the network grows, the machine that hosts the proxy server should be upgraded. The problem isn't so much with the proxy server as it is with the amount of traffic that has to flow through a single gateway.

One way around the proxy server slowdown is to add multiple proxy servers to the same network connection. The servers can be configured differently so they share the total network traffic load. One server can handle traffic from one subnet of users, one to another, and so on.

 Before you start investing in multiple proxy servers, make sure your Internet connection is robust enough to handle the amount of traffic your network is experiencing.

Working with Client Configurations

You have to configure each client program to work with the proxy server. For example, when you set up a proxy server, you must configure a Web browser to support the connection. A typical setup for Internet Explorer is shown in Figure 5-8. No proxy server is specified for FTP and Gopher connections because the browser can use the **SOCKS** standard, a set of protocols that enable applications that don't specifically have a proxy server assigned to them to use a proxy server, to make those connections via the proxy server's gateway.

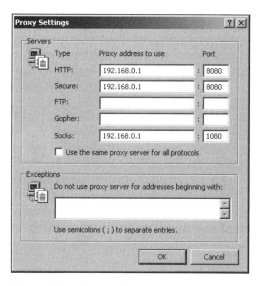

Figure 5-8 Each client on the network must be configured to access the proxy server

Such configurations are easy to perform once or twice, but when multiplied across dozens or even hundreds of client computers, the time and effort involved can be substantial. To help with this situation, most proxy servers will let you access a **configuration file** from which the browsers on your network can automatically retrieve the proxy settings. The file shown in Figure 5-9 contains the default settings for NetProxy; you can edit the **JavaScript** to include (if you have one) the **static IP address** of the server that hosts the proxy server(s).

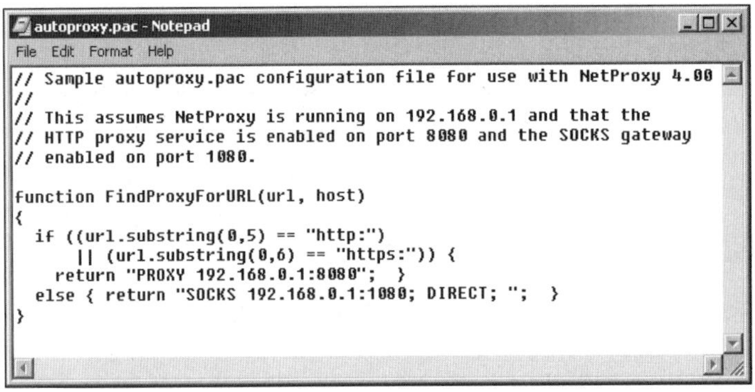

```
// Sample autoproxy.pac configuration file for use with NetProxy 4.00
//
// This assumes NetProxy is running on 192.168.0.1 and that the
// HTTP proxy service is enabled on port 8080 and the SOCKS gateway
// enabled on port 1080.

function FindProxyForURL(url, host)
{
  if ((url.substring(0,5) == "http:")
    || (url.substring(0,6) == "https:")) {
    return "PROXY 192.168.0.1:8080";  }
  else { return "SOCKS 192.168.0.1:1080; DIRECT; ";  }
}
```

Figure 5-9   A proxy server configuration file

You can give the individual users in your organization instructions on locating the configuration file, as described in Hands-On Project 5-3, to save yourself considerable time and effort.

Working with Service Configurations

Similarly, you have to have a separate proxy server available for each service protocol you expect to use on the network. That doesn't mean, of course, that you have to have a separate proxy server setup for every instance. You can set up a dedicated proxy that handles one type of traffic that is especially vulnerable to attack, such as SMTP. On the other hand, services that can receive an especially heavy load, such as HTTP, might also run more efficiently if they are given a dedicated proxy server—such as the proxy server Squid—designed to work especially with HTTP.

More commonly, though, organizations use a general-purpose firewall that includes a proxy server that monitors all inbound and outbound traffic. You should certainly configure HTTP and DNS, as well as SMTP and POP3 for e-mail. The range of options available with NetProxy is shown in Figure 5-10.

   Services for which no proxy server is available can make use of the SOCKS generic proxy, which is described later in this chapter.

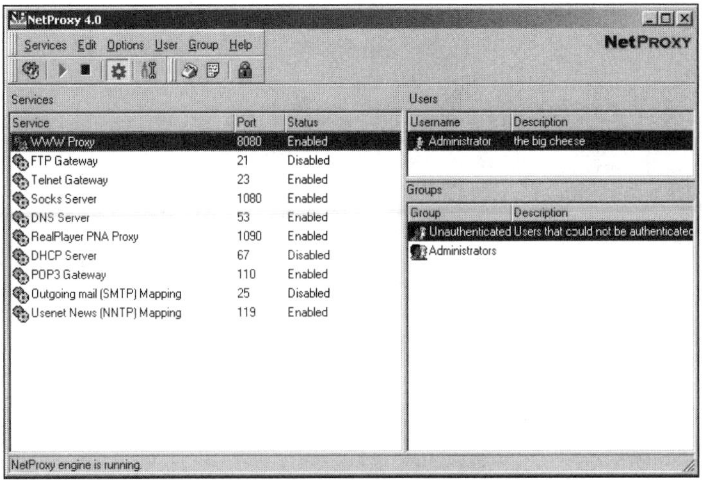

Figure 5-10   Each service needs to be configured to use a proxy server

Creating Filter Rules

You can set up rules such as allowable hosts that can bypass the proxy. You can filter out URLs. You can also set up rules that enable internal users to send outbound requests only at certain times. For an organization that only works during daylight hours, cutting off communications (except e-mail messages that might come in overnight) can be an important security level in the evening and overnight hours. During those hours, the protection ensures that no Trojan horses that may have found their way into a system can try to connect to the Internet.

 You can also set up rules governing the length of time a session can last. Cutting off a session after a lengthy amount of time, such as an hour, can stall hackers who manage to get in to your system and attempt to run executables from one of your host machines.

Recognizing the Single Point of Failure

When you have a proxy server routing all traffic into and out of a network, you provide a single point of ingress and egress. You also provide a single point of failure for the network. If the proxy server crashes due to a hacker's efforts, your network could be totally cut off from the Internet.

This problem isn't unique to proxies, of course. Routers and firewalls that lie between your internal network and the Internet can provide the same failure point. Firewall hardware or software packages that include proxy servers will have other means of enabling traffic to flow with some amount of protection, such as packet filtering. You can also use load-balancing systems, such as the Windows Load Balancing feature of Windows 2000

Advanced Server, to create multiple proxies that are in use simultaneously and thus make your system less vulnerable—if one proxy ceases to function, the others will still work.

Recognizing Buffer Overflow Vulnerabilities

Proxy servers can fall victim to a number of problems that result from misconfiguration or built-in vulnerabilities. The most common problem is a buffer overflow, which occurs when a program (in this case, a proxy server) attempts to store more data in a temporary storage area (a buffer) than that area can hold. The resulting overflow of data (some of which might even contain executable code intended to cause harm to a network) renders the program nonfunctional.

Some proxy servers have been known to fall victim to buffer overflow problems. The problem might be a request that comes in with numerous quotation marks, which causes the server to get confused and freeze, or the problem might be a request that comes in with a very long DNS name, which the proxy server is unable to resolve. After the proxy server has ceased to function, an unscrupulous individual can attempt to execute code on the server or execute commands by assuming the administrator's privileges. The only way to combat such vulnerabilities is to check the Web site of the manufacturer of the proxy server you are using and install any security patches that have been provided for such vulnerabilities.

CHOOSING A PROXY SERVER

Proxy servers come in different varieties. Some, like WinGate, are commercial products primarily used by home and small business users. Others, like Squid, are designed to protect one type of service (Web or FTP) and to serve Web pages stored in cache. Most proxy systems are part of a **hybrid firewall**—a firewall that combines several different security technologies, such as packet filtering, application-level gateways, and VPNs. Others, like NetProxy, are true standalone proxy servers.

The following sections give you an overview of the different types of proxy servers with which you should be familiar. The types are transparent, nontransparent, and SOCKS based.

Transparent Proxies

Transparent proxies can be configured to be totally invisible to an end user. A transparent proxy sits between two networks like a router. The firewall intercepts outgoing traffic and directs it to a specific computer, such as a proxy server. The individual host does not know its traffic is being intercepted; in addition, the client software doesn't have to be configured, which makes network administrators very happy.

Nontransparent Proxies

Nontransparent proxies, also called explicit proxies, require the client software to be configured to use the proxy server. Every FTP client, chat program, browser, or e-mail software you use must have the ability to house a proxy server. All target traffic is forwarded to the proxy at a single target port. Typically, the SOCKS protocol is used to do this.

Nontransparent proxies are more complicated to configure because each client program must be set up to route all requests to a single port. However, nontransparent proxies provide greater security. Clients can have their routing entries removed so that only the proxy server knows how to reach the Internet. Figure 5-11 shows a configuration to use a nontransparent proxy.

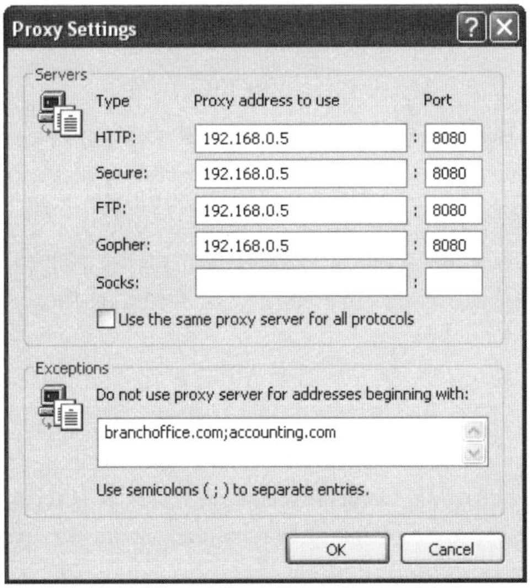

Figure 5-11   Nontransparent proxies use a single port number and IP address

Notice that, in Figure 5-11, an exception has been made for local networks. If you have a local network that you don't want to have to go through the proxy, such as a branch of your own company, you should list it here. All traffic from that network will access needed resources directly.

SOCKS-Based Proxies

SOCKS is a protocol that enables the establishment of generic proxy applications—applications designed to act on behalf of many different services and particularly those such as FTP, NetMeeting, and other programs that don't work with other proxy software. SOCKS is known for its flexibility; it can help developers set up firewalls and virtual private networks (VPNs) as well as proxies.

The term SOCKS is derived from sockets, a TCP/IP protocol used to establish a communication session. A socket is also an identifier consisting of an IP address and port number, such as 172.16.0.1:80. WinSock, for instance, is the name of a DLL that implements Sockets for Windows.

SOCKS Features

The SOCKS protocol is typically used to direct all traffic from the client to the proxy using a target port of TCP/1080. (TCP 8080 may be used as well.) SOCKS acts as a transparent proxy. SOCKS is important to know about because it provides a number of security-related advantages, including the following:

- SOCKS functions as a **circuit-level gateway**. It functions at the Session layer, filtering internal traffic that leaves the network being protected. Because it works at the Session layer, it can work with virtually any TCP/IP application.
- SOCKS can encrypt data passing between client and proxy.
- It uses a single protocol to both transfer data via TCP and UDP and to authenticate users.

SOCKS has one disadvantage, and it's a big one from the standpoint of proxy servers: it does not examine the data part of a packet. It does hide IP addresses of internal clients, however, and it does recreate packets before passing them on. Thus, it does provide protection against passing on malformed packets.

SocksCap

SocksCap, a free SOCKS application available from Permeo Technologies (the originators of the SOCKS protocol), has a graphical interface that enables you to quickly configure applications to use SOCKS. In Figure 5-12, a chat application has been configured, and Microsoft Messenger is about to be added.

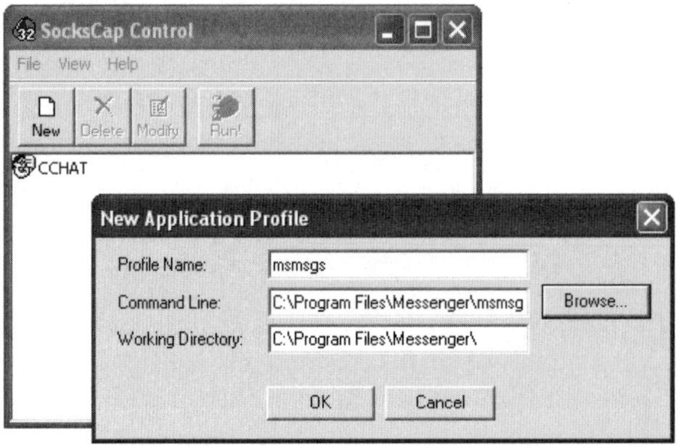

Figure 5-12 SocksCap provides a graphical interface for identifying applications to use a proxy server

PROXY SERVER-BASED FIREWALLS COMPARED

You can choose from a number of firewalls that are based on proxy servers (that is, proxy servers either play an important role in their makeup or are their primary function). Your choice depends on the platform you are running and the number of hosts and services you need to protect.

T.REX Open-Source Firewall

T.REX is an open-source UNIX-based firewall solution based on the well-known open-source product Trusted Information System Firewall Toolkit (TIS Firewall Toolkit). It can handle URL blocking as well as encryption and authentication. The firewall's CD-ROM contains installation scripts that can help expedite installation, but configuration can be complex due to an extremely long user manual. T.REX runs on AIX 4.2.x and later, Solaris 2.6 and later, and Linux Red Hat 7.1 and later. Choose T.REX only if you are looking for a free UNIX-based solution and you are already proficient with proxy server configuration.

You can find out more about T.REX at *www.opensourcefirewall.com/*.

Squid

Squid is a high-performance and free open-source application that is specially designed to act as a proxy server and cache files for Web and FTP servers. Squid isn't a full-featured firewall. It performs access control and filtering, and it is especially good at quickly serving files that are held in cache.

Squid runs on all UNIX-based systems. One nice feature is that the program is popular and well known enough that developers have come up with plug-in applications that enhance its functionality. Add-on applications include a banner ad filter created by the privacy organization Junkbusters; a log analyzer called Calamaris (*http://cord.de/tools/squid/calamaris/*), and a content filter called Jeanne (*www.ists.dartmouth.edu/IRIA/projects/d_jeanne.htm*). Squid is an excellent choice if you want to protect a Unix-based network and you are on a budget.

You can find out more about Squid at *www.squid-cache.org/*.

WinGate

WinGate by Deerfield.com is the most popular proxy server for home and small business environments. Early versions suffered from a default configuration that enabled external users to connect to the proxy as though their computers were internal clients. In particular, the default configuration allowed the port used for administering WinGate (Port 808) to be open to an outside attack. Current versions don't have that problem.

Currently, WinGate comes in three versions: Home for home users, Standard for small businesses, and Pro for larger enterprises. The Home version is primarily intended to provide Internet connection sharing (a feature that is built in to more recent versions of Windows anyway). The Standard version adds a proxy server, URL redirection, logging, and authentication. The Pro version adds database integration and remote administration. Choose WinGate if you want to protect a small network and are looking for a well-documented Windows-based program that offers customer support and frequent upgrades.

 WinGate's home on the Web is at *www.wingate.com*.

Symantec Enterprise Firewall

Formerly known by the name Raptor, Symantec Enterprise Firewall by Symantec Corp. combines proxy services with encryption, authentication, load balancing, and packet filtering in a single full-featured firewall package. It filters content using a technology it calls WebNOT, which enables administrators to limit access to Web sites that contain unauthorized content. It also contains one nice feature for Windows users: configuration can be handled through a snap in to the Microsoft Management Console (MMC). Choose this product if you are looking for a commercial firewall that has proxy servers built in and that is a little more full featured than WinGate.

 Symantec Enterprise Firewall is designed to run on Windows NT/2000 and Solaris systems. You can find out more about the product at *http://enterprisesecurity.symantec.com/products/products.cfm?ProductID=47*.

Microsoft Internet Security & Acceleration Server

Microsoft Internet Security & Acceleration Server 2000 (ISA) is Microsoft's proxy server product, replacing the previous product Microsoft Proxy Server. It's a complex, full-featured firewall that includes stateful packet filtering as well as proxy services, NAT, and intrusion detection. ISA is designed to compete with FireWall-1, Symantec Enterprise Firewall, and other high-performance firewall products.

ISA does more than cache files and provide an application proxy gateway. First of all, it comes in two editions: Standard Edition and Enterprise Edition. The Standard Edition is a standalone product that supports up to four processors; the Enterprise Edition is a multiserver product with centralized management and no limit on the number of processors supported. Both versions require Windows 2000 Server or Windows 2000

Advanced Server with Service Pack 1 installed. However, both versions can be installed on a standalone basis for networks that don't use Active Directory.

 You can find out more about ISA at *www.microsoft.com/isaserver*. You can also download a trial version of the software that you can try out for 120 days.

REVERSE PROXIES

5

Most proxies act primarily on behalf of their internal hosts—receiving, rebuilding, and forwarding outbound requests. However, you can improve security as well as enhance performance by setting up a reverse proxy, which is a type of service that acts as a proxy for *inbound* connections. It can be used outside the firewall to represent a secure content server to outside clients, preventing direct, unmonitored access to your server's data from outside your company. A reverse proxy setup is shown in Figure 5-13.

Why use a reverse proxy when the primary clients you want to protect are those on the internal network rather than those on the external Internet? Performance, for one thing: reverse proxies cut down on unnecessary requests, which reduces the load on the company's Web server. Another reason is privacy, which can be critical to a company's bottom line if that company sells to the public and receives sensitive information such as customers' credit card numbers. A reverse proxy that is set up outside the firewall as a stand-in for a Web server can protect sensitive information stored on that Web server that must remain secure, such as a database of credit card numbers.

 In practice, a company that does retail sales online should store customer data on a computer that has no direct connection to the Internet (not a Web server) for maximum security.

How do reverse proxy servers work? When someone on the Internet makes a request to connect to your company's Web server, the request goes first to the reverse proxy server. The proxy server then forwards the client's request through a specific port to the Web server. The Web server relays the reply through the passage back to the reverse proxy server. The proxy, in turn, rebuilds the data packets from scratch (as proxies do) and sends the retrieved information to the client as if the proxy were the actual Web server. If the content server returns an error message, the proxy server can intercept the message and change any URLs listed in the headers before sending the message to the client. This prevents external clients from getting a glimpse of the redirection path of any URLs that point to the internal content server.

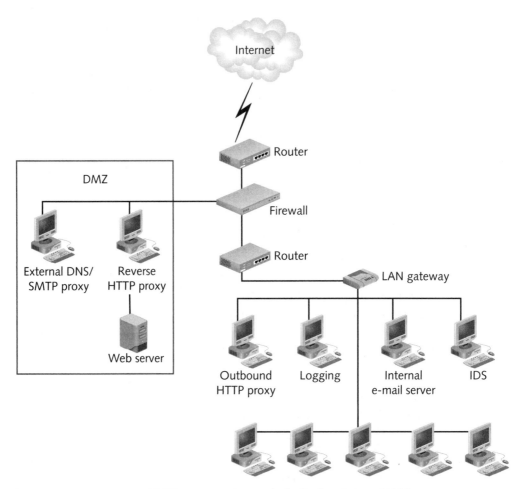

Figure 5-13 A reverse HTTP proxy acting on behalf of an internal Web server

By standing in for the public Web server, the reverse proxy server provides an additional barrier for the internal network. In the event of a successful attack, the hacker is more likely to be restricted to only the information involved in a single transaction, as opposed to having access to the entire data stores of the organization. The unauthorized user is unable to connect to the actual Web or database server because only the reverse proxy server is allowed such access.

When a Proxy Service Isn't the Correct Choice

You don't have to set up a proxy server. Some organizations find that it slows down traffic excessively. Other times, users who need to communicate using a messaging system find that the need to authenticate via the proxy server makes connection impossible. In that case, you can have external users connect to the firewall directly using Secure Sockets Layer (SSL) encryption. This presupposes that the firewall has a static IP address, however, which may or may not be the case.

Another alternative to using an organization's own proxy server is to use the proxy server of an Internet Service Provider (ISP). However, there's a downside: you have to depend on how well the ISP has configured the server. In fact, it may not be configured correctly and may actually slow down some Web sites unnecessarily.

 You can find publicly accessible proxy servers online, but they won't give you any improvement in security. If you're curious, you can find a list of publicly accessible proxy servers at *http://tools.rosinstrument.com/proxy/*.

The primary reason for using someone else's proxy server would be to speed up performance by being able to access Web pages kept in the proxy server's cache rather than having to access the original Web sites for every request. However, most Web pages these days are dynamic rather than static; they generate their contents on the fly based on an individual request, so caching is of no value in such cases. You're better off installing and configuring your own proxy server, even if you have only a small home or business network to protect.

Chapter Summary

❑ Proxy servers were originally developed as a tool for caching frequently accessed pages and serving them to external clients in place of the real Web server. Proxy servers still perform this function, but because more and more Web page contents are generated dynamically by a database means caching is less of a benefit than it was previously.

❑ Among the biggest benefits that application proxies provide is their ability to conceal the hosts on an internal network through a variety of strategies. The most powerful is the ability to completely regenerate packets and forward them to their destination on the originating host's behalf. Such packets contain IP source information pertaining to the proxy server, not the originating host. In addition, proxy servers can be configured to do packet filtering and NAT. In addition, because the proxy server completely regenerates packets, they eliminate the chance that attacks that start with mangled IP packet data will ever reach an internal host.

❑ Proxy servers should be used in conjunction with packet filters and firewalls to provide a complete security solution. Proxy servers can be standalone products; they may also be part of a complete firewall solution such as CheckPoint FireWall-1. A proxy can be located on either a dual-homed host or a screened host, but a firewall should sit between it and the external network for maximum security.

❏ Another benefit of using proxies is their ability to provide detailed log file information about who attempts to access the proxy. Because proxies provide a single checkpoint through which all communications flow, this gives you a reliable way to monitor network activity. To keep log files from becoming too unwieldy, you should only log the services you consider to be most critical.

❏ Proxy servers do have downsides, such as slowdowns in performance and providing a single failure point for a network, but their ability to work with many different client programs (through the SOCKS standard) and their high level of protection clearly offset these disadvantages.

Key Terms

alerting — A feature of some proxy servers that enables them to notify a network administrator if an unauthorized access attempt is in progress.

application-level gateway — *See* proxy server.

application proxy — *See* application-level gateway.

cache — A section of disk space set aside for storage, usually to help speed up performance of applications that need the resources stored there.

circuit-level gateway — A protocol that works at the Session layer to monitor internal traffic leaving a protected network.

configuration file — A file that contains configuration information for an application.

event — A specific request or response associated with an attempt to access a networked resource such as a dropped packet, a hangup, a response, and so on.

gateway — A point in a network through which data is allowed to pass.

holes — Vulnerable points in a network through which unauthorized users might be able to access supposedly protected resources.

hybrid firewall — A firewall that combines several different security methods, such as packet filtering, application-level gateways, and VPNs.

JavaScript — A low-level programming language that is primarily used to add functionality to Web pages.

log file — A text file set up to store information about access to networked resources; the information might be the time the request was made, the IP address of the machine making the request, the name of the file being requested, and so on.

parameters — Aspects of a filtering rule that enable an application (such as a proxy server) to determine how the rule is to be enforced; aspects might include length of time, the IP address of a host, and so on.

proxy server — Software that functions on behalf of end users within a network, reading the data part of IP packets and acting on behalf of end users, receiving requests and passing on replies. In the process, the gateway shields internal hosts from direct contact with external hosts on the Internet.

proxy service — *See* proxy server.

reverse proxy — A proxy server that is configured to monitor inbound rather than outbound traffic.

SOCKS — A protocol that applications can use for proxy servers when proxy servers don't exist for them.

static IP address — An IP address that does not change, in contrast to a dynamic IP address that is generated by a server each time a computer connects to a network.

StuffIt — A popular application for the Macintosh that is used to compress and transport groups of files across a network or from one computer to another.

URL redirection — The ability of some proxy servers to key in on the host, file, or directory being requested, as listed in the HTTP header, and direct the request to a specific location.

Zip archive — A compressed file that holds multiple files and that is created by the popular applications WinZip or Gzip.

5

REVIEW QUESTIONS

1. Why were application-level proxies originally developed?

    a. to shield internal users from the Internet

    b. to store popular Web pages in cache

    c. to filter offensive content

    d. to provide improved logging as compared to packet filters

2. Name two things that proxy servers do that are similar to the way packet filters do them.

3. Name two things that proxy servers do better than packet filters.

4. Consider the following: You are asked to explain to a group of end users how the company proxy server functions. You create an analogy in which an individual makes a purchase and delivery on behalf of someone else. The head of the IT department shakes his head to indicate that you've missed something. Why is this analogy inadequate as a way of understanding how proxy servers function? What function is missing from such an oversimplified description?

5. Reassembling IP packets adds more time to network communications, so there must be some benefit to doing so. Give two reasons why it's good for proxy servers to reassemble packets before sending them on their way.

6. The most effective way proxy servers conceal internal clients is by
   _____.

   a. inserting new source IP addresses into headers

   b. completely regenerating new requests

   c. using Network Address Translation (NAT)

   d. using Internet Connection Sharing (ICS)

7. Which of the following is not a disadvantage or complication of using a proxy server gateway?

   a. single point of configuration

   b. slower performance

   c. single point of failure

   d. multiple services need to be configured

8. Explain why you would want to use load balancing in conjunction with a proxy server gateway.

9. A proxy server that receives traffic from all services at a single port, such as a SOCKS server, is called a(n) _____ proxy.

   a. transparent

   b. nontransparent

   c. reverse

   d. application gateway

10. When would you want to dedicate a proxy server to a single service?

    a. when you want to limit logging to a dedicated machine

    b. when the service runs on a server that is accessible by the public

    c. when the service is particularly vulnerable to attack

    d. when the service sees an especially high amount of traffic

11. On what does a proxy server focus in an HTTP header to redirect a request to a specific URL?

    a. the host being requested

    b. the referer—the site the client visited before the request was made

    c. the directory or file being requested

    d. the file extensions the client can handle

12. Consider the following: You run an external Web site that lists catalog items for sale. The overwhelming number of requests your company receives from the Internet are HTTP requests. You need to distribute the traffic load more evenly, and you need to protect sensitive client information contained on your Web server. What two proxy server approaches could help you achieve these goals?

13. A proxy server should never be located so that it has a direct interface on the Internet. True or False?

14. Which of the following functions at the Session layer of the OSI model?

    a. authentication

    b. packet filtering

    c. a SOCKS gateway

    d. a reverse proxy

15. Which of the following is a downside of using a reverse proxy?

    a. The reverse proxy creates more log files for an administrator to review.

    b. The reverse proxy slows down network performance.

    c. Log files show only connection attempts by the proxy server, not attempts by external clients.

    d. It can act as a proxy only for a single Web server.

16. Which of the following is a disadvantage of using SOCKS?

    a. Clients need to be configured to work with it.

    b. It does not examine the data part of a packet.

    c. It does not work with every TCP/IP application.

    d. It does not examine the header part of a packet.

17. What feature is built into Apache so that, as a result, it is unnecessary for a proxy server to perform the same function?

    a. processing of Java and other scripts

    b. virtual server capabilities

    c. packet filtering

    d. URL redirection

18. Why consider using authentication if a proxy server completely separates internal clients from the Internet?

    a. It can protect sensitive directories.

    b. It enhances security.

    c. It can protect user privacy.

    d. none of the above

19. How could you protect an internal network overnight when no employees are present? (Choose all that apply.)

    a. completely disconnect the internal network from the Internet after hours

    b. set up a rule that blocks all traffic through the proxy after hours

    c. block all traffic except SMTP and POP after hours

    d. turn off the proxy server after hours

20. Within application-level firewalls, what is the purpose of parameters such as time, IP address, or port number?

5

HANDS-ON PROJECTS

Project 5-1: Install and Configure NetProxy

There are many proxy server programs you can install and work with, but for the purposes of lab testing, a good way to start is to download a freely available program that you can keep in the lab and use on an ongoing basis if you wish. The program is free for single-user use. You can install the program on any Windows 2000 or XP workstation.

The NetProxy software (and the steps that follow) both assume that the workstations on your network use reserved IP addresses in the range 192.168.0.0/24 and that they are dynamically generated by a server using Dynamic Host Control Protocol (DCHP). If the workstation on which you install NetProxy uses a different IP address, substitute your machine's actual IP address for the one NetProxy instructs you to enter by default.

1. Double-click the **Internet Explorer** icon on your desktop.

2. In the browser's Address box, type **www.grok.co.uk**, and then press **Enter**. The home page of the Grok Developments Ltd. Web site opens.

3. Click the **Downloads** link. The Download NetProxy page opens.

4. Click the link **Get It!** across from NetProxy Server v4. The Download NetProxy page opens.

5. Click the link that represents the closest geographic location to you. Your browser goes to the selected download site. Follow the instructions on the download site to download NetProxy to your computer.

6. Double-click the file you downloaded (when this was written the current version was named np401.exe; the name may be different when you try to download the file). Follow the installation steps to install the program.

7. When your computer restarts and the Windows desktop is visible, click **Start**, point to **Programs** (**All Programs** in Windows XP), point to **NetProxy**, and click **NetProxy Configuration**. The Net proxy window opens.

8. To configure NetProxy, click the **Configuration Wizard** button on the NetProxy toolbar. (This button isn't labeled, but it looks like a pair of pliers and a wrench.) The NetProxy window opens. Click **Yes**, and then click **OK**. The NetProxy 4.0 window opens.

9. Fill out the details that apply to your Internet connection in the ISP's Server Details section. For instance, in the WWW Proxy Server text box, enter the IP address of your machine and the port on which you access the Web (this will probably be either Port 80 or 8080).

10. Fill out the rest of the boxes with the IP address of your primary DNS server, mail server names, and newsgroup server names.

11. In the Connection section, click the **Connect to the Internet using a modem or ISDN adaptor** option button if you use a dial-up modem to connect to the Net. Otherwise, leave the Connected to the Internet permanently option button selected.

12. Click **OK**.

 If you are unable to enter an address in the DNS Server box, you can still continue to configure and test NetProxy.

5

13. If your computer lab uses a set of IP addresses different than 192.168.0.0/24, click **Options** and click **Firewall**. (Otherwise skip to Step 17.)

14. In the Incoming Firewall Rules dialog box, click **Add**. The Add Incoming Firewall Rule dialog box opens.

15. In the IP address range text box, enter the IP address range your network uses. Leave **All Services** displayed in the Service box, and then click **OK**. The new address range is added to the list in the Incoming Firewall Rules dialog box.

16. Click **OK** to close the Incoming Firewall Rules dialog box and return to the NetProxy window.

17. Click **Options** and click **Logging**. The Access Logging dialog box opens.

18. Check the boxes next to **WWW proxy requests** and to any other services you want to log, and then click **OK**.

19. After you have NetProxy configured, stop any other firewall programs, such as Tiny Personal Firewall, that are currently running, to ensure that they don't interfere with NetProxy.

20. Connect to any Web site, such as *www.course.com*. Is the Web browser's performance slower than usual?

21. Start a text editor such as Notepad by clicking **Start**, pointing to **Programs** (**All Programs** in Windows XP), pointing to **Accessories**, and then clicking **Notepad**.

22. Click **File** on the menu bar, click **Open**, and then click **All Files** on the Files of type drop-down menu in the Open dialog box.

23. Navigate to the log file for NetProxy, which is contained in C:\Program Files\NetProxy4 (or in the location where you installed the program). The file-name ends with the extension .log and begins with a number (for example, 2002617.log). (If you cannot find a log file, click **Options** and click **Logging** from the NetProxy toolbar. In the Access Logging window, check the location specified in the Log file directory box.) Double-click the file to open it. How many log entries were created by that single Web site access? What is the difference between the different log entries? Record the answers in a lab book or word processing file.

Project 5-2: Configure a Client to Work with a Proxy

As stated in the chapter, every client that expects to do communications through the proxy server gateway needs to be configured to work with that gateway. The most obvious example is a Web browser that will have a proxy acting on its behalf to connect to Web sites and retrieve information. Assume you have a proxy server at 192.168.0.1 running Web services on Port 8080. You'll need to configure your Web browser to work with NetProxy for your own personal use; if you're setting up a proxy in a corporate setting, you'll need to either instruct employees how to do this or do the configuration for them.

1. Double-click the **Internet Explorer** icon on your desktop.

2. Click **Tools** and then click **Internet Options** to open the Internet Options dialog box.

3. Click the **Connections** tab to bring the Connections options to the front.

4. If you use a dial-up modem connection to connect to the Internet, click on the connection in the Dial-up settings box to select it, and then click **Settings**. Because in your lab you probably connect via a LAN, click **LAN Settings**.

5. In the Local Area Network (LAN) Settings dialog box, check the **Use a proxy server for your LAN** check box, and then click **Advanced**.

6. In the Proxy Settings dialog box, type the address of your proxy server in the HTTP: text box, and enter the port your proxy uses for HTTP service in the adjacent Port text box.

7. If you use different proxy servers for different services, repeat Step 6 for each of the services you plan to use: FTP, e-mail, and so on. Otherwise, check the **Use the same proxy server for all protocols** check box.

8. If you regularly need to connect to a computer on your local network, you don't need to access that machine through the proxy server. Enter the machine's name (and any other computers' names to which you need to connect) or IP address in the Exceptions text box.

9. Click **OK** to close the Proxy Settings, Local Area Network (LAN) Settings, and Internet Options dialog boxes in succession and return to the Internet Explorer window.

10. Connect to a remote Web site, such as *www.grok.co.uk/*. When you connect to the Internet through your proxy server, what message appears in your browser's status bar?

11. Exit Internet Explorer and return to the Windows desktop.

Project 5-3: Use an AutoConfigure File to Configure Browsers

An autoproxy.pac file is a special text file that contains details of the proxy settings to be used by client web browsers. It's an effective way to configure multiple browsers: you can send end users the following simple steps to have their browsers retrieve the configuration files so that they can begin using the proxy to surf the Web. After the browser is configured to retrieve the file, the browser will then automatically configure itself to use the appropriate proxy ports and services. NetProxy ships with a sample autoproxy.pac file in the NetProxy program folder. This text file can be edited with any text editor to match your own requirements.

1. Click **Start**, point to **Programs** (or **All Programs** in Windows XP), point to **Accessories**, and click **Notepad** to start Windows' built-in text-editing program.

2. Click **File** on the menu bar and click **Open**.

3. In the Open dialog box, navigate to the NetProxy directory which, by default, is installed in C:\Program Files\NetProxy4.

4. Click **All Files** on the Files of type drop-down list at the bottom of the Open dialog box to open the autoproxy.pac file.

5. Open the **autoproxy.pac** file. Check the JavaScript in the autoproxy.pac file to make sure the IP address and port number both apply to your proxy configuration. For instance, by default, the file contains the following line:

```
return "PROXY 192.168.0.1:8080";   }
```

If your proxy server is, for example, at 207.34.0.1:8080, change the line to read as follows:

```
return "PROXY 207.34.0.1:8080";   }
```

6. Change the line with the SOCKS server address in it, changing it to match your configuration information.

7. Click **File** on the menu bar, and then click **Exit**.

8. Click **Yes** if you are prompted to save any changes you made.

9. Double-click the **Internet Explorer** icon on your desktop.

10. Click **Tools** and then click **Internet Options** to open the Internet Options dialog box.

11. Click the **Connections** tab to bring the Connections options to the front.

12. If you use a dial-up modem connection to connect to the Internet, select the connection in the Dial-up settings box, and then click **Settings**. Because in your lab you probably connect via a LAN, click **LAN Settings**.

13. In the Local Area Network (LAN) Settings dialog box, check the **Use automatic configuration script** check box.

14. In the Address box, enter the address leading to the automatic configuration script in this format:

```
http://proxy.server.ip-address:port/autoproxy.pac
```

For instance, if your NetProxy PC has the IP address 192.168.0.1 and the Web proxy service is running on Port 8080 (the default), then the LAN Settings dialog in Internet Explorer would be as follows:

```
http://192.168.0.1:8080/autoproxy.pac
```

5

15. Click **OK** twice to return to the Internet Explorer window.

16. Close Internet Explorer and return to the Windows desktop.

Project 5-4: Configure an Application To Use SOCKS

Some applications aren't covered by proxy servers. They need to use the SOCKS protocol, which provides them with a generic proxy application they can use to send and
receive information on a network. Most proxy server programs include an implementation of SOCKS as a built-in feature.

To learn more about SOCKS, it's useful from an educational standpoint to download an
application that's designed specifically to implement the SOCKS protocol. The following steps show you how to set up an application to use SocksCap, an application that is
free to use for educational purposes. It works on any Windows 2000 or XP workstation.

> The following exercise assumes that you have a firewall program, such as Tiny
> Personal Firewall or Sygate Personal Firewall, already running on your work-
> station. SocksCap is designed to work in conjunction with existing proxy
> servers; thus, the following steps also assume that you have installed and con-
> figured NetProxy as described in Hands-On Project 5-1.

1. Double-click the **Internet Explorer** icon on your Windows desktop.

2. Enter **http://www.socks.nec.com/reference/sockscap.html** in the address
   box. The SOCKS Reference Software page opens.

3. Read the information on the page about system requirements for using SocksCap,
   and then scroll down the page and click the link **Download SocksCap**. The
   Download page opens.

4. Select the version of SocksCap that matches your computer system, and then
   click **Download**.

5. Follow the steps on subsequent screens to download and install SocksCap. After
   the program is installed, the SocksCap icon appears (if you instructed the installation program to install an icon on your desktop). Double-click the **SocksCap**
   icon or click **Start**, point to **Programs** (**All Programs** in Windows XP), click
   SocksCap V2, and click **SocksCap V2** to start the software.

6. Click **File** and click **New** on the SocksCap menu bar to choose an application to
   run under SOCKS. The New Application Profile dialog box opens.

7. Click **Browse** to open the Browse for Application dialog box.

8. Locate an application on your computer that operates by connecting to the
   Internet and that isn't likely to be covered by a proxy server program. A likely
   program is your Web browser, an instant-messaging application, or an audio or
   video player. Double-click the executable file for the application, which will have
   the filename extension .exe. The pathname and application name are added to the
   New Application Profile dialog box.

9. Click **OK**. The application name is added to a list in the main SocksCap window.

10. Select the application you just added, and then click **Run** on the SocksCap toolbar.

11. The application's window starts up. What happens after the application starts? Note the answer in your lab notebook or in a word-processing program.

12. Click **File** on the menu bar and click **Exit** to exit SocksCap and return to your Windows desktop.

Project 5-5: Test Proxy Server Network Address Translation (NAT)

5

This project assumes that you have one workstation in your lab that is running NetProxy and at least one other workstation that has a network connection to it. For the purposes of this project, we refer to the remote workstation as the "Remote Machine" and the one with the proxy software as the (you guessed it) "Proxy Machine."

1. Start the Remote Machine and its associated firewall software. Set up logon auditing on the Remote Machine, as described in Hands-On Project 2-5. (Make sure you activate account logon auditing.)

2. Start up the Proxy Machine.

3. Make sure NetProxy is running on the Proxy Machine. To verify this, click **Start**, point to **Programs** (**All Programs** in Windows XP), point to **NetProxy**, and click **NetProxy Configuration**.

4. In the NetProxy window, click the **Enable/Disable NetProxy** button. The message "NetProxy is running" should appear in the status bar of the NetProxy window.

5. Make note of the Proxy Machine's IP address (see Hands-On Project 1-5 if you need a refresher).

6. Log on to the Remote Machine from the Proxy Machine. (Usually, when you attempt to access a shared folder on the remote machine, you are prompted to log on, unless automatic logon has been enabled.)

7. Switch to the Remote Machine. View this machine's event log by clicking **Start** and clicking **Control Panel**. (In Windows 2000, click **Start**, point to **Settings**, and then click **Control Panel**.)

8. Double-click **Administrative Tools** to open the Administrative Tools window.

9. Double-click **Event Viewer** to display the Event Viewer Management Console.

10. In the left half of the Event Viewer, click **Security**.

11. Make a note of the logon from the remote computer. What machine is identified as having logged on? Record the result in your lab notebook or a word-processing program.

Project 5-6: Make a Telnet Connection, and Then Block It

Telnet is a program that is used to connect computers to one another over a network. NetProxy, by default, sets up a proxy gateway for Telnet on port 23. You can test the gateway using another workstation in your network. One workstation needs to have NetProxy running, and the other needs to be able to connect to the NetProxy workstation.

1. Start NetProxy on the workstation that hosts this application (to verify that NetProxy is running, refer to Steps 3-4 in Hands-On Project 5-5).

2. Make sure Telnet service is described as Enabled in the NetProxy window. (If it's not, right-click **Telnet Gateway**, and then click **Enable** from the context menu that appears.

3. Go to the other workstation, click **Start**, and click **Run** to open the Run dialog box.

4. Type **telnet**, and then click **OK** to launch Telnet.

5. At the command prompt, type **open** *IP address*, where *IP address* is the IP address of the computer to which you want to connect, and then press **Enter**. What message do you see? Record the answer in a lab notebook or word-processing document.

6. Type **open** *IP address* **23**, where *IP address* is the IP address you entered earlier. You should see a connection message. Press **Enter**. Leave the Telnet window open.

7. Go the NetProxy computer, and double-click **Telnet Gateway**. The Telnet Gateway dialog box opens.

8. In the Bind to text box, replace the default All Interfaces with any IP address that does not exist on your network, such as 10.0.0.23, and then click **Apply**.

9. Return to the other workstation. In the Telnet window, type **open IP address**, and then press **Enter**. What message do you see? Record the answer in a lab notebook or word-processing document.

10. Type **Quit**, and then press **Enter**. The Telnet window closes.

11. Return to the NetProxy workstation. In the Telnet Gateway box, click **All Interfaces** on the Bind to drop-down list, and then click **OK**. The Telnet Gateway box closes and you return to the NetProxy window.

12. Click **Services** on the menu bar and click **Exit** to close NetProxy and return to the Windows desktop.

CASE PROJECTS

Case 5-1: Use Private IP Addresses and Share a Connection

You are hired as the network administrator of a small start-up company with a limited budget. You are instructed to configure the LAN so that the company makes use of a single dynamic IP address it has obtained from its ISP as part of its low-cost Internet access account but that also gives three other computers Internet access as well. How could you do this?

Case 5-2: Repair a Default Configuration

You are called in by a small business that is experiencing performance problems with one of its network computers. The five workstations in the company share a connection to the Internet using the WinGate proxy server. The complaint is that the computer that hosts WinGate is running slowly and that their Internet connection is slower than normal. What would you look for as the cause of the problem, and how would you remedy it?

Case 5-3: Troubleshooting Slow Proxy Performance

After installing a proxy server gateway, you notice a significant performance drop on your network. You have installed a single proxy server on the perimeter of your network that handles all services. Name some strategies for improving performance.

Case 5-4: Do a Batch Configuration

You install a proxy server system in a mid-size organization with about 100 separate hosts distributed among several subnets. You are faced with the task of configuring all client software on all 100 hosts to access the proxy so that employees can send and receive e-mail and other Internet services. Yet, you have to get everyone online within a day or two. How could you perform the batch configuration quickly?

5

6

AUTHENTICATING USERS

After reading this chapter and completing the exercises, you will be able to:

- ◆ Understand why authentication is a critical aspect of network security
- ◆ Describe why firewalls authenticate and how they identify users
- ◆ Describe user, client, and session authentication
- ◆ List the advantages and disadvantages of popular centralized authentication systems
- ◆ Be aware of the potential weaknesses of password security systems
- ◆ Understand the use of password security tools
- ◆ Be familiar with common authentication protocols used by firewalls

The firewall security strategies, such as packet filtering, that were discussed in previous chapters are used to authenticate machines rather than individuals. This chapter discusses the ability of some firewalls to perform a stronger level of authentication—to reliably determine whether a person or entity is whom they claim to be. This authentication is important because if an unauthorized user "fools" the firewall and gains access to the wrong resources, the whole purpose of the firewall has been defeated. For this reason, many firewalls support user authentication schemes to support their other security approaches.

In this chapter, you will explore different aspects of authentication as it is performed by firewalls. First, you'll get an overview of what authentication is and why it is important to network security in general. Then you'll focus on how and why firewalls perform authentication services. This is followed by an introduction to the main types of authentication performed by firewalls: client, user, and session authentication. After this, you'll examine different types of centralized authentication methods that firewalls can use, including Kerberos, TACACS+, and RADIUS. Because passwords are a critical part of all of the aforementioned authentication schemes, you'll explore password security issues, followed by a section on special password security tools, including one-time passwords. The chapter ends with a section on the different authentication protocols used by full-featured enterprise-level firewalls such as Check Point FireWall-1.

THE AUTHENTICATION PROCESS IN GENERAL

Authentication is the act of identifying users and providing network services to them based on their identity. Most types of authentication require the user to supply to the authenticating firewall or server one of the following:

- A piece of information, such as a password

- Proof of physical possession of something, such as a **smart card** (which is a plastic card with an embedded microchip that can store data about the owner)

- A piece of information that is part of your physical identity, such as a fingerprint, voiceprint, or retinal scan

 You are probably already familiar with smart cards without realizing it. If you have a bank card that enables you to withdraw cash from a debit account, you have made use of a smart card. Along with the card (something you have) you also need to enter a PIN (something you know, the bank's equivalent of a password) to authenticate yourself to the bank's network. After you are authenticated, the ATM recognizes you by name and gives you access to your account.

In the field of network computing, authentication takes one of three specific forms (listed from the lowest to the highest level of security):

- **Basic authentication:** A server maintains a local file of usernames and passwords that it refers to for matching the username-password pair being supplied by a client. This is the most common form of authentication, the weakness of which is that passwords can often be forgotten, stolen, or accidentally revealed.

- **Challenge-response authentication:** The authenticating computer or firewall generates a random code or number (the challenge) and sends it to the user who wishes to be authenticated. The user resubmits the number or code and adds his or her secret PIN or password (the response). If the code and PIN or password match the information stored on the authenticating server, the user gains access to the requested resources.

- **Centralized authentication service:** A centralized server handles three separate and essential authentication practices: authentication, authorization, and auditing. Authentication, as you have already seen, is the process of identifying someone who wishes to use network services. Authentication is the process of determining what users are and are not allowed to do on the network based on their identity. **Auditing** is the act of recording information (usually in a log file) of who was or was not authenticated and what level of authorization that individual was granted.

Each of these types of authentication requires a user to enter a password at some point. This might be called one-factor authentication: the user only needs to know one item (the password) to initiate the authentication process. Physical objects such as smart cards or other kinds of physical **tokens** offer a more stringent level of two-factor authentication in which users need to have something (the token) and know something (the PIN or password) to gain access. Two-factor authentication can be used to strengthen any of the aforementioned systems, but it most commonly used with a centralized authentication server.

 The use of **biometrics** (retinal scans, fingerprints, and the like) for authentication is mainly used by large security-minded entities such as banking institutions and credit card centers for regulating access to sensitive information, but it is gaining ground in the general corporate world as well.

HOW FIREWALLS IMPLEMENT THE AUTHENTICATION PROCESS

Most operating systems are equipped with authentication schemes. Web servers can be configured to authenticate clients who want to access certain protected content. Firewalls, too, can perform **user authentication**. In fact, many organizations depend on firewalls to provide more secure authentication than conventional systems. Authentication is a key function because firewalls exist to give external users (such as mobile users and telecommuters) access to protected resources.

Authentication comes into play when a firewall is called upon to apply its set of rules to specific individuals or groups of users. For instance, the IT staff may need access to all computers in the organization, and, thus, a higher level of security is needed to ensure that the right individuals have such a level of access. On the other hand, the head of a company's accounting department may need remote access to the company once a quarter or once a year—not frequently enough to warrant the establishment of a VPN between the two companies' LANs.

In such cases, the firewall uses authentication to identify individuals so that it can apply rules that have been associated with those individuals. Some firewalls use authentication to give employees access to common activities such as accessing the Web or using FTP to transfer files. Some try to identify the user associated with a particular IP address; after the user is authorized, the IP address can then be used to send and receive information with hosts on the internal network.

The exact steps that firewalls follow to do authentication may vary from one firewall configuration to another, but the general process is the same:

1. The client makes a request to access a resource.

2. The firewall intercepts the request and prompts the user for name and password.

3. In return, the user submits the information to the firewall.

4. The user is authenticated.

5. The request is checked against the firewall's rule base.

6. If the request matches an existing allow rule, the user is granted access.

7. The user accesses the desired resources.

The "plain English" version of the exchange between external client and authenticating firewall is illustrated in Figure 6-1.

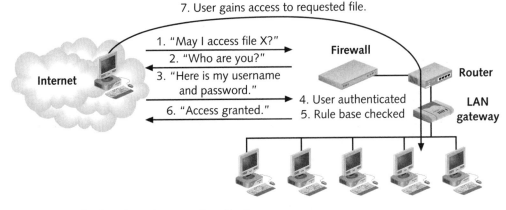

Figure 6-1   Basic external user authentication

TYPES OF AUTHENTICATION WITH FIREWALLS

Some firewalls, like Check Point FireWall-1, provide for a variety of different authentication methods. FireWall-1, in particular, provides for a user to be authenticated through user, client, or session authentication.

User Authentication

User authentication is the simplest type of authentication, and the one with which you are most likely to be familiar. Upon receiving a request, a program prompts the user for a username and password. When the information is submitted, the software checks the information against a list of usernames and passwords in its database. If a match is made, the user is authenticated.

In NetProxy, the freeware proxy server program examined in Chapter 5, user authentication is handled by opening the program's configuration window and then choosing New from the User menu (see Figure 6-2).

6

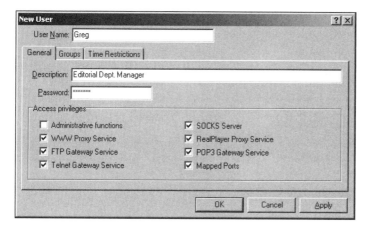

Figure 6-2   NetProxy user authentication

User authentication is useful for the many different individuals who might need to legitimately gain access to your internal servers:

- Employees who work remotely or who are traveling

- Contractors who work on-site

- Freelancers who work off-site

- Visitors who want to do some work or take a look at your system from your offices

- Employees in branch offices

- Interns who work for you

- Employees of partner companies

- Members of the public who may need to get into your internal network to make purchases, change contact information, or review account information

Individuals in the preceding list should be added to your **Access Control Lists (ACLs)** so that approved users are easier to authenticate. The ACLs can be organized by directory or even individual files, but most often ACLs are organized by groups of users because this simplifies administration. How you organize the ACLs depends on how many users you have, how many resources you need to protect, and how much time you have available to administer the ACL.

Client Authentication

Of course, not every outside user can or should gain access to everything on the network. The problem: how do you verify users' identity so you can give them controlled access? Client authentication will help you establish limits to user access.

Client authentication is similar to user authentication but with the addition of usage limits. The user authenticates with the firewall by successfully submitting a username and password contained in a database. The firewall then enables the user to access the desired resources for a specific period of time (for instance, one hour) or for a specific number of times (three accesses, for instance).

As an example of client authentication, consider that NetProxy lets you assign time limits by double-clicking the name of a user group you have previously set up and then editing the settings in the Time Restrictions tab (see Figure 6-3).

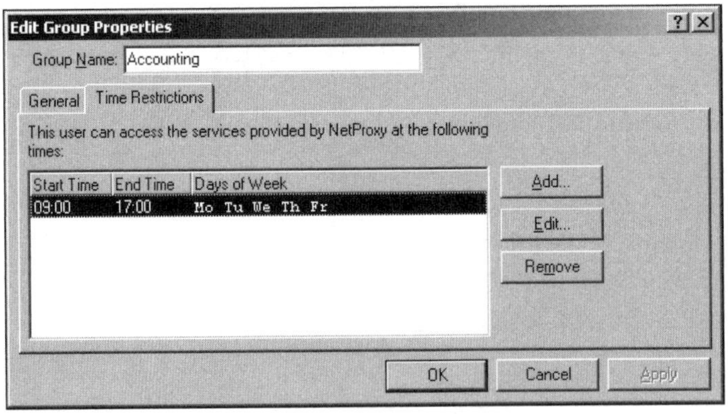

Figure 6-3   Setting time limits for a user group

In configuring client authentication, you need to set up one of two types of authentication systems:

- A **standard sign-on** system, in which the client, after being successfully authenticated, is allowed to access whatever resources the user needs or perform any desired functions, such as transferring files or viewing Web pages

- A **specific sign-on** system, in which the client is required to authenticate each time the user wants to access a server or use a service on the network being protected

Session Authentication

Session authentication calls for authentication to be made whenever a client wishes to connect to a network resource and establish a session (a period when communications are exchanged). Session authentication can be used with any service. The client wishing to be authenticated contains a software agent that provides for authentication; the server or firewall detects the agent when the connection request is made. When necessary, the firewall intercepts the connection request and contacts the agent. The agent performs the authentication, and the firewall allows the connection to the required resource.

Because some advanced firewalls give you multiple choices of authentication methods, which one should you choose? The choice depends on the OS of the client and the applications you need to authenticate. Choose User Authentication if the protocols you want authorized users to use include FTP, HTTP, HTTPS, rlogin, or Telnet. Client Authentication or Session Authentication should be used when only a single user is coming from a single IP address. Table 6-1 gives the reasons for using each service.

Table 6-1   Authentication methods

Method	Used Under These Conditions
User Authentication	• You want to scan the content of IP packets. • The protocol in use is HTTP, HTTPS, FTP, rlogin, or Telnet. • You need to authenticate for each session separately.
Client Authentication	• The individual user to be authenticated will come from a specific IP address. • The protocol in use is *not* HTTP, HTTPS, FTP, rlogin, or Telnet. • You want a user to be authenticated for a specific length of time.
Session Authentication	• The individual user to be authenticated will come from a specific IP address. • The protocol in use is *not* HTTP, HTTPS, FTP, rlogin, or Telnet. • You want a client to be authenticated for each session.

6

CENTRALIZED AUTHENTICATION

Large corporations can easily develop a complex set of security requirements that can be difficult to maintain. They require you to put in different types of authentication control for different purposes. Fortunately, deploying a centralized authentication server can greatly simplify such enterprise-wide authentication. This centralized server maintains all the authorizations for users regardless of where the user is located and how the user connects to the network.

In a centralized authentication setup, a server—which is sometimes referred to as an **Access Control Server (ACS)**—alleviates the need to provide each server on the network with a separate database of usernames and passwords, each of which would have to be updated individually if someone changed a password or a new user was added. The process of centralized authentication is illustrated in Figure 6-4: a client on a local network makes a request to access a program held on an application server, but it first has to authenticate using the authentication server. Two levels of trust are involved: the client trusts that the authentication server holds the correct information, as indicated by number 2 in Figure 6-4, and the application server trusts that the authentication server will correctly identity and authorize the client, as indicated by number 3 in Figure 6-4.

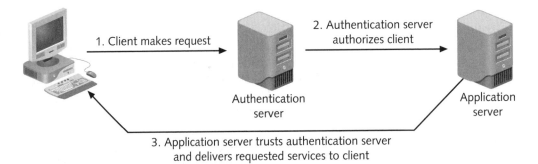

Figure 6-4   Centralized authentication

The scenario illustrated in Figure 6-4 has a substantial downside: the authentication server becomes a single point of failure. Organizations that use this method should also have emergency plans in place to get the server back online to limit downtime.

Centralized authentication can make use of a number of different authentication methods. The following sections examine some of the most common ones, including Kerberos, TACACS+, and RADIUS.

Kerberos Authentication

Kerberos was developed at the Massachusetts Institute of Technology (MIT) in the university's Athena Project. Kerberos is designed to provide authentication and encryption through standard clients and servers. Instead of a server having to trust a client over an untrusted network, both client and server place their trust in the Kerberos server. Kerberos provides an effective network authentication system that is used internally on Windows 2000 and XP systems. It also has backward compatibility with Microsoft's NTLM protocol, which is used in NT 4.0 and earlier.

Although Kerberos is useful on internal networks, it is not recommended for authentication of outside users because it uses **cleartext** passwords. Remote users should make use of encrypted transmissions or **one-time passwords**, which are discussed later in this chapter.

The Kerberos system of granting access to a client that requests a service is quite involved (and thus quite secure). The steps are as follows:

1. The client requests a file or other service.

2. The client is prompted for a username and password.

3. The client submits a username and password. The request goes to an Authentication Server (AS) that is part of the Kerberos system. The AS creates an encrypted code called a **session key** that is based on the client's password plus a random number that is associated with the service being requested. The session key functions as a **Ticket–Granting Ticket (TGT)**.

4. AS grants the TGT.

5. The client presents the TGT to a **Ticket–Granting Server (TGS)**, which is also part of the Kerberos system and that may or may not be the same server as the AS.

6. The TGS grants a session ticket. The TGS forwards the session ticket to the server holding the requested file or service.

7. The client gains access.

The Kerberos Authentication Server is also known as a Key Distribution Center (KDC). In Windows 2000 or XP, a domain controller also functions as an authentication server. The Kerberos server must be highly secured because such a strong level of trust is placed in it.

One great advantage of using the Kerberos ticket system is that passwords are not stored on the system and thus cannot be intercepted by hackers. The tickets issued are specific to the individual user who made the request and to the services the user is attempting to access. Tickets typically have a time limit (typically, eight hours, though this can be configured by the security administrator). Before a ticket expires, the client may make additional requests using the same ticket without having to reauthenticate. Another advantage is that Kerberos is widely used in the UNIX environment, which enables authentication to take place across operating systems: a Windows client can be authenticated by a UNIX server, and vice versa. The authentication process is illustrated in Figure 6-5.

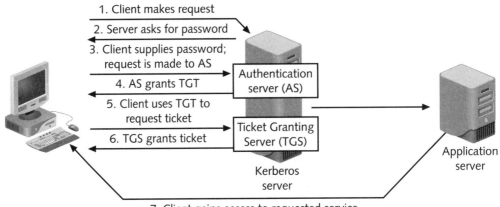

Figure 6-5   Kerberos authentication

  You can download trial versions of both the Kerberos client and server from MIT Software Release Team Releases page (*http://web.mit.edu/swrt/releases.html*).

TACACS+

Terminal Access Controller Access Control System (TACACS+)—commonly called "tac-plus"—is the latest and strongest version of a set of authentication protocols developed by Cisco Systems. TACACS+ replaces its less-secure predecessor protocols, TACACS and XTACACS. All of these protocols provide what Cisco has dubbed the **AAA services** that form an essential part of a dial-up environment:

- Authentication

- Authorization

- Auditing

TACACS+ and its predecessor protocols all provide authentication for dial-in users and are used primarily on UNIX-based networks. TACACS+ uses the **MD5** algorithm (a formula that produces a 128-bit code called a **message digest**) to encrypt data. It provides centralized authentication services so that a network access server such as a router or firewall doesn't have to handle dial-in user authentication. You might have to use

TACACS+ or RADIUS (described in the following section) if your firewall doesn't support authentication or if your authentication needs are so extensive that they might slow down other tasks the firewall is called on to perform.

 You can find more information about the MD5 algorithm and other security tools on the CERT Web site at *http://www.cert.org/tech_tips/security_tools.html*.

Remote Authentication Dial-In User Service (RADIUS)

Remote Authentication Dial-In User Service (RADIUS) is the other common protocol used to provide dial-in authentication. Note that RADIUS still transmits authentication packets unencrypted across the network, which means they are vulnerable to attacks from packet sniffers. RADIUS is generally considered to provide a lower level of security than TACACS+, even though it's more widely supported.

TACACS+ and RADIUS Compared

If you expect to have to authenticate remote users who need to dial in to your network, chances are you'll use either TACACS+ or RADIUS. The following sections go into more detail in comparing these two protocols. They examine strength of security, filtering characteristics, proxy characteristics, and NAT characteristics of both TACACS+ and RADIUS.

Strength of Security

As you go through the information in this section of the chapter, keep the information in Table 6-2 in mind:

Table 6-2   Characteristics of TACACS+ versus RADIUS

TACACS+	RADIUS
Uses TCP	Uses UDP
Full packet encryption between client and server	Encrypts only passwords –other information is unencrypted
Independent authentication, authorization, and accounting	Combines authentication and authorization
Passwords in the database may be encrypted	Passwords in the database are in clear text

All the items in Table 6-2 point to the fact that TACACS+ provides stronger security than RADIUS. TCP is considered more secure than User Datagram Protocol (UDP), an alternative network communications protocol. It's considered more secure because, when a host sends a TCP packet, it expects a packet to be sent in response with the ACK bit sent to show that a connection has been established. ACK stands for

Acknowledgement, one of the flags in the TCP header part of a packet, which indicates that the destination computer has received the packets that were previously sent. UDP, in contrast, is considered "connectionless." If a UDP packet is sent, an acknowledgement packet is neither expected nor needed. If the destination host doesn't receive the packet, it simply asks for the packet to be re-sent.

TCP traffic can be filtered by firewalls based on the presence of the ACK bit. TACACS+ also does full-packet encryption; TACACS+ handles accounting (i.e., auditing or logging) as well as authentication and authorization; RADIUS stores passwords in clear text. Note, however, that if you use both a firewall and an authentication server, the encryption benefits of TACACS+ aren't so dramatic because the firewall will receive communications directly from the Internet, and the firewall and authentication server will communicate with one another over a trusted network. RADIUS can be an equally viable solution in this type of network configuration.

Filtering Characteristics

TACACS+ uses TCP Port 49, so if you use it, you need to set up rules that enable clients to exchange authorization packets with the TACACS+ or RADIUS server. RADIUS uses UDP Port 1812 for authentication and UDP Port 1813 for accounting. Table 6-3 shows a set of packet-filtering rules that enables users on an internal network that is protected by a firewall to be authenticated through a TACACS+ or RADIUS server.

Table 6-3   Filtering rules for TACACS+ and RADIUS

Direction	Protocol	Source Port	Destination Port	Remarks
Inbound	TCP	All ports > 1023	49	Enables external client to connect to internal TACACS+ server
Outbound	TCP	49	All ports > 1023	Allows internal TACACS+ server to respond to external clients
Inbound	UDP	All ports >1023	1812	Allows external client to connect to internal RADIUS server
Outbound	UDP	1812	All ports > 1023	Allows internal RADIUS server to respond to external client
Inbound	UDP	All ports > 1023	1813	Enables accounting when external client connects to RADIUS server
Outbound	UDP	1813	All ports > 1023	Enables accounting when internal RADIUS server responds to a client

Proxy Characteristics

One important thing to note is that RADIUS doesn't work with generic proxy systems. However, a RADIUS server can function as a proxy server, speaking to other RADIUS servers or other services that do authorization, such as Windows domain authentication.

TACACS+, in contrast to RADIUS, works with generic proxy systems. Because some TACACS+ systems use the same IP address to generate the key, you may need a dedicated proxy that has its own encryption key.

NAT Characteristics

RADIUS doesn't work with NAT. Addresses that are intended to go through NAT need to be static, not dynamic.

TACACS+ should work through NAT systems, but because TACACS+ supports encryption using a secret key shared between server and client, there is no way for the server to know which key to use if differing clients make use of different keys. Static IP address mappings work best because some TACACS+ systems use the source IP address to create the encryption key.

6

PASSWORD SECURITY ISSUES

Many authentication systems depend in part or entirely on passwords. The simplest forms of authentication require typing a user name and a reusable password. This method is truly secure for controlling only outbound Internet access because password guessing and eavesdropping attacks are likely on inbound access attempts.

The following sections provide you with security issues that you need to be aware about to keep your network from being accessed by unauthorized users.

Passwords That Can Be Cracked

Systems that rely on passwords for authentication can be **cracked** (i.e., accessed by an unauthorized user) in a number of different ways:

- Find a way to authenticate without knowing the password
- Uncover the password from the system that holds it
- Guess the password

Passwords that are transmitted or stored in cleartext (plain, unencrypted text) are easy to crack because they are readable. Systems that exchange **hashed** passwords (passwords that have been encrypted) that a hacker can copy and reuse as is (that is, in their encrypted format) without having to actually know the unencrypted password also create vulnerabilities. You can avoid both by ensuring that your network's authorized users protect passwords effectively and observe some simple security habits.

User Error with Passwords

Passwords have a number of built-in vulnerabilities. The more obvious ones include:

- Passwords are often easy to guess because they haven't been thought through by users.
- Passwords are often stored on sticky notes or papers displayed in readily visible areas.
- Passwords can be uncovered by "social engineering"—fooling users into giving out information.

You can reduce the chances that passwords will be stolen or guessed by telling individual users to choose passwords that are complicated enough not to be guessed easily. They should also be coached to memorize the passwords rather than store them in writing and to never give out the passwords to anyone.

Lax Security Habits

Large organizations can't keep tabs on everyone who works outside the office and who needs to access internal resources. In addition, in partner organizations, passwords might get copied and shared in ways the original organization can't control.

To maintain some level of integrity, some corporations draw up a formal **Memorandum of Understanding (MOU)** with their partner companies. In an MOU, both parties formally agree to observe a set of rules of behavior. The MOU usually states what outsiders can do on the network or with passwords and states that any other use is forbidden. An MOU spells out who bears responsibility for critical resources as well as system maintenance, and it lists who to contact in case questions arise or help is needed.

PASSWORD SECURITY TOOLS

Password-based authentication can be undone by poor security habits on the part of users who don't manage their passwords well. Such weaknesses can be offset by passwords that are generated for one-time use with each session and then discarded. In addition, Linux makes use of a "shadow password system" that also makes passwords difficult if not impossible to crack.

One-Time Password Software

The many problems associated with passwords and the ease of cracking them are alleviated by a one-time password. Two types of one-time passwords are available:

- *Challenge-response passwords:* The authenticating computer or firewall generates a random number (the challenge) and sends it to the user who enters a secret

PIN or password (the response). If the code and PIN or password match the information stored on the authenticating server, the user gains access.

- *Password list passwords:* You enter a seed phrase, and the password system generates a list of passwords you can use. You pick one from the list and submit it along with the seed phrase to gain access.

For inbound access, one-time passwords using a scheme, such as Bellcore's S/KEY, provide a higher level of security. Users type a different password each time they connect. (See the section on S/Key later in this chapter for a more detailed description.)

An even higher level of security is realized by some firewalls when they have the ability to work with hardware devices called token generators that automatically generate and display the next password the user types. (See the sections on SecurID and Axent Pathways Defender later in this chapter for more information.)

The Shadow Password System

Linux stores passwords in the **/etc/passwd** file in encrypted format. The passwords are encrypted using a one-way hash function: an algorithm that is easy to compute when encrypting passwords but very difficult to decrypt.

The algorithm begins to encrypt the password after receiving a randomly generated value called the **salt**. The salt has one of 4096 possible values. Hackers can possibly determine passwords by compiling a database of words and common passwords that can be generated with all of the 4096 possible salt values. The hacker can then compare the encrypted passwords in your /etc/passwd file with their database; if they find a match, they can gain access to your computer or network. Such an attack is called a **dictionary attack**.

The **shadow password system**, which is a feature of the Linux operating system that enables the secure storage of passwords, stores passwords in another file that has restricted access. In addition, passwords are stored only after being encrypted by a randomly generated value and an encoding formula. The key is then stored along with the encrypted password. When a user enters a password, it is encrypted using the same formula and then compared to the stored password; if the passwords match, the user is granted access to the requested system resources.

OTHER AUTHENTICATION SYSTEMS

Most firewalls that are capable of handling authentication make use of one or more well-known systems. Check Point FireWall-1, for instance, handles the two centralized authentication protocols discussed earlier in this chapter, RADIUS and TACACS+. In addition, FireWall-1 can provide access control to other authentication systems, including those mentioned in the following sections.

Single-Password Systems

FireWall-1 supports the use of relatively simple authentication systems. The following simple authentication systems require a user to enter a single password to be authenticated:

- *Operating system password:* FireWall-1, like other firewall programs, gives you the option of forwarding all authentication requests to the operating system of the bastion host on which it resides.

- *Internal firewall password:* If you do not make use of a centralized authentication server, you can have FireWall-1 function as the repository of static usernames and passwords. In this case, users are required to enter the account name and password information associated with FireWall-1 itself to be authenticated.

One-Time Password Systems

FireWall-1 overcomes the problems associated with a single-password system. Each time the user wishes to authenticate and access resources, a different password is required. As long as the secret key used to generate the password is not divulged, the scheme is secure because hackers cannot pretend to be a particular user by intercepting a password. You should be familiar with the following three types of systems.

Single Key (S/Key)

The S/Key one-time password authentication system uses multiple-word rather than single-word passwords: the user begins by specifying a single-word password and by specifying a number (n) that represents the number of times the password is to be encrypted. The password is then processed by a hash function n times, and the resulting encrypted passwords are stored on the server.

When users attempt to log in, the server prompts them for the password. The server then processes the password $n-1$ times; the result is compared with the stored password set. If the result is the same, the user is granted access. S/Key has the great advantage that it never stores the original password on the server, so the original password cannot be intercepted or "sniffed" by a hacker.

SecurID

SecurID, an authentication system developed by RSA Security Inc., makes use of a highly touted feature called **two-factor authentication**. As the name implies, it requires two things from the user to authenticate:

- *A physical object:* In this case, a SecurID authenticator (or token) that takes the form of a card or "fob;" the token that generates a unique code that is supplied to the user (Figure 6-6 gives a sampling of available tokens.)

- *A piece of knowledge:* In this case, the PIN associated with that authenticator

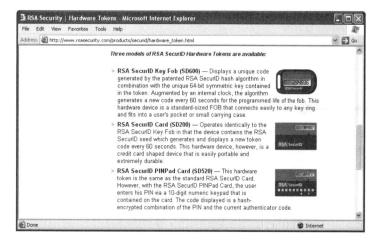

Figure 6-6 SecurID tokens

The SecurID tokens generate a random code every 60 seconds; the code, along with the associated PIN, is submitted to the authentication server. SecurID is the most frequently used one-time password solution with FireWall-1.

Axent Pathways Defender

Axent Pathways Defender is another two-factor authentication system: it requires the administrator to purchase a Defender Token (either a hardware keypad or a software-based keypad) that is used to enter and submit PIN numbers to the authentication server. A **challenge–response** system is used: when you log in to the network, the server responds by sending you a random password—a one-time numeric code. You respond by submitting the same numeric code along with your PIN.

Certificate-Based Authentication

FireWall-1 supports the use of digital certificates, rather than passwords, to authenticate users. The organization using FireWall-1 would have to set up a Public Key Infrastructure (PKI) that generates keys to users. The user receives a code called a public key that is generated using the server's private key and uses the public key to send encrypted information to the server. The server receives the public key and can decrypt the information using its private key.

802.1x Wi-Fi Authentication

IEEE 802.1x is one of the fastest growing standards being used in connection with enterprise networks today. It's popular because it supports wireless Ethernet connections (sometimes called "Wi-Fi").

This relatively new protocol isn't supported by FireWall-1, but it deserves mention because of the increasing popularity of wireless networks in corporate settings. Wireless networks make it easy for users to connect to the network without having to string cables. At the same time, they present the security administrator with a considerable challenge: without some kind of authentication, any hacker with a laptop computer equipped with a wireless network card who ventures within a few hundred feet of the wireless network can potentially connect to it.

The 802.1x protocol provides for authentication of users on wireless networks. Windows XP can be configured to use such authentication, which also requires the use of a smart card or digital certificate (see Figure 6-7).

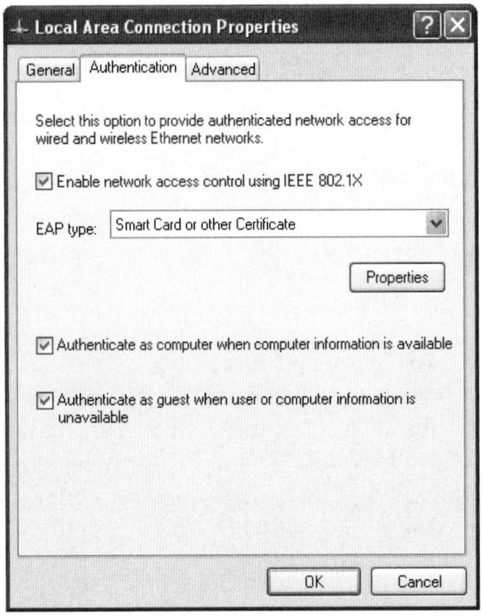

Figure 6-7   Windows XP for 802.1x wireless network authentication

Wi-Fi makes use of Extensible Authentication Protocol (EAP), which enables a system that uses Wi-Fi to authenticate users on other kinds of network operating systems. For instance, the EAP-MD5 type enables a Windows XP user to authenticate with Ethernet LANs and the EAP-TLS type works with 802.11b WLANs.

CHAPTER SUMMARY

❐ This chapter provided you with an overview of how and why firewalls authenticate and described various configurations, protocols, and authentication schemes they employ. Firewalls authenticate when they need to assign different levels of authorization to different users and groups. By determining that users or computers are really who or what they claim to be, the firewall can then grant access to the needed network resources.

❐ Firewalls can make use of many different authentication schemes, including user, client, and session authentication. But in general, they all require a user to supply either something they have (such as a smart card) or something they know (such as a password), or both. (The latest authentication systems make use of something that is a physical attribute of the individual, such as a fingerprint or voiceprint.) To obtain the needed pieces of information, firewalls make use of various types of authentication.

❐ In a centralized authentication system, the firewall works in tandem with an authentication server. The authentication takes over some or all of the job of maintaining (or generating) usernames and passwords and receiving login requests, as well as auditing—the process of recording who is and who is not authenticated and what level of access is granted. Kerberos is a centralized authentication system used by Windows and UNIX, whereas TACACS+ and RADIUS are systems used to authenticate remote users who dial in to the network.

❐ Passwords are an important part of virtually every authentication system and take one of two general forms. Single-word, static password systems receive a password from a user, compare it against a database of passwords, and grant access if a match is made. However, such simple password security is vulnerable to the ability of hackers to determine passwords, to user error, and to bad security habits.

❐ Some of the vulnerabilities of password systems can be offset by using one-time passwords that are generated dynamically each time the user wishes to log on to the network. A secret key is used to generate a single- or multiple-word password. Hardware devices might also generate one-time passwords that, when combined with PIN numbers previously assigned to users, provide an authentication system that is especially difficult to crack.

Key Terms

AAA services — Cisco Systems' term for the three primary functions of a centralized authentication server: authentication, authorization, and auditing.

Access Control Lists (ACLs) — Lists of individual users or computers that can access a set of networked resources.

Access Control Server (ACS) — A server that hosts centralized authentication software, such as RADIUS, and that performs authentication, authorization, and auditing functions.

auditing — The process of keeping records of who is or is not authenticated and what level of authorization those individual users are given.

authentication — The act of identifying users and providing network services to them based on their identity.

basic authentication — A server maintains a local file of usernames and passwords that it refers to for matching the username-password pair being supplied by a client.

biometrics — The use of unique physical characteristics such as fingerprints and retinal patterns to identify someone.

centralized authentication service — A centralized server handles three separate and essential authentication practices: authentication, authorization, and auditing.

challenge-response — A type of authentication in which the authentication server sends the user a challenge, usually a numeric code. To authenticate, the user needs to respond by resubmitting the code and a secret PIN or password.

challenge-response authentication — The authenticating computer or firewall generates a random code or number (the challenge) and sends it to the user who wishes to be authenticated.

cleartext — Plain, unencrypted text.

client authentication — Same as user authentication but with additional time limit or usage limit restrictions.

crack — The act by an unauthorized individual of determining—by guessing, brute force, or deception—someone else's supposedly secret password.

dictionary attack — An attack in which a hacker compiles a database of commonly used words and passwords that can be encrypted using all 4096 possible salts and compares its database of encrypted terms against the encrypted passwords found in the /etc/passwd directory on Linux. If a match is found, the actual password is known and access is gained.

/etc/passwd — Contains the encrypted passwords on a Linux system.

hashed — Encryption using a complex formula called an algorithm.

Kerberos — A simple authentication method that uses a Key Distribution Center (KDC) to issue tickets to those who want to gain access to resources.

MD5 — An algorithm used to provide a 128-bit encrypted output called a message digest that is considered very secure.

Memorandum of Understanding (MOU) — An agreement in which various parties agree to observe rules of behavior governing network use and passwords.

message digest — The encrypted data file that results from processing a message through an algorithm such as MD5.

one-time password — A password that is generated using a secret key and that is used only once, when the user authenticates. Different passwords are used for each authentication session.

Remote Authentication Dial-In User Service (RADIUS) — A centralized dial-in authentication service that uses UDP. RADIUS is thought to provide a lower level of security than TACACS+, even though it's more widely supported.

salt — A randomly generated value that is used to encrypt passwords in the Linux environment.

session authentication — Authentication that is required any time the client establishes a session with a server or other networked resource. Authentication is done by software called a session authentication agent that resides on the client computer.

session key — A temporary key issued by a Kerberos Authentication Server that is based on the client's password and that functions as a Ticket-Granting Ticket (TGT).

shadow password system — A feature of the Linux operating system that enables the storage of passwords so they can't be discovered by unauthorized users who attempt to break into a system.

smart card — A card that contains embedded authentication information and that can be read by a card reader—for example, an ATM machine.

specific sign-on — A type of client authentication in which the client is required to be authenticated each time the user wants to access a server or use a service.

standard sign-on — A type of client authentication in which the client, after being authenticated, is given access to all network resources and the ability to perform all desired functions (copying, viewing Web pages, transferring files, and so on).

Terminal Access Controller Access Control System (TACACS+) — TACACS+—commonly called "tac-plus"—is the latest and strongest version of a set of authentication protocols for dial-up access developed by Cisco Systems.

Ticket-Granting Server (TGS) — An element in the Kerberos authentication system. The TGS accepts a TGT from a client and generates a session ticket, which gives the client access to requested services.

Ticket-Granting Ticket (TGT) — A part of the Kerberos authentication system; a random number is generated that is associated with the service being requested by a client. The session key serves as a TGT, which is presented to a TGS which, in turn, grants a session ticket that permits access to the requested resources.

token — Any kind of physical object (a smart card, for example) that is used to identify someone on a network.

two-factor authentication — A system that requires users to authenticate themselves by supplying two separate things—ideally, something they know (a password) and something they possess (an identification card).

user authentication — Basic authentication in which an individual user supplies a username and static password to access networked resources.

REVIEW QUESTIONS

1. What distinguishes user authentication from the other security approaches used by firewalls? (Choose all that apply.)

    a. Usernames and passwords are used rather than IP addresses.

    b. Individuals are authenticated rather than devices.

    c. Many users can be given access to a resource, not just one.

    d. Many resources can be opened up to an authorized user as opposed to a single resource to a device.

2. Regarding firewalls, which of the following statements is true?

    a. The proxy gateway receives the request first.

    b. The packet filter is used first.

    c. The user is authenticated first.

    d. The firewall decides on the fly, depending on who is trying to connect.

3. Two-factor authentication is based on _____. (Choose all that apply.)

    a. something you want

    b. something you know

    c. something you have

    d. someone you know

4. An authenticating server that responds to a login request by generating a random number or code and expecting to receive that code plus a secret password in return is making use of _____.

5. Name the three *As* associated with AAA services.

6. Kerberos is not recommended for authenticating users who are on what kind of network?

    a. intranet

    b. external private network

    c. virtual private network

    d. external network

7. Why is Kerberos considered less secure than other authenticating methods?

    a. It generates public keys.

    b. It uses cleartext passwords.

    c. It uses one-time passwords.

    d. It works only with certain operating systems.

8. Authentication systems such as Kerberos and RADIUS are more complex to set up and use than other systems, so what is the advantage of using them?

9. A document that spells out the correct use of passwords is called a(n) _____.

    a. Memorandum of Understanding (MOU)

    b. Acceptable Use Policy

    c. Security policy

    d. rulebase

10. A two-factor authentication system requires the user to submit a password and a _____. (Choose all that apply.)

    a. username

    b. smart card

    c. token

    d. PIN

11. Which of the following is *not* a common type of authentication on networks?

    a. biometrics

    b. passwords

    c. signature

    d. smart cards

12. When does a firewall need to authenticate?

13. Centralized authentication requires what kind of trust? (Choose all that apply.)

    a. A client must trust the authentication server.

    b. A client must trust the application server.

    c. The application server must trust the client.

    d. The application server must trust the authentication server.

14. Kerberos makes use of service-granting items called _____.

    a. packets

    b. tickets

    c. certificates

    d. tokens

15. Before you can obtain a ticket from a Kerberos server, you must first obtain a(n) _____.

6

16. Which of the following is an advantage of TACACS+ over RADIUS? (Choose all that apply.)

    a. handles accounting

    b. uses TCP instead of UDP

    c. stores passwords in encrypted form

    d. all of the above

17. Why is a one-time password system considered more secure than a basic authentication system? Provide at least two reasons.

18. If TACACS+ provides a much stronger level of security than RADIUS, why would you consider using a RADIUS server to authenticated dial-in users?

19. Which authentication protocol creates one-time passwords that consist of multiple words?

    a. TACACS+

    b. SecurID

    c. S/Key

    d. Kerberos

20. Why is authentication important with wireless networks?

HANDS-ON PROJECTS

Project 6-1: Set Up User Authentication

NetProxy, the freeware proxy server program used in Chapter 5, also has a user authentication feature you can set up. By default, authentication isn't set up on NetProxy; all users have unlimited access to all applications covered by the proxy server. If you set up authentication, you can configure the program to give specific users or groups access to specific services. You can also set up time limits that govern how long they can use each service. NetProxy uses its own custom authentication protocol, called NPAuth. The NPAuth protocol is administered by a small, freeware application that you have to download and install on all client machines that use NetProxy to make external connections.

This and subsequent exercises assume that you have a Windows XP or 2000 Professional workstation available with NetProxy installed and running on it. You will also need the program WinZip to extract the authentication software (you can get the software at *www.winzip.com/*). If you need instructions on how to download and install NetProxy, refer to Hands-On Project 5-1.

1. Double-click the **Internet Explorer** icon on your desktop.

2. In the browser's Address box, type **www.grok.co.uk**, and then press **Enter**. The home page of the Grok Developments Ltd. Web site opens.

3. Click the **Downloads** link. The Download NetProxy page opens.

4. Click **Get It!** across from NetProxy Authentication Client for Windows. Click **Save**, and then choose a location for the download. The software is downloaded to your computer.

5. Double-click the file you downloaded, **npauth.zip**, to open the file in WinZip. Click **I Agree**, if necessary, to open WinZip.

6. Click **Extract** on the WinZip toolbar to extract the files to the directory of your choice.

7. Navigate to the directory where you chose to install NetProxy. Double-click **NPAuth.exe** to install the software in your system tray. (An icon labeled NP indicates that the software is installed and running.)

8. Double-click the **NetProxy Authentication Client** icon in the system tray.

9. In the NetProxy Authentication Client dialog box, type the username and password you want to use to access the Internet.

10. Click **OK** to close the NetProxy Authentication Client dialog box.

11. Click **File** on the menu bar and click **Close** to close Internet Explorer and return to the Windows desktop.

Project 6-2: Create a User Account

After you have obtained and installed the NetProxy Authentication Client, you can set up one or more user accounts so that only authenticated users can access the Web or use other services from behind NetProxy. This project assumes that you have a Windows 2000 or XP workstation running NetProxy and that the NetProxy Authentication Client is visible in the system tray. You also need to configure your Web browser to work with NetProxy.

1. If you configured NetProxy to run as a service and the program is already running, double-click the **NetProxy Engine** icon in the system tray. If NetProxy is not already running, click **Start**, point to **Programs**, point to **NetProxy**, and click **NetProxy Configuration**. The NetProxy 4.0 window opens.

2. Click **WWW Proxy** in the Services section of the NetProxy 4.0 window. Notice that, by default, Unauthenticated is selected in the Groups section.

3. In the Groups section, click **Administrators** to deselect Unauthenticated.

4. Click **User** and click **New**. The New User dialog box opens.

5. Type a name for your new user in the User Name text box (for this exercise, use your own name). Type a description in the Description text box (this is optional) and type a password for yourself in the Password text box.

6. In the Access Privileges section of the New User dialog box, make sure a check mark appears in the check box next to each of the services the user can access. When you're done, click **OK**. The New User dialog box closes and you return to the NetProxy window.

7. Click the **NetProxy Configuration Wizard** button on the NetProxy 4.0 toolbar.

8. Click **Require user authentication**, and then click **OK**.

9. When a NetProxy dialog box appears informing you that any existing NetProxy settings will be overwritten, click **Yes**.

10. Make sure the words "NetProxy engine is running" appear in the status bar at the bottom of the NetProxy window. (If the words "NetProxy Engine is Disabled" appear, click the **Enable/Disable Proxy Engine** button on the NetProxy toolbar to start the program.)

11. Double-click the **Internet Explorer** icon on your desktop to start the browser.

12. When the NetProxy Authentication Client dialog box opens, enter a false username and password. What message appears?

13. Click **File** on the menu bar and click **Close** to close the Internet Explorer window.

14. Restart Internet Explorer.

15. When the NetProxy Authentication dialog box opens, enter the correct username and password you established in Step 5. Click **OK**. Your browser's default startup page should open.

16. Double-click the **NetProxy Engine** icon in the system tray.

17. Click **WWW Proxy** and then click **Unauthenticated**. This enables others to use this workstation to access the Web without having to be authenticated.

18. Click **Close**.

19. Click **File** on the menu bar and click **Close** to close Internet Explorer and return to the Windows desktop.

Project 6-3: Create a User Group

Setting up authentication for a group enables you to grant a particular level of authorization to a group of users. By creating a group of users, all of whom have access to the same level of services or at the same time, you make configuration easier and more convenient. This exercise assumes that you have two or more individual users configured for authentication, as described in Hands-on Project 6-2.

> You don't necessarily have to install NPAuth on each workstation that you want to authenticate. If there is no NPAuth client running on a workstation, NetProxy will attempt to use the standard HTTP Proxy Authentication protocol to grant or deny access to the Web. During Web browsing, if the Web browser being used supports proxy authentication, the user will be presented with a dialog box into which a username and password can be entered.

1. Double-click the **NetProxy Engine** icon in the system tray to start NetProxy. If the program is not running in the system tray, click **Start**, point to **Programs**, point to **NetProxy**, and click **NetProxy Configuration** to open the NetProxy 4.0 window.

2. Click **Group**, and then click **New**. The New Group dialog box opens.

3. In the Group Name text box, type **Accounting**.

4. In the Description text box, type **Accounting Dept. Managers**.

5. In the Access privileges section, check all check boxes except RealPlayer Proxy Service and Telnet Gateway Service.

6. Click **OK**. The New Group dialog box closes and you return to the NetProxy 4.0 window. The name of the group appears in the Groups section of the window.

7. In the Users section of the NetProxy 4.0 window, double-click the name of the user you want to add to the Accounting group. The Edit User Properties dialog box opens.

8. Click the **Groups** tab to bring it to the front. The Groups tab opens with two boxes: Member of (which should be empty) and Not member of (which contains the groups available to you).

9. Click **Accounting** to highlight it, and then click **Add** to move Accounting to the Member of list box.

10. Click **OK** to close the Edit User Properties dialog box.

11. Repeat Steps 7 through 10 for each user you want to add to the group.

12. Click **Services**, and then click **Exit** to close NetProxy—unless you want to move on to the next exercise, in which case you should leave the NetProxy 4.0 window open.

Project 6-4: Configure Time-Based Authentication

When you set up authentication for a group of users as described in Hands-On Project 6-3, it becomes easy to set up usage restrictions for that group based on time. One of the most useful ways to protect a network with a proxy-based firewall is to establish time restrictions. By identifying when individuals can make use of network services, you prevent unauthorized use of those services during "off hours" by employees and unauthorized users alike.

1. Double-click the **NetProxy** icon in the system tray to start NetProxy. If the program is not running in the system tray, click **Start**, point to **Programs**, point to **NetProxy**, and click **NetProxy Configuration** to open the NetProxy window.

2. Double-click the **Accounting** group in the Groups section of the window. (If you did not create this group in Hands-On Project 6-3, double-click **Administrators**.) The Edit Group Properties dialog box opens.

3. Click the **Time Restrictions** tab to bring it to the front.

4. The default time entry is highlighted; this entry allows use of NetProxy 24 hours a day, 7 days a week. Click **Edit** to change the default settings.

5. In the Edit Access Time dialog box, type **09:00** in the first time text box (next to Between) and **17:00** in the second time text box. (NetProxy uses the military form of expressing time; 17:00 is equivalent to 5:00 p.m.)

6. Uncheck the **Saturday** and **Sunday** check boxes, leaving the other five boxes checked.

7. Click **OK**. The new time setting—Start Time 09:00, End Time 17:00, Mo Tu We Th Fr—should appear in The Edit Group Properties dialog box.

8. Click **OK** to close the Edit Group Properties dialog box and return to the NetProxy 4.0 window.

9. Click **Services**, and then click **Exit** to close NetProxy and return to the Windows desktop.

Project 6-5: Set Up Authentication for a Dial-Up Connection

Windows 2000 supports several different authentication protocols for dial-up connections. This exercise assumes that your lab workstation uses Windows 2000 and has a direct connection to the Internet via a LAN. For the purposes of this exercise, you'll set up a nonfunctioning dial-up connection and then configure it so that anyone using that connection needs to authenticate before connecting to your network.

1. Click **Start**, point to **Settings**, point to **Network and Dial-Up Connections**, and click **Make New Connection**. The Network Connection Wizard opening screen opens.

2. Click **Next** to move to the next screen.

3. Under Network Connection Type, leave the default option, Dial-up to private network, selected.

4. Click **Next**.

5. Under Phone Number to Dial, type **123-4567**, and then click **Next**.

6. Under Connection Availability, click **Only for myself**, and then click **Next**.

7. In the last screen, leave the default label in the Type the name you want to use for this connection text box, and then click **Finish**. The Connect Dial-up Connection dialog box opens.

8. Click **Properties**.

9. Click the **Security** tab to bring it to the front.

10. Click **Require secured password** in the Validate my identity as follows: list box.

11. Click **OK**. The Dial-up Connection Properties dialog box closes and you return to the Connect Dial-up Connection dialog box.

12. In the User name: and Password: text boxes, type a user name and password that you will use to authenticate yourself when dialing up the network. Leave the Save password box unchecked.

13. Click **Cancel** to close the dialog box.

14. Click **Start**, point to **Settings**, and click **Control Panel**.

15. Double-click **Network and Dial-Up Connections**.

16. Right-click the icon for the "fake" connection you just created and click **Delete**.

17. When asked to confirm that you want to delete the connection, click **Yes**.

Project 6-6: Setting Up IEEE 802.1x Authentication

Windows XP supports the 802.1x standard, and you can configure your LAN connection to use it. By configuring your Windows XP workstation to use 802.1x, you require other computers in your local network to authenticate themselves before they access your shared files.

For the authentication system to really work, you need to have a RADIUS server on your network and either a smart card (a card that contains identification information on it) or a digital certificate. Even if you don't have one of these items, you can set up 802.1x on your workstation so that you can become acquainted with this type of authentication. You must be logged in as a member of the Administrators group on your computer to configure authentication.

1. Click **Start**, and then click **Control Panel**. In Classic View, double-click **Network Connections**, and double-click **Local Area Connection**.

2. In the Local Area Connection Status dialog box, click **Properties**.

3. Click the **Authentication** tab.

4. If necessary, check the **Enable network access control using IEEE 802.1x** check box. The EAP type list becomes active.

5. If necessary, click **Smart Card or other Certificate** in the EAP type list box.

6. If necessary, click the **Authenticate as computer when computer information is available** check box. This instructs Windows XP to prompt you to authenticate yourself if you are not currently logged on to the network.

7. If necessary, click the **Authenticate as guest when user or computer information is unavailable** check box. This enables you to authenticate as a guest if your username and password information are not accessible for some reason.

8. Click **OK** to close the Local Area Connection Properties dialog box, click **Close** in the Local Area Connection Status dialog box, and then close the Network Connections window to return to the Windows desktop.

Project 6-7: Setting Up Authentication Using Check Point NG (Optional Project)

Check Point NG, the latest version of the Check Point firewall tools, lets you choose the authentication schemes you want to use. The following exercise assumes you have set up Check Point NG and that you have configured the firewall object itself with the name Local_Gateway.

1. Click **Start**, point to **Programs** (**All Programs** on Windows XP), point to **Check Point Management Clients**, and click **Policy Editor NGFP2**. Enter your username and password, and then click **OK**.

2. From the menu bar, click **Manage** and click **Network Objects**.

3. Scroll down the list of objects in the Network Objects dialog box, click **Local_Gateway**, and then click **Edit**. If you do not see Local_Gateway in the list of objects, click **London_Gateway** and edit it for the purposes of this exercise.

4. Click **Authentication** in the list of topics on the left side of the Check Point Gateway – Local_Gateway dialog box.

5. Under Enabled Authentication Schemes, click the check box next to the authentication schemes you want the firewall to support. The available options are S/Key, SecurID, OS Password, VPN-1 & FireWall-1 Password, RADIUS, AXENT Pathways Defender, and TACACS.

6. Click the **Authentication Failure Track** list arrow and click an option that indicates how you want to be notified if someone attempts to log on to the network unsuccessfully. Options include None, Mail Alert, Popup Alert, and Log.

7. Click **OK** to close the Check Point Gateway – Local_Gateway dialog box, and then click **Close** to close the Network Objects dialog box.

8. Click **Manage** and click **Users and Administrators**.

9. Click **New** and then click **Template**.

10. In the Login Name text box of the User Template Properties dialog box, type **Berlin_Branch_Office**.

11. Click the **Authentication** tab.

12. Click **S/Key** in the Authentication Scheme list box.

13. Click **Local_Gateway** in the Installed on list box.

14. Click **MD5** in the Method section.

15. Click **OK** to close the dialog box, and then click **Close** in the Users dialog box.

16. Click **File**, and then click **Exit**. Click **Yes** if asked to save your changes.

CASE PROJECTS

Case 6-1: Single-user authentication

You need to restrict your company's rank-and-file employees to using the Internet only during regular working hours (9 a.m. to 5 p.m., five days a week). However, as network administrator, you want to be able to access the network at any time of the day or night, seven days a week. How would you meet the needs of the employees and yourself?

Case 6-2: Group Authentication

A group of freelance designers who work at home, some of whom dial in to the Internet and some who have DSL or cable modem connections, needs to gain access to a set of your company publication files to design them. How would you enable this?

Case 6-3: Supplementing Password-Based Authentication

Your network employs basic authentication that centers on usernames and passwords. However, you have two ongoing problems. The first is that usernames and passwords are frequently lost by negligent users. In addition, hackers have, on occasion, fooled employees into giving up their authentication information. What two things could you do to strengthen the use of basic username and password authentication?

6

Case 6-4: Providing Centralized Access to Your User Database

You have configured your firewall, Check Point NG, to authenticate a group of 100 users who are in your company. You set up the database of users using your firewall's own user management software, User Manager NG. As your network grows and security items are added, other network components need to access the same database of users. How would you provide the other network components with access to the database of users?

ENCRYPTION AND FIREWALLS

After reading this chapter and completing the exercises, you will be able to:
◆ Understand the role encryption plays in a firewall architecture
◆ Know how digital certificates work and why they are important security tools
◆ Analyze the workings of SSL, PGP, and other popular encryption schemes
◆ Enable Internet Protocol Security (IPSec) and identify its protocols and modes

Firewalls are designed to inspect packets of information when they reach the perimeter of a network. As you've already learned, a firewall inspects each packet, and, based on the content of the packet and the rules in its rulebase, the firewall either sends the packet to the appropriate location or drops it.

What happens if the packet's contents have been corrupted in transit? What happens if the packet has been intercepted before it gets to the firewall and mangled by a hacker? The firewall itself can't control what happens to packets before they reach or after they leave the network being protected. This is one reason why firewalls and other security applications encrypt the contents of packets leaving the network being protected and are prepared to decrypt incoming packets.

This chapter discusses how and why encryption is used in a network and how to use encryption in a way that complements the firewall's activities rather than making them more difficult. It also discusses encryption applications, such as **Pretty Good Privacy (PGP)**, Secure Sockets Layer (SSL), and **Internet Protocol Security (IPSec)**, and schemes that can form part of a firewall architecture. By encrypting the data that passes into and out of your network, you help protect your hardware and data in a way that is different, but just as effective, as packet filtering, proxy services, and other firewall functions.

Why Your Firewalls Need To Use Encryption

Encryption turns ordinary information into encoded **ciphertext** to preserve the authenticity, integrity, and privacy of the information that passes through the security perimeter. In other words, encryption is the process of concealing information to render it unreadable to all but the intended recipients. As important as encryption is, a 1997 survey by the CIO Institute and *Government Executive* magazine was still able to show that four out of five civilian agency security managers didn't know how much they were being attacked or by whom.

Of course, firewalls didn't always perform encryption-related functions. They originally focused on basic features like IP forwarding and Network Address Translation (NAT). The problem was that, although such approaches provided protection at the network level, they didn't account for application-level problems, such as executable code that finds its way into a system. In fact, many of the attacks that plague companies both small and large—even those that are already protected by firewalls—occur as a result of executable code that is either tampered with before it reaches the firewall or, more commonly, that makes it past the firewall in malicious e-mail attachments or HTTP downloads.

The sections that follow explain the important role that encryption plays in many firewalls. In the process, you will learn the following:

- Hackers will take advantage of firewalls that don't use encryption.

- Encryption creates costs in terms of CPU resources and time.

- Encryption preserves data integrity.

- Organizations can increase confidentiality by using encryption.

- User authentication relies on encryption.

- Encryption plays a fundamental role in enabling virtual private networks (VPNs).

Hackers Take Advantage of a Lack of Encryption

Firewall vendors added encryption to their products to provide protection against "active attacks," which are also known as **session hijacks**. These are attacks involving a communication session that has already been established between a server and a client. The hacker inserts confusing or misleading commands into packets, thus disabling the server and enabling the hacker to gain control of the session. These are different from "passive attacks," such as packet sniffing, in which a program scans for open ports that can be compromised.

As you can see in Figure 7-1, the unencrypted packet is vulnerable at points A and B.

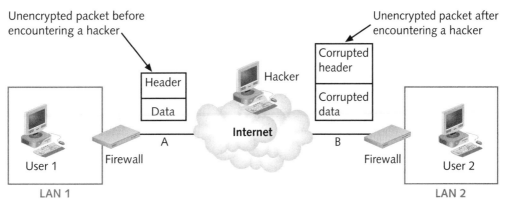

Figure 7-1   A vulnerable, unencrypted packet

With encryption, however, an attack such as X or Y is rebuffed, as shown in Figure 7-2.

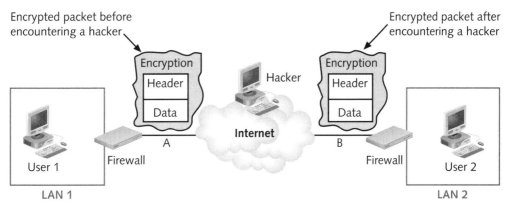

Figure 7-2   A protected, encrypted packet

The Cost of Encryption

Before you decide whether to use a firewall that has the ability to encrypt communications, be aware that encryption can be a very CPU-intensive process. The bastion host (which is an application server that has an interface on the Internet; you'll learn more about bastion hosts in Chapter 8) that hosts your firewall should be robust enough to manage encryption along with the other security functions you call on it to perform. In addition, encrypted packets may need to be padded to uniform length to ensure that some algorithms work effectively.

Ideally, when firewalls encrypt data the encryption is transparent to the end user. However, on busy networks, encryption can result in slowdowns that can increase the time it takes to perform individual tasks. In addition, the need to choose an encryption method and monitor how well encryption works adds another item to a busy system administrator's list of responsibilities. The burden placed on system administrators can have tangible results in how well the network works and on whether intrusion attempts are detected during, for example, the reviewing of firewall log files.

Preserving Data Integrity

One reason for encrypting information is to preserve its integrity, which is the accuracy of the information's contents. If a packet is encrypted, hackers cannot get at it and corrupt or mangle the contents in ways the original author never intended.

Although encryption minimizes the risk that information will be corrupted, it isn't foolproof. Even encrypted sessions can go wrong as a result of **man-in-the-middle attacks**: attacks in which a hacker intercepts part of an encrypted data session to gain control over the data being exchanged. Such attacks involve encrypted codes called keys and are discussed in more detail in the section "Generating Public Keys."

Another service related to data integrity that encryption can perform is **nonrepudiation**, which is the ability to prevent one participant in an electronic transaction from denying that it performed an action. Nonrepudiation uses encryption to ensure that an electronic transaction occurred, that an action was performed by the legitimate originating party, and that the party that was supposed to receive something as a result of the transaction actually received that result. Specifically, an encrypted code called a **digital signature** is attached to the files that are exchanged during the transaction so that each party can ensure the other's identity. Nonrepudiation is an important aspect of establishing trusted communications between corporations or other organizations that do business across a network rather than face to face.

Maintaining Confidentiality

The most obvious reason to encrypt data is to keep it confidential. You want to render the information unreadable to all but the intended recipients. The reason computers are stolen frequently is that the information such devices can contain is more valuable than the hardware itself. The computer insurance agency Safeware, Inc. (*www.safeware.com*) has stated that, in 1999, 319,000 laptops and 27,000 desktop computers were reported stolen. In addition, a widely reported survey by the American Society for Industrial Security claims that Fortune 1000 companies experienced data-related losses of more than $45 million in 1999. Such losses are especially hard to document or verify because many companies lose data to thieves, hackers, and disgruntled employees without even knowing it.

One memorable data-integrity incident in September 2000 indicates how quickly sensitive data can be lost: The CEO of a well-known wireless communications company had just used his laptop to make a slide show presentation at a conference in California. When the CEO left the podium to chat with members of the audience, the laptop was stolen. Although the computer was password protected, the password could conceivably be cracked using a number of specialized software programs. In addition, the computer reportedly contained proprietary information about the company's wireless technologies that would be of value to foreign governments.

Authenticating Network Clients

A cashier who accepts payment from customers in a brick-and-mortar retail store can know with reasonable certainty that the customers are who they claim to be. Presumably, the customers hand over some sort of photo identification, such as a driver's license. The cashier and the store both place trust in the state or other government agency that issued the ID that the person's identity is actually correct.

On the Internet, requests for information reach a firewall at the perimeter of a network. The firewall, like any individual Internet user, needs to trust that the person's claimed identity is genuine. Firewalls that handle encryption, as well as specialized encryption software, can also be used to identify individuals who possess "digital ID cards" that include encrypted codes. These codes include digital signatures, **public keys**, and **private keys**—all codes that are generated by complex algorithms. Users on the Internet can exchange these codes like digital ID cards, enabling them to identify each other. The same codes can be used to encrypt and decrypt e-mail messages as well as files.

Enabling VPNs

A VPN joins two separate LANs. Encryption is an integral part of VPNs and is used to accomplish two types of goals:

- Encryption enables the firewall to determine whether the user who wants to connect to the VPN is actually authorized to do so.
- Encryption is used to encode the payload of the information to maintain privacy.

VPNs are complex and important types of firewall functions, and as such, are beyond the scope of this chapter. Turn to Chapter 9 for more information on VPNs.

DIGITAL CERTIFICATES AND PUBLIC AND PRIVATE KEYS

Some administrators use a third-party's certification of identities. In such a case, a **digital certificate** is needed. A digital certificate is an electronic document that contains an encrypted series of numerals and characters called a digital signature, which authenticates the identity of the person sending the certificate.

The basis of digital certificates and digital signatures are keys. They enable holders of digital certificates to encrypt communications (using their private key) or decrypt communications (using the sender's public key).

In this part of the chapter, we discuss both digital certificates and the use of public and private keys.

Digital Certificates

Digital certificates are important from the standpoint of firewalls because they are used to transport encrypted codes called public and private keys through the firewall from one host to another. Digital certificates help ensure the identity of the individual who owns the digital certificate, and as such, they provide another layer of security in an organization's firewall architecture.

The following sections examine aspects of digital certificates, including the establishment of an infrastructure for exchanging public and private keys, the need to view and verify someone's digital certificate, and the difference between client- and server-based digital certificates.

The Private Key Infrastructure

Many organizations make use of a **Lightweight Directory Access Protocol (LDAP)** directory, which holds publicly available information about digital certificates as well as individual users in the organization and the organization's network. All of these elements make up a **Public-Key Infrastructure (PKI)**, which is needed to make digital certificates and public and private key distribution possible within an organization.

A PKI is a framework that enables the distribution of digital certificates and public and private keys, and that underlies many of the popular and trusted security schemes in use today, such as PGP and SSL.

Viewing a Digital Certificate

You can view digital certificate information and (provided you trust the organization that issued the digital certificate) be certain that the owners of the digital certificates are who they claim to be. The digital certificate created by the freeware version of PGP, shown in Figure 7-3, contains the basic information: the owner's name, a digital ID (here called a Signer KeyID), and a timestamp (the date the digital certificate was issued).

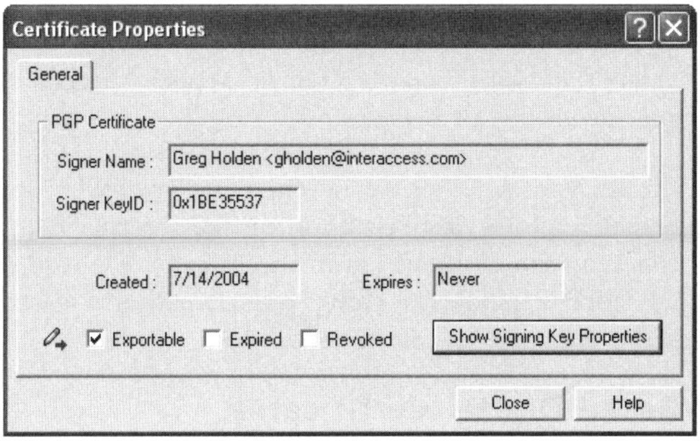

Figure 7-3 The basic information associated with a digital certificate

If you click the Show Signing Key Properties button shown in Figure 7-3, you can view more information about the owner's key, including the size of the key, the formula that was used to create it, and the digital "fingerprint" (see Figure 7-4). This "fingerprint" is a unique set of characters (these can be either a set of English language words or hexadecimal characters) that identifies it as belonging to the owner.

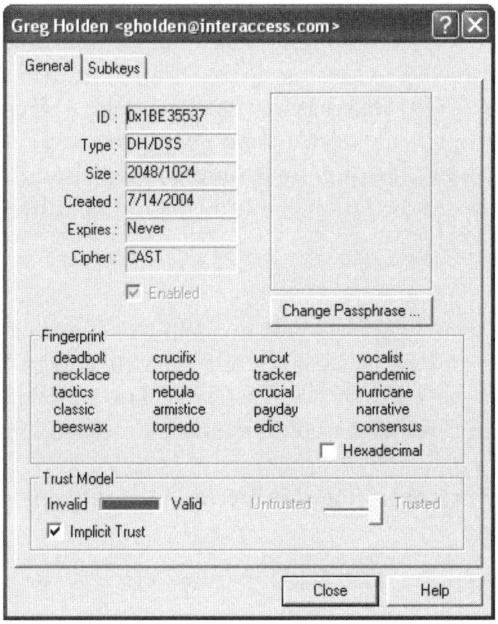

Figure 7-4 Signing key properties

Some applications (like Microsoft Internet Explorer) use the term "thumbprint" rather than "fingerprint" to describe the digital signature associated with a digital certificate. Either one is a set of words or characters that, by its complex nature, identifies itself as the owner's.

You can view digital certificates you already have by checking your Web browser—for instance, by starting up Internet Explorer, clicking Tools on the Internet Explorer menu bar, clicking Options, and clicking the Content tab in the Internet Options dialog box. Click Certificates, and then click Personal to view your own digital certificates and Other People to view digital certificates you've obtained from others.

Client- and Server-Based Digital Certificates

There are two types of digital certificates a firewall will encounter:

- *Client-based digital certificates*. These are digital certificates that an individual user obtains from a **Certification Authority (CA)**, a company that issues them and vouches for the owner's identity. Users install the digital certificate on their individual computers and use it for identification to Web sites and other individuals.

- *Server-based digital certificates*. These are digital certificates issued by a CA to a company that issues them to individuals.

For the digital certificate system to work, both individuals and organizations that use them need to place a good deal of trust in the CA that grants digital certificates and verifies the identity of their owners. Trust also has to be placed in a **Registration Authority (RA)**—a server located in the network where people can apply to obtain a digital certificate that they can distribute. The RA holds information about users in the network; the CA issues digital certificates based on the information held by the RA.

Keys

A **key** is a value that is generated by an algorithm and that can also be processed by an algorithm to encrypt text or to decrypt text that has already been encrypted. The length of the key determines how secure the level of encryption is. The following sections examine aspects of keys that pertain to firewall-based encryption: public and private keys, the need to generate public keys, the need to securely manage private keys, the need to use a key server either on your network or on the Internet, and the differences between private and public key servers.

Public and Private Keys

A key can be very long, containing 1024, 2048, or even 4096 individual bits of data. A private key is a secret code that is generated by an algorithm and that the holder never shares with anyone else. The public key is another block of encoded information that is generated when the private key is processed by the same algorithm: the public key can be exchanged freely with anyone online. Both are used in the creation of digital certificates in that the holder's private key is used to generate a public key that becomes part of the digital certificate.

A public key generated by the encryption program PGP is shown in Figure 7-5.

Figure 7-5   A public key is part of a public-private key pair

An Encrypted Communication Session

One of the most popular key-exchange systems is the public-private key system: users exchange public keys freely on the Internet but keep the private keys that are used to generate those public keys secret. The private keys are used to decrypt communications encrypted with the public keys.

A typical encrypted communication might work like this:

1. Two users obtain digital certificates and public-private key pairs from a CA such as VeriSign (*www.verisign.com*). They pay a yearly fee to the CA to keep the digital certificate from expiring.

2. The two users exchange public keys with one another, by attaching the key to an e-mail message, pasting the key into the body of an e-mail message, or posting the key on a public key server where it can be downloaded.

3. One user sends an e-mail message to the other that is encrypted. It can be encrypted in one of two ways: the message itself might be encrypted, or an attachment to the message might be encrypted. The encryption is done using the recipient's public key.

4. The recipient receives the message from the other user, whose identity seems to be authentic because that person has the recipient's public key. The recipient decrypts the message using his or her private key.

This exchange is illustrated in Figure 7-6.

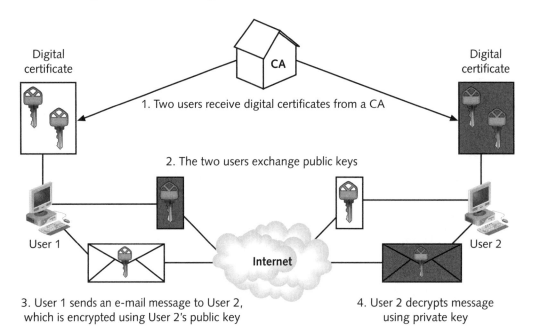

Digital certificate

CA

Digital certificate

1. Two users receive digital certificates from a CA

2. The two users exchange public keys

User 1

Internet

User 2

3. User 1 sends an e-mail message to User 2, which is encrypted using User 2's public key

4. User 2 decrypts message using private key

Figure 7-6 Public keys are exchanged to encrypt communications

The words "seems to be authentic" had to be added to the preceding Step 4 because of the possibility of a man-in-the-middle attack. In such an attack, a hacker is able to intercept the public key that is exchanged during a public-private key encryption session. The hacker then substitutes his or her own public key for that of the intended recipient. As a result, the hacker can impersonate the intended recipient. Armed with a public key, the hacker can potentially gain the ability to read messages between the two individuals even though they are being encrypted.

 You can protect yourself from a man-in-the-middle attack in different ways depending on what is being compromised. If Windows 2000 or NT is being attacked, disable NetBIOS or use NTLMv2, which employs 128-bit encryption. If Internet Explorer 5.5 is being used, upgrade to a more recent version.

Public keys come in many sizes. The encryption program you use should give you a choice of how many data bits the key should contain. The larger the number of bits, the harder the key is to exchange with other users, and the more memory it consumes. As shown in Figure 7-7, a 2048-bit key size is recommended by the Key Generation Wizard that opens when you first set up the program Pretty Good Privacy (PGP).

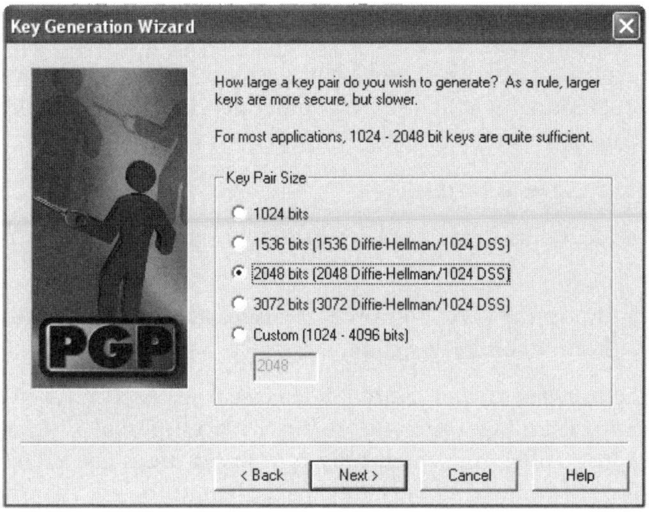

Figure 7-7   Encryption software lets you choose the size of your public and private keys

When you first install Check Point FireWall-1, you are prompted to enter one hundred characters of random text. FireWall-1 uses that text to generate your private key (see Figure 7-8).

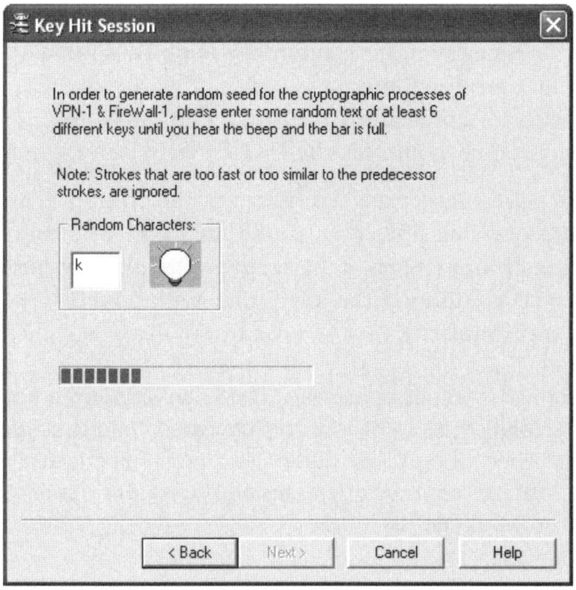

Figure 7-8   FireWall-1 uses random text that you enter to generate keys

Managing Keys

Keys are valuable objects on a network. A key that is issued to one individual needs to be used by that individual alone; if it is used by someone else by mistake, the goal of ensuring identity is defeated.

Key management comes in several forms:

- *Manual distribution*: Users agree on a set of shared secrets, and keys are issued manually.

- *Use of a CA*: Rely on the CA's resources to issue, store, and distribute keys, and to destroy them when they expire.

- *Use of a Key Distribution Center (KDC) to manage keys*: A KDC is usually used not with public-private key distribution, but with a different system—symmetric cryptography—in which only one key is used. The KDC issues a **session key**—a key that exists only during the length of the communication between hosts.

Obviously, manual key distribution is suitable only for small organizations. Key management can be very involved when keys are issued to hundreds or even thousands of different individuals. When dozens or hundreds of keys are involved, key management becomes complex, and the use of a CA or KDC is recommended.

Using a Key Server That Is on Your Network

If you decide to manage keys in-house, you have a number of options for where the **key server**—the program that holds and distributes keys—should be located. One option is to integrate the key server with an application platform: The same host that runs an organization's Web server, for instance, could handle PKI services (see Figure 7-9).

If you run a computer that is a Web server *and* a key server, the computer would need to have enough memory and processing power to handle the range of duties it is called upon to perform. Although the computer has to perform two important and resource-intensive duties, the advantage of combining the key server with a Web server or other type of server is cost savings and simplicity.

If you want more information about key servers, there's an excellent article on options for the establishment of a PKI infrastructure called "Infrastructure Design Considerations When Using Client Certificates." You'll find it at the SANS Organization's reading room (*http://rr.sans.org*). Click Encryption & VPNs, and then scroll down to find the article.

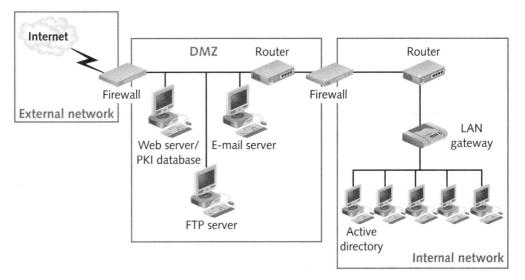

Figure 7-9   A key server combined with a Web server

Using an Online Key Server

Rather than hosting a key server within your own network, you can make use of a public key server on the Internet. Key servers that are available on the Internet should be used with PGP only in connection with software development projects. Other key servers used by an organization should be located on a computer located in-house (for greater security). After you install PGP, for instance, you can access the public key server at *http://pgpkeys.mit.edu.* You can then use this key server to extract keys or add your own keys to it so that others can get them (see Figure 7-10).

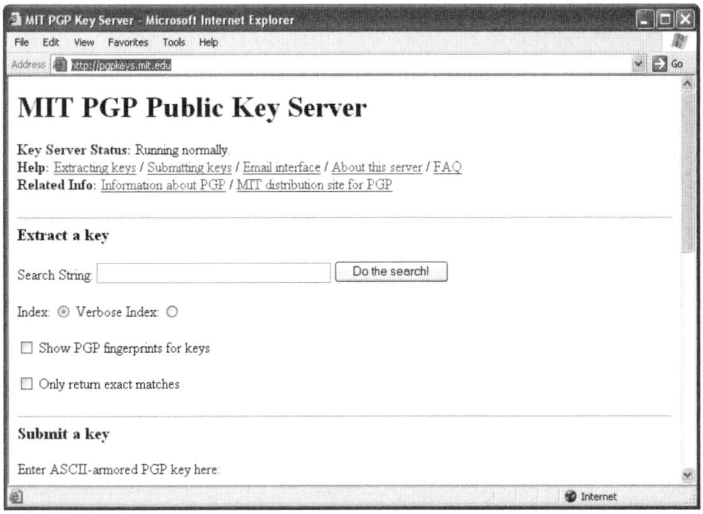

Figure 7-10   A public key server gives anyone a place to exchange keys

After someone else gets your public key from the server, that person can use your key to encrypt an e-mail message to you. Although it might seem like just anyone can obtain your public key from the server, in reality, they first have to know that the digital certificate is stored on the server, and they need an identifier such as a KeyID to extract the digital certificate. Both of these pieces of information should come from the key holder.

ANALYZING POPULAR ENCRYPTION SCHEMES

An encryption scheme is a way of protecting the integrity, privacy, and authenticity of information that is transmitted from one location to another along a network. There are many encryption schemes in use on the Internet and in corporate networking today. A firewall that is expected to receive and process encrypted communications needs to recognize multiple encryption schemes.

Accordingly, Check Point FireWall-1 uses a proprietary encryption scheme called FWZ that generates and manages keys for the firewall. FireWall-1 also recognizes IPSec, an IETF-standardized encryption protocol based on the IP protocol that encrypts IP header information. ISAKMP/OAKLEY is another IETF-standardized protocol, commonly called Internet Key Exchange (IKE). IKE is discussed in more detail in Chapter 9; in addition, you can read a good article on IPSec and IKE at *www.microsoft.com/technet/ treeview/default.asp?url=/technet/columns/security/robi/robich06.asp*.

The most popular encryption schemes in use on the Internet are examined in the following sections. These schemes include **symmetric key encryption** and **asymmetric key encryption**, PGP, and SSL.

Symmetric Versus Asymmetric Encryption

In symmetric encryption, both keys are private—both keys must be kept secret at all times, or the session will no longer be secure. Symmetric key sessions can be very efficient when used on an individual session basis but don't work well when scaled up to the communications needs of large organizations. A diagram of a simple symmetric key exchange is shown in Figure 7-11. User A has a secret key, which encrypts a message. The message is sent along the Internet to User B, who decrypts it using the same symmetric key. Note that at no time are the actual keys exchanged because they must be kept private or the data can be easily compromised by anyone who obtains the key.

The problem of scalability is a drawback with the symmetric key system. Suppose an organization has 100 individuals who need to exchange information. Each user would need separate keys for transmitting data with other individuals; it wouldn't make sense to use the same key to encrypt data for two or more different people—everyone would be able to decode everyone else's messages. Thus, a user would need 100 separate keys. In fact, each user would need 100 separate keys, which would require the organization to purchase literally thousands of keys.

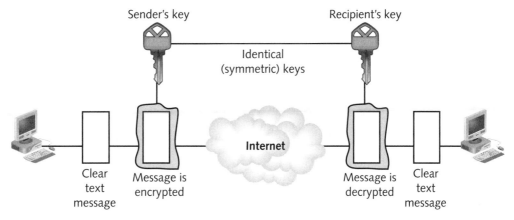

Figure 7-11 Symmetric key encryption

The need for thousands of keys is alleviated by the use of asymmetric encryption, which uses only one user's private key and public key. These keys are used to generate unique session keys that are exchanged by users during a particular session. Asymmetric (public–private) keys use different keys for client and server. Only the private key must be kept secret; the public key can be exchanged, as shown in Figure 7-12.

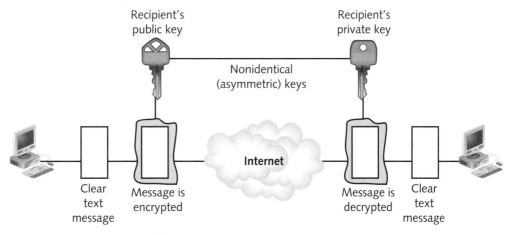

Figure 7-12 Asymmetric key encryption

Asymmetric encryption scales better than symmetric encryption, but it also has its disadvantages:

- It's slower than symmetric encryption.
- Only a few public key algorithms, such as RSA and ElGamal, are available that are secure and easy to use for both encryption and key exchange.

A solution is to use a hybrid system that combines the advantages of both asymmetric and symmetric encryption systems. This hybrid system is called Pretty Good Privacy (PGP). We discuss it next.

PGP

PGP is a **hybrid** system that uses both symmetric and asymmetric keys. The goal is to gain the advantages using both systems: the speed of symmetric cryptography combined with the scalability of asymmetric cryptography. PGP works by using symmetric cryptography to generate a random session key that is used for only one communications session. For example, the session key might be used to encrypt an e-mail message or an individual file.

After the file or message is encrypted, the session key is itself encrypted—this time using the public key half of the asymmetric public-private key pair. The recipient of the encrypted message (or the person who wants to open the encrypted file) uses his or her private key to decode the session key. The session key is then used to decode the message or file.

If you use PGP, you are given the chance to use one of two encryption schemes to generate your public and private key pairs:

- **Rivest-Shamir-Adleman (RSA) encryption:** This is used for older versions of PGP. Two large prime numbers are processed through an algorithm; the level of security depends on how large the prime number is and whether it is a "strong" prime number that is especially difficult to factor. RSA encryption is slow, and it is not in the public domain; it must be licensed from RSA Labs. You'll find a detailed explanation of how the RSA algorithm works at *http://world.std.com/~franl/crypto/rsa-guts.html.*

- **Diffie-Hellman encryption:** This formula is considered stronger than RSA. It uses two large numbers that are processed by an algorithm. These two publicly known numbers, only one of which needs to be a prime number, enable two users to exchange a public key over an insecure medium such as the Internet. When you use Diffie-Hellman, you create two keys: a master or "signing key" and an encryption key. The master key is never exchanged. You'll find a good explanation of Diffie-Hellman encryption at *www.linuxjournal.com/article.php?sid=6131.*

The Diffie-Hellman implementation of PGP uses two separate keys: a master key and an encryption subkey. One advantage of this system is that you can generate multiple encryption subkeys that are based on your master key. One use for multiple encryption subkeys is to change the encryption key over the life of your digital certificate: if the digital certificate lasts three years, for instance, you might create separate subkeys, one specified to be used during each year (see Figure 7-13).

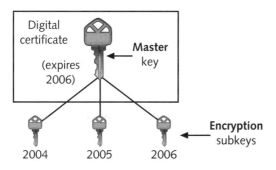

Figure 7-13   Multiple encryption subkeys can be generated from one master key

In the scenario illustrated in Figure 7-13, if one encryption key becomes compromised, you can use a different subkey to generate a new encryption key, without having to generate an entirely new public-private key pair. PGP enables you to keep track of your subkeys, and to generate new ones, in the Subkeys tab of the Properties dialog box for your key pair (see Figure 7-14).

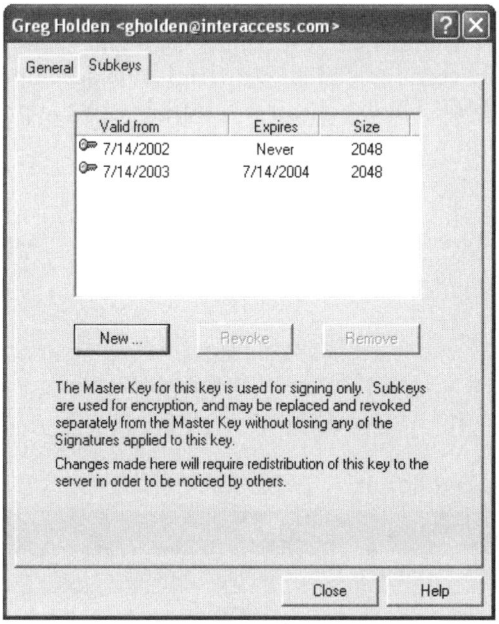

7

Figure 7-14   Diffie-Hellman encryption lets you create subkeys, each of which can generate its own encryption key

X.509

X.509 is a standard set of specifications for assembling and formatting digital certificates and encrypting data within them and is a commonly used type of PKI. X.509 digital certificates are promoted and developed by PKIX, a working group of the **Internet Engineering Task Force (IETF)**. Each X.509 implementation makes use of a root CA. The CA issues a digital certificate, extracts the attached public key, and assures it is trusted. X.509 is popular because it is widely used and well trusted.

X.509 and PGP Compared

The general perception among casual users is that X.509 digital certificates must always be issued by a CA and that, in contrast, PGP digital certificates call for individual users to certify one another's identity, forming a so-called "Web of Trust." In fact, the system isn't so simple: Individuals as well as CAs can issue X.509 digital certificates. However, the perception of trust with X.509 is important, and the perception that CAs must always be involved makes it easy to bring new users into a trusted network.

PGP does not make use of the CA concept. Each user signs his own digital certificate. The program also gives users the ability to **wipe** files from hard disk, which provides better protection than simply deleting a file and sending it to the Windows Recycle Bin. Conventionally deleting a file still leaves traces of that file on your hard disk. When you wipe a file with PGP, all traces of it are deleted permanently.

Another advantage of PGP is that it is available both in freeware and commercial versions. You can try out the freeware version, which was originally developed by Phil Zimmerman and is maintained by MIT. Then, if you are satisfied with the product, you can purchase the commercial version, which is available on the PGP Corporation Web site at *www.pgp.com/display.php?pageID=2*.

Hands-on Project 7-1 covers the installation and configuration of the freeware version of PGP.

Note that digital certificates created using PGP are different from those that use the X.509 standard. Table 7-1 compares the two encryption schemes.

Table 7-1   X.509 versus PGP digital certificates

Aspect of Digital Certificate	X.509	PGP
Issuer	Not same as subject: CA	Same as subject
Number of authentications	1	At least 1
Subject	Owner's public key	Owner's public key
Signer of digital certificate	CA root signed **hash**	Owner's signed hash; recipient's signed hash

SSL

SSL is a secure way to transmit data, such as the personal information associated with a consumer who makes a purchase on a retail Web site, over the Internet. Note that SSL can cause problems for firewalls that can't interpret SSL data. At this writing, more firewalls are expected to implement SSL acceleration, which will enable firewalls to **terminate** SSL connections. However, processing the encrypted data will add to firewall latency, which is the slowdown in performance that results from encryption and other functions.

An actual SSL session makes use of both symmetric and asymmetric keys. The asymmetric keys are used to start an SSL session, but symmetric keys are then dynamically generated for the bulk of the transfer.

The following lists the steps involved in an SSL data transaction:

1. Client connects to Web server using SSL protocol.

2. The two machines arrange a "handshake," during which they authenticate each other and determine what formulas and protocols will be used to encrypt and exchange information. The client sends the server its preferences for "cipher settings," the SSL version number, and a randomly generated number to be used later.

3. The server responds with SSL version number and its own cipher preferences, along with its digital certificate. The digital certificate tells the client who issued it, a data range, and the public key of the server. The server may ask the client for its own digital certificate at this point.

4. The client verifies that the date and other information on the digital certificate is valid. The domain name on the digital certificate is checked to see if it matches the domain name of the server. If it matches, the client generates a "pre-master" code and sends it to the server using the server's public key. The client's digital certificate is also sent if one was requested by the server.

5. The server uses its private key to decode the pre-master code sent by the client. The server generates a "master secret" that will be used by both client and server to generate session keys—symmetric keys that will be used only for the duration of the session because of their efficiency.

6. The session keys are generated and used to encrypt the data going from client to server.

USING IPSEC ENCRYPTION

Firewalls can create VPNs using IPSec. IPSec creates a secure IP connection between two computers, operates under the Application layer, and is transparent to the user. An IPSec-enabled computer can automatically protect e-mail, Web traffic, and file transfers using FTP. If you choose to install a firewall that supports encryption, you are very likely to use IPSec, so it pays to know something about this powerful and increasingly popular protocol.

For many businesses that need to exchange information securely over the Internet, a VPN based on IPSec is the approach of choice.

Understanding IPSec

Other encryption methods discussed in this chapter, such as PGP, encrypt e-mail messages or other content. IPSec works differently—it encrypts the IP connections between computers. IPSec, which is supported by both Windows 2000 and XP as well as Linux, the Mac OS, and other operating systems, is a set of standards and software tools. It was created by the IETF as a set of protocols that would function with both IP Version 4 (IPv4) and IP Version 6 (IPv6). IPv6 is the newest version of IP; it supports 128-bit addressing and contains other improvements to IPv4. It can also be used as an extension to IPv4 in systems, such as Windows 2000, that do not yet support IPv6.

Windows 2000 does support IPv6 with a free upgrade from Microsoft (you can find it at *http://msdn.microsoft.com/downloads/sdks/platform/tpipv6.asp*). Microsoft does not recommend the implementation of IPv6 in Windows 2000 in production environments as yet because applications, other operating systems, and network infrastructure don't widely support the new protocol.

IPSec allows a packet to specify a mechanism for authenticating its origin, ensuring data integrity, and ensuring privacy. Two computers that both have IPSec enabled authenticate each other when they establish a connection and then can transfer data using encryption. In addition, you can send data from one IPSec-enabled machine to another in tunnel mode, as though the two machines were on a VPN but without the expense and trouble of actually installing VPN hardware and/or software.

Modes of IPSec

IPSec works in two modes: **transport mode** or **tunnel mode**. You can specify the use of one or the other mode in your security policy. The one you choose depends on the type of network you have and whether it uses NAT. In transport mode, IPSec authenticates two computers that establish a connection. It can also optionally encrypt data sent between the computers. In tunnel mode, IPSec encapsulates packets sent between two connected computers and can optionally encrypt them as well.

Note that tunnel mode encrypts packet headers rather than the data payload of packets. If your network uses NAT, you should probably use transport mode. You should do so because tunnel mode is incompatible with NAT: tunnel mode encrypts packet headers, but NAT alters those headers as they pass through the network, with the result that they may be interpreted as invalid by a firewall at the receiving network and then dropped.

IPSec Protocols

In each of its two modes, IPSec can make use of two different protocols: **Authentication Header (AH)** and **Encapsulation Security Payload (ESP)**.

AH

AH is an IPSec protocol that adds a digital signature to packets to protect against repeat attacks, spoofing, or other tampering. It is used to verify that parts of the packet headers, such as the source and destination IP addresses, have not been altered on the way from the client to the IPSec-enabled host. If the packet fails this verification test, it is dropped. The signature and authentication header are added to a normal TCP/IP packet header, which retains its IP header and TCP header information, as shown in Figure 7-15.

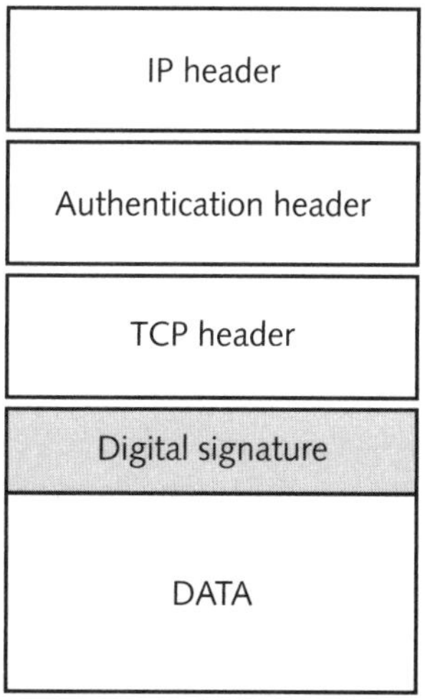

```
┌─────────────────────────┐
│       IP header         │
├─────────────────────────┤
│  Authentication header  │
├─────────────────────────┤
│       TCP header        │
├─────────────────────────┤
│    Digital signature    │
├─────────────────────────┤
│                         │
│         DATA            │
│                         │
└─────────────────────────┘
```

Figure 7-15   Authentication header and digital signature added to a TCP/IP packet

AH has one big drawback: it is incompatible with NAT. NAT changes the IP addresses of packets when they leave the network; such changes will be interpreted as security violations by AH. For that reason, AH is not frequently used.

ESP

ESP is a more robust IPSec protocol than AH, providing both confidentiality and message integrity. ESP encrypts the data payload of an IP packet (see Figure 7-16).

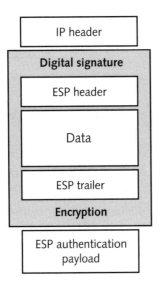

Figure 7-16   ESP data encryption

As you can see, a digital signature as well as an ESP header and trailer enclose the data part of a packet that is protected with ESP. In addition, an ESP authentication payload is added to the end of the packet for even stronger protection. However, ESP has a downside: it can cause problems with firewalls that use NAT.

In transport mode, ESP conceals the port number information in packet headers. Such changes will be seen as a violation by an IPSec-compliant device running in transport mode, and the packets will be dropped. In tunnel mode, ESP conceals the TCP or UDP header information of packets. However, if your firewall uses **Static Network Address Port Translation (NAPT)** and IPSec using the ESP protocol, packets will pass through because only the IP address information is translated—and because the client initiates the connection to the remote server over UDP Port 500 to begin the data exchange. When this "handshake" part of the connection is complete and the client sends actual packets to the NAPT device, the source port and IP address is concealed, but the NAPT device forwards the packet to the remote host anyway because a connection was already established with that remote host.

If you use a VPN device such as Cisco Systems' Cisco 3060 and its associated VPN client, and your existing firewall uses NAT, you should use static NAPT and configure the Cisco 3060 to use EPS in tunnel mode.

Components of IPSec

Besides its two modes and two protocols, IPSec uses a number of other components to protect communications:

- **IPSec driver:** Software that performs protocol-level tasks needed to encrypt, decrypt, authenticate, and verify packets.

- **Internet Key Exchange (IKE):** A protocol that generates security keys (very long sequences of numerals and characters generated by algorithms) for IPSec and other protocols.

- **Internet Security Association Key Management Protocol (ISAKMP):** An IPSec protocol that enables two computers to reach agreed-upon security settings and securely exchange security keys so they can communicate with encryption.

- **Oakley:** A protocol that uses the Diffie-Hellman algorithm to generate a master key as well as session-specific keys that can be used for IPSec communications.

- **IPSec Policy Agent:** A Windows 2000 service that retrieves IPSec policy settings from Active Directory and applies them upon system startup.

How To Choose the Best IPSec Mode for Your Organization

The combination of two modes (transport mode and tunnel mode) plus two protocols (AH and ESP) give you four possible choices on how to use IPSec, as illustrated in Table 7-2.

Table 7-2   IPSec communications alternatives

IPSec Protocol and Mode	When To Use
ESP plus Transport mode	You need to preserve both data integrity and confidentiality and your network does not use a VPN.
AH plus Transport mode	You need to preserve data integrity but communications aren't critical and you don't need confidentiality.
ESP plus Tunnel mode	You need to preserve data integrity and confidentiality and aren't using NAT—and, your network uses a VPN.
AH plus Tunnel mode	You use a VPN and your firewall performs NAT.

Given that ESP conceals IP header information and tunnel mode can both encapsulate and encrypt packets, ESP plus tunnel mode provides you with the best level of protection.

Enabling IPSec

If you're a network administrator and your security policy specifies IPSec, you need to select a group policy security setting for any computers that need to communicate with enhanced security. When a computer initiates a session with another IPSec-enabled computer, the following happens:

1. The IPSec driver and the ISAKMP retrieve the IPSec policy settings.

2. ISAKMP negotiates between hosts, based on their policy settings, and builds a security association (SA) between them.

3. The Oakley protocol generates a master key that is used to secure IPSec communications.

4. Based on the security policy established for the session, the IPSec driver monitors, filters, and secures the Transport layer against network traffic.

You need to define an IPSec policy at the group policy level if you work in a Windows 2000 domain. If you are not in a Windows 2000 domain, you define IPSec policy at the local policy level, as shown in Figure 7-17.

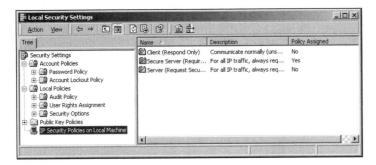

Figure 7-17   IPSec policy set at the local policy level

In Windows 2000 or XP, you choose one of the following predefined IPSec policy levels:

- *Client (Respond Only)*: A computer itself does not initiate communications using IPSec but can participate when another computer requires it.

- *Server (Request Security)*: A middle-ground policy in which a host requests that IPSec be used to communicate, but if the other computer is not configured for IPSec, the two machines can still communicate.

- *Secure Server (Require Security)*: The highest IPSec security level—a host with IPSec enabled will only communicate with other IPSec-enabled hosts.

IPSec cannot be used through any process that translates addresses, such as a firewall that does NAT. If you need to use IPSec between a private and public network through a firewall, you need to open two ports if you use ESP and one port if you use AH. For IPSec AH traffic, open IP protocol ID 51. For IPSec ESP traffic, open IP protocol ID 50 and UDP Port 500.

Keep in mind that the higher the security level you choose, the greater the negative effect on network performance. For more about IPSec and tunneling, see Chapter 9.

Limitations of IPSec

The preceding details about IPSec might well suggest that it can create a perfectly secure encrypted means of communication between two computers. In fact, IPSec has a number of limitations:

- If the machine that runs IPSec-compliant software has already been compromised, none of the communications that come from that machine, including IPSec communications, can be trusted.

- IPSec encrypts the IP connection between two machines—it does not encrypt the body of e-mail messages or the content of other communications. (It can encrypt e-mail, but only at the level of the IP addresses used to transmit and receive the messages; it doesn't encrypt the individual words within a message.)

- IPSec is usually used to encrypt IP information at the gateway of one network and decrypt it at the gateway of the receiving network. It's not an end-to-end (in other words, end user to end user) security method.

- Whereas digital certificates are used to authenticate individual users, IPSec only authenticates machines. You can't use IPSec to ensure that the person you expect to be using a machine is actually operating it.

- IPSec doesn't prevent hackers from intercepting encrypted packets and attempting to learn about a network by reading the unencrypted parts of packets, such as source and destination gateway addresses, packet size, and so on.

Despite these limitations, IPSec does create secure connections between machines that communicate using IP, particularly over untrusted networks. Many organizations use IPSec to create a VPN linking several different branch offices, which can then communicate over the Internet.

 You'll find an excellent FAQs about IPSec, explaining the advantages and disadvantages of the protocol, at *www.freeswan.org/freeswan_trees/freeswan=1.91/*.

CHAPTER SUMMARY

This chapter introduced you to an important tool used to protect a network and its individual users: encryption. Encryption is the process of concealing information so as to render it unreadable to all but the intended recipients. Consider the following aspects of encryption that were covered in this chapter:

◻ The purpose of encryption is to preserve the integrity and confidentiality of information and to authenticate individual users. Encrypted code is an important part of a digital certificate, which is an electronic document that contains a digital signature as well as information about the authenticity of the digital certificate's owner.

◻ Many digital certificates are used to transport public keys from one user or computer to another. Public keys are blocks of encoded information consisting of many bits (1024, 2048, or 4096, for example) of digital information. A public key is exchanged freely on the Internet and is generated by a private key—another long block of encoded information that is generated by a formula called an algorithm. This key is always kept secret by its owner.

◻ Organizations and individuals can receive digital certificates from a CA. Digital certificates and public and private keys can be issued by a RA, which is part of an organization's PKI. PGP, in contrast, issues its own digital certificates, which users exchange with one another to establish a "Web of Trust."

◻ Some firewalls, such as Check Point FireWall-1, use their own encryption schemes and support the use of several popular encryption methods. Encryption can also be used by specialized software, such as PGP. Web servers also support SSL encryption to secure Web-based communications. All of these methods protect information as it passes between one network and another.

◻ PGP is a hybrid system that makes use of both asymmetric and symmetric cryptography. Symmetric cryptography makes use of only one key to encrypt and decrypt communications, while symmetric cryptography uses a public-private key pair. SSL encrypts communications between a client and server on the Web, whereas IPSec conceals IP header information in individual packets.

◻ Whereas digital certificates are used to authenticate individual users, IPSec authenticates machines. IPSec is frequently used in establishing a VPN for secure, encrypted communications.

KEY TERMS

asymmetric key encryption — Encryption that involves the use of public and private keys (also called public key encryption).

Authentication Header (AH) — An IPSec protocol that adds a digital signature to packets to protect against repeat attacks, spoofing, or other tampering.

Certification Authority (CA) — An entity that grants digital certificates and verifies the identity of their owners.

ciphertext — Ordinary text that has been rendered unreadable as a result of encryption.

client-based digital certificates — Digital certificates that a user obtains from a CA, which issues them and vouches for the owner's identity.

Diffie-Hellman encryption — Stronger than RSA; it uses two large numbers that are processed by an algorithm.

digital certificate — An electronic document issued by a CA that contains a digital signature and other information, and that verifies the identity of the possessor.

digital signature — A series of numerals and characters generated by an encryption process that is easily transportable, can be time-stamped, and is commonly used to authenticate the identify of the person who possesses it.

Encapsulation Security Payload (ESP) — One of two protocols available for use with IPSec. It is considered more robust than the other IPSec protocol, AH, because it encrypts the data part of packets as well as the headers.

encryption — The process of encoding and decoding information to preserve its integrity, maintain privacy, and ensure the identity of the users participating in the encrypted data session.

hash — An encrypted password created by an algorithm called a hash function that is used to protect information. A hash is also called a fingerprint or digest and can be used as part of a digital certificate.

hybrid — A security method (for example, PGP) that uses both symmetric and asymmetric cryptography to obtain the advantages of both approaches.

Internet Engineering Task Force (IETF) — A group of individuals and organizations that seeks to keep the Internet running smoothly and safely.

Internet Key Exchange (IKE) — A protocol that generates security keys for IPSec and other protocols.

Internet Protocol Security (IPSec) — An IETF-standardized encryption protocol based on the IP protocol that encrypts IP header information and is used to authenticate computers.

Internet Security Association Key Management Protocol (ISAKMP) — An IPSec protocol that enables two computers to reach agreed-upon security settings and securely exchange security keys so they can communicate with encryption.

IPSec driver — Software that performs protocol-level tasks needed to encrypt, decrypt, authenticate, and verify packets.

IPSec Policy Agent — A Windows 2000 service that retrieves IPSec policy settings from Active Directory and applies them upon system start-up.

key — A value that can be processed by an algorithm to encrypt text or to decrypt text that has already been encrypted.

key server — A program that holds and distributes keys on a network.

Lightweight Directory Access Protocol (LDAP) — A database that holds names of users and digital certificates and is publicly available. Any client can connect to the database using LDAP to verify someone or something's identity.

7

man-in-the-middle attack — An attack in which a hacker intercepts the public key being exchanged by two individuals using encryption. The hacker substitutes his or her own public key to impersonate the recipient.

nonrepudiation — The use of encryption to prevent one participant in an electronic transaction from denying that it performed an action. Nonrepudiation uses digital signatures to ensure that an electronic transaction occurred, that an action was performed by the legitimate originating party, and that the party that was supposed to receive something as a result of the transaction actually received that result.

Oakley — A protocol that uses the Diffie-Hellman algorithm to generate a master key as well as session-specific keys that can be used for IPSec communications.

Pretty Good Privacy (PGP) — A personal encryption system developed by Phil Zimmerman that uses both symmetric and asymmetric encryption; it relies on a "Web of Trust" in which users authenticate one another by exchanging public keys.

private key — One of two keys used in public key cryptography. The private key is never exchanged but is used to generate a public key that can be exchanged freely on the Internet.

public key — One of two keys used in public key cryptography. Individuals who want to encrypt communications exchange their public keys and then use those keys to perform the encryption.

Public-Key Infrastructure (PKI) — A system used to store, distribute, and manage public and private keys within an organization.

Registration Authority (RA) — A networked resource that individuals can use to apply for digital certificates.

Rivest-Shamir-Adleman (RSA) encryption — Used for older versions of PGP.

server-based digital certificates — Digital certificates issued by a CA to a company that issues them to individuals.

session hijacks — Attacks that involve a communication session that has already been established between a server and a client.

session keys — Symmetric keys that are used only for the duration of one communications session because of their efficiency.

Static Network Address Port Translation (NAPT) — Makes use of static rather than dynamic IP addresses and conceals the source IP address and source port number when a packet leaves the public interface of a router or firewall.

symmetric key encryption — The use of only one key to encrypt information, rather than a public-private key system. The same key is used to encrypt and decrypt a message; both sender and recipient must have the same key.

terminate — Drop or end a communication session.

transport mode — One of two communications modes supported by IPSec. In transport mode, IPSec authenticates two computers that establish a connection. IPSec also encrypts communications in transport mode without using a tunnel.

tunnel mode — One of two communications modes supported by IPSec. In tunnel mode, IPSec encapsulates IP packets and can optionally encrypt them.

wipe — Remove all traces of a file from a disk permanently.

REVIEW QUESTIONS

1. Encryption is used to protect data that is _____.
   a. leaving the internal network
   b. passing through the Internet to a remote server
   c. leaving a remote network's gateway on the way to an internal network's firewall
   d. arriving at the perimeter of the network being protected

2. Encryption preserves what aspect of digital data passing between networks? (Choose all that apply.)
   a. integrity
   b. authenticity
   c. accuracy
   d. reliability

3. Which function of a firewall might not be compatible with encryption?
   a. proxy services
   b. packet filtering
   c. NAT
   d. none of the above

4. Which of the following aspects of firewalls is made worse by encryption?
   a. operating system compatibility
   b. latency
   c. the need for load balancing
   d. complexity

5 An attack in which a hacker intercepts a public key is called a _____.
   a. denial of service attack
   b. trojan horse
   c. man-in-the-middle attack
   d. brute force attack

6. What is the difference between a digital signature and a digital certificate?

7. What is the main advantage of using symmetrical encryption?
   a. security
   b. authenticity
   c. integrity
   d. speed

7

8. What is the advantage of using asymmetrical encryption?

   a. speed

   b. authenticity

   c. security

   d. integrity

9. You handle security for a corporation with 10 branch offices and 5,000 employees. You are tasked with issuing security keys to each of these employees. How would you handle this?

10. Which of the following provides for authentication?

    a. IPv4

    b. tunnel mode

    c. Oakley

    d. transport mode

11. IPSec can save you the time and expense of installing a _____.

    a. firewall

    b. VPN

    c. subnet

    d. bastion host

12. What does an IPSec policy do?

    a. It defines the level of security to be used by IPSec-enabled computers.

    b. It decides whether to encrypt data.

    c. It specifies whether to use transport mode or tunnel mode.

    d. It specifies whether IPv6 or IPv4 is to be used.

13. In what environment would you specify an IPSec policy in Group Policy?

    a. in any mid- to large-scale corporate environment

    b. in a Windows 2000 domain

    c. in a specified user group

    d. in a workgroup

14. X.509 digital certificates make use of _____.

    a. the Internet Engineering Task Force (IETF)

    b. a root digital Certificate Authority (CA)

    c. a Public Key Infrastructure (PKI)

    d. a Key Distribution Center (KDC)

15. As you learned in this chapter, IPSec has two modes and two protocols. Which combination of modes and protocols gives you the highest level of protection? Explain your answer.

16. What can digital certificates authenticate that IPSec cannot?

    a. groups

    b. packets

    c. machines

    d. individuals

17. Digital certificates contain digital signatures and public keys as well as detailed information about the digital certificate holder. However, the quality of all that information depends on one thing that neither you nor the digital certificate holder can control. What is it?

    a. the strength of the encryption method

    b. the identity of the digital certificate holder

    c. the reliability of the Certificate Authority (CA)

    d. the level of effort with which the public or private keys can be "cracked"

18. What function of PGP can effectively erase unencrypted files from hard disks?

    a. wiping

    b. signing

    c. importing

    d. exporting

19. Which of the following is a "hybrid" security scheme that uses both symmetric and asymmetric encryption? (Choose all that apply.)

    a. digital certificates

    b. Internet Protocol Security (IPS)

    c. Secure Sockets Layer (SSL)

    d. Pretty Good Privacy (PGP)

20. What do the terms "thumbprint" or "fingerprint" mean in the context of encryption?

HANDS-ON PROJECTS

Project 7-1: Install and Configure PGP

You can gain a good deal of experience with encryption by installing and configuring the free version of the highly-regarded program PGP. With PGP, you obtain your own keys, import someone else's public key so that you can exchange encrypted e-mail messages with that individual, encrypt files, authenticate yourself to other users, and import X.509 digital certificates. To get started, you need to install and configure the program on a Windows 2000 or XP workstation, as described in the following steps.

You need to have WinZip (if you use Windows) or WinRAR (if you are on Linux) already installed on your workstation to extract the PGP files. PGP Freeware can be downloaded only by users in the U.S. and Canada; it cannot be exported to other countries. If you live outside the U.S. or Canada and want to make use of PGP technology, visit the Network Associates site to download a 30-day trial version of a commercial product that incorporates PGP into its operations, such as McAfee Desktop Firewall (*www.mcafeeb2b.com/ products/desktop-firewall/default.asp*).

1. Double-click the **Internet Explorer** icon on your Windows desktop.

2. Type **http://web.mit.edu/network/pgp.html** in the Address box, and then press **Enter**. The MIT Distribution Center for PGP (Pretty Good Privacy) Web page opens.

3. Scroll down the page, and click the link for the version of PGP that matches your workstation's operating system. PGP Freeware is available for Linux, Unix, the Mac OS, and many versions of Windows.

4. The PGP Distribution Authorization Form opens. Fill out the form by choosing options from the various menus, and then click **Submit**. The Welcome to the PGP Freeware Distribution Page opens.

5. Click the link for the version of PGP that you want, and download the file to your computer.

6. Save the PGP files in a directory on your computer. Open WinZip to unzip the PGP file. Then double-click the file **setup.exe** to install the software. Follow the steps presented to you by the installation wizard to install the program. In the screen of the wizard entitled Select Components, make sure the boxes are checked next to **PGP Microsoft Exchange/Outlook Pulgin**, **PGP Microsoft Outlook Express Plugin**, **PGP Key Management (required)**, and **PGP User's Guide**.

7. When installation is complete, PGP starts and you are presented with the first screen of Key Generation Wizard. Click **Next** to follow the steps shown in the wizard to have PGP generate your own public/private key pair.

8. Unless you expect to exchange messages with individuals who use older versions of PGP, choose the Diffie-Hellman/DSS algorithm to generate your key pair. It's a newer algorithm and considered stronger than the other RSA formula that is supported by PGP. Also select a standard 2048-bit key size.

9. Click **Next**. Click **Key pair never expires**, and then click **Next**.

10. In the Passphrase box, type a passphrase. Retype the passphrase in the Confirmation box, and then click **Next**.

11. When you are asked if you want to send your key to the root server, leave the box unchecked.

12. Click **Finish**. The Key Generation Wizard closes and the PGPkeys window opens, showing all of the keys on your keyring. (PGP automatically gives you a set of keys, or keyring, belonging to the program's developers.)

13. Double-click your own DSS exportable signature to open it. The Certificate Properties dialog box opens.

14. Click **Show Signing Key Properties**. What does the digital "fingerprint" of your key consist of? (Give two versions.) Write the answer in your lab book or in a word-processing document.

15. Click **Close** to close the Properties dialog box for your key, and then click **Close** to close the Certificate Properties dialog box and return to the PGPkeys window.

16. Click **File** and then click **Exit**. Click either **Save Backup Now** or **Don't Save** in the PGPkeys dialog box.

Project 7-2: Use a Public Key Server

A key server is a site on the Internet that stores keys so that PGP users can exchange them. The public key server provided by MIT at *http://pgpkeys.mit.edu* lets you upload your own key to the server so that others can view it or import it to their own version of the PGP software. In this project, you'll first post your PGP public key to the server. Then, you or another student can extract the key to your Windows 2000 or XP work-station by following these steps. (You can even recruit a classmate to extract your key; you, in turn, can extract that student's key.)

> When you submit your key to the public key server, the server forwards it to other key servers around the world; they, in turn, forward the key to other servers as well, so be sure you want to do this. If you need more help with the PGP public key site, go to the Help page for the PGP Public Key site at *http://pgpkeys.mit.edu/extracthelp.html*.

1. Click **Start**, point to **Programs** (or **All Programs** in Windows XP), point to **PGP**, and then click **PGPtray** to add the PGPtray to the system tray, if necessary. Click the **PGPtray** icon in the Windows system tray, and then click **PGPkeys** on the pop-up menu. The PGPkeys window opens.

2. Click your own name in the list of keys available to you in your keyring to highlight it.

3. Click **Keys** and click **Export**. The Export Key to File dialog box opens.

4. Select a directory on your computer where you want to export the ASCII (plain text) version of your public key, and then click **Save**.

5. Click **Start**, point to **Programs** (**All Programs**, if you use Windows XP), point to **Accessories**, and click **Notepad**.

6. Click **File** and click **Open**. In the Open dialog box, click **All Files** from the Files of type list box. Then locate the plain text version of your key (the file name will be your own name plus the .asc extension). Click on the file to select it, and then click **Open**.

7. View your public key file, and then click **Edit** and click **Select All** to highlight the entire file.

8. Click **Edit** and click **Copy** to copy the public key file to your computer's clipboard.

9. Click **Start**, point to **Programs** (or **All Programs** in Windows XP), and click **Internet Explorer** to launch your Web browser.

10. Type **http://pgpkeys.mit.edu** in the Address box, and then press **Enter**. The MIT PGP Key Server Web page opens.

11. Scroll down the Web page to the Submit a Key section. Click in the large text box to position the cursor within it. Then press **Ctrl+V** to paste the key you copied earlier.

12. Click the **Submit this key to the keyserver!** button. A Web page opens stating that the key has been added to the server.

13. Click your browser's **Back** button to return to the MIT PGP Key Server Web page. To verify that your own key has been added, type the KeyID in the Search String box at the top of the page, and then click **Do the search!**. A Web page should appear with information verifying your identity as the holder of the key. What information is provided on this page? Write down the answer in a word-processing document or a lab manual.

 To find your KeyID, expand your name in the list of keys in the PGPkeys window. Double-click your DSS exportable signature to display the Certificate Properties dialog box. Copy or write down the code in the Signer KeyID box: this is the number you use to search for a key on the Key Server Web site.

14. Obtain the KeyID of one of your classmates. Type it in the Search String box on the MIT PGP Key Server Web page, and click **Do the search!**.

15. On the Web page that displays the key holder's information, click the **KeyID** link. The user's public key opens on a separate Web page. You can now add your classmate's key to your keyring, as described in the following project.

Project 7-3: Import Someone Else's Public Key

After you obtain someone else's public key from a key server, you can add it to your PGP keyring. Then you can exchange encrypted e-mail messages with that individual. The following steps assume you are using a Windows 2000 or XP computer.

1. Double-click the **Internet Explorer** icon on your desktop to start your browser.

2. Type **http://pgpkeys.mit.edu** in your browser's Address box, and then press **Enter**. Type the KeyID for the individual whose key you want to obtain in the Search String box, and then click **Do the search!**.

3. Click the **KeyID** link on the Web page that opens with information about the holder of the key you have found. The plain-text version of the key opens on a separate Web page.

4. Click **Edit** and click **Select All** to highlight the public key in the browser window.

5. Click **Edit** and click **Copy** to copy the key to your computer's clipboard.

6. Click the **PGPtray** icon in your Windows system tray, and click **PGPkeys** on the pop-up menu. The PGPkeys window opens.

7. Press **Ctrl+V** or click **Edit** and click **Paste** on the PGPkeys menu bar. The Select key(s) dialog box opens, displaying the name of the owner of the key you are pasting.

8. Highlight the name of the key holder, and then click **Import**. The name is added to the list of keys in your keyring.

9. Click **File** and click **Exit** to close the PGPkeys window.

7

Project 7-4: Encrypt and Sign an E-Mail Attachment

PGP comes with several plug-ins that can be used to automatically encrypt and decrypt e-mail messages and attachments. However, the plug-ins work primarily with the e-mail program Eudora, and not with all versions of Outlook or Outlook Express. No matter what e-mail program you use, however, after you have obtained a public/private key pair from the PGP software, you can encrypt an e-mail attachment using Windows Explorer. You then can send it in the body of an e-mail message or from a public key server to someone whose public key you have already obtained (see Project 7-2).

1. Prepare the file you want to attach. You can use virtually any file except the plain-text version of your own public key file, which PGP regards as already encrypted.

2. Click **Start**, point to **Programs** (or **All Programs** in Windows XP), point to **Accessories**, and click **Windows Explorer**.

3. In the Windows Explorer window, locate the file you want to encrypt. Right-click the file, point to **PGP**, and click **Encrypt & Sign** from the pop-up menu. The PGPshell – Key Selection Dialog box opens.

4. Click and hold on the name the recipient—whose PGP key you should already have on your keyring—and drag that person's name into the **Recipients** box near the bottom of the PGPshell – Key Selection dialog box. If you obtained a classmate's key as described in Project 7-2, drag that person's name into **Recipients**. Otherwise, drag your own name into **Recipients**.

Selecting the recipient as described in Step 4 tells PGP to encrypt the attachment using the recipient's public key. The recipient can then decrypt the message using his or her private key.

5. Click **OK**. The PGPshell – Enter Passphrase dialog box opens.

6. In the box labeled "Enter passphrase for above key:" type the passphrase you created when you first installed and configured PGP (see Project 7-1) in the text box. Then click **OK**.

7. The PGPshell – Enter Passphrase dialog box closes, and the file is encrypted.

8. In the Windows Explorer window, check the directory where the original file is located. You should now see two versions of the file: what are they, and what file extension is unique to the second version? Write the answer in a lab manual or word-processing program.

9. Open your e-mail program and compose a message to the recipient you identified in Step 4. (If you are the recipient, address the e-mail message to yourself.)

10. Attach the encrypted file and send the message.

11. If you sent the message to a classmate, ask that person to check his or her e-mail and open the file when it arrives. If you sent the message to yourself, check your own e-mail and open the file.

12. Click the attachment (if you use Netscape Messenger) or right-click the attachment (if you use Outlook Express) and save it to your Windows desktop. The PGPtools – Enter Passphrase dialog box opens. Enter your passphrase so PGP can use your private key to decrypt the file, and then click **OK**.

13. The PGP log dialog box opens, notifying you that the attachment was decrypted and that it came from a valid digital certificate holder. Close PGPlog.

14. Check your desktop: the encrypted file should be there, along with the decrypted file you originally encrypted.

Project 7-5: Generate a Subkey

If you generate your private-public key pair using the Diffie-Hellman encryption scheme (as described in Project 7-1), you gain the ability to generate subkeys that are associated with your "master" key. By setting up one or more subkeys, you can create or revoke encryption keys without having to generate a new public-private key pair. The following steps assume you are using a Windows 2000 or XP computer.

1. Click the **PGPtray** icon in the Windows system tray, and click **PGPkeys** from the pop-up menu to open the **PGPkeys** window.

2. Right-click your own name in the list of keys in your keyring, and click **Key Properties** from the pop-up menu. The Properties dialog box for your key opens.

3. Click the **Subkeys** tab to bring it to the front.

4. Click the **New** button.

5. In the New Subkey dialog box, select a size for your subkey in the Key Size list box. What standard key size options are available to you? If you try to enter a custom key size, how large a size can you enter? Write the answers in a word-processing document or lab manual.

6. If you want to choose a start date other than the default date (today's date), click the **Start Date** list arrow. A miniature calendar opens. Click a date to select it (you can move from month to month by clicking the arrows at the top of the miniature calendar).

7. Select an expiration date. If you want the subkey to never expire, check **Never**. If you want to specify an expiration date, click the **Date** button, and select a date from the miniature calendar that opens when you click the **Date** list arrow.

8. Click **OK**. The PGP Enter Passphrase for Key dialog box opens.

9. Type your PGP private key passphrase, and then click **OK**. PGP generates your subkey, and the subkey is listed in the Subkey window.

10. Click **Close** to close the Properties dialog box for your key.

11. Click **File** and click **Exit** to close the PGPkeys window and return to the Windows desktop.

Project 7-6: Import an X.509 Digital Certificate from a Root CA

PGP creates its own digital certificates, which you can use to sign e-mail attachments and other communications you exchange with other individuals. You can also import digital certificates that use the X.509 protocol into PGP, so that PGP can use those digital certificates if needed. You can obtain such digital certificates from a variety of CAs such as VeriSign or Thawte. Your Web browser also comes with digital certificates from a number of such CAs, so it's easiest to use one of those resources first. The following steps apply to Windows 2000 or XP computers.

The freeware version of PGP that you downloaded and installed in Project 7-1 does not actually support importing of X.509 digital certificates. You need to download a trial version of the commercial version of PGP to actually use this feature. However, it's still useful to follow the steps now so that you'll know what to do if, in future, you do work with an encryption program that does support X.509 digital certificates.

1. Double-click the **Internet Explorer** icon on your Windows desktop to start your Web browser.

2. Click **Tools** and click **Internet Options** to open the Options dialog box.

3. Click the **Content** tab to bring it to the front.

4. Click **Certificates**.

5. In the Certificates dialog box, click the **Trusted Root Certification Authorities** tab to bring it to the front.

6. Scroll down the list of digital certificates, and click **VeriSign Individual Software Publishers CA** if you have this option. Be sure to select a digital certificate with an expiration date that has not yet occurred. (If you don't have a VeriSign digital certificate, pick one from Thawte or another CA.)

7. Click **View**. The Certificate dialog box opens.

8. Click the **Details** tab to bring it to the front.

9. Scroll down the list of certificate details, and click **Public key**. The key code opens in the bottom half of the Certificate dialog box.

10. Click **Copy to File**. The Certificate Export Wizard opens.

11. Click **Next**.

12. In the Export File Format screen, click **Base-64 encoded X.509 (.CER)**, and then click **Next**.

13. In the File to Export screen, type a filename for the file, such as **VeriSign.cer** or **Thawte.cer**, and then click **Next**.

14. Click **Finish**, then click **OK** when a dialog box opens stating that the export was successful.

15. View the digital certificate you just exported by clicking **Start**, pointing to **Programs** (or **All Programs** in Windows XP), pointing to **Accessories**, and clicking **Notepad**.

16. Click **File** on Notepad's menu bar and click **Open**, and locate the file you just exported. Click **Open**.

17. When the file opens, click **Edit** and click **Select All**.

18. Click **Edit** and click **Copy** to copy the digital certificate to your computer's clipboard.

19. Click the **PGPtray** icon in your system tray, and click **PGPkeys** on the pop-up menu.

20. Press **Ctrl+V** to paste the digital certificate into PGPkeys. Click **Import** in the Select keys(s) dialog box.

21. Click **Edit** and click **Options** on the PGPkeys menu bar.

22. In the PGP Options dialog box, click the **CA** tab to bring it to the front.

23. Click **Select Certificate**. The Select X.509 Certificate dialog box opens with the digital certificate you just exported displayed in it.

24. Click the name of the X.509 digital certificate to highlight it, and then click **OK**. You return to the PGP Options dialog box. What is different about the dialog box now? Write the answer in a word-processing document or lab manual.

25. Type the URL for the CA, such as **http://www.verisign.com**, in the URL text box.

26. Click **OK** to close PGP Options.

27. Click **File** and click **Exit** to close PGPkeys and return to the Windows desktop.

CASE PROJECTS

Case 7-1: Analyzing Security Problems

You are assigned to set up members of a partner company with user accounts that will give them access to critical files on your network. However, you have heard that the company has had security problems in their own network and you don't entirely trust that they will always exchange "genuine" communications with you that have not been intercepted by hackers. How would you ensure that communications you appear to receive from the partner company are authentic?

Case 7-2: Encryption

You want to encrypt communications with a coworker in another network, but you don't necessarily want to go through the effort of setting up a VPN because your communications are going to be sporadic, not regular. How would you set up an easy, low-cost system for encrypting communications?

Case 7-3: An Intercepted Key

The digital key you use to sign e-mail messages has become compromised; you realize that someone has intercepted your public key and is attempting to impersonate you online. What can you do to make your key more secure that's quicker and easier than reinstalling a key and not as drastic as deleting the key altogether?

Case 7-4: Working with a Confidential File

You need to encrypt—not only from users on the Internet, but from your own coworkers—a confidential personal file that contains financial information. How would you make the file unreadable to outsiders while at the same time deleting any unencrypted versions of the file from your hard disk?

7

Case 7-5: Applying Encryption to the Workplace

You are employed by a company that makes corrugated boxes for use by shippers, retail stores, and moving companies. You regularly receive supplies of corrugated paper from a trusted supplier. However, when the supplier raises its rates, your company switches to a new supplier that is untrusted and untested. Management comes to you shortly after the change with the following problem: the new supplier denies that it sent a shipment of 10,000 feet of corrugated paper. Even though shipments are recorded and billed electronically and there are records of the transaction, the new supplier contends that the old supplier actually sent the shipment, pretending to be the new supplier. How can you prove the new supplier actually sent the shipment and thus provide a nonrepudiation service for your company?

8

CHOOSING A BASTION HOST

After reading this chapter and completing the exercises, you will be able to:

♦ Understand the general requirements for installing a bastion host
♦ Select the attributes—memory, processor speed, and operating system—of the bastion host
♦ Evaluate different options for positioning the bastion host, both physically and within the network
♦ Configure the bastion host
♦ Provide for backups of the bastion host operating system and data
♦ Establish a baseline performance level and audit procedures
♦ Connect the bastion host to the network

The effectiveness of a network security configuration depends on many things, and one of them is the **bastion host** that runs the firewall software or other services on the network perimeter. A bastion host is a server that (usually, but not always) has an interface on the Internet and that has been specially **hardened** (in other words, made as secure as possible) and configured to provide a limited range of services. The term *bastion* comes from medieval times and was originally used to describe a fortress or castle that has been built in such a way that it is difficult if not impossible for outsiders to invade. This describes the goal of a bastion host as well because it is a particularly secure point in a network.

The trend among corporations and other organizations is to turn to the Internet to exchange data rather than using private networks or leased lines. Such a strategy reduces telecommunications cost while decreasing the burden placed on the organization's technical support staff. A company might want to set up a public FTP server to enable customers to transfer files to and from the company's network. Universities regularly enable students to download software that they need to do their assignments, such as word-processing and spreadsheet programs, from FTP servers, for example. Such servers need to be made especially secure bastion hosts due to their public accessibility.

The bastion host is your organization's public face on the Internet. Because it is highly exposed on the network perimeter, a bastion host needs to be highly secured. Setting up a bastion host requires you to be systematic and thorough to a higher degree than you may be used to; backups, detailed record-keeping, and auditing are essential steps. This chapter discusses how to properly configure a bastion host. In particular, you'll learn about the general requirements that apply to most bastion hosts, factors to take into consideration when selecting a host machine, possible locations for the bastion host, and how to decide what functions the host should perform.

Installing a Bastion Host: General Requirements

A bastion host can be any server that hosts a Web server, e-mail server, FTP server, or other network service. However, it typically provides only one service because, as more services are offered on the bastion host, the greater the chance that a security vulnerability will result on one of the services installed on the system.

Both the hardware and software that make up a bastion host should be familiar to the network administrator. He or she uses the bastion host to facilitate configuration and to perform troubleshooting. The machine should present intruders with only a minimal set of resources and open ports: a bare bones configuration reduces the chances of attack and has the extra benefit of boosting efficiency. The fewer the resources and openings on the system, the more secure the host is.

A simple, bare-bones server may not be what the management of your own organization has in mind, however—at least initially. You're likely to receive a request from management to "install a real strong bastion host to keep out hackers." More likely, the words "bastion host" won't be used at all: you'll simply be directed to "install a firewall and keep the Web server secure." The bastion hosts don't need to contain the latest and most expensive processor/memory combinations, however. Rather, the most important requirements for a bastion host are your own level of comfort with the system, its security, and its reliability. In general, the steps you need to follow to secure a bastion host can be broken down as follows:

1. Obtain a machine with sufficient memory and processor speed.

2. Choose and install the operating system.

3. Determine where the host will fit in the network configuration, and put it in a safe and controlled physical environment.

4. Enable the host to defend itself.

5. Install the services you want to provide, or modify existing services.

6. Remove services and accounts that aren't needed.

7. Back up the system and all data on it, including log files.

8. Run a security audit.

9. Connect the machine to the network.

These are the steps that will be detailed in the sections that follow. Throughout the process, you'll develop the highest level of security if you adopt an approach that can be described as "healthy paranoia." Assume that you will be attacked, that you don't know where the attack will come from, and that you cannot trust even resources with which you are familiar.

The concept of Defense in Depth (DiD) requires hardening the system at multiple levels to minimize the possibility of intrusion. When moving data from the bastion host to other computers inside your network, that information will go through some of those layers. It's likely that, as described later in this chapter, because of its high security configuration, your bastion host will be placed in a particularly vulnerable location on the **Demilitarized Zone (DMZ)** and outside the internal LAN. Log file and system data, which needs to be backed up regularly, should go through the firewall that protects the internal LAN to screen it for viruses and other vulnerabilities such as mangled packets.

A single device alone will not enforce the security policy. However, securing the bastion host will go a long way toward creating a secure network perimeter.

8

SELECTING THE HOST MACHINE

Choose a combination of machine type and software that you are familiar with and can work on easily if you need to. You don't want to be repairing or rebuilding a machine under pressure and have to learn to operate it at the same time.

Do You Need More Than One Machine?

One thing you're going to have to decide is whether you are going to have one or more bastion hosts on the perimeter. It's ideal to have only one service on each bastion host, but this means if you have a firewall program, a Web server, an FTP server, a DNS server, and an SMTP server on the perimeter, you would need to obtain and configure five separate bastion hosts. For many organizations, this isn't always practical. The cost of obtaining multiple hosts might well be prohibitive. On the other hand, the risk of losing proprietary information can be greater.

When you're analyzing the cost of one or more bastion hosts, it's often a good idea to conduct a comprehensive risk analysis of all the resources in your organization. Even if your own company may not be able to lay out sizeable expenditures on separate hardware devices to protect every segment of your network topology, you should encourage them to at least conduct a threat assessment that identifies the most valuable information you have—the information that needs to be protected by the proper bastion host or other hardware. Refer to the list of network resources you used to develop a security policy in Chapter 2. Note that you'll have to perform the usual balancing act between cost-effectiveness and security: get as many bastion hosts as you can afford to maximize security, but on the other hand, you can combine two or more services on the bastion host if you need to save money.

No matter how many bastion hosts you purchase, be sure to get machines that have CD-RW drives, removable disk drives, or tape drives so that you can make backups.

Memory Considerations

RAM is always important when operating a server, but because the bastion host may be providing only a single service on the network, you aren't likely to need multi-gigabytes worth of RAM. Don't forget that you'll probably need to operate a program that maintains, **rotates** (in other words, moves the current log file to a storage area and opens a new log file), and clears outdated log files, in addition to the services you provide on the bastion host.

Hard disk storage space, on the other hand, should be in the multi-gigabyte category because you'll be accumulating vast quantities of **log files**—records detailing who accessed resources on the server and when the access attempts occurred. You'll need to review and analyze this information either manually or by making use of log file analysis software. You should also create a **page file** on your hard disk so that you can make use of additional memory if needed.

Processor Speed

Processor speed is the rate at which the logic circuitry of microprocessor within a computing device processes the basic instructions that make the device operate. You can tell how fast a processor is by checking your computer's system information for the clock speed of the processor, which may be called the Central Processing Unit (CPU). The clock speed is expressed in MHz (megahertz). Because the bastion host is integral to network security, you should obtain a machine with the fastest processor you can afford.

Keep in mind that the speed of the machine doesn't depend solely on the type or number of processors within it. The speed of a computer's operation on a network is also a factor of available bandwidth: a fast computer won't be able to move traffic quickly if the speed of its own Internet connection is slow.

Some security administrators believe that a slower machine used as a bastion host actually helps to deter would-be attackers because a slower machine, when it's at work, doesn't have as many resources sitting unused as a faster machine. If resources aren't available, a hacker cannot exploit them. In the real world, this doesn't mean that you should look for a slow, outdated computer to function as a bastion host; rather, it means that to keep costs down or to be able to afford multiple bastion hosts, you don't necessarily have to look for the most expensive or full-featured computer. If you are running a Web server on a bastion host, by all means get the fastest processor you can afford, so that the server will operate more smoothly and quickly on the network.

 As more firewalls are required to add Secure Sockets Layer (SSL) encryption to their list of features, as described in Chapter 7, processor speed will become even more critical so that the firewall doesn't add latency to the network.

Choosing the Operating System

Where the bastion host operating system is concerned, the most important consideration is your own familiarity with the system. If you are a UNIX person, choose UNIX. Or choose Linux if this is what you use most often. Or go with Windows. The supervisors in your organization aren't going to necessarily concern themselves with what operating system you install: their priority is that the machine protects the internal network, that you are able to get it up and running, and that you can maintain it smoothly.

UNIX and Linux Hosts

UNIX is the most popular operating system used to provide services on the World Wide Web. It contains an extensive set of software tools for development and auditing, and there is plenty of online documentation explaining how to configure the various varieties of UNIX.

The security patches you install must correspond to the operating system you choose. If you are using HP-UX, install HP-UX security patches; for AIX, install AIX patches, and so on. Installing security patches is no small undertaking. You might have six, eight, or even a dozen to install. It can also be time consuming and demanding to keep up with new patches as they come out. However, you can do this by visiting the operating system manufacturer's Web site on a periodic basis to check for the release of such patches. You may also want to install supplemental security software such as TCP Wrapper and SSH.

You also need to do logging through the **syslog** daemon; be sure to configure syslog to record messages to files. It's also useful to pick a version of UNIX that includes a utility called **chkconfig**, which reports on the services that are currently started—you can check the list of services to see if all of them are absolutely necessary or whether they should be stopped.

Windows 2000/XP Hosts

Windows 2000 and XP are also excellent choices for bastion host operating systems because of their reliability and widespread use as servers. If your network already uses Windows, the choice of Windows for the bastion host is a natural one.

If you plan to run Windows 2000 or XP on a bastion host that is intended to function solely as a Web server, you should disable the NetBIOS interface, Server service, and Workstation service as they are not needed. Also be sure to set up logging for the following events: account logon and logoff, object access, policy changes, privilege use, and system events (restart and shutdown).

Keep Your Operating System Updated

Whatever system you decide, be sure to pick a version of that system that is stable and secure. You can check these Web sites for updates that you need for your operating system:

- Windows 2000 Server (*www.microsoft.com/windows2000/server/default.asp*)

- Windows XP Professional (*www.microsoft.com/windowsxp/pro/default.asp*)

- Red Hat Linux (*www.redhat.com*)

- Linux Home Page (*www.linux.org*)

- The FreeBSD Project (*www.freebsd.org*)

- The SANS Institute's list of the Top Twenty Most Critical Internet Security Vulnerabilities, which includes subsections on UNIX and Windows vulnerabilities (*www.sans.org/top20.htm*)

- The U.S. Department of Energy's Computer Incident Advisory Capability (CIAC) site (*www.ciac.org/ciac/*), which lists newly discovered security advisories right on its home page

 Along with making sure your bastion host's operating system has the latest patches installed, make sure your system of choice can reliably provide the services you want to make available on the public DMZ.

POSITIONING THE BASTION HOST

Bastion hosts sit on the perimeter of the network. They should provide a buffer between the Internet and the internal network that is being protected. That much is straightforward, but beyond that, you do have several options for locating the host, both physically and logically within the network configuration.

Physical Location

The physical location of a bastion host is often overlooked in the process of configuring and installing it. The physical location is defined as the exact building and room in which the device is located. The room itself should be properly ventilated, with adequate cooling and a backup power system. If your organization has a specially designated server room with all the proper environmental controls (sprinklers and air conditioning) as well as the required physical security devices (deadbolt locks and alarm systems), then this is where the bastion host should be physically located. If, on the other hand, your organization does not have an isolated server room available, then at the very least, the bastion host and other critical servers should be located in a locked server cabinet that has proper ventilation and cooling and that has backup power available.

Many companies decide to **co-locate** Web servers and other bastion hosts off-site. Co-location can result in greater security and improved network **uptime** (the time the server is online). Companies that specialize in hosting services (such as NTT/Verio, shown in Figure 8-1) are protected against storms and other natural disasters. They also have electrical backup systems that can keep them online in case of power outages.

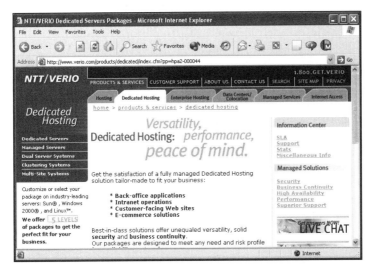

Figure 8-1   Co-locating a server can increase security and network uptime

Many hosting services are available. Because some are more secure than others, the selection of a hosting services is a process that should not be undertaken lightly or too quickly. Be sure to get references, interview the staff, and get reports on the hosting service's uptime, backup resources, environmental and security protection, and everything else about the reliability of the company. The hosting service must be able to adhere to the company's stated security, legal, and regulatory requirements. How do you determine whether a host is able to meet those requirements? Here are some specific suggestions:

- Do research and ask questions. Get an idea of how much of a track record the host has—how long has it been around? Are there any financial warning signs such as layoffs or other cutbacks?

- Get bios of senior staff. Gauge their experience and expertise. Encourage your IT professionals to visit the hosting service and get their own personal references.

- Pin the hosting service down on all the start-up fees it is going to charge as well as other fees that might come as a surprise. The contract you sign with the host should outline additional monthly fees for data backup and recovery (often these items are included in the main fee). Also, make sure you understand whether there will be any fees for help desk support and any fees for placing support calls to the host.

- Get a **Service-Level Agreement (SLA)**, a document that defines an agreed-upon level of service that the host will provide, and adjust it to fit your needs. A good SLA serves as a complete service agreement. It should address availability, response time, reliability, and monthly fees.

- Do a risk-benefit analysis. Try to quantify what you'll gain by outsourcing—how much staff time or money will you save by hiring a hosting service? Also, try to estimate how much it would cost to perform the desired function in-house.

- Ask for references. Talk to current customers; in addition, try to locate any independent software vendors (ISVs). ISVs provide to the hosting services the software that they need to lease to end users like you. These ISVs are good places to turn to for references on hosting services.

- Shop around. It's not uncommon for companies to solicit information from a dozen or more hosting services and then request full proposals from five of those companies.

Contracts typically range from 12 to 36 months, though they can get even longer. Don't get sucked into signing a long-term contract unless you're really sure of the hosting service's future.

On the downside, co-locating makes it more complicated for the administrator, who has to configure and maintain the bastion host remotely. It also extends the network perimeter into the domain of the company that is hosting the bastion host. Theoretically, this should be a highly secure network, but because it's not *your* network, you don't have ultimate control over the security measures it employs.

Network Location

A DMZ is a network of publicly accessible servers, such as Web and FTP servers, that is connected to the firewall but that is isolated from the internal network to protect internal users from intrusions and attacks. Because it has been specially secured and is prepared to defend itself against attacks, the logical location for a bastion host is in the highly vulnerable public DMZ, as shown in Figure 8-2.

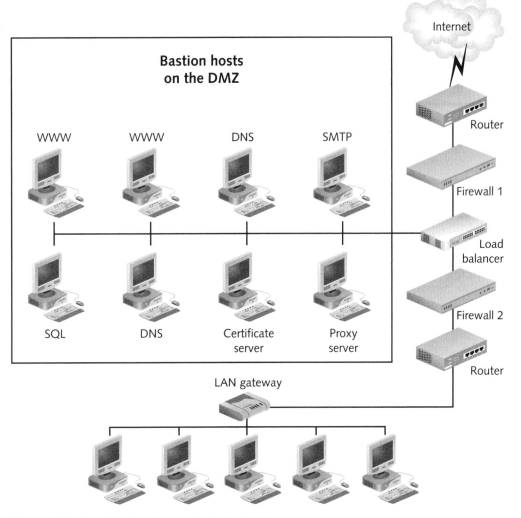

Figure 8-2   Locating bastion hosts in the DMZ

A bastion host can, however, be located at any point in a network that is considered vulnerable or where an extra level of security is needed. A bastion host should be part of a strategy of DiD, which calls for a network to be hardened at many different levels. Accordingly, a single hardened bastion host that is placed on the DMZ should not be relied upon as the sole source of security for a network. All servers or other components of the DMZ (such as routers) should be secured as well. Ideally, if one machine in the DMZ suffers a security breach, the entire DMZ will not be compromised, only weakened—and the internal network will not be compromised, either.

Securing the Machine Itself

When you install a bastion host, you need to take special steps to protect it both physically and in terms of the operating system. If you have an extra workstation available, consider using it as a spare server that you can connect to the network in case of disaster. Having spare equipment available is only one small-scale strategy that forms part of an organization's disaster recovery plan. Other aspects of such a plan include:

- How often you back up data, either on the bastion hosts or other hosts
- How to store data off-site securely (companies like Iron Mountain can collect tapes and store them at special facilities run by IBM or Comdisco)
- Where to find temporary office space in case of disaster (ideally, you should arrange for such space before the disaster occurs)
- Hardware/software insurance you might need
- How often to test your disaster program

The availability of bastion hosts is just one aspect of disaster recovery. Strategies for data backup and recovery should balance the need to balance budgets with techniques, such as co-location and contracting with businesses that specialize in data recovery, which can help a company get back online after a natural disaster or terrorist attack.

Selecting a Secure Location

Because of its prominent role in the network security configuration, you should not leave the bastion host out in the middle of an office or in a high-traffic area. The host should be physically located in a room to which only a limited number of individuals have access. Ideally, it will be protected by an alarm system that has a battery backup and that is connected to a central alarm service that can notify the police in case of trouble. A physical computer lock and cable attaching the machine to the table or rack on which it sits will provide even more protection.

Set up a password-protected screen saver on the bastion host, and configure it with a short time delay so that the screen saver switches on quickly after you finish working on the machine. Use a blank screen saver because it consumes fewer resources than an animated one.

Installing the Operating System Securely

Sometimes, the most vulnerable part of a computer (regardless of whether it is to function as a bastion host) is the operating system. When it comes to securing a bastion host, securing the operating system that is to run on that host is one of the most important activities you can undertake. In terms of the operating system, even if the machine comes with a version of a particular operating system installed, chances are that you should reinstall an operating system that you consider to be more secure and do so with a minimum configuration. For instance, if the installation disk gives you the option of a stripped-down installation, such as the HP-UX option "64-Bit Minimal HP-UX (English Only)," you should choose it. This option bypasses the installation of X-Windows and other unneeded items or services.

On a Windows 2000 or XP bastion host, create two partitions: one for the operating system (this should be the C: drive) and one for the Web server, DNS server, or other software you plan to run on the host (this could be the D: drive or another drive).

 To create a partition, you need to have Administrator status on the computer. You can then open Computer Management, click Disk Management, right-click the unallocated region of a disk drive (if there is one) of the disk drive you want to partition, and click New Partition. Then follow the steps shown in the New Partition Wizard. (Note that if there is no unallocated space on the disk drive, the New Partition option will not appear.)

Use only the NTFS file system for file storage because the NTFS security features, such as auditing and permission-level protection, are not available on the FAT file system. (In addition, NTFS meets the U.S. Government's C-2 security classification.) Install only the most essential components, such as the Microsoft Management Console, Data Sources, and the like.

Reinstalling the system is time consuming, but when you do the installation yourself from scratch, you gain a great deal of control and can decide exactly what you want to install.

Virus protection software should certainly be included on a Windows-based bastion host (antivirus software does not exist for the UNIX file system). A DNS server that is located on a bastion host in the DMZ should be configured to prohibit unauthorized zone transfers.

Documenting Your Work

It's important to document the steps you go through to secure the machine and locate backups, Emergency Recovery Disks (ERDs), and the like. Why? In case of a system crash, you want to be able to move quickly to get the host up and running again. You don't want to consume valuable time looking for such resources. You also want to make it easy for other personnel to do the repair work if you're not there when the problem occurs. To document your work, prepare a simple word-processed document. Consider giving the document a title that will quickly tell your coworkers exactly what it contains, such as "Steps to Follow in Case a Bastion Host Crashes."

Make sure your instructions include the following information:

- Name and location of the bastion host
- The bastion host's IP address and domain name
- Bastion host operating system
- Location of backup files

- What to do in case the system crashes

- The levels of the patches (if any) that have been made to the bastion host's operating system

- Any customized scripts that have been developed to support the host

Also document how you decided which services to install on each bastion host. If you can't install a single service on each host, state why you grouped the services as you did. Important services (such as HTTP) should go on one host, whereas less important services (such as chat) should go on another. Put trusted services on one bastion host, and allocate the other to services that are less trusted.

Configuring Your Bastion Host

A security policy becomes important when deciding what role the bastion host will play. Look to your security policy to determine which resources need to be protected and which threats need to be addressed. A policy that puts an emphasis on connectivity will result in a host that has a minimum of services. For instance, consider a policy that advocates a more restrictive "Deny-All" approach (an approach in which the firewall will block *everything* by default and specifically allow only those services you need on a case-by-case basis). Such an approach might call for the bastion host to function as a proxy server—a server that conceals hosts on the internal LAN by processing requests on their behalf.

The following sections describe some of the important aspects of configuring a bastion host.

Making the Host Defend Itself

Some organizations have set up a **honey pot** server: a machine that is purposely placed in the DMZ to attract hackers and direct them away from the actual servers being protected. It is supposed to be bait that is used to catch hackers. A honey pot machine is configured the same as a normal bastion host, but it requires users to log on. The honey pot bastion host seems to be a real network server and contains Web server, FTP, or DNS services, but it is not connected to any other machines on the network, and it does not contain any files of any value. If the honey pot machine is compromised, the rest of the DMZ—as well as the internal LAN—will hopefully remain secure.

 You may also hear a honey pot bastion host referred to as a "victim machine" or a "sacrificial goat."

You may also want to set up an Intrusion Detection System (IDS) on the bastion host to notify you or other IT staff of possible intrusion attempts. You have two options for installing an IDS system. You can place a host-based IDS system, such as Tripwire (*www.tripwire.com*) directly on the host itself, or a network-based IDS, such as Network Sensor by RealSecure (*www.iss.net*), on the firewall or router that protects the bastion hosts in the DMZ.

Selecting Services To Be Provided

When you perform a clean install of the operating system, you have the opportunity to choose services that you'll need, such as the primary service or services, a back-up utility, logging, and the like.

Whether the primary service you want to run on the bastion host is a Web server, FTP server, e-mail server, or proxy server, make sure the server software is the latest version. Also make sure you install any security patches or updates that are available. Table 8-1 contains URLs for the latest versions of various operating systems.

Table 8-1   Latest versions of operating systems

OS	Where To Find the Latest Version
Linux	*www.redhat.com*
AIX	*www.ibm.com/servers/aix*
HP-UX	*www.software.hp.com/OE_products_list.html*
Solaris	*www.sun.com/solaris*
Windows 2000	*www.microsoft.com/windows2000/*
Windows XP	*www.microsoft.com/windowsxp/*

It's a good idea to install a system patch that guards against an application that can be subject to **buffer overflow**. In a buffer overflow, a program or process attempts to store more data than can be held in a temporary disk storage area called a buffer. In a buffer overflow attack, a computer is flooded with more information than it can handle, and some of it may contain instructions that could damage files on the computer or disclose information that is normally protected—or give the hacker root access to the system.

 Whenever you install software on the bastion host, observe extreme caution: make sure you are using the latest available version of the software and that any security patches have been added to the program. For an extra measure of safety, you should consider installing the software on another workstation first to ensure that the product is secure.

Special Considerations for UNIX Systems

UNIX makes use of a utility called **security_patch_check**, which automates the process of analyzing security patches that are already on the system and reporting on patches that should be added. You should become very familiar with this utility.

On a UNIX host, run a **Trusted Computing Base (TCB)** Check, which makes sure that any software you run is a trusted program. (The TCB is a group of software, including the system kernel, that maintains security data on a UNIX machine.) You should also consider enabling some sort of system logging. On UNIX, enable inetd logging if you plan to run the inetd daemon on the server.

Log files are likely to take up a lot of room on the bastion host, and yet they are essential to monitoring network security. Be sure to provide sufficient room for log files to grow, and increase log file buffer size as much as possible. Keep in mind that a central logging server can be set up to handle logging for all critical servers on the network. Typically, a central logging server is a secure system with an extra-large storage capacity. It gives you a central location from which to search all log files for malicious activity.

Special Considerations for Windows Systems

If you are configuring a bastion host using a Windows 2000 or XP computer, you should make use of two utilities that Microsoft has provided to help harden the systems. Microsoft Baseline Security Analyzer (*www.microsoft.com/technet/treeview/default.asp?url=/technet/security/tools/Tools/MBSAhome.asp*) performs an analysis of the current Windows 2000 or XP configuration. It identifies hotfixes and patches that are necessary and isolates vulnerabilities such as open Guest accounts and anonymous connections being enabled (see Figure 8-3).

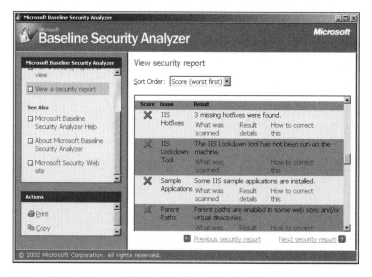

Figure 8-3   *Microsoft Baseline Security Analyzer*

Running the Baseline Security Analyzer after you do a clean install of the operating system on the bastion host is a good way to identify obvious vulnerabilities. Another piece of software, the IIS Lockdown Tool, is intended to turn off the Windows 2000 or XP built-in Web server, Internet Information Server (IIS), plus any services that depend on it.

Finally, Windows 2000 contains a number of files in the %SystemRoot%\system32 folder that aren't needed and can be deleted for extra security. See Table 8-2 in the "Disabling Unnecessary Services" section of this chapter for a list of these files.

Disabling Accounts

As with most operating systems and application software, default accounts may be created during installation. Accordingly, you should delete all user accounts from the bastion host. They aren't needed because individual users should not be able to connect to the host from their workstation. Each user account on the bastion host increases the chances of a security breach.

You should rename the Administrator account as another way to deter hackers. Many hackers are able to gain access to computers through Administrator accounts that use the default account name "Administrator" and that are never assigned a password. Renaming such accounts and using passwords that contain at least 6 or 8 alphanumeric characters can prevent these obvious attacks. You can, as an additional measure, keep an account called Administrator to serve as a honey pot account. The real account could be renamed, but a "dummy" account called Administrator could still be set up by copying the original account, naming the copy Administrator, disabling the account, and stripping it of all rights and membership.

8

Disabling Unnecessary Services

One of the most important bastion host configuration tasks is the elimination of unnecessary services. These services (such as FTP, Telnet, or SMTP) listen on open ports that can provide hackers with entry points.

Perhaps the most important services you should disable are those that enable the host to do routing or IP forwarding—unless, of course, the host is intended to function as a router. Also take out hardware features you won't use, such as floppy disk drives. However, you may well have to include some capacity to write data to a tape or a CD-ROM to make a binary disk image of the bastion host, as described in the section "Handling Backups" later in this chapter.

Table 8-2 lists the services that a network administrator should typically disable for UNIX and Windows 2000/XP systems.

Obviously, when you are stopping or removing services, you should not disable any **dependency services**—services that the system needs to function correctly. It's advisable to stop services one at a time. Each time a service is stopped, test the system to make sure it still functions properly by opening an application, copying a file, or performing another simple task. If the system runs slowly or fails to perform the task, you need to restore the service you disabled most recently. On the other hand, if the system continues to work correctly after you disable a service, don't simply move on to the next one: get in the habit of documenting every single change you make and recording how the system reacts so that you have a record you can call upon in case you have to troubleshoot that same system at a later date.

Table 8-2 Services and features to disable on a bastion host

UNIX Services and Other Features	Windows 2000/XP Services and Other Features
All services from within /etc/inetd.conf	Guest access account
All accounts except Administrator	All accounts except Administrator
Links to any start-up scripts in the /etc/rc.d directories that start network services	Sample scripts for Internet Information Server (IIS), located in the iissamples folder in the inetpub folder; delete only if you plan to run bastion host as a Web server running IIS; otherwise disable IIS altogether
The X window system	The %SystemRoot%\system32/os2 folder
The PPP-RUN fileset	These unnecessary files in the system32 folder: %SystemRoot%\system32\ntvdm.exe %SystemRoot%\system32\krnl386.exe %SystemRoot%\system32\psxdll.dll %SystemRoot%\system32\psxss.exe %SystemRoot%\system32\posix.exe %SystemRoot%\system32\os2.exe
Any network services except those you will be running on the bastion host	Any network services except those you will be running on the bastion host
SNMP daemons; you may not be able to completely remove these daemons but you can disable them	
The swagentd (SD-UX) daemon	
The sendmail daemon; disable only if you don't plan to run mail services on the bastion host	
The rpcbind daemon; disable only if you don't plan to run RPC services	

Be sure to disable any routing services on the bastion host because routing can be exploited by intruders. Any routing services that enable the bastion hosts to direct traffic to hosts on the internal network represent a security weakness. In addition, pay special attention to services that cannot be disabled. You'll have to leave them running, but make a list of such dependency services so that you can check them first in case of trouble.

Limiting Ports

For reasons that should be obvious (you want to eliminate as many possible points of entry to hackers), you should stop traffic on all but the ports you actually need to provide services on the network. On a bastion host that is intended to function as a Web server, for instance, you need only enable traffic on TCP Port 80 and Port 443 for SSL traffic.

After the bastion host has been configured, you can use a package of hacker-style tools called NetScanTools or NMAP/NMAPNT to scan your system for active ports (see Figure 8-4). You can then close any ports that are being used by "unknown" or unneeded services.

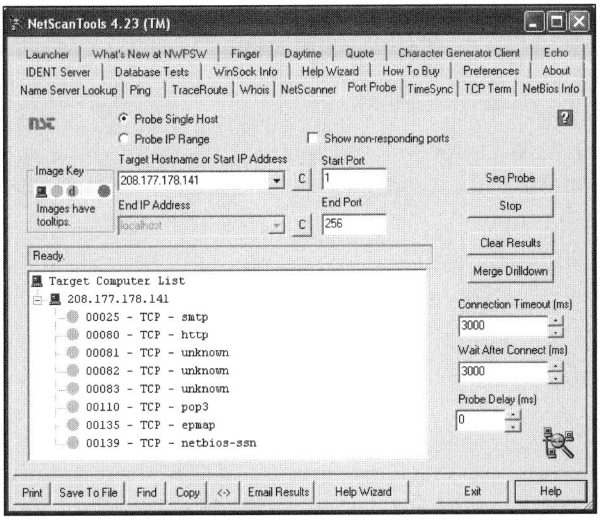

Figure 8-4   NetScanTools can do a port scan of your bastion host

Installation and use of NetScanTools for port scanning is described in Hands-On Project 8-4. Hands-On Project 8-1 covers how to set up packet filtering on Windows 2000 or XP using the TCP/IP Security box. You can use this utility to block traffic on all but the necessary ports.

HANDLING BACKUPS

Having gone through the effort to harden and secure a bastion host, you should now take steps to back up the data on the machine so that you can restore it if needed. If the system becomes corrupted by a virus or a worm that replicates itself throughout the system, you can restore part or all of it from scratch using the backup you've made.

The best kind of backup is a **binary drive image**, which is a mirror image of all the data on a hard disk or partition that includes not only files but applications and system data. Some commercial applications are available for creating a binary drive image. They include Norton Ghost by Symantec Inc. (*www.symantec.com*) and Drive Image by PowerQuest Corporation (*www.powerquest.com/driveimage/*).

You can also, of course, back up the system by copying all of the relevant files to disk or by using the system's built-in back-up utility, if one is available. A detachable CD-RW drive, removable hard drive, or removable tape drive would be ideal. You can make a backup of the system and data and then detach the drive and store it in a safe location.

AUDITING THE BASTION HOST

After you put the host online, the last step is to **audit** the system by testing it for vulnerabilities and evaluating its performance. The effectiveness of a bastion host configuration can be evaluated by asking yourself two questions:

- How well does the bastion host protect itself from attack? You can use one of the hacker tools mentioned earlier (NetScanTools or NMAP/NMAPNT) to research this after the machine is online.

- How well does the bastion host protect the internal LAN behind it from attack? This is something you judge by reviewing the bastion host's log files' unsuccessful accesses and other possible intrusion events.

You need to establish a **baseline** for system performance. A baseline is a level of performance that you consider acceptable and that the system can be compared against. The process of establishing a baseline is called **benchmarking**: Benchmarking requires that you check system logs, event logs, and performance information and record the information you uncover. Check the server on a daily or weekly basis after it is first installed, and compile a month's worth of log files that you can analyze. Take a snapshot of system logs (in other words, record a typical day's worth of activity in a text file) to see how the system normally runs. Print out system and event logs, and store them in case you need to refer to them when testing the system in the future.

When you configure the bastion host, do not use a production Web server or you may disable certain functionality. First apply hardening actions to a Web server in a mock production environment. After you verify that the server is functional, perform the same steps on a production server.

CONNECTING THE BASTION HOST

After all of the configuration and auditing is complete, you can finally connect the server to the network. When the bastion host is up and running, test the system and check it against your baseline level of performance to make sure it's still functioning correctly. A program called IPSentry can monitor your network performance and send you alerts in case of trouble (see Figure 8-5).

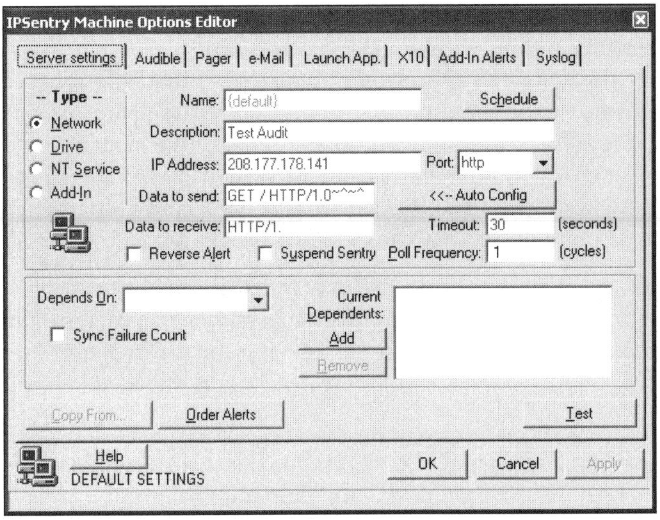

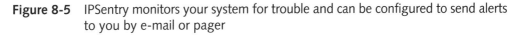

Figure 8-5 IPSentry monitors your system for trouble and can be configured to send alerts to you by e-mail or pager

Continue to audit the host on a periodic basis—daily or weekly, depending on how much time you can devote to it. An automated service such as WebScan by E-Soft, Inc. (*www.securityspace.com/smysecure/index.html*) can test the system on a monthly basis and provide you with a detailed security report.

CHAPTER SUMMARY

❏ In this chapter, you learned about the requirements for successfully configuring and maintaining a bastion host. A bastion host is a specially hardened computer that is located on the network perimeter and that hosts firewall software and/or publicly accessible services such as Web, FTP, and e-mail servers. Because of its exposed position, extra steps need to be taken to ensure that the bastion host is secure and that it functions reliably.

❏ When choosing the combination of hardware and operating system that the bastion host will comprise, be sure to choose systems that you are familiar with so that you can handle configuration and troubleshooting as the need arises. RAM is important if you plan to run a Web server, but other requirements for the bastion host are not as extensive because (aside from log analysis software) few other applications should be run on it. Processor speed also isn't the most critical consideration when choosing hardware for a bastion host.

❏ The bastion host should be placed on the perimeter of the network. The logical location for a bastion host that is intended to provide DNS services or publicly available services is on the DMZ. A bastion host that hosts firewall software should be in a room with limited access and with back-up power and air conditioning.

◻ Next, you need to decide what function the bastion host will be called upon to perform. Besides running public services, the bastion host can function as a proxy server. Some bastion hosts are set up as honey pot servers that intentionally attract intruders but that are not connected to any computers on the internal network. Log files should be recorded and reviewed on the server, and security patches that guard against buffer overflows and other problems should be installed. Any unnecessary services or accounts on the bastion host should be disabled. In particular, routing services should be disabled so that they cannot be exploited by intruders.

◻ After the bastion host software has been installed and a minimal operating system is in place, you should back up all of the system data so that it can be restored quickly in case it becomes corrupted. A binary drive image is a mirror image of all the information on a hard disk or partition. It can be created by a number of commercial applications, such as Norton Ghost.

◻ Finally, along with saving backups of the system and data on the bastion host, you need to audit the system. You should test it for vulnerabilities and evaluate its performance. First, establish a baseline for acceptable system performance. Then, regularly monitor the system to see how it compares with the baseline. Software programs are available to test the bastion host for vulnerabilities and to monitor how frequently the bastion host goes offline due to problems with the network, the operating system, or the services provided by the host.

KEY TERMS

audit — To test a system for performance qualities or vulnerabilities.

baseline — The minimum level of service or performance that is determined to be acceptable and that is used for comparison in future tests of a system.

bastion host — An application server that has been specially hardened and configured to function on a network perimeter with an interface on the Internet.

benchmark — A level of performance that you consider acceptable and against which the system can be compared.

binary drive image — A copy of a floppy or hard disk that includes all information on it, including the operating system, applications, and individual files.

buffer overflow — A situation where a program or process attempts to store more data than can be held in a temporary disk storage area called a buffer. This can result from a common type of attack called a buffer overflow attack.

chkconfig — A UNIX utility that reports on the services that are currently started so that you can verify whether all of them are absolutely necessary.

co-locate — To host a Web server at an ISP or Web-hosting service's facility for greater security.

Demilitarized Zone (DMZ) — A network of publicly accessible servers, such as Web and FTP servers, that is connected to the firewall but that is isolated from the internal network to protect internal users from intrusions and attacks.

dependency services — Services that an operating system or application needs to function properly.

hardened — A term used to describe a computer that has been secured by removing all unnecessary applications, file shares, permissions, and services and installing security software.

honey pot — Something (a server or an Administrator account, for example) that is configured to intentionally attract hackers so that they can be identified and caught without causing any harm to your system.

log file — A file that contains information about accesses and events that have occurred on a server, operating system, or individual application.

page file — An area of disk memory that is allocated for applications or data when RAM or other memory resources are running low.

rotate — Delete old log file entries and replace them with fresh entries.

security_patch_check — A UNIX utility that automates the process of analyzing security patches that are already on the system and reporting on patches that should be added.

Service-Level Agreement (SLA) — A document that defines an agreed-upon level of service that the host will provide.

syslog — A UNIX utility that records log messages to files.

Trusted Computing Base (TCB) — A collection of software on UNIX, including the system kernel, that maintain relevant security information.

up time — The time a server is online and available.

REVIEW QUESTIONS

1. To minimize the chance that security vulnerabilities will arise, a bastion host should ideally be limited to one _____.

   a. network interface

   b. service

   c. processor

   d. user with administrative privileges

2. A bastion host provides only one network service, and that service is a firewall. True or False?

3. Which of the following is a function that is required to a greater degree with configuring a bastion host than with other firewall-related tasks? (Choose all that apply.)

   a. setting up rules

   b. auditing

   c. making backups

   d. testing the system

4. If it's ideal to run only one service on a bastion host, what is the obstacle to configuring multiple hosts on a network? What's to stop you from recommending the installation of as many bastion hosts as you have services? (Choose all that apply.)

   a. complexity

   b. security holes

   c. network slowdowns

   d. cost

5. The speed with which a bastion host works is a function of _____.

   a. whether the LAN uses regular or fast Ethernet

   b. bandwidth

   c. processor speed

   d. brand name

6. What's the purpose of going through the time and effort of documenting every step involved in bastion host configuration?

7. What is the name given to a server that is placed on the DMZ and whose sole purpose is to direct hackers away from bastion host servers?

   a. a reverse firewall

   b. a decoy server

   c. a honey pot server

   d. a mirror site

8. What are the primary characteristics of the attitude of "healthy paranoia" that you should adopt when configuring a bastion host? Name three specific qualities.

9. Processor speed becomes an even more critical consideration when choosing a bastion host if you plan to perform _____ on it.

   a. Network Address Translation (NAT)

   b. encryption

   c. authentication

   d. logging

10. The ideal operating system for a bastion host is _____.

   a. one with which the administrator is familiar

   b. UNIX

   c. Linux

   d. Windows 2000 with Service Pack 2 or higher

11. What is a benefit of establishing a bare-bones configuration on a bastion host?

    a. less work for the administrator

    b. greater efficiency

    c. reduced chance of attack

    d. less memory consumption

12. What characteristics should you look for when finding a room where the bastion host will be physically located?

13. A honey pot bastion host is set up like any other bastion host, except that _____. (Choose all that apply.)

    a. a logon is required

    b. users who connect are infected with viruses

    c. the server is isolated

    d. the server is filled with "dummy" information

14. Which of the following is among the criteria for grouping services on the same bastion host? (Choose all that apply.)

    a. popularity

    b. trust

    c. complexity

    d. importance

15. Among the most important services you can disable on the bastion host is _____. (Choose all that apply.)

    a. IP forwarding

    b. logging

    c. serving

    d. routing

16. When working on a bastion host configuration, you are asked by a manager, "Why are you spending so much time securing a single computer?" Give a good, comprehensive reply.

17. What are dependency services?

    a. services that the public depends on

    b. services that the company depends on

    c. services that the internal network depends on

    d. services that operating systems depend on

18. Why back up a system after you configure it?

8

19. Give at least three important considerations when choosing a bastion host OS—and put the most important one first.

20. What do you need to consider when evaluating the effectiveness of the bastion host configuration during the audit process? (Choose all that apply.)

    a. how much traffic the host can handle

    b. how well the host protects itself

    c. how well the host protects the internal network

    d. how quickly the host responds to client requests

HANDS-ON PROJECTS

Project 8-1: Configure an FTP Server as a Bastion Host

This exercise leads you through the steps involved in configuring a bastion host that is designed to serve as a public FTP server. Before you actually obtain and configure the server, however, you need to review your organization's security policy and make sure the bastion host conforms to its guidelines. The steps that follow assume that you are setting up a Windows 2000 computer as a bastion host and that your security policy calls for you to follow the concept of "least privilege," in which you decide to first restrict all transmissions through the gateway except a specific set of services. You need to have Microsoft Internet Explorer version 5.01 or later to use the Microsoft Baseline Security Analyzer.

The steps in this project assume that you have Internet Information Server (IIS) running on your computer. If you do not, you can ignore the steps that pertain to IIS and continue with the remaining steps in the project.

1. Obtain the machine and place it in a secured room with air conditioning and an alarm system.

2. Install the new system from scratch using the Microsoft Windows 2000 CD, wiping away the old system.

3. Double-click the **Internet Explorer** icon on the Windows desktop.

4. In the Address box, type the address of the CERT Coordination Center's Web site (**www.cert.org**) and then the SANS Web site (**www.sans.org**) for any security advisories regarding Windows 2000.

5. In the Address box, type the address of the Windows 2000 Web site (**www.microsoft.com/windows2000**) and click the **Security information** link.

6. Check the Maintain Security with Windows 2000 page for any obvious Service Packs or patches you need to add to the system, and download them as needed.

7. In your browser's Address box, type the URL of the Microsoft Baseline Security Analyzer page (**www.microsoft.com/technet/treeview/default.asp?url=/ technet/security/tools/Tools/MBSAhome.asp**), then press **Enter**.

8. Scroll down to the Download Now section of the page and click the link supplied to download the Security Analyzer.

9. When the File Download dialog box opens, click **Open this file from its current location**, and then click **OK**.

10. Follow the steps indicated in the installer to install the baseline analyzer. Double-click the **Microsoft Baseline Security Analyzer** icon on your desktop to scan your system for any hotfixes or security patches you might need. Download and install any software that is listed in the Security Analyzer's report, which appears automatically when the scan is complete.

11. Return to Internet Explorer, where the Microsoft Baseline Security Analyzer page should still be displayed. Click **IIS Lockdown Tool** in the list of links on the left side of the page. This tool stops any IIS dependency services as well as IIS itself. Download the tool, and when prompted, click **Run this program from its current location**, and then click **OK** to install it.

12. Follow the steps shown in the Internet Information Services Lockdown Wizard.

13. When the Select Server Template screen appears, click **Other (Server that does not match any of the listed roles)**, and then click **Next**.

14. In the Internet Services dialog box, make sure the box next to **File Transfer service (FTP)** is checked, and uncheck **E-mail service (SMTP)**.

15. Accept the defaults, and then click **Finish** to complete running the lockdown tool.

16. Click **Start**, point to **Settings**, and click **Control Panel**.

17. Double-click **Administrative Tools**.

18. Double-click **Computer Management**.

19. Click **Local Users and Groups**.

20. Double-click the **Users** folder in the right pane of Computer Management.

21. Double-click **Guest**.

22. Check the box next to **Account is disabled**, if it is not already checked.

23. Click **OK**.

24. Repeat Steps 21 through 23 for any accounts other than Administrator.

25. Close Computer Management and return to Administrative Tools.

26. Double-click **Local Security Policy**.

27. Double-click **Local Policies** in the left side of Local Security Settings.

28. Double-click **Security Options** in the right side of Local Security Settings.

29. Double-click **Additional restrictions for anonymous connections** in the right half of Local Security Settings.

30. Click **No access without explicit anonymous permissions** on the Local policy setting list.

31. Click **OK**.

32. Double-click **Audit Policy**, which is under Local Policies on the left side of Local Security Settings.

33. Set the event policies listed in the right half of Local Security Settings to the following (double-click each one of the events and check the boxes next to **Success** and/or **Failure** in the Properties dialog box for that particular event policy):

    ⊓ Audit account logon events (Success, Failure)

    ⊓ Audit account management (Success, Failure)

    ⊓ Audit directory service access (Failure)

    ⊓ Audit logon events (Success, Failure)

    ⊓ Audit object access (Failure)

    ⊓ Audit policy change (Success, Failure)

    ⊓ Audit system events (Success, Failure)

34. Close Local Security Settings, close Administrative Tools, and return to the Control Panel.

35. Double-click **Network and Dial-Up Connections** in the Control Panel window.

36. Double-click **Local Area Connection** (if your computer has a direct connection to the Internet) or the icon that represents your Internet connection.

37. Click **Properties**.

38. Click **Internet Protocol (TCP/IP)** and then click **Properties**.

39. Click **Advanced**.

40. Click the **Options** tab.

41. Click **TCP/IP Filtering**, and then click **Properties**.

42. Click **Permit Only** above TCP Ports, and then click **Add**.

43. Type **20** in the TCP Port text box in the Add Filter dialog box, and then click **OK**.

44. Click **Add** under TCP Ports.

45. Type **21** in the TCP Port text box in the Add Filter dialog box, and then click **OK**.

46. Click **Permit Only** above IP Protocols, and then click **Add**.

47. Type **6** (the TCP protocol number) in the IP Protocol text box of the Add Filter dialog box, and then click **OK**.

48. Click **OK** to close TCP/IP Filtering, Advanced TCP/IP Settings, Internet Protocol (TCP/IP Properties), and Local Area Connection Properties in succession. Do *not* restart your machine when prompted to do so.

49. Close Network and Dial-Up Connections to return to the Control Panel window.

50. Double-click **Administrative Tools**.

51. Double-click **Services**.

52. In the Services dialog box, turn off services you don't need, except EventLog, FTP Publishing Service, NTLM Security Support Provider, Protected Storage, and Remote Procedure Call (RPC).

53. Click **Start** and click **Shut Down**. When prompted, click **Restart** to reboot the computer. After the computer restarts, log in as Administrator.

54. Click **Start**, point to **Programs** (**All Programs** on Windows XP), point to **Accessories**, and click **Command Prompt** to open a command prompt window.

55. Type **netstat -a** and press **Enter**.

56. Review the services that are listening on the computer. The names of the services aren't listed, but the port numbers are, in the form [*Computer name*]:*port*. Match the port numbers with the services. Only a minimal number of services should be listening. Any unnecessary ports should be blocked in the IP Filtering dialog box.

57. Click **Start** and click **Run**.

58. In the Open text box of the Run dialog box, type **syskey**, and then click **OK**.

59. When the Securing the Windows NT Account Database dialog box opens, click **OK** to encrypt system account passwords.

60. Remove the following unnecessary files from the %SystemRoot% folder (%SystemRoot% is an arbitrary placeholder that represents your actual root folder, which may be C:\Windows or C:\WINNT or something different depending on how you installed the operating system):

   - %SystemRoot%\system32\ntvdm.exe

   - %SystemRoot%\system32\krnl386.exe

   - %SystemRoot%\system32\psxdll.dll

   - %SystemRoot%\system32\psxss.exe

   - %SystemRoot%\system32\posix.exe

   - %SystemRoot%\system32\os2.exe

   - %SystemRoot%\system32\os2ss.exe

61. Delete the **os2srv.exe** file from the %SystemRoot%\system32 folder.

62. Connect the machine to the network.

63. Do a security audit as described earlier in this chapter.

8

Project 8-2: Create an Emergency Repair Disk (ERD)

If you use a Windows 2000 workstation as a bastion host, you should create an Emergency Repair Disk (ERD) for that machine. In case the host becomes corrupted, you can then reboot from the ERD and repair the system from the disk as well. You create an ERD using the built-in application Backup. You'll need a Windows 2000 workstation and a blank floppy disk to perform this exercise.

1. Click **Start**, point to **Programs**, point to **Accessories**, point to **System Tools**, and then click **Backup**. The Welcome to the Windows 2000 Backup and Recovery Tools window opens.

2. Click the **Emergency Repair Disk** button.

3. The Emergency Repair Disk dialog box prompts you to insert a disk into your floppy disk drive. Insert a disk, and then check the box next to **Also backup the registry to the repair directory**.

4. Click **OK**.

5. The Emergency Repair disk notifies you of the progress of reading system data and then writing the data to the floppy disk. When the copying is complete and you receive the message that the emergency repair diskette was saved successfully, click **OK**.

6. Close the dialog box.

Project 8-3: Create an Automated System Recovery Set

Windows XP handles backup and recovery options differently than Windows 2000. For example, the Backup utility does not give you the opportunity to create an Emergency Recovery Disk (ERD). Rather, you create an Automated System Recovery Set by following these steps.

1. Click **Start**, point to **All Programs**, point to **Accessories**, point to **System Tools**, and then click **Backup**.

2. Depending on your system configuration, either the Backup Utility window or the Backup or Restore Wizard opens. If the Backup or Restore Wizard opens, click **Advanced Mode**. Click **Automated System Recovery Wizard**.

3. When the first screen of the wizard opens, click **Next**.

4. Insert a blank floppy disk into your computer's floppy disk drive. Click **Next**.

5. When the Completing the Automated System Recovery Preparation screen opens, click **Finish**. The Backup Progress window opens and presents you with a series of dialog boxes informing you of the progress creating the ASR set.

6. When you are prompted to insert the next "tape" in your disk drive, click **Cancel**, and then click **Close**. This cancels the ASR creation before it is finished; if you really wanted to create an ASR set, you would need to insert multiple floppy disks.

7. Click the **Restore and Manage Media** tab in the Backup Utility window.

8. In the What to restore pane of the Backup window, click the **plus sign (+)** next to **File**.

9. Click the **plus sign** next to **Backup.bkf**.

10. Click **C:** to select the C: drive backup files you created. How many files are listed in the right pane of the Backup window? Which files were copied? Record the answer in a lab book or word-processing document.

11. Click the **Close** box to close Backup and return to the Windows desktop.

Project 8-4: Test Your Bastion Host

Download and install NetScan Tools 4 to analyze your workstation just as you would analyze a bastion host. You will need a Windows XP or 2000 workstation to complete this project. If you download a Zip archive version of NetScan Tools, you will also need to have WinZip installed. (If you do not have WinZip available, you can download a self-extracting version of the program.)

1. Open Internet Explorer.

2. Type **www.netscantools.com/nstmain.html** in the Address box and press **Enter**. Your browser displays the NetScan Tools Product Information page.

3. Click **here** in the sentence "Download the 30 day trial here."

4. Scroll down to the Download Links section of the page and click one of the download links. If you have WinZip installed, click the file with the .zip filename extension. If you do not have WinZip installed, click the self-extracting file with the .exe extension.

5. When the File Download dialog box opens, click **OK**, and then click **Save** to download the file. When the download is complete, WinZip automatically opens.

6. If you downloaded the .zip version of NetScan Tools, extract the files using WinZip. If you downloaded the .exe version, double-click it to extract the files. When you have extracted the files, double-click the **Setup.exe** file to install the program. Accept all default settings when installing.

7. When the application starts, click **OK**, click **Continue and Start NetScanTools 4.3**, and then click **Close** in the Tip of the Day window.

8. Click the **Port Probe** tab to bring it to the front.

9. Type your computer's IP address or hostname in the Target Hostname or Start IP Address text box, and then click the **Seq Probe** (Sequential Probe) button.

10. When the IMPORTANT NOTICE TO END USER dialog box opens, read the user agreement and then click **I Accept**.

11. NetScanTools probes your workstation for active ports and the services that are running on them. You probably found ports that run common services such as HTTP and POP3. Did you find any that you don't recognize or that came up as "unknown"? Record them in a lab manual or word-processing document.

12. Close NetScanTools and return to the Windows desktop.

8

Project 8-5: Monitor Your Network Availability

A program called IP Sentry is intended to monitor the availability and performance of a network server, such as a bastion host. It comes with an Event Log Monitor add-on that can be very useful for auditing a bastion host.

You need a Windows XP workstation equipped with Windows Script Host (cscript.exe) to perform this project. To determine whether Windows Script Host is present, do a search for the file cscript.exe or open a Command Prompt window, type cscript.exe, and then press Enter. If the program is present, you will see the line "Microsoft® Windows Script Host Version 5.6." If the program is not present, you can obtain it from Microsoft's Web site by going to the site and doing a search for "Windows Script Host."

1. Double-click the **Internet Explorer** icon on your desktop.

2. Type the URL **www.ipsentry.com/scr/bnd.overview.asp** in your browser's Address box, and then press **Enter**. The IPSentry page opens.

3. Click **Download** to go to the Download Software page. Filling out the form is optional; leave the form blank, click **Next**, and follow the steps shown on subsequent pages to download and install IPSentry.

4. Double-click the **IPSentry** icon on your desktop. Click **OK** in the Tips window.

5. When the End-User License Agreement dialog box opens, click **I Agree**. A window opens, notifying you that IPSentry has started. The IPSentry Options dialog box also opens.

6. Click the **Server/Machine Monitoring** tab in the IPSentry Options dialog box.

7. When a dialog box opens notifying you that you need to set defaults, click **OK**. The IPSentry Machine Options Editor dialog box opens.

8. In the Description text box, type the name **Test Audit** for this auditing configuration.

9. In the IP Address text box, type your workstation's IP address.

10. Click **ICMP-Ping** in the Port list.

11. Click **Test** to send a test message to your workstation to make sure IPSentry is functioning.

12. Click **OK**.

13. Click the **e-Mail** tab.

14. Under the Enabled? heading, click **Yes**.

15. Type your SMTP e-mail server name in the SMTP server text box, your username in the User text box, and the password you use to retrieve e-mail in the Pwd text box.

16. In the From text box, type your e-mail address.

17. In the To text box, type an e-mail address where you want IPSentry to send an alert notification. You can arrange with a classmate to receive such a message.

18. In the Subject text box, type **IPSentry Alert Message**.

19. Click **OK**. The IPSentry Machine Options Editor dialog box closes and you return to the IPSentry Options dialog box, where an entry now exists for your test configuration.

20. Click **OK**.

21. When the Backup Current Configuration dialog box opens, choose **No**.

22. The IPSentry v.4.5.0 dialog box remains open, presenting a list of status messages about the program and its monitoring activities. Click **View**, then click **Statistics**.

23. Your Web browser launches and displays a set of statistics for your workstation. Because you just installed and started IPSentry, there aren't many statistics. Where would you go to determine how often your workstation was offline?

24. Click **File**, then click **Close** to close the statistics page.

25. In the IPSentry v.4.5.0 dialog box, click **File** and then click **Exit** to exit the program. When prompted if you want to terminate IPSentry, click **Yes** to exit the program and return to your Windows desktop.

Project 8-6: Download Service Packs and Hotfixes

If you use a version of Windows to run a bastion host, it's critical to obtain the latest service packs, hotfixes, and updates for the system—and to update them on a regular basis. (This is obviously important for any Windows workstation as well.) Go to the Microsoft TechNet site and learn how to quickly find and install the updates you need.

1. First, check to see if your current operating system has any service packs installed by clicking **Start**, pointing to **Settings** and clicking **Control Panel** on Windows 2000 or, on Windows XP, simply clicking **Control Panel**.

2. Double-click **System**. The General tab of the System Properties window should display your operating system and Service Packs (if any). Write down the name of the Service Pack that is currently installed.

3. Click **OK** to close System Properties. Close the Control Panel.

4. Double-click the **Internet Explorer** icon on your desktop.

5. Type **www.microsoft.com/technet/treeview/default.asp?url=/technet/security/current.asp** in the Address box, and then press **Enter**. The HotFix & Security Bulletin Service Web page opens.

6. Click on your workstation's operating system on the Product list. Click the Service Pack you are running on the Service Pack list. (If you don't have a Service Pack installed, leave **All** selected.)

7. Click **Go**.

8. Make a note of any security bulletins that are available for your workstation. Click one to read about it; scroll down the bulletin page to the links where security patches are available. Make a note of the security problem, and discuss with your instructor whether or not you should install the patch on the workstation.

9. Click your browser's **Back** button until you return to the HotFix & Security Bulletin Service Web page, and then click the link **Service Packs** on the right side of the page under the heading Hot Fix Central.

10. Scroll down the Service Packs page and click the link for your operating system if there is one. If there is no link for your system, click Windows 2000 to see what's available for it.

11. Make a note of the latest Service Packs and hotfixes available for your system in a lab notebook or word-processing document. Does your lab workstation have the latest Service Pack installed? Are there any hotfixes available that were released after your current Service Pack was released? If you think you need a hotfix or Service Pack, tell your instructor and see if you should install it. (Installation instructions are found farther down on the page where the Service Packs and hotfixes are listed.)

12. When you are done, close Internet Explorer and return to the Windows desktop.

CASE PROJECTS

Case 8-1: Analyze Bastion Host Requirements

You have been asked by upper management to install a bastion host to improve security between the company network and the Internet. You have also been asked to report on the primary requirements for obtaining bastion hosts and to list how expensive they will be (i.e., to describe the most expensive aspects of creating the bastion host). You suspect that management has determined that a host is needed without really understanding what one is. You decide to focus on three primary bastion host requirements and to provide a detailed description in two or three sentences. What three requirements would you list? What description would you give?

Case 8-2: Bastion Host Load Balancing

You have two bastion hosts in the DMZ. One provides Web and FTP services, the other DNS and SMTP. Performance is slow on the Web/FTP server due to unexpectedly heavy traffic. What are your options for lightening the load on the host?

Case 8-3: Review System Logs

A review of your system logs reveals that attempts have been made to log on to your workstation using the Administrator account at times when the Administrator was not working (such as the middle of the night). What could you do to identify the individual who is attempting to log on?

Case 8-4: Add Intrusion Detection

You configure a bastion host to function as a mail server on the public DMZ. After a few months, as a result of an intrusion in another part of your network, a change is made to your company's security policy to the effect that intrusion detection must be enabled on all publicly accessible servers. How does this affect the configuration of your mail server bastion host?

8

9

SETTING UP A VIRTUAL PRIVATE NETWORK

After reading this chapter and completing the exercises, you will be able to:

♦ Understand the components and essential operations of virtual private networks (VPNs)

♦ Describe the different types of VPNs

♦ Create VPN setups such as mesh or hub-and-spoke configurations

♦ Choose the right tunneling protocol for your VPN

♦ Enable secure remote access for individual users via a VPN

♦ Observe best practices for configuring and maintaining VPNs effectively

In the corporate world, businesses routinely are called upon to join two or more LANs to facilitate corporate communications. The goal is secure point-to-point communications: a secure line that is used to connect one host to another and that can be accessed by no one else. Private **leased lines** have traditionally been used to connect remote users or branch offices to a central administrative site. However, private leased lines, such as **frame relay** high-speed network connections, don't scale well; as a company grows and undertakes e-commerce transactions with the public via the Internet, the cost of using the leased lines and the complexity of the technology used to support them both rise considerably.

The growth and widespread use of the Internet has produced a solution to the need for private communication channels: **virtual private networks (VPNs)**. VPNs function like "virtual" private leased lines; they encapsulate and encrypt the data being transmitted, and they use authentication to ensure that only approved users can access the VPN. However, rather than using an expensive leased line, VPNs provide a means of secure point-to-point communications over the public Internet. In this chapter, you'll learn how to set up a VPN for your organization.

VPN COMPONENTS AND OPERATIONS

The need for VPNs for e-commerce and telecommuting is increasing their popularity. Many telecommunications companies provide IP VPN services. VPNs can be set up with special software or with firewall software that includes VPN functionality. Many firewalls have VPN systems built into them in a single hardware or software package because the rules that apply to the VPN are part of the firewall's existing security policy. If they are set up correctly, VPNs can represent a critical component in an organization's perimeter security configuration.

The goal of VPNs is to provide a cost-effective and secure way to connect businesses to one another and remote workers to office networks. If remote branch offices were to connect to one another using a LAN-based file-sharing protocol, such as NetBIOS or AppleTalk, the results could be disastrous: the company's sensitive personnel information, job data, and accounting department records could all become accessible to intruders who are able to either guess or obtain valid usernames and passwords.

Because multinational corporations may well need to connect branch offices in various countries, VPNs provide an ideal means of communication. In addition, mobile salespeople and other staff need to be able to connect to the home office to obtain information at any time and from virtually any location. The following sections provide an overview of VPN architecture that enables such access. First, you learn about the essential components that make up a VPN. Then, you get a rundown of how VPNs enable data to be accessed securely. Finally, you learn about the advantages and disadvantages of using VPNs compared to leased lines and how VPNs extend a network's boundaries.

Components Within VPNs

VPNs consist of two different types of components: hardware devices and the software that performs security-related activities. This section briefly discusses the physical devices that can be used to create a VPN.

In terms of hardware, the following statements are true:

- A VPN can have two **endpoints** or **terminators**. Endpoints are hardware or software devices that perform encryption to secure data, authentication to make sure the host requesting the data is an approved user of the VPN, and **encapsulation** to protect the integrity of the information being sent.

- A VPN can have a **tunnel**. A tunnel is a secure channel used by the VPN and runs through the Internet from one endpoint to another.

The term *tunnel,* which is almost always used when discussing VPNs, can be misleading. It implies that there is a single cable joining one endpoint to another and that no one but approved users can send or receive data using that cable. In reality, a VPN uses a *virtual* tunnel, which is a series of connections between two endpoints that makes use of Internet-based hosts and servers to conduct data from one "hop" to another just like any other TCP/IP data transmission.

Note The use of the Internet's system of networks, subnetworks, and servers keeps costs down and makes it relatively easy to set up a VPN, at least compared to leased lines. However, the use of the Internet adds a level of uncertainty to VPN communications because so many systems are involved. See "Advantages and Disadvantages of VPNs" later in this chapter for more detailed discussion on this point.

In drawings of networks that employ VPNs, you'll often see a single line used to join the two endpoints, as shown in Figure 9-1.

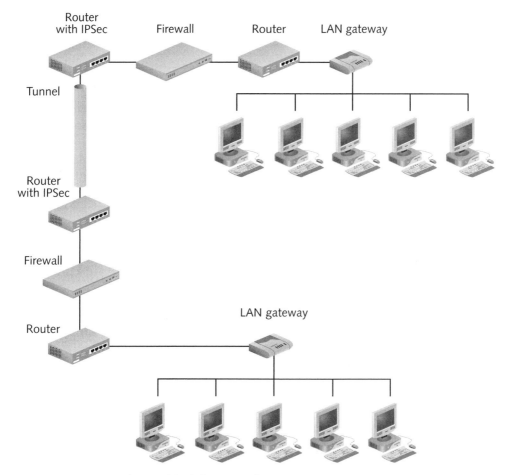

Figure 9-1 A greatly simplified diagram of a VPN

This simplified view of a VPN conveys the general notion that it is a communications path through the Internet that provides a heightened degree of security for two participants. After you understand that fundamental aspect of VPNs, you should then understand how

VPNs actually create that secure communications channel. In reality, the packets traverse the public Internet with all its complexities, as shown in Figure 9-2.

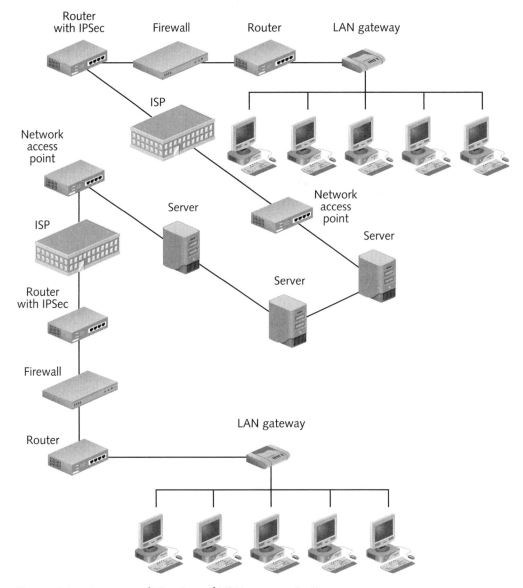

Figure 9-2   A more realistic view of VPN communications

Figure 9-2 illustrates one set of endpoints for a VPN: routers that support Internet Security Protocol (IPSec). Each LAN's communications first go to its ISP's server, then to a **Network Access Point** (a point that is on a high-speed part of the Internet called the backbone) and several intermediate servers.

In reality, even Figure 9-2 is greatly simplified because the ISPs involved may or may not be connected to the Internet backbone, and there are probably more than three servers that lie between one LAN and the other. Not only that, but more than one VPN may be involved as different offices that are part of the same corporation attempt to share information. For professionals in the fields, diagrams such as Figure 9-3 are more commonly encountered.

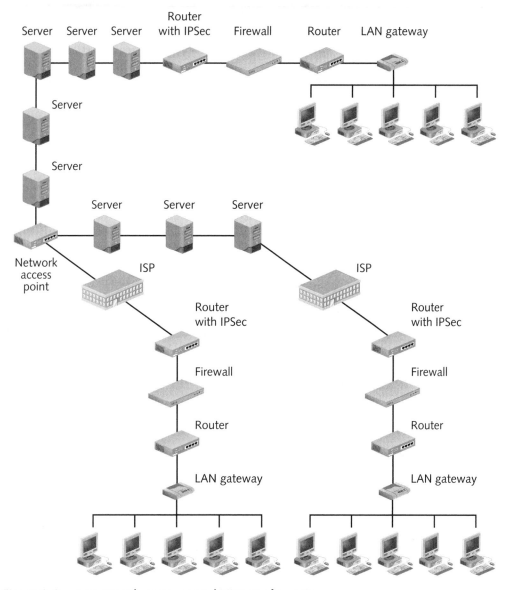

Figure 9-3   A commonly encountered VPN configuration

The devices that form the endpoints of the VPN (these are often said to "terminate" the VPN) can be one of the following:

- A server running a tunneling protocol

- A VPN appliance, which is a special hardware device devoted to setting up VPN communications

- A firewall/VPN combination; many high-end firewall programs support VPN setups as part of their built-in features.

- A router-based VPN; routers that support IPSec can be set up at the perimeter of the LANs to be connected. (These are also sometimes called **IPSec concentrators**.) IPSec concentrators use a complex set of security protocols to protect information, including Internet Key Exchange (IKE), which provides for the exchange of security keys between the machines in the VPN.

 IPSec is discussed in detail in Chapter 7.

The final components in a VPN scenario are certificate servers, which manage certificates if the system calls for it, and client computers that run VPN client software, which lets remote users dial in to the LAN over the VPN.

Essential Activities of VPNs

Because the VPN uses the public Internet to transfer information from one computer or LAN to another, the data needs to be well protected. It's this protection that really gives VPNs the ability to be very secure. This section discusses the essential activities included in every VPN:

- IP encapsulation

- Data payload encryption

- Encrypted authentication

All three of these activities must be present in a genuine VPN; each of the three is described in the following sections.

IP Encapsulation

You already know that information that passes to and from TCP/IP-based networks travel in manageable chunks called packets. VPNs protect packets by performing IP encapsulation, the process of enclosing a packet within another one that has a different IP source and destination information in order to provide a high degree of protection.

The benefit of encapsulating IP packets within other packets is that the source and destination information of the actual data packets (the ones being encapsulated) are completely hidden. The VPN encapsulates the actual data packets within packets that use the source and destination addresses of the VPN gateway. The gateway might be a router that uses IPSec, or a VPN appliance, or a firewall that functions as a VPN and that has a gateway set up.

What's more, because a VPN tunnel is being used, the source and destination IP addresses of the actual data packets (the ones being encapsulated) can be in the private reserved blocks that are not usually routable over the Internet, such as the 10.0.0.0/8 addresses or the 192.168.0.0/16 reserved network blocks. The IP packets that enclose the actual data packets have source and destination addresses of the gateway devices, such as routers, that direct packets to and from the network.

Data Payload Encryption

One of the big benefits of using VPNs is the fact that they encrypt the data portion of the packets that pass through them. They don't encrypt the header information within packets, only the data payload that the packets carry. The encryption can be performed in one of two ways:

- *Transport method:* The host encrypts traffic when it is generated; the data part of packets are encrypted but not the headers.

- *Tunnel method:* The traffic is encrypted and decrypted in transit, somewhere between the source computer that generated it and its destination. In addition, both the header and the data portions of packets are encrypted.

The level of encryption applied by the firewall or VPN hardware device varies: the higher the number of data bits used to generate keys, the stronger the encryption. As you'll recall from Chapter 7, a key is a value that is generated by a formula called an algorithm. The length of a key determines just how strong the encryption is. A key can also be processed by an algorithm to encrypt text, or to decrypt text that has already been encrypted.

Encrypted Authentication

Some VPNs use the term **encryption domain** to describe everything in the protected network and behind the gateway. The same cryptographic system that is used to protect the information within packets can be used to authenticate computers that use the VPN. Authentication is essential because hosts in the network that receive VPN communications need to know that the host originating the communications is an approved user of the VPN.

Hosts are authenticated by exchanging long blocks of code called keys that are generated by complex formulas called algorithms. Two types of keys can be exchanged in an encrypted transaction:

- *Symmetric keys:* The keys are exactly the same. The two hosts exchange the same secret key to verify their identities to one another.

- *Asymmetric keys:* Each participant has a different secret key called a private key. The private key is used to generate a public key. The participants in the transaction exchange their public keys. Each can then use the other's public key to encrypt information, such as the body of an e-mail message. When the recipient receives the encrypted message, he or she can decrypt it using the private key.

Symmetric key encryption is faster and more efficient, but asymmetric key encryption is more secure because hackers who intercept public keys can't use them to decrypt information, only to encrypt information.

 The choice and implementation of a key distribution system is another complication facing anyone who wants to set up a VPN. For more on keys and symmetric/asymmetric keys, algorithms, and key distribution systems, see Chapter 7.

Advantages and Disadvantages of VPNs

The primary advantage of using VPNs as opposed to leased lines is economic. VPNs are far less expensive to establish and maintain than leased lines, which can cost several thousand dollars per month. They allow the use of private address space in communications, which means you can have more machines on a network. VPNs also allow the packet encryption/translation overhead to be done on dedicated systems, decreasing the load placed on production machines.

Another advantage is control. Because you control the physical setup, you can decide exactly at what level data that passes through the VPN will be encrypted, whether that is at the physical level or at the application level. The fact that all traffic that passes through the VPN *is* encrypted is itself an advantage over leased lines, which do not provide for encryption.

VPNs do have some significant downsides. They are complex and, if configured improperly, can create significant network vulnerabilities. Leased lines may be more expensive, but the chance of introducing vulnerabilities is not as great because they create point-to-point connections. They also make use of the unpredictable and often unreliable Internet over which you have little or no control. This turns up particularly often in multinational VPNs. Packets being routed through various hubs might encounter slowdowns or blockages that you can neither predict nor solve. You then have to explain to administration that the problem is occurring thousands of miles away and you'll just have to wait until it is fixed there.

Another problem involves authorization: if your VPN's authorization is not configured properly, you can easily expose your corporate network. In addition, some vendor solutions have more documented security issues than others.

The advantages and disadvantages of VPNs are summarized in Table 9-1:

Table 9-1   Advantages and disadvantages of VPNs

Advantages	Disadvantages
Less expensive than leased lines	VPNs can still be expensive, especially if you use multiple VPN appliances
Scalability and flexibility; allows many different computers to communicate over many different networks	Uses the unregulated and often unreliable Internet
All traffic that passes through the VPN is encrypted	Complexity
You can control how the VPN is configured	VPN client software may not be compatible with all desktops; testing needs to be done, which can be time consuming

VPNs Extend a Network's Boundaries

High-speed Internet connections such as cable modem and DSL lines are changing the role of VPNs in the corporate setting. Only a few years ago, when high-speed connections were expensive and relatively hard to come by, remote users primarily used VPNs to dial into a network using their dial-up modems. They were connected to the corporate network through the VPN only for the length of the phone call. Because many ISPs charged by the minute or placed restrictions on the number of hours a customer could be connected each month, the remote user was likely to hang up as soon as business was completed.

Now, it's increasingly likely that the contractors, vendors, and stay-at-home employees who connect to an organization's internal network through a VPN will have a high-speed connection that is "always on." Unless you specifically place limits on how long such employees can use the VPN, they can potentially be connected to your network around the clock as well. The problem is that each VPN connection extends your network to a new location that is out of your control. Each such connection can open up your network to intrusions, viruses, or other problems. You need to take extra care with users who connect to the VPN through always-on connections. Here are some suggestions for how to deal with the increased risk:

- *Use of two or more authentication tools to identify remote users:* **Multifactor authentication** adds something the user possesses, such as a token or smart card, and something physically associated with the user, such as fingerprints or retinal scans. For such a system to work, each remote user would have to have a smart card reader, fingerprint reader, retinal scanner, or other potentially expensive device along with his or her computer.

- *Integrate virus protection:* Make sure each user's computer is equipped with up-to-date virus software that scans the computer continually, screening out any viruses as soon as they enter the system. After files are encapsulated, encrypted, and sent through the VPN tunnel, any viruses in those files will make it through the firewall into the corporate network. Virus-scanning software needs to be present on the network to catch any viruses, of course; however, requiring vendors, partners, or contractors to use their own anti-virus software will reduce the chance of viruses entering the system in the first place.

- *Set usage limits:* Tell any VPN participants that they need to terminate the VPN session as soon as they are done with it.

Such provisions should be written into any agreements you reach with business partners or contractors. They should also be part of your company's security policy and explained to employees during orientation or during any security "consciousness raising" sessions you conduct with them.

TYPES OF VPNs

In general, you can set up two different types of VPNs. The first type links two or more networks and is called a **site-to-site VPN**. The second type makes a network accessible to remote users who need dial-in access and is called a **client-to-site VPN**. The two types of VPNs are not mutually exclusive—many large corporations link the central office to one or more branch locations using site-to-site VPNs, and they also provide dial-in access to the central office by means of a client-to-site VPN.

Because of their cost effectiveness, VPNs are growing steadily in popularity. Accordingly, you can choose between a number of options for configuring VPNs: hardware systems, software systems, and hybrids that combine both hardware and software. When choosing a system, keep in mind that any type of VPN, whether it consists of hardware or software or both, needs to be able to work with any number of different operating systems or types of computers.

 There's a Web site devoted solely to the subject of finding VPN hardware and software and providing reviews of different products. Visit Find VPN at *http://findvpn.com/providers/vpnware.cfm.*

VPN Appliances

One way to set up a VPN is to use a hardware device such as a router that has been configured to use IPSec or another VPN protocol (see the section "Tunneling Protocols Used with VPNs" later in this chapter for a run-down on these). Another option is to obtain a **VPN appliance**, a hardware device specially designed to terminate VPNs and join multiple LANs. VPN appliances can permit connections between large numbers of users or multiple networks, but they don't provide other services such as file sharing and printing.

One VPN appliance that has a strong reputation is the SonicWALL series of VPN hardware devices. This series is comprised of nine different VPN products. At one end is a product designed for the small business or a branch office. It can support 10, 25, or 50 simultaneous VPN connections along with stateful packet filtering, network address translation (NAT), and even anti-virus protection. A Web-based interface and wizard installations make this SonicWALL product good for installations that require basic VPN support with a minimal amount of management.

At the high end of the series is a product that can support up to 500 concurrent VPN connections at speeds over 1.5 Gbps. Designed to deliver a high performance VPN solution, this VPN appliance even comes with redundant power supplies that can be replaced without turning the unit off. It provides mission-critical safety for large organizations that need the highest level of security.

Another widely-used VPN appliance is the Symantec Firewall/VPN appliance. Similar to the SonicWall, the Symantec Firewall/VPN appliance is a series of different models. Each model is an integrated security VPN networking device that provides secure and cost-effective Internet connectivity between locations. The Symantec Firewall/VPN is designed for small businesses and remote offices, and supports up to 40 simultaneous VPN connections. For larger dispersed organizations, Symantec Firewall/VPN offers a solution for extending firewall protection and VPN access to satellite offices or branch locations, and even provides a remote VPN for traveling users.

The Symantec Firewall/VPN security has a Web-based management interface that enables both remote and local administration. Because it contains a built-in local area network (LAN) auto-sense switch, system set up is easy, with no additional devices required to connect networking systems to the appliance. To ensure continuous connectivity, the Symantec Firewall/VPN appliance features an automatic backup that enables dial-up connections using an external modem in the event of a service disruption.

The advantage of using hardware systems is illustrated in Figure 9-4. They enable you to connect more tunnels and users than software systems. If the server goes offline or crashes for some reason (as shown in the left half of the figure), the hardware VPN appliance doesn't go offline (as shown in the right half of the figure).

 The ISP Planet Web site held a side-by-side comparison of four VPN appliances and asked readers to vote for the best product. Read about how the appliances compared to one another at *www.isp-planet.com/technology/ vpn/vpn_conclusion.html*.

Software VPN Systems

Software VPNs are generally less expensive than hardware systems, and they tend to scale better for fast-growing networks. One of the popular software VPN products is F-Secure VPN+. This product supports traveling employees who need private access to a corporate LAN or intranet from any dial-up location, IT staff who need the ability to secure internal networks and partition parts of the network, and corporate partners who require secure connections to a company's data network for business collaboration. F-Secure VPN+ supports Windows, Linux, and Solaris Sparc clients and servers as well as gateways.

F-Secure VPN+ uses a policy manager system for enterprise-wide software distribution, policy creation, and management. Security settings for the entire corporate network using VPN can be made from the administrator's computer. Settings can be based on "role-based policies." This allows multiple configuration profiles for end users to be created; examples might include "out-of-office,", "at-home," or "in-office." In addition, all installations and maintenance can be performed from a single central location.

Another widely-used software VPN is Novell BorderManager VPN services. This software-based VPN supports both the TCP/IP protocol as well as IPX/SPX (another LAN protocol), which is found on older Novell networks. BorderManager can support up to 256 sites per tunnel and can handle up to 1,000 dial-in users per server. Novell BorderManager VPN clients run on Windows 95, 98, NT 4.0, 2000, Me, and XP.

In addition, Novell BorderManager VPN services integrate with Novell's directory service, known as eDirectory, to simplify VPN management and administration. Novell BorderManager authenticates all users through the Novell eDirectory to ensure that only authorized users are permitted to access the VPN. Administrators can control access through the same interface used to manage other network users, as it is not necessary to maintain a separate directory of information for VPN users.

In addition to F-Secure and Novell, another software-only VPN product is Check Point FireWall-1. Additional coverage of Check Point is available in Appendix B.

VPN Combinations of Hardware and Software

You may also use VPN systems that implement both VPN appliances and client software. The Cisco 3000 Series VPN Concentrator is another family of five different models of products. Supporting from 100 to over 10,000 simultaneous VPN users, the Cisco 3000 Series VPNs provide solutions for the smallest office or branch location to the largest enterprise setting. Access levels can be set either by the individual user or by groups, which allows for easy configuration and maintenance of company security policies.

The Cisco 3000 Series VPN Concentrator gives users the choice of operating in one of two modes: client mode and network extension mode. In client mode, the 3000 Series acts as a software client, enabling users to connect to another remote network via a VPN. Supported software clients include Windows, Linux, Solaris, and Apple Macintosh. In network extension mode, the 3000 Series acts as a hardware device enabling a secure site-to-site VPN connection.

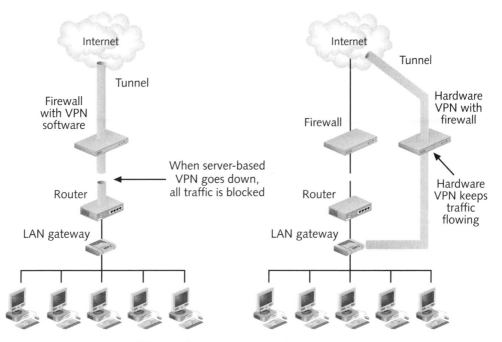

Figure 9-4   Hardware VPNs can keep networks online

VPN Combinations of Different Vendors' Products

You may also be forced to operate a VPN system that is "mixed" not only in terms of using both hardware and software, but also by different vendors. You might have one company that issues certificates, another that handles the client software, another that handles the VPN termination, and so on. The challenge is to get all of these pieces to talk to one another and communicate with one another successfully. To do this, pick a standard security protocol that is widely used and that all the devices support, such as IPSec, which is described later in this chapter and in Chapter 7.

VPN SETUPS

If you have only two participants in a VPN, the configuration is relatively straightforward in terms of expense, technical difficulty, and the time involved. However, when three or more networks or individuals need to be connected, several options arise. Those options—a mesh configuration, a hub-and-spoke arrangement, and a hybrid setup—are explained in the sections that follow.

Mesh Configuration

In a **mesh configuration**, each participant (that is, network, router, or computer) in the VPN has an approved relationship, called a **security association (SA)**, with every other

participant. In configuring the VPN, you need to specifically identify each of these participants to every other participant that uses the VPN. Before initiating a connection, each
VPN hardware or software terminator checks its routing table or **SA table** to see if the
other participant has an SA with it. A mesh configuration is shown in Figure 9-5.

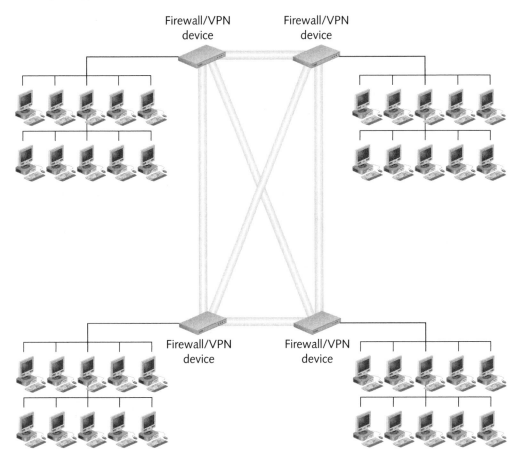

Figure 9-5   A mesh VPN configuration

In Figure 9-5, four separate LANs are joined in a mesh VPN. Each LAN has the ability to
establish VPN communications with all of the other participants in the LAN. If a new LAN
is added to the VPN, all other VPN devices will have to be updated to include information
about the new users in the LAN. Thus, each host can be added to the state table. In addition, every host that needs to use the VPN in each of the LANs must be equipped with
sufficient memory to operate the VPN client software and to communicate with all other
hosts in the VPN. The problem with VPNs is the difficulty associated with expanding the
network and updating every VPN device whenever a host is added. For fast-growing networks, a hub-and-spoke configuration is preferable. We discuss it next.

Hub-and-Spoke Configuration

In a **hub-and-spoke configuration**, a single VPN router contains records of all SAs in the VPN. Any LANs or computers that want to participate in the VPN need only connect to the central server, not to any other machines in the VPN. This setup makes it easy to increase the size of the VPN as more branch offices or computers are added. Figure 9-6 illustrates a hub-and-spoke configuration.

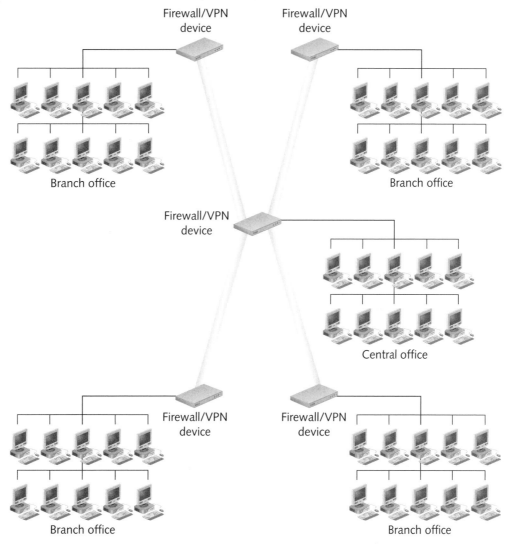

Figure 9-6   A hub-and-spoke VPN configuration

In Figure 9-6, the central VPN router resides at the organization's central office because that is most common for a hub-and-spoke VPN to have all communications go through the central office where the main IT staff resides. A hub-and-spoke VPN is ideally suited for communications within an organization that has a central main office and a number of branch offices.

The problem with hub-and-spoke VPNs is that the requirement that all communications flow into and out of the central router slows down communications, especially if branch offices are located on different continents around the world. In addition, the central router must have double the bandwidth of other connections in the VPN because it must handle both inbound and outbound traffic at the same time. The high-bandwidth charge for such a router can easily amount to several thousand dollars per month. However, in a situation where all communications need to go through the central office anyway, a hub-and-spoke configuration makes sense because of the heightened security it gives to all participants.

Hybrid Configuration

As organizations grow, a VPN that starts out as a mesh design or hub-and-spoke design often evolves into a mixture of the two. This is a common scenario, and you don't need to feel you should switch to one configuration or another exclusively.

Because mesh configurations tend to operate more efficiently, the central core linking the most important branches of the network should probably be a mesh configuration. However, as branch offices are added, they can be added as spokes that connect to a central VPN router at the central office.

Any critical communications with branch offices that need to be especially fast should be part of the mesh configuration. However, far-flung offices such as overseas branches can be part of a hub-and-spoke configuration. A hybrid setup that combines the two configurations benefits from the strengths of each one—the scalability of the hub-and-spoke option and the speed of the mesh option.

 If at all possible, try to have the branch offices that participate in the VPN use the same ISP. That will minimize the number of "hops" between networks.

Configurations and Extranet and Intranet Access

Whether you use a hub-and-spoke, mesh, or hybrid configuration, creating VPNs that connect business partners and other branches of your own organization raise a number of questions and considerations that go beyond physical considerations.

Each end of the VPN represents an extension of your corporate network to a new location—you are, in effect, creating an **extranet**. The same security measures you take to protect your own network should be applied to the endpoints of the VPN. Each remote user or business partner should have firewalls and anti-virus software enabled, for instance.

VPNs can also be used to give parts of your own organization access to other areas through a corporate **intranet**. An example would be a large corporation that has its facilities spread across several different buildings in separate locations. A VPN can allow the IT staff in one location to monitor servers in the other location, or accounting staff to adjust the financial records or job records in a server located in another building, for instance. Leaving the VPN connection "always on" opens the possibility that unscrupulous staff can gain access to sensitive corporate resources they are not allowed to use. With VPN users inside your organization, you need to establish usage limits and set up anti-virus and firewall protection just the same as with other users, as indicated in Figure 9-7.

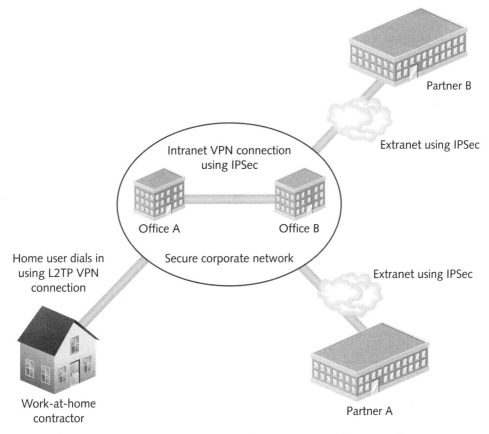

Figure 9-7   VPNs help create extranet and intranet access for networks

TUNNELING PROTOCOLS USED WITH VPNS

In the past, firewalls that provided for the establishment of VPNs used **proprietary** protocols. Such firewalls would only be able to establish connections with remote LANs that used the same brand of firewall. Today, the widespread acceptance of the IPSec protocol with the Internet Key Exchange (IKE) system means that proprietary protocols are used far less often. In this section of the chapter, we discuss the IPSec protocol and others so that you have a strong basis for making the right choice of protocol in your VPN.

IPSec/IKE

IPSec is a standard for secure encrypted communications developed by the Internet Engineering Task Force (IETF). IPSec, which is described in detail in Chapter 7, will be only briefly summarized here as it pertains to VPNs. IPSec provides for encryption of the data part of packets, authentication to guarantee that packets come from valid sources, and encapsulation between two VPN hosts.

IPSec provides two security methods: Authenticated Headers (AH) and Encapsulating Security Payload (ESP). AH is used to authenticate packets, whereas ESP encrypts the data portion of packets. You don't have to make a choice to use one or the other; both methods can be used together.

IPSec can work in two different modes: transport mode and tunnel mode. Transport mode is used to provide secure communications between hosts over any range of IP addresses. Tunnel mode is used to create secure links between two private networks. Tunnel mode is the obvious choice for VPNs; however, there are some concerns about using tunnel mode in a client-to-site VPN because the IPSec protocol by itself does not provide for user authentication. However, when combined with an authentication system like Kerberos, IPSec can authenticate users.

IPSec is commonly combined with IKE as a means of using public key cryptography to encrypt data between LANs or between a client and a LAN. IKE provides for the exchange of public and private keys. The key exchange is used to tell the hosts wishing to initiate a VPN connection that each is a valid user of the system. IKE can also determine which encryption protocols should be used to encrypt data that flows through the VPN tunnel. The process of establishing an IPSec/IKE VPN connection works like this:

1. The host or gateway at one end of the VPN sends a request to a host or gateway at the other end asking to establish a connection. (Both hosts have obtained the same key, called a pre-shared key, from the same trusted authority.)

2. The remote host or gateway generates a random number and sends a copy of the number back to the machine that made the original request.

3. The original machine encrypts its pre-shared key using the random number and sends the pre-shared key to the remote host or gateway.

4. The remote host decrypts the pre-shared key and compares it to its own pre-shared key or, if it has multiple keys, a set of keys called a keyring. If the pre-shared key matches one of its own keys, the remote host encrypts a public key using the pre-shared key and sends it back to the machine that made the original request.

5. The original machine uses the public key to establish a security association (SA) between the two machines, which establishes the VPN connection.

 Even though many firewalls support IPSec and IKE, they sometimes use different versions of these protocols. If your VPN uses more than one kind of firewall and you plan to implement an IPSec/IKE VPN, check with the manufacturers of those firewalls to see if their product will work with the other firewalls you have, and ask about any special configuration you have to perform.

PPTP

Point-to-Point Tunneling Protocol (PPTP) is commonly used by remote users who need to connect to a network using a dial-in modem connection. PPTP uses Microsoft Point-to-Point Encryption (MPPE) to encrypt data that passes between the remote computer and the remote access server. It's an older technology than the other dial-in tunneling protocol, L2TP, but it is useful if support for older clients is needed. It's also useful because packets sent using PPTP can pass through firewalls that perform Network Address Translation (NAT)—in contrast to L2TP, which is incompatible with NAT but provides a higher level of encryption and authentication.

L2TP

Layer 2 Tunneling Protocol (L2TP) is an extension of the protocol long used to establish dial-up connections on the Internet, **Point-to-Point Protocol (PPP)**. L2TP uses IPSec rather than MPPE to encrypt data sent over PPP. It provides secure authenticated remote access by separating the process of initiating a connection by answering a phone call from the process of forwarding the data encapsulated in PPP communications. Using L2TP, a host machine can make a connection to a modem and then have its PPP data packets forwarded to another, separate remote access server. When the data reaches the remote access server, its payload is unpacked and forwarded to the destination host on the internal network.

PPP Over SSL/PPP Over SSH

Point-to-Point Protocol (PPP) over Secure Sockets Layer (SSL) and **Point-to-Point Protocol (PPP) Over Secure Shell (SSH)** are two UNIX-based methods for creating VPNs. Both combine an existing tunnel system (PPP) with a way of encrypting data in transport (SSL or SSH). As you probably know already, PPP can be used to establish a connection between two hosts over an IP system.

SSL is a public key encryption system used to provide secure communications over the World Wide Web (see Chapter 7 for more on SSL). SSH is the UNIX secure shell, which was developed when serious security flaws were identified in Telnet. SSH enables users to perform secure authenticated logons and encrypted communications between a client and host. SSH requires that both client and host have a secret key in advance—a **pre-shared key**—in order to establish a connection.

Which protocol should you use in a VPN you establish, and why? Table 9-2 lists the protocols mentioned in this section along with situations in which they might be used.

Table 9-2   VPN protocols and their uses

Protocol	When To Use
IPSec/IKE	Rapidly becoming the protocol of choice for VPN connections of all sorts and should be used when the other protocols are not acceptable
PPTP	When a dial-up user has an old system that doesn't support L2TP and needs to use PPP to establish a VPN connection to your network
L2TP	When a dial-up user needs to establish a VPN connection with your network (L2TP provides stronger protection than PPTP)
PPP Over SSL	When a UNIX user needs to create a VPN connection "on the fly" by connecting to the SSL port on a server
PPP Over SSH	When a UNIX user needs to create a VPN connection "on the fly" over the UNIX secure shell (SSH) and both parties know the secret key in advance

ENABLING REMOTE ACCESS CONNECTIONS WITHIN VPNs

If users in disparate locations need to connect to the home office via a VPN, you need to set up a remote access connection. A VPN is a good way to secure communications with users who need to connect remotely by either dialing into their ISP and establishing a connection to the corporate network or by using their existing cable modem or DSL connection to the Internet to initiate the VPN connection to the corporate network. To enable a remote user to connect with a VPN, you need to issue that user VPN client software. You should also make sure the user's computer is equipped with anti-virus software and a firewall. You may need to obtain a key for the remote user if you plan to use IPSec to make the VPN connection as well.

If one or more remote users who want to make a VPN connection to you reside overseas, you may encounter the problem of having to find a phone provider that will have dial-up numbers in all locations. Some providers may not cover the foreign countries you want; you may have to sign up with several different providers to obtain dial-up access from certain locations.

 If you decide to outsource your VPN needs and use a telecommunications company to set up an IP-based VPN, make sure the provider will be able to provide dial-up numbers that potential VPN clients will need.

Configuring the Server

One step in setting up a client-to-server VPN is configuring the server to accept incoming connections. If you use a firewall-based VPN, you need to identify the client computer. Check Point FireWall-1, for instance, calls this process defining a network object.

The major operating systems include their own ways of providing secure remote access. In Linux, you use the IP Masquerade feature built into the Linux kernel to share a remote access connection. A part of IP Masquerade, called VPN Masquerade, enables remote users to connect to the Linux-based firewall using either PPTP or IPSec.

Windows XP and 2000 include a Network Connections Wizard that makes it particularly easy to set up a workstation to accept incoming VPN connections, with one limitation: the Remote Access Server that is used to provide the connection has the ability to permit only one incoming connection at a time. It's primarily intended to let one individual user connect to his or her home workstation from a remote location. However, if one connection is all you need, the wizard (see Figure 9-8) is a useful tool.

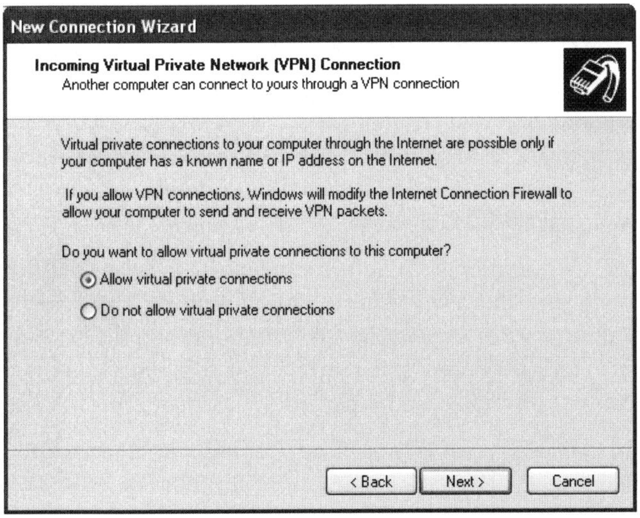

Figure 9-8   Windows XP can accept one incoming VPN connection

After the remote workstation is connected, the Windows XP workstation will see the dialog box similar to the one shown in Figure 9-9. (A Windows 2000 workstation displays a network connection icon in the system tray.) Either party can then terminate the connection at any time by clicking the Disconnect button.

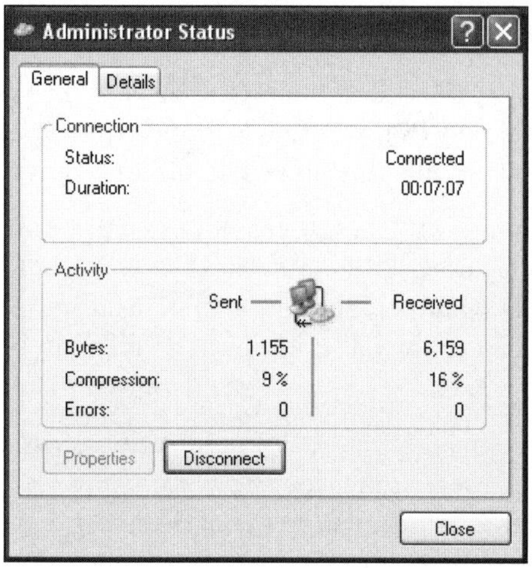

Administrator Status ? ✕

General | Details

Connection

Status: Connected
Duration: 00:07:07

Activity

Sent ——— 🖥️ ——— Received

Bytes: 1,155   6,159
Compression: 9 %   16 %
Errors: 0   0

Properties | Disconnect

Close

Figure 9-9   Windows hosts that are connected via a VPN see this dialog box

Configuring Clients

After you set up the server, you then need to configure each client that wants to use the VPN. This either involves installing and configuring VPN client software or, in the case of a Windows-to-Windows network, using the Network Connection Wizard. FireWall-1 uses client software called SecuRemote that, when installed on a client computer, enables connections to another host or network via a VPN.

The most important things to consider are whether your client software will work with all client platforms, and whether the client workstation is itself protected by a firewall. All users who dial in to the LAN using a VPN extend the LAN and open up a new "hole" through which viruses and hackers can gain access. The requirement that remote users protect laptops and other computers with firewalls can be part of your organization's VPN policy.

VPN BEST PRACTICES

The successful operation of a VPN depends not only on its hardware and software components and overall configuration, but also on a number of other best practices. These include security policy rules that specifically apply to the VPN, the integration of firewall packet filtering with VPN traffic, and auditing the VPN to make sure it is performing acceptably.

The Need for a VPN Policy

In a corporate setting, the VPN is likely to be used by many different workers in many different locations. A VPN policy is essential for identifying who can use the VPN and for ensuring that all users know what constitutes proper use of the VPN. This can be a separate standalone policy, or it may be a clause within a larger security policy.

The policy should spell out who should be permitted to have VPN access into your corporate network. For example, vendors might be granted access to the network through a VPN connection, but they may only be allowed to access information pertaining to their own company's accounts. The vendor VPN solution should have controls that allow the administrator to restrict where they can go on the corporate network. On the other hand, managers and full-time employees who access the network through a VPN while traveling should be granted more comprehensive access to network resources.

The policy should also state whether authentication is to be used and how it is to be used, whether **split tunneling** (two connections over a VPN line) is permitted, how long users can be connected using the VPN at any one session, whether virus protection is included, and so on.

 SANS provides a sample VPN Policy in PDF format at *www.sans.org/ newlook/resources/policies/Virtual_Private_Network.pdf*.

Packet Filtering and VPNs

When configuring a VPN, you must decide early on where encryption and decryption of data will be performed in relation to packet filtering. You can either decide to do encryption and decryption outside the packet-filtering perimeter or inside it. Figure 9-10 shows encryption and decryption outside the packet-filtering perimeter.

In the scenario shown in Figure 9-10, the firewall/VPN combination is configured to perform transport encryption. Packets are encrypted at the host as soon as they are generated. Already-encrypted packets pass through the packet filters at the perimeter of either LAN and are not filtered. The problem with this scenario is that, if the LAN that generates the communications has been infected by a virus or been compromised in some way, the packets that pass through the packet filters could be infected and could then potentially infect the destination LAN as well.

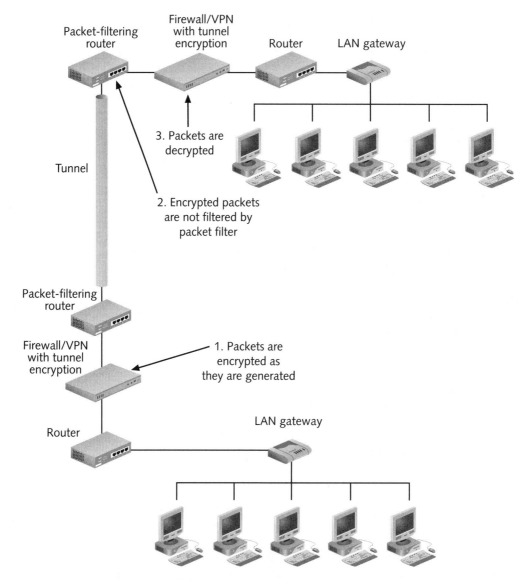

Figure 9-10 Encryption and decryption done outside the packet filter perimeter

Figure 9-11 illustrates the alternative: encryption and decryption are performed inside the packet-filtering perimeter using the tunnel method. Keep in mind that the network configurations illustrated in this figure and Figure 9-10 depict a packet filter that is separate from the firewall (this is done for clarity of explanation). In fact, packet filtering might be done by the firewall itself; the same firewall may provide VPN services. At the same time, a separate VPN appliance may be used instead of a firewall-based VPN.

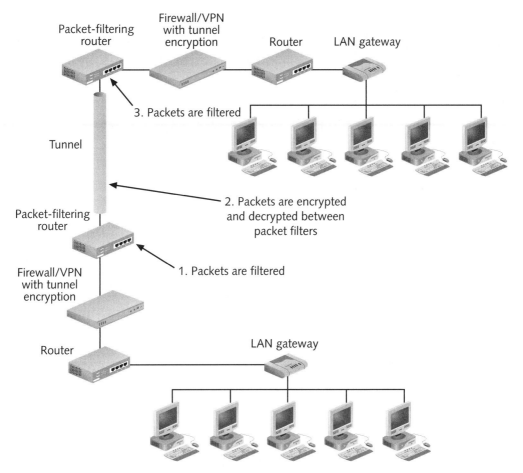

Figure 9-11   Encryption and decryption performed inside the packet-filtering perimeter

As a result of the scenario illustrated in Figure 9-11, packet filtering is performed before the data reaches the VPN. Mangled packets can be dropped before they reach the firewall/VPN, thus providing additional protection for the destination LAN.

PPTP Filters

PPTP is commonly used when older clients need to connect to a network through a VPN or when a tunnel must pass through a firewall that performs NAT. For PPTP traffic to pass through the firewall, you need to set up packet filtering rules that permit such communications. Incoming PPTP connections arrive on TCP port 1723. In addition, PPTP packets use Generic Routing Encapsulating (GRE) packets that are identified by the protocol identification number ID 47. Table 9-3 shows the filter rules that you would use for remote users at IP addresses 211.208.30.1 and 105.40.4.10.

Table 9-3 PPTP packet-filtering rules

Protocol	Transport Protocol	Source IP	Source Port	Destination IP	Destination Port	Action
PPTP	TCP	211.208.30.1, 105.40.4.10	Any	(remote access server's IP address)	1723	Allow
GRE	ID 47	Any		(remote access server's IP address)		Allow

L2TP and IPSec Packet-Filtering Rules

Because L2TP uses IPSec to encrypt traffic as it passes through the firewall, you need to set up packet-filtering rules that cover IPSec traffic. Table 9-4 shows the filter rules that you would use for remote users at IP addresses 211.208.30.1 and 105.40.4.10.

Table 9-4 PPTP packet-filtering rules

Protocol	Transport Protocol	Source IP	Source Port	Destination IP	Destination Port	Action
IKE	UDP	211.208.30.1, 105.40.4.10	500	(remote access server's IP address)	500	Allow
AH	ID 51	Any		(remote access server's IP address)		
ESP	ID 50	Any		(remote access server's IP address)		Allow

Auditing and Testing the VPN

After the VPN is installed, you need to test the VPN client on each computer that might use the VPN. In an organization with many different workstations, this can be a time-consuming prospect. There's no easy way around this, but you can choose client software (which is installed as part of the test) that is easy for end users to install on their own to save you time and effort.

To give you an idea of how testing of a VPN client might work, consider the following step-by-step scenario:

1. You issue VPN client software and a certificate to the remote user.

2. You call the remote user on the phone and lead him or her through the process of installing the software and storing the certificate.

3. If you are using IPSec, you verify with the remote user that the IPSec policies are the same on both the remote user's machine and on your VPN gateway.

4. You tell the user to start up the VPN software and connect to your gateway. (Hopefully, you'll be able to remain on the phone while the end user connects but if the remote user has only one telephone line and a dial-up connection to the Internet, you may have to communicate by e-mail.)

5. If there are any problems connecting to the gateway, tell the remote user to write down or report the error message exactly to help you correctly diagnose the problem.

6. After the connection is established, the remote user should authenticate by entering his or her username and password when prompted to do so.

After the testing of the client is done, you need to check the VPN to make sure files are being transferred at an acceptable rate and that all parts of the VPN remain online when needed. To give you an idea of how testing of file transferring might work, consider the following step-by-step scenario:

1. After the remote user connects to your network, tell him or her to start up a Web browser and connect to your server.

2. Enter the username and password needed to access the server when prompted.

3. Locate the files to be transferred.

4. Copy the files from the corporate network to the remote user's computer (or vice versa).

5. Keep track of how long the file transfers take.

6. Open the files after they are transferred to make sure they transferred completely and work correctly.

7. The remote user should disconnect from the corporate network when he or she is finished transferring files.

If part of the network goes down frequently, switch to another ISP—preferably, an ISP that also serves another part of the VPN. If you find yourself needing to switch to another ISP, consider using the following questions to help determine which ones can help you (and which ones cannot):

- How often does your network go offline?

- Do you have back-up servers that will keep customers like me online if the primary server goes down?

- Do you have back-up power supplies in case of a power outage?

- How far are you from the network backbone? (Two or three hops is considered close; the closer to the backbone the ISP is, the faster the connection.)

CHAPTER SUMMARY

This chapter examined the configuration and operations of Virtual Private Networks (VPNs), which extend security beyond a single LAN to include partner LANs and remote users who need dial-in access to the network. VPNs provide businesses with a cost-effective alternative to private leased lines. In contrast to leased lines, VPNs use the public Internet to connect two or more separate LANs or to link one or more remote users with a LAN. Many firewalls include VPN services among their list of features. Consider the following points covered in this chapter:

❑ VPNs consist of two main types of hardware: endpoints or terminators, and the tunnel through which the data passes. The endpoints perform the three essential functions of a VPN: encryption of data, authentication of hosts, and encapsulation of data packets within other packets.

❑ VPNs have advantages and disadvantages over leased lines. On the plus side, VPNs are less expensive than leased lines. They allow users to address packets using private addresses that are not normally routable on the Internet because the packets are encapsulated in other packets that contain the source and destination IP addresses of the VPN gateways involved. They also give the network administrator control over how information is encrypted. On the downside, VPNs are complex and, because they make use of the public Internet, you have little or no control over exactly how data gets from one LAN to another.

❑ VPNs fall into one of two general categories: site-to-site VPNs or client-to-site VPNs. A company can make use of both systems and does not have to choose one or the other. Some VPN systems make use of hardware terminators such as routers or appliances, which can connect large numbers of users. Others use software programs, which tend to scale better than hardware-based VPNs. VPN devices that make use of both hardware and software are also available.

❑ In terms of exactly how sites are connected in a VPN, you have two basic options: a mesh configuration or a hub-and-spoke configuration. A mesh configuration works well when small numbers of computers are involved and the company that is running the VPN is not expected to grow rapidly—each VPN device has to be configured separately to accept all other VPN devices. A hub-and-spoke configuration works better for larger, faster-growing organizations because configuration is only done at the hub computer. On the other hand, hub-and-spoke setups might work more slowly because all traffic is required to pass into and out of a central VPN device.

❑ A variety of tunneling protocols is available for use with VPNs, but currently the most popular is Internet Security Protocol (IPSec) coupled with Internet Key Exchange (IKE). IPSec handles the encapsulation and encryption of data while IKE provides for user authentication through public key cryptography. Other protocols such as PPTP and L2TP are specially designed to provide remote dial-in access to the VPN for individual users.

❑ In setting up a VPN, you'll probably be called upon to provide access for remote users. This requires you to set up a remote access server as well as client software on each remote workstation to be included in the VPN. All remote computers should be protected by firewalls, and client software should be chosen to work with any software or hardware combinations used by the client workstations. You'll also need to set up packet-filtering rules to allow dial-in access.

❐ To successfully operate and maintain a VPN, a number of best practices should be followed. For instance, security policies that apply specifically to the VPN should be included. In addition, the VPN should be audited and tested periodically to make sure it is operating at an acceptable level.

KEY TERMS

client-to-site VPN — A VPN that makes a network accessible to remote users who need dial-in access.

encapsulation — The act of enclosing one data structure within another structure; in the context of this chapter, an IP packet is enclosed within another IP packet.

encryption domain — The computers, routers, and other devices in a network that is protected by a gateway that performs encryption.

endpoint — One end of a VPN. The endpoint is provided by a router, VPN appliance, or firewall that sits at the perimeter of a network and does authentication, encapsulation, and encryption.

extranet — An extension of your corporate network to a new location.

frame relay — A telecommunications service that enables data to be transmitted in units called frames between endpoints in a wide area network or two points in a local area network.

hub-and-spoke configuration — A VPN configuration in which a single VPN router maintains records of all SAs; any device that wishes to participate in the VPN need only connect to the central router.

intranet — An internal network that uses Web servers, Web browsers, and other Internet-based software to enable communication and allow information to be shared.

IPSec concentrator — A device that terminates VPN connections.

Layer 2 Tunneling Protocol (L2TP) — An extension to Point-to-Point Protocol (PPP) that enables dial-up users to establish a VPN connection to a remote access server.

leased line — A connection used for network communications, such as a frame relay setup, that is leased from the telecommunications company that owns and operates it.

mesh configuration — A VPN configuration that is used to connect multiple computers that each have a security association (SA) with all other machines in the VPN.

multifactor authentication — The use of two or more authentication tools (something the user knows, such as a password; something the user has, such as a smart card; and something physically associated with the user, such as a fingerprint) to identify remote users.

Network Access Point — A network exchange facility where Internet Service Providers (ISPs) can connect to one another and to a high-speed part of the Internet called the "Internet backbone."

9

Point-to-Point Protocol (PPP) — A protocol that enables computer users to establish a dial-up modem connection with a remote access server. PPP is still used to give many individuals dial-up access to the Internet.

Point-to-Point Protocol (PPP) over Secure Shell (SSH) — A protocol used to give UNIX users VPN access to a remote network by means of the UNIX secure shell, which uses secret key encryption to authenticate participants.

Point-to-Point Protocol (PPP) over Secure Sockets Layer (SSL) — A protocol used to give UNIX users VPN access to a remote network using SSL to encrypt data sent between client and server.

Point-to-Point Tunneling Protocol (PPTP) — A protocol developed by Microsoft for granting VPN access to remote users over dial-up connections; it has since been replaced by L2TP.

pre-shared key — A secret key that both parties must have beforehand to establish a secure VPN connection.

proprietary — A term used to describe something that is owned by a company and that can be used only in that company's products.

SA table — A list of all the machines or individuals that have a security association (SA).

security association (SA) — A relationship that enables two computers or individuals to trust one another and share information over a network.

site-to-site VPN — A VPN that links two or more networks.

split tunneling — The establishment of two connections over a single VPN line.

terminator — A device that provides an endpoint for a VPN session, such as a router, a VPN appliance, or a firewall; *See* IPSec concentrator.

tunnel — A series of connections between Internet-based hosts and servers that conducts data from one hop to another between VPN endpoints.

virtual private network (VPN) — A system for point-to-point communications that encapsulates and encrypts data and uses authentication, and that uses the Internet to join users to a remote LAN.

VPN appliance — A hardware device specially designed to terminate VPNs and join multiple LANs.

REVIEW QUESTIONS

1. What do VPNs do that firewalls cannot do?

   a. encrypt data

   b. conceal IP source and destination addresses

   c. protect packets after they leave the local network

   d. authenticate users

2. Which of the following is a limitation of using leased lines to set up a private network?

    a. complexity

    b. cost

    c. scalability

    d. all of the above

3. Which of the following is a limitation of using a VPN rather than a leased line?

    a. scalability

    b. cost

    c. reliability

    d. all of the above

4. Why would you choose a VPN that is built into a firewall rather than a VPN appliance or a router? (Choose all that apply.)

    a. convenience

    b. lower cost

    c. higher security

    d. less complexity

5. Each of the following is a valid configuration of VPN except _____.

    a. hardware systems

    b. flash systems

    c. hardware and software systems

    d. hybrid systems

6. In the context of VPNs, why is the term *tunnel* misleading?

7. Which of the following is a downside of using a proprietary VPN protocol?

    a. Such protocols are often limited to working only with the same brand of firewall.

    b. Such protocols provide a weak level of encryption.

    c. Such protocols limit you to choosing one type of encryption.

    d. Such protocols do not provide for authentication.

8. Why is authentication an essential part of a VPN? (Choose all that apply.)

    a. It provides for groups of users who want to connect to the VPN.

    b. It guards against an unauthorized user using an authorized remote user's computer and dialing in to the network.

    c. It's important to know that the host originating the connection is an approved user.

    d. It makes for a stronger level of encryption.

9. How are the participants in a VPN actually authenticated?

   a. They submit approved passwords.

   b. They are identified by username.

   c. They exchange keys.

   d. They use a digital signature.

10. Which of the following protocols does *not* provide for client-to-site authentication on its own?

   a. PPTP

   b. PPP over SSH

   c. IPSec

   d. L2TP

11. Which of the following is a benefit of setting up a VPN rather than a leased line? (Choose all that apply.)

   a. reliability

   b. cost savings

   c. speed

   d. control

12. Which of the following is a special consideration you need to take into account when setting up multinational VPN?

   a. the reliability of the foreign ISP connection

   b. the language barrier

   c. different protocols

   d. different electrical systems

13. Why would you consider purchasing a VPN appliance rather than installing less expensive VPN software? (Choose all that apply.)

   a. Appliances are easier to configure than software VPNs.

   b. Appliances can handle more connections than software VPNs.

   c. Appliances are more reliable than software VPNs.

   d. Appliances stay online if the server crashes.

14. Aside from the fact that they're less expensive, under what circumstances does using a software VPN give you an advantage over a VPN appliance?

   a. if your network lacks sufficient bandwidth to allow a VPN appliance

   b. if you need software that's easier to configure than a VPN appliance

   c. if the company being protected works in financial or government services

   d. if the company being protected is growing quickly

15. A record that a VPN terminator checks to see if a security association exists is called a(n) _____ .

   a. rule base

   b. SA table

   c. state table

   d. security log

16. A mesh VPN configuration is ideal in what situation?

   a. when the company is small and not growing quickly

   b. when the participants all use the same ISP

   c. when many different software and hardware platforms are involved

   d. when the participants are located in the same state

17. A hub-and-spoke VPN configuration is ideal in what situation? (Choose all that apply.)

   a. if a mesh configuration is too slow

   b. if the number of participants is growing quickly

   c. if a single configuration point is needed

   d. if many different hardware and software platforms are involved

18. Which VPN protocol is most widely used today?

   a. PPP Over SSH

   b. PPTP

   c. L2TP

   d. IPSec with IKE

19. Tunnel mode seems like the obvious choice in using IPSec to secure communications through a VPN tunnel; what's the potential drawback with it?

   a. It requires the use of a Certificate Authority (CA).

   b. It doesn't provide for user authentication.

   c. It doesn't provide for strong-enough encryption.

   d. It doesn't work with all computers or operating systems.

20. PPTP is an older VPN protocol that is mainly used with older client computers, but it has one advantage over the more recent L2TP. What is it?

   a. It links sites as well as clients.

   b. It is compatible with firewalls.

   c. It is compatible with packet filtering.

   d. It is compatible with NAT.

Hands-on Projects

Project 9-1: Set Up a VPN Client Connection

VPN connections can take one of two forms: site-to-site or client-to-site. To set up a client-to-site connection, in which a remote user could dial in to a network over a VPN, you need to configure the client computer. Windows XP lets you establish a VPN client connection with a VPN network by following these steps.

1. Click **Start**, and then click **Control Panel**.

2. Double-click **Network Connections**. If necessary, click **Switch to Classic View**.

3. Under Network Tasks in the headings on the left side of the Network Connections window, click **Create a new connection**. Supply dialing information, if you are prompted to do so.

4. In the first screen of the New Connection Wizard, click **Next**.

5. In the second screen, click **Connect to the network at my workplace**, and then click **Next**.

6. In the third screen, click **Virtual Private Network connection**, and then click **Next**.

7. In the fourth (Connection Name) screen, type the name of the company you want to connect to in the Company Name text box. For this exercise, enter your school's name. Click **Next**.

8. In the Public Network screen, click **Do not dial the initial connection** because, if you have a direct connection to the Internet, you are already connected. Click **Next**.

9. In the VPN Server Selection screen, type the IP address or host name of the computer to which you connect at the remote network. For this exercise, type **192.168.0.0**, and then click **Next**.

10. In the final screen, click **Finish** to close the wizard. The Connect (Company Name) dialog box opens, where (Company Name) is the name you entered in Step 7. Type in your username and password, and click **Connect**. The computer you are trying to connect to needs to be configured as a VPN server for the connection to actually work (in Project 9-3). If it is not, click **Cancel**.

Project 9-2: Change VPN Connection Properties

If you have a dial-up connection to a remote VPN, you may occasionally need to change your settings. Your company might require you to select a new password periodically for enhanced security, for instance; or, you might need to set up authentication if it is not provided for already as part of the connection. Follow these steps to change connection settings on a Windows XP workstation.

1. Click **Start** and then click **Control Panel**.

2. Double-click **Network Connections**. If necessary, click **Switch to Classic View**.

3. Scroll down to the Virtual Private Network section, and double-click the icon for your VPN connection. The Connect (Company Name) dialog box opens.

4. In the Password text box, type a new password if you need to.

5. If you need to set up authentication, click **Change settings of this connection** under the Network Tasks heading on the left side of the Network Connections dialog box. The (Company Name) Properties dialog box opens.

6. Click the **Security** tab to bring it to the front.

7. Check the **Automatically use my Windows logon name and password (and domain if any)** check box if you want to use your Windows logon information for authentication. If your VPN uses IPSec, click **IPSec Settings** and check the **Use pre-shared key for authentication** check box. Then click **OK**.

8. Click **OK** to close (Company Name) Settings and return to Network Connections.

Project 9-3: Set Up Your Workstation to Function as a VPN Server

9

A Windows XP computer that has an always-on Internet connection, such as a T-1 line or DSL or cable modem connection, can function as a VPN server for an incoming connection from a single workstation or network gateway. This enables you to connect to the Windows XP computer from a remote computer running another version of Windows or XP itself. The VPN server workstation must have a known IP address—ideally, a static IP address, or at least one that is not generated dynamically. You must also be logged in as an administrator of your workstation to configure VPN access.

1. Click **Start**, and then click **Control Panel**.

2. Double-click **Network Connections**. If necessary, click **Switch to Classic View**.

3. Click **Create a new connection** under Network Tasks.

4. Click **Next**.

5. In the Network Connection Type screen, click **Set up an advanced connection**, and then click **Next**.

6. In the Advanced Connection Options screen, make sure **Accept incoming connections** is selected, and then click **Next**.

7. In the Devices for Incoming Connections screen, check the box next to the modem or other device you want to use for the incoming connections. If you have a direct connection to the Internet through a LAN, you may see the options WAN Miniport and Direct Parallel. If so, check the **WAN Miniport** check box, if available, and then click **Next**.

8. In the Incoming Virtual Private Network (VPN) Connection, select **Allow virtual private connections**, and then click **Next**.

9. In the User Permissions dialog box, check the boxes next to the names of the users to which you want to grant access to your workstation. Check only the names you are sure you want to connect; keep the list of selections as short as possible, and do not select Guest.

10. Double-click the names of each of the selected users. In the User Permissions dialog box, confirm the name and password, and then click **OK**.

11. Click **Next**.

12. In the Networking Software screen, click the networking software you want to use, and then click **Next**.

13. Click **Finish** to complete the wizard.

Project 9-4: Define Check Point FireWall-1 VPN Network Objects

An essential prerequisite for working with Check Point FireWall-1 is the establishment of network objects. In the case of a VPN, you need to define each of the networks that will have a security association. You use the FireWall-1 GUI interface or Policy Editor to open Network Properties, where you then define the local and remote networks that will use the VPN. Once the two networks are defined, you can then go on to set up the VPN and set up rules for it, as described in subsequent projects.

 If you don't have two real networks you want to connect, use an IP address of 192.168.164.1 with a subnet mask of 255.255.255.0 for the first network and an IP address of 192.168.164.2 with a subnet mask of 255.255.255.0 for the second network.

1. Click **Start**, point to **Programs**, point to **Check Point Management Clients**, and click **Policy Editor NG FP2** to open the Check Point Policy Editor window. Type your password and click **OK**.

2. Click **Manage** and then click **Network Objects** to open the Network Objects dialog box.

3. Click **New** and then click **Network** to open the Network Properties dialog box.

4. In the General tab, type the name **Local_Network** in the Name text box to set up your own network object.

5. In the Network Address text box, type the first IP address in your network. (For example, if your address range is 192.168.164.00/24, type **192.168.124.0**.)

6. In the Net Mask text box, type your own subnet mask: such as **255.255.255.0**.

7. Click **OK**.

8. Repeat Step 3.

9. Type the name **Remote_Network** for the remote network in the VPN.

10. Repeat Steps 5-7, but type in the information that pertains to your remote network to define it as a network object.

11. When you're done, click **Close** to close the Network Objects dialog box.

Project 9-5: Define an Encryption Domain for a FireWall-1 VPN

FireWall-1 uses the term *encryption domain* to describe an area that is behind a gateway and protected by encryption. In a VPN, two gateways use encryption to protect two separate networks. Your job is to define two network objects for the VPN: the two gateways that will use encryption to protect their networks. The following project assumes that you have defined two network objects called Local_Network and Remote_Network, as described in the preceding project.

1. If you do not have the Policy Editor open from the previous project, click **Start**, point to **Programs**, point to **Check Point Management Clients,** and click **Policy Editor NG FP2** to open the Check Point Policy Editor window. Type your password, and then click **OK**.

2. Click the **+ (plus sign)** next to Network Objects.

3. Locate and double-click **Local_Network**.

4. In the list of categories (General Properties, Topology, NAT, VPN) in the left side of Check Point Gateway, click **VPN**.

5. Check the **IKE** check box, and then click **Edit**. The IKE Properties dialog box appears.

6. Make sure that the **DES** and **3DES** check boxes are checked. Also make sure that the **MD5** and **SHA1** check boxes are checked.

7. Check the **Pre-Shared Secret** check box. (You need to check **Public Key Signatures** only if you are using certificates; leave it unchecked for now.)

8. Click **OK** to close the IKE Properties dialog box.

9. Click **Topology** in the list of categories on the left side of the Workstation Properties dialog box.

10. Click **Manually Defined** under VPN Domain.

11. Click **All_Intranet_Gateways** from the drop-down list.

12. Click **OK** to close the Check Point Gateway dialog box. Then click **OK** to close the Network Objects dialog box.

9

Project 9-6: Define the Remote Gateway and Configure Authentication

After you have defined the local gateway for your site-to-site VPN, you need to define the remote gateway. The process of defining the remote gateway is almost identical to defining the local gateway except that, this time, you have the opportunity to create a shared secret for authentication. (You don't define the shared secret when you define the local gateway, only when you define the remote gateway.)

1. If necesarry, click **Start**, point to **Programs**, point to **Check Point Management Clients**, and then click **Policy Editor NG FP@** to open the Check Point Policy Editor window.

2. Click the **+ plus sign** next to Network Objects, if necessary.

3. Locate and double-click **Remote_Network**.

4. In the IKE Properties dialog box, click **Pre-Shared Secret**.

5. Click **Edit Secrets**.

6. In the Shared Secret dialog box, click **Local_Gateway** under the Peer Name column.

7. If a dialog box saying this feature is not supported in local mode appears, click **OK**. If the Edit Secret dialog box opens, type a secret word, phrase, or code in the Enter secret text box. What kind of "secret" could you enter here? What qualities would make a good secret? Write the answer in a lab manual or word processing document.

8. Click **Set**.

9. Click **OK** to close the Shared Secret dialog box, and click **OK** again.

10. Click **Topology**.

11. Click **Manually Defined**, and click **All_Intranet_Gateways** from the drop-down list.

12. Click **OK** to close the Check Point Gateway dialog box. Then click **OK** to close the Network Objects dialog box. If a dialog box appears telling you that you cannot configure anti-spoofing, click **OK**.

Project 9-7: Establish VPN Rules

In FireWall-1, you add rules to the existing Policy Editor rule base to cover the operation of the VPN. You need to add only two rules to enable the key exchange that sets up encrypted traffic between the two networks. You also need to add Encrypt to the Action column in the rule base.

1. Click **Start**, point to **Programs**, point to **Check Point Management Clients**, and click **Policy Editor NG FP2** to open the Check Point Policy Editor window. Type your password, and then click **OK**.

2. If necessary, click **Rules**, point to **Add Rule**, and click **Below**. Click **Desktop Security – Standard** in the Rule Base pane of the Policy Editor.

3. In Inbound Rules, right-click the heading **Action** and click **Query Column**.

4. In the Rule Base Query Clause dialog box, click **Encrypt** in the Not in list column, and then click **Add** to move Encrypt to the In List column.

5. Click **Close**.

6. Repeat Steps 3 and 4 for Outbound Rules.

7. Click **Rules**, point to **Add Rule**, and choose **Below**.

8. In the Inbound Rules section, scroll down to the new rule at the bottom of the list. Right-click **Any** under the Source column and click **Add**. The Add Object dialog box appears.

9. Click **Local_Gateway**, then click **OK**.

10. In the Inbound Rules section, right-click **Any** under the Destination column, and click **Add**. The Add Object dialog box appears.

11. Click **Remote Gateway**, and then click **OK**.

12. Right-click **Accept** under the Action column, and click **Encrypt**.

13. Right-click **None** under the Track column, and choose **Log**.

14. Highlight the Inbound Rules section. Click **Rules**, point to **Add Rule**, and click **Below** to set up the second VPN rule.

15. Right-click **Any** under the Source column, and click **Add**. The Add Object dialog box appears.

16. Click **Remote_Gateway**, then click **OK**.

17. Highlight the Outbound Rules section. Right-click **Any** under the Destination column, and click **Add**. The Add Object dialog box opens.

18. Click **Local_Gateway**, and then click **OK**.

19. Right-click **Accept** under the Action column, and click **Encrypt**.

20. Right-click **None** under the Track column, and click **Log**.

21. Click **File** and click **Save**.

22. Click **File** and click **Exit** to close the Check Point Policy Editor and return to the Windows desktop.

Project 9-8: Install a Symantec Enterprise Virtual Private Network 7.0

One of the most common VPNs found in the information security environment is made by Symantec. Symantec Enterprise Virtual Private Network 7.0 provides a software VPN method. In this project, you install the Symantec Enterprise Virtual Private Network 7.0.

Symantec Enterprise Virtual Private Network 7.0 30-day evaluations are available for download from Symantec at *www.symantec.com/downloads*. For this lab, you must obtain the software license key. If you do not, the software will be installed on a 30-day evaluation basis only. This lab assumes that you have conducted the download prior to starting the lab.

The method in this lab installs the Symantec Enterprise Virtual Private Network 7.0 as a standalone system without the Management Console.

1. Log on as **Local Administrator**.

2. Depending on what level of encryption you need, browse to one of the following directories on the distribution CD:

   SYMC_fw_vpn\DES

   SYMC_fw_vpn\3DES (stronger encryption)

3. Double-click the **setup.exe** file to begin the installation and display the Symantec Enterprise VPN 7.0 Welcome screen.

4. Click the **Next** button to proceed to the License Agreement screen.

5. After reading the license agreement, click the **Yes** button to accept the terms of the agreement and display the Product License Key screen.

6. If you do not possess a software license key, click **Evaluation Install** and click **Next**.

7. You will be presented with a Product Selection window. Perform the following:

   a. Select **Symantec Enterprise VPN**.

   b. Uncheck the **Symantec Raptor Management Console** check box.

   c. Leave the **Documentation** check box checked.

   d. Click **Next** to proceed to the Destination Drive screen.

8. Choose the destination drive in which you wish to install the Symantec Enterprise VPN files. Ensure that the Space listing indicates the required amount is available.

9. Click **Next** to proceed to the Install Selected Components screen. Verify the components selected for installation and click **Next**.

10. The Setup Screen will appear and begin to show the progress of the installation. Upon completion of the files being copied, the Symantec Enterprise VPN Configuration screen will be displayed. Choose a network interface to be the Inside and click the **Add >>** button to move it to the Inside box. Note that you may be notified that an Inside adapter cannot have a Default Gateway set. See the documentation included with the installation for the section containing the Configure Network settings for further assistance.

11. After setting both the Inside and Outside network interfaces, click **OK** to proceed to the Local Management Password screen.

12. Type your password, press **Tab**, and type your password again for verification. After you are satisfied with your password, click **Next**.

13. Upon leaving the Password screen, the installation will be complete. Restart your system when prompted.

Project 9-9: Install a Symantec Enterprise VPN Client 7.0

To connect to a VPN server, a remote user must have a VPN client installed on his or her host machine. It is not always a requirement to have the same vendor software on both ends of a VPN, but it does minimize configuration and management. In this project, you install the Symantec Enterprise VPN Client.

Symantec Enterprise VPN Client 7.0 30-day evaluations are available for download from Symantec at *www.symantec.com/downloads*. For this lab, you must obtain the software license key. If you do not, the software will be installed on a 30-day evaluation basis only. This lab assumes that you have conducted the download prior to starting the lab.

1. Log on as **Local Administrator**.
2. With your Symantec Enterprise VPN Client CD in the required drive, browse to the **VPNClient** directory.
3. Depending on what level of encryption you need, browse to one of the following directories on the distribution CD:

   \DES

   \3DES (stronger encryption)
4. Select the directory for the operating system on which you are installing the client.
5. Double-click the **setup.exe** file to begin the installation and display the Symantec Enterprise VPN Client 7.0 Welcome screen.
6. Click the **Next** button to proceed to the License Agreement screen.
7. Select **Yes, I wish to read the Release Notes now** to open the release notes document. When finished reading the release notes, close them to continue the installation.
8. Click **Next** to continue with the installation.
9. From the Destination Location screen, select the directory where you intend to install the Symantec Enterprise VPN Client; the C:\Program Files\Symantec\VPNClient directory will be selected as the default location.
10. Click **Next**.
11. From the Symantec Enterprise VPN Client Installation Options screen, check the **Create a Start Menu folder** and **Add to desktop** options.
12. Click **Next**.
13. From the Select Program Folder, accept the default location for the program folder (Symantec Enterprise VPN Client) and click **Next**.
14. The Installation Review screen will appear. Verify the configuration selected for installation. Note that you can click **Back** to change settings. If satisfied with the configuration, click **Next**.
15. After a couple minutes, the setup will be complete and you will be asked to restart your machine. You must do this to use your newly installed client. Select **Yes, I want to restart my computer now** and click **Finish**.

9

CASE PROJECTS

Case 9-1: Setting Up a VPN

You have been hired by a small company that has set up a VPN. The VPN includes two business partners with which the company needs to communicate on a regular basis. You set up a simple mesh configuration, going from office to office to do the initial configuration, which includes SA table listings for all devices in the VPN. The VPN operates smoothly until your company purchases another business that has branch offices located overseas. You are given the assignment of expanding the VPN to include the new employees. You are told that all internal LANs should be able to communicate with one another and are informed in confidence that more acquisitions may be in store. You are happy about the prospect of travelling overseas to extend the VPN, but the prospect of updating four or more VPN devices around the world on a regular basis seems impractical to say the least. What should you do to help the VPN grow?

Case 9-2: Improving Communication

Your company (the same one mentioned in the previous Case 9-1) does indeed follow through with the purchase of a distribution center located in another state. You are told, however, that only the central office and one branch office will need to communicate with the distribution center to send delivery instructions and maintain shipping records. You are told that speed is of the essence in getting updated records, particularly at budget time each spring. What is the best way to expand the VPN in this case?

Case 9-3: Dealing with Communication Slowdowns

After you have the newly expanded VPN mentioned in Case 9-2 up and running, you notice significant slowdowns in communications, particularly with one Asian branch office. What are your options for speeding up communications with this single office? Give two alternatives.

Case 9-4: Viruses on VPNs

Your VPN uses transport mode to send traffic to other VPN participants. The network administrator of one of the LANs in the VPN e-mails you an alert stating that his network has been infected with the W32.Klez virus. Because all communications between your LAN and his LAN go through a VPN, you feel reasonably confident that you won't be infected. Nevertheless, the next day a computer on your machine reports that its antivirus software has isolated the same virus. How could this have happened, and what steps can you take to reduce the chances of its happening again?

10

BUILDING YOUR OWN FIREWALL

After reading this chapter and completing the exercises, you will be able to:

♦ List and define the two categories of firewalls

♦ Explain why desktop firewalls are used

♦ Explain how enterprise firewalls work

The importance of installing a firewall as part of a total network security system should never be underestimated. Used alongside antivirus scanners, virtual private networks (VPNs), encryption, and host intrusion detection software that identifies holes in the network, firewalls play a critical role in protecting a network by "keeping the bad guys out."

Which firewall product should you use? A quick search of the Internet reveals that there are a wide variety of firewalls available. Some firewalls are hardware appliances that are installed next to routers or switches and provide protection for the entire enterprise. Other firewalls are software-only packages that can either run on a Linux or Windows server to protect the network or be installed on a local computer to protect a single device. The cost of these firewalls range from free Internet downloads to tens of thousands of dollars. Which should you choose?

The answer, of course, is that there is no one firewall that is the best for every situation. Whereas an expensive appliance firewall may be the top choice for one business, a free software-only package may be the ideal solution somewhere else. The key is to first develop a security policy and then select the firewall that best supports that policy by providing the type and level of protection that is required.

In this chapter we will look at common types of firewalls found today. These firewalls are representative of the types of firewalls that are available for enterprise, small office home office (SOHO), and single computer protection. We will explore the features of these firewalls that provide the necessary protection to help keep a network or a computer secure.

ENTERPRISE VERSUS DESKTOP FIREWALLS

There are a variety of different ways in which firewalls can be categorized. One of the most common ways is by its platform: Is the firewall a separate hardware appliance or is it software that runs on a separate computer? Until recently hardware appliances were generally firewalls that protected the entire network or network segment, while software-only firewalls protected just a single computer. However, with the increasing popularity of low-cost Linux servers (which can even function on a pre-Pentium computer), these software-only servers can now protect entire networks.

Today firewalls are more often classified as either enterprise or as desktop firewalls. An enterprise firewall is one that protects the entire network or a network segment. This is illustrated in Figure 10-1. An enterprise firewall can be either a separate hardware appliance or a software-only firewall that is installed on a server running Linux, Windows, or another operating system.

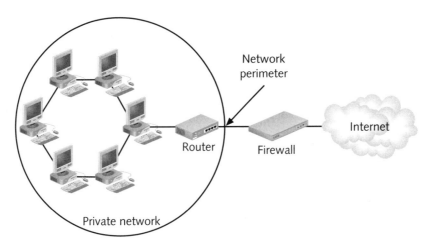

Figure 10-1   Enterprise firewall

A desktop firewall, on the other hand, is a software-only firewall that is intended to be installed on one client computer on the network and provide protection only to that device. Also known as personal firewalls, these software-only firewalls today have generally replaced separate hardware firewalls for protection of a single device. A network that is protected by both an enterprise firewall and desktop firewalls is seen in Figure 10-2. Desktop firewalls intercept and inspect all data that enters or leaves the computer. Traffic can generally be blocked by the IP address, port address, or the application.

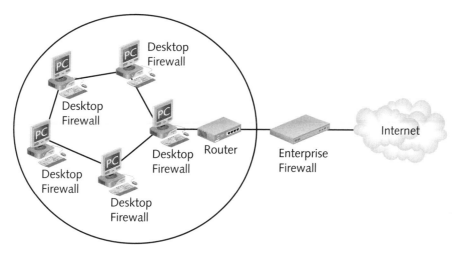

Figure 10-2 Desktop firewall

Yet why would a desktop firewall be needed if the entire network were already protected by an enterprise firewall? The answer is that users in a network protected by an enterprise firewall can compromise the security provided by that firewall. As seen in Figure 10-3, an employee may bring from home a **wireless access point**, a device used to connect wireless computers to a wired network, and connect it to the wired network in his or her office. This unauthorized device, sometimes called a **rogue access point**, could enable an unauthorized user with a wireless computer to access the network behind the enterprise firewall. In addition, a user could accidentally introduce a worm to the network by bringing in an infected CD-ROM or diskette and installing it on their personal computer. A desktop firewall can help protect the network by providing additional security at each network device.

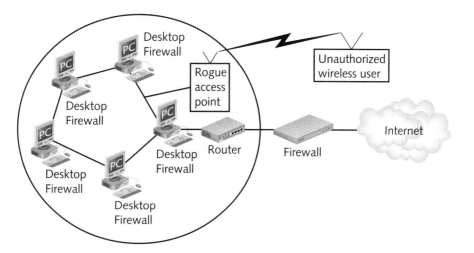

Figure 10-3 Rogue access point

10

One of the criticisms of desktop firewalls is that they are difficult to manage. For example, users could change settings on their desktop firewall without the knowledge of the network manager and thus compromise security. However, a new breed of desktop firewalls provide centralized management that allows administrators to download a security policy file from a single server to all desktop firewalls and prevent any user changes to the policy. These systems can also upload a status report from the client to the server regarding any suspicious activity.

Because most industry experts today classify firewalls as either enterprise or desktop firewalls, this chapter will look at firewalls in that same way. First we will explore several popular desktop firewalls and then look at the larger and more powerful enterprise firewalls.

DESKTOP FIREWALLS

Desktop firewalls have gained increased popularity in recent years. This is due to the fact that they can supply a second level of security at the user's computer. Used along with enterprise firewalls, desktop firewalls can make a system much more difficult for an unauthorized user to break into. Three of the most popular desktop firewalls are Tiny Personal Firewall, Sygate Personal Firewall and ZoneAlarm.

 Versions of all of these desktop firewalls—Sygate Personal Firewall, Tiny Personal Firewall, and ZoneAlarm—are available as free downloads over the Internet. Each of the vendors of these products also offers for sale a companion product that has expanded features.

Tiny Personal Firewall

Tiny Personal Firewall, a product of Tiny Software, Inc. (*www.tinysoftware.com*), is well known as a solid desktop firewall product. Tiny Personal Firewall is unique among most desktop firewalls in the advanced security features that it includes. In addition to providing firewall protection, antivirus protection can also be integrated into Tiny Personal Firewall. This allows a single package to protect against network attacks, worms, and viruses.

Tiny Personal Firewall is based on a technology that has been certified by the ICSA, an independent group that tests and certifies firewalls. Only those firewalls that pass the ICSA tests, which include event logging, administrative functions, persistence, security, and documentation, can receive the ICSA certification. Once a firewall is certified, it remains installed and operational at the ICSA labs. This enables ICSA to not only test any upgrades or patches to the firewall but also to verify that it continues to protect against the latest security attacks that continue to arise.

Figure 10-4 shows the Tiny Personal Firewall software. Tiny Personal Firewall is made up of several different components called "engines." The basic firewall is called the Firewall engine. The Firewall engine performs stateful packet inspection. This engine can be set to permit, deny, or ask the user for permission for the packet to pass based on the packet's contents. Security administrators can set the policies for the Firewall engine and then distribute these policies to all desktops using the Management Server function. Administrators can also create trusted address groups and then create filtering rules that apply to these groups. These trusted address groups can be based on a single IP address, a subnet, or a range of network IP addresses.

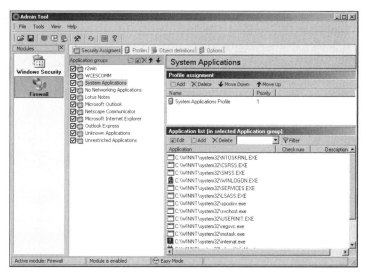

Figure 10-4   Firewall engine

In addition to filtering network activity based on the TCP/IP protocol, the Firewall engine also supports rules that link to specific applications. Known as an Application Filter, this service provides an additional level of security beyond that of low-level packet inspection. An Application Filter, for example, can prevent an unauthorized application from directly accessing the network or communicating with an unwanted source. This filtering is based on the application program and not on the contents of a packet.

Apart from checking incoming and outgoing packets the Firewall engine can also detect if permitted packets are sent by unauthorized applications. A rogue application program could infiltrate a computer by e-mail or from a floppy disk. This program "pretends" to be a regular and known program but it has a malicious intent. The program replaces the original executable program on the hard drive and then tries to send data out from the computer. Such an application is called a Trojan horse.

Trojan horse programs can sometimes be caught with anti-virus software.

The Firewall engine uses a method to ensure that the application program on the computer is the real program and not a Trojan horse. It accomplishes this by creating and checking **MD5 signatures** of application programs. An MD5 signature is a unique number (also called a **checksum**) that is generated based on the contents of application programs. Checksums are illustrated in Figure 10-5. When the application program is executed for the first time, the Firewall engine displays a dialog box asking the user if it will permit the program to access the network. If the answer is yes then the Firewall engine creates an MD5 signature for the application program. This signature is then checked whenever the application program attempts to communicate over the network. If a Trojan horse replaces the application program the MD5 signatures will no longer match and it is denied access to the network.

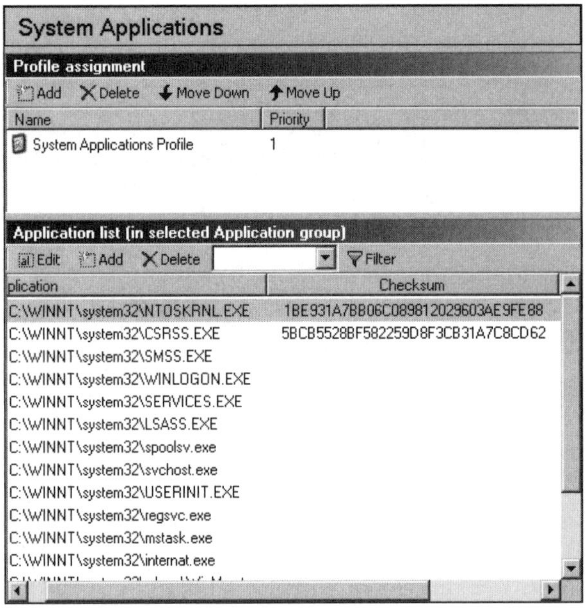

Figure 10-5 Checksums

In addition to the Firewall engine, Tiny Personal Firewall includes an Intrusion Detection System (IDS) engine. The purpose of the IDS is to monitor the Firewall engine. The IDS engine is also signature based: it compares the content of each packet with a predefined set of signatures. If the content of the packet matches an IDS signature then an event for the report is generated. The event includes information that can be used to identify the packet, such as the source IP addresses, the port, and the packet contents. The IDS engine report is seen in Figure 10-6.

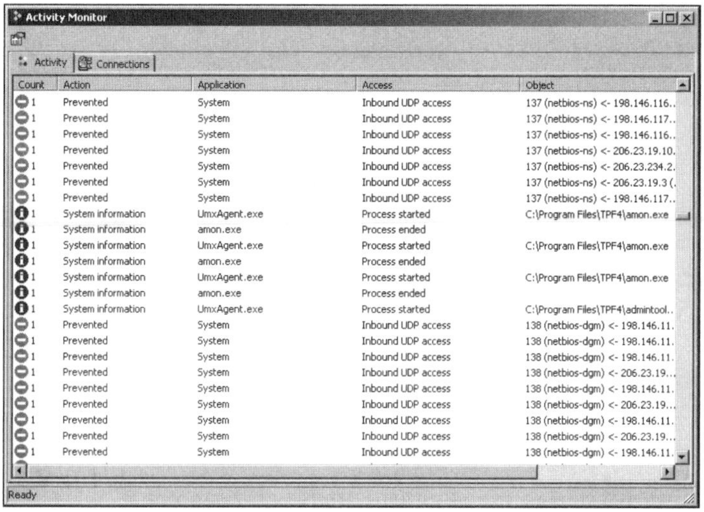

Figure 10-6   IDS engine

In addition the protection of the Firewall engine and IDS engine, Tiny Personal Firewall also uses what is called **sandbox** technology. Sandbox technology creates a closed environment (sandbox) around an application and restricts its access to resources. Within this closed environment the program can perform its regular functions. However, when the application program attempts to access an unauthorized resource outside the sandbox it is prevented from doing so. The types of resources that the sandbox protects include device drivers, the registry database that contains all the configurations of the computer, and the file system. Sandbox technology shields and constantly monitors application programs to protect the privacy and integrity of the computer system.

Sandbox technology protects computers and networks against attacks generated through the programs that run in a Web browser, such as ActiveX, Java applets, Javascript, or VisualBASIC script. These programs provide what is known as **active content**, such as an animated icon, and provide enhanced functions to static Web pages. However, in the wrong hands active content programs can perform the following functions:

- **Theft of information and data**—Active content programs can access data and files on the computer or network and send them to another computer via e-mail or through unrestricted ports.

- **Remote access via the Internet**—An active content program can create a proxy on the computer that allows unauthorized computers on the Internet to remotely access all the resources on the computer or network.

- **Manipulate communication**—Active content programs can filter, manipulate, or falsify information received from another computer. In addition, they could impersonate the computer user and send malicious e-mails from the user's e-mail account or start destructive actions.

10

- **Deletion of files**—An active content program could delete system or user files in the background while running on the computer.

- **Denial of service**—By changing the configuration of the operating system or applications an active content program can cripple a system and make it unusable.

The Tiny Personal Firewall sandbox protects these computer resources against unauthorized access. This is done by allowing the user to indicate which resources, called objects, are to be protected. Figure 10-7 shows the objects that can be protected. Some of the more frequently used objects and their descriptions are summarized in Table 10-1.

Figure 10-7   Objects that can be protected

Table 10-1   Sandbox objects

Object	Description	Protection
Registry	Database of system configurations	Prevents active content from securing unauthorized access to resources
Services	Provide important tasks of OS	Prevents Trojan horse from being installed
Devices	Hard drives, floppies, CD-ROMs	Prevents active content from reformatting hard drive
OLE	Cooperation between programs	Prevents unauthorized access to other programs and data
Spawning	Spawned program inherits security	Prevents unauthorized access to other programs and data

By default, a spawned application inherits the security environment of the application that invokes it. For example, when opening an attachment in an e-mail program (Outlook), the e-mail program invokes or spawns a word processor (Word). An active content program could manipulate spawning to provide it with unauthorized levels of security.

Tiny Personal Firewall has gained a reputation as being a full-featured desktop firewall. The firewall along with the additional security that is provided through its sandbox technology has made Tiny Personal Firewall one of the more attractive desktop firewalls available.

Sygate Firewalls

Sygate Technologies (*www.sygate.com*) has a reputation as an industry leader in providing enterprise-wide security solutions. Sygate's products are designed to protect corporate networks and desktop systems from intrusion and prevent malicious attackers from gaining control of the corporate information network.

Sygate offers a broad range of desktop firewall products. These products range in design from enterprise-based security systems to personal firewall systems. The Sygate Secure Enterprise is their top-of-the-line product that combines protection with centralized management. Secure Enterprise is made up of the Sygate Management Server (SMS) and Sygate Security Server. The Sygate Security Server firewall provides protection to network users by inspecting both inbound as well as outbound traffic. It also checks all components and Dynamic Link Libraries (DLLs) to ensure that no tampering has taken place. The Sygate Security Server also works with other protocols besides TCP/IP, such as Appletalk.

The SMS enables security managers to create a global security policy that applies to all users and groups. Subgroups can be created within the global group. Any changes to a parent group are automatically inherited by all of its subgroups. For example, in Figure 10-8 the global policy prevents any users from using File Transfer Protocol (FTP). However, the subgroup "Technical Staff" is provided access to FTP. Because policies of parent groups are inherited by their subgroups and these subpolicies override global policies, all subgroups beneath "Technical Staff" can have FTP access.

The Sygate Management Server also allows security managers to create multiple policies based on the user's location or the task they are performing. For example, one policy can apply to all users logged into the local network while another policy can apply to users connecting to the network by a VPN. Policies can be based on IP address, Media Access Control (MAC) address, the application that is being run, or even time of day.

10

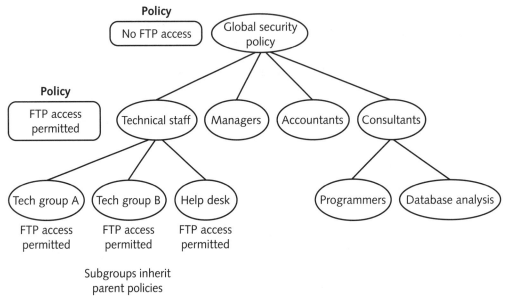

Figure 10-8   Subgroups inherit policy

Sygate Secure Enterprise can also produce detailed reports of actions by the firewall. Each rule that makes up a policy can be assigned a severity level from 0 to 15. Whenever an attempt is made to breach that rule an entry into the report log is generated, with those incidences with the highest severity level appearing first in the report. In addition, security managers can create bar, line and pie charts showing the IP address, protocol, time, application being run, and severity of the attack.

Sygate Personal Firewall Pro is Sygate's product that is also designed for business users but lacks many of the centralized management features found in Secure Enterprise. Sygate Personal Firewall Pro 5.0 has a reputation for providing in-depth low-level tools for protecting computers from a variety of attacks, including attempts to modify the Windows Registry. The Personal Firewall Pro main screen is seen in Figure 10-9.

Personal Firewall Pro blocks or allowing specific services and applications instead of restricting specific TCP network ports. Personal Firewall Pro's security settings can be set to automatically allow everything to pass through the firewall, to allow nothing to pass, or to ask the user each time for permission, which is the default setting. This is seen in Figure 10-10. Sygate's security is so restrictive that by default it requires the user to grant permission for a Web browser to access the Internet.

Although firewall restrictions based on services and applications instead of by TCP port are frequently found on desktop firewalls, many industry security professionals prefer to have the flexibility to use either approach.

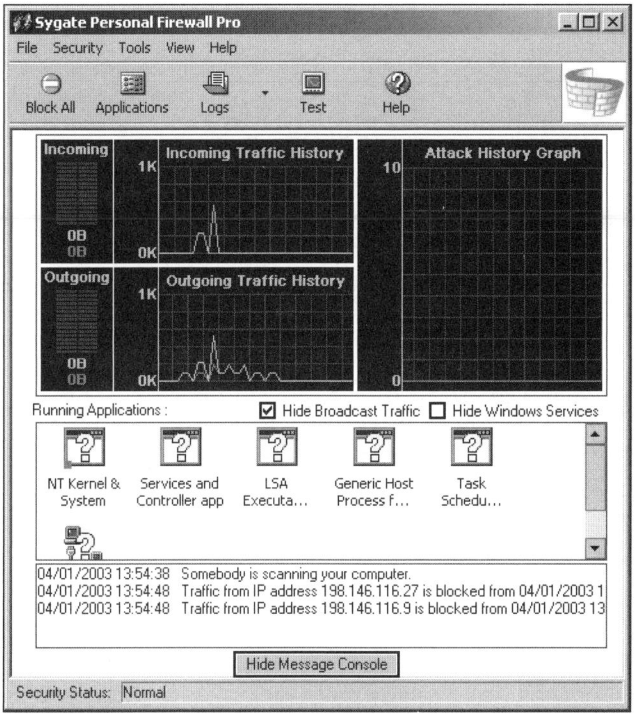

Figure 10-9   Personal Firewall Pro

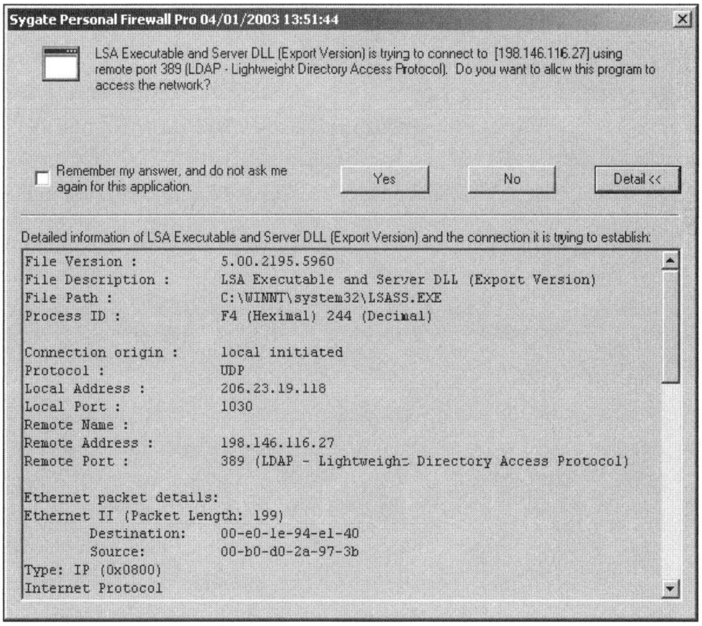

Figure 10-10   Asking for permission

Sygate Personal Firewall Pro can treat individual program device drivers as if they were network applications. This ensures that the application program on the computer is the real program and not a Trojan horse. It accomplishes this by creating and then checking the signatures of application programs. Sygate calls this a **fingerprinting system**. Personal Firewall Pro determines if programs have changed since being registered. If a fingerprint changes because of a virus or Trojan horse, Personal Firewall Pro asks the user whether to block or allow it the application.

 Personal Firewall Pro can also separately inspect and fingerprint each Dynamic Link Library (DLL) that is loaded by an application.

The Personal Firewall Pro provides a great deal of flexibility over the rules that govern the firewall. Rules can be set based on applications, Media Access Control (MAC) addresses, protocols, and network devices. For example, a rule can be created to block all Hypertext Transport Protocol (HTTP) traffic using TCP Port 80 using the Microsoft Internet Explorer browser originating from the 192.168.x.x subnet of a network from the time 11:30 PM to 5:00 AM.

 Personal Firewall Pro can send an e-mail notification when an attack on the firewall occurs.

The Personal Firewall Pro contains additional features that are not commonly found on most desktop firewall products. For example, by clicking on a Test icon, a user can be connected to the Sygate Online Services and execute a series of security tests on the firewall. In addition, Personal Firewall Pro protects against MAC and IP spoofing. Personal Firewall Pro also restricts a Web browser program from revealing information about itself and the operating system that the computer is running. Both VPN and integrated anti-virus protection are also included. These additional features are seen in Figure 10-11.

Sygate also offers Sygate Personal Firewall as a desktop firewall for home users. Personal Firewall, which is available free over the Internet, has the same basic features as Personal Firewall Pro but lacks some of the high-end features such as VPN support and advanced protection against Trojan horses. Sygate Office Network firewall and Sygate Home Office Network firewall round out its firewall product line.

Sygate has a reputation for providing solid firewall security with a variety of additional features. It is one of the leading desktop firewall vendors in the industry.

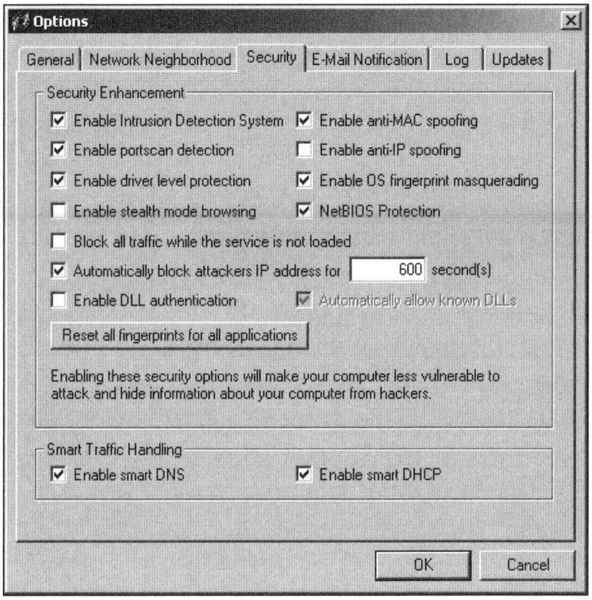

Figure 10-11   Additional features

ZoneAlarm Firewalls

Perhaps the best-known software desktop firewalls are products from Zone Labs (*www.zonelabs.com*) known as ZoneAlarm. ZoneAlarm has gained a strong following among users as a very flexible but rock-solid desktop firewall that has many advanced features. ZoneAlarm is available in three product configurations. ZoneAlarm Pro is a full-featured desktop firewall, while ZoneAlarm contains fewer features but is available as a free download. Integrity is the name of Zone Lab's high-end enterprise product, which integrates centralized management features.

> **Note**
> ZoneAlarm will not run on Windows 95 because of the security weaknesses in that version of the operating system. It does run on Windows 98, ME, NT, 2000 and XP.

The ZoneAlarm program is made up of the following four interlocking security services:

- Firewall
- Application Control
- Internet Lock
- Zones

The ZoneAlarm firewall interface is seen in Figure 10-12. The firewall is bi-directional, meaning that it provides protection from both incoming and outgoing traffic. If an unknown outside source attempts to connect to a computer, a pop-up window alerts the user to the intrusion attempt and prompts whether to grant or deny access. These settings are configurable by the user, as seen in Figure 10-13.

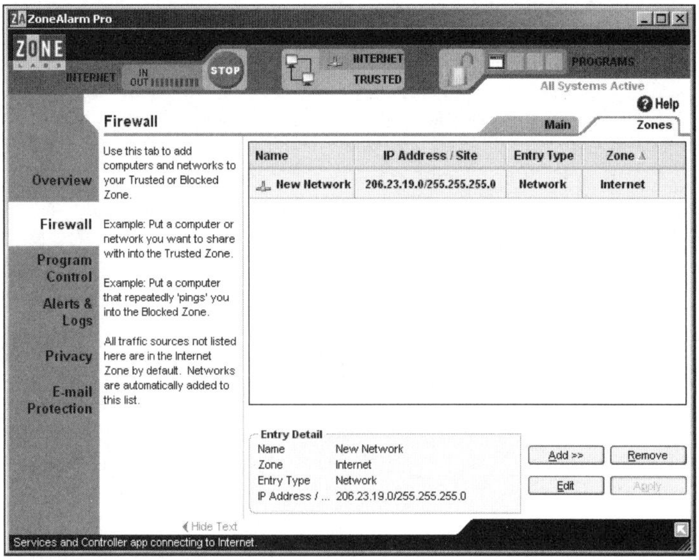

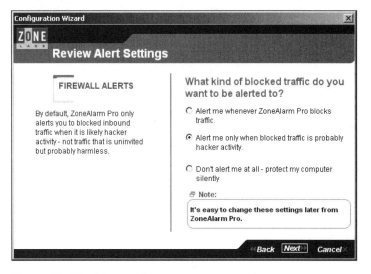

Figure 10-12   ZoneAlarm firewall

Figure 10-13   User settings

The ZoneAlarm firewall uses fingerprints to identify all components of a program as well as the program itself. This prevents a Trojan horse or other malicious code that pretends to be an approved program from gaining control of the computer. ZoneAlarm also stops potentially malicious active content, including JavaScript and ActiveX controls, from harming the computer. The firewall's settings are seen in Figure 10-14.

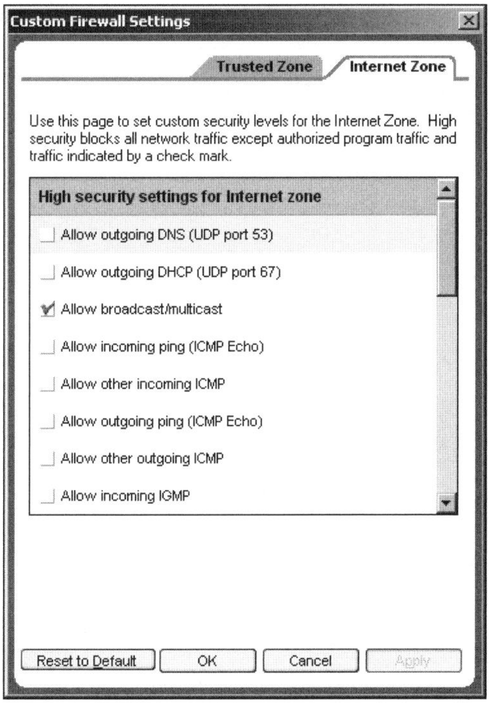

Figure 10-14 Firewall settings

The Application Control allows users to decide which applications can or cannot use the Internet. Internet Lock blocks all Internet traffic while the computer is unattended or while the Internet is not being used. It can be activated automatically with the computer's screensaver or after a set period of inactivity. This is illustrated in Figure 10-15.

ZoneAlarm's Zones monitors all activity on the computer and sends an alert when a new application attempts to access the Internet. ZoneAlarm is designed for use on both traditional wired as well as wireless networks. A network status display details information about which networks are active and whether they are "trusted" or "untrusted." As a new network is identified, either wired or wireless, a dialog box appears that allows the user to name the network and assign it as either a trusted or untrusted zone. Zone management allows users to easily share files with computers and networks that are trusted while blocking untrusted networks. Zone security is seen in Figure 10-16.

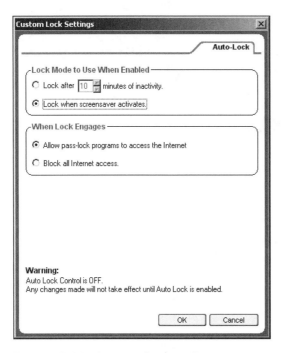

Figure 10-15   Internet Lock settings

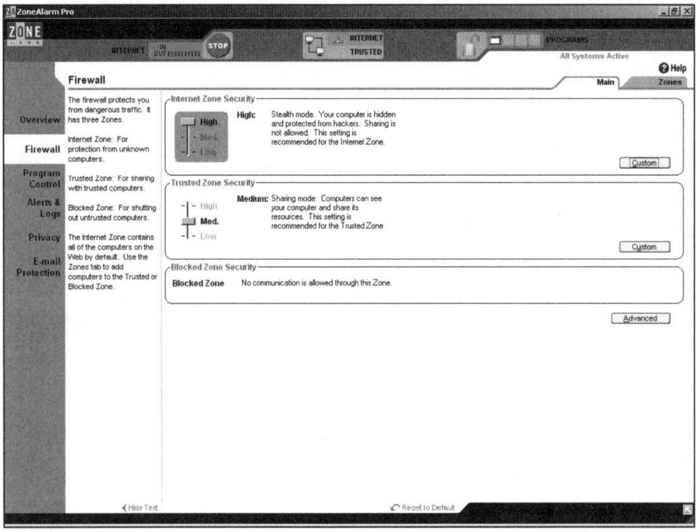

Figure 10-16   Zone security

A feature known as AlertAdvisor includes information about potential break-ins as well as logging facilities for real-time analysis of the alert. The logging capabilities are seen in

Figure 10-17. A graphical utility maps the location of the computer that is attempting to break into the network to make tracking the offender easier. The origins of the blocked network probes are plotted on a map for quick identification of their source. In addition, ZoneAlarm searches out the intruder's location using server-based methods so the user's computer does not reveal its identity to the potential intruder.

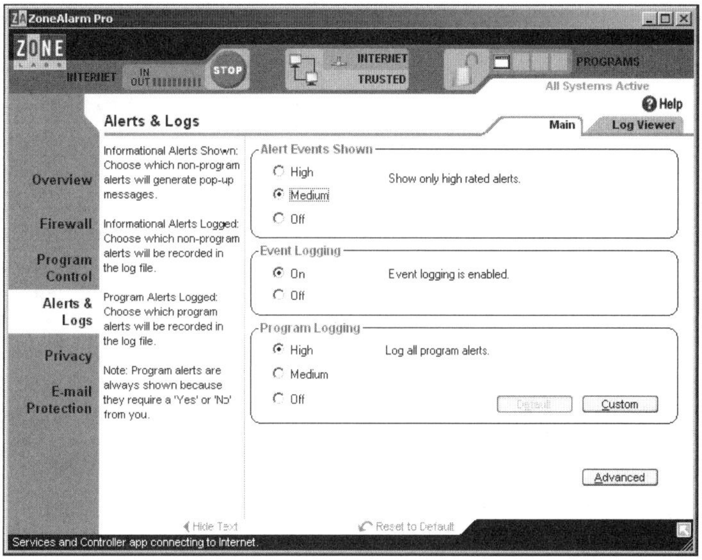

Figure 10-17   Logging options

ZoneAlarm can also block cookies and popup advertisements.

ZoneAlarm includes logging, which provides log filtering, sorting, and analysis of attempted break-ins. In addition, ZoneAlarm also has the capacity to work with proxy server applications.

ZoneAlarm's long list of features and its history of strong performance have made it a favorite among users as a desktop firewall. It provides a comprehensive system for protecting computers from intrusion.

ENTERPRISE FIREWALLS

Although desktop firewalls have gained increased popularity in recent years, enterprise firewalls still perform the bulk of the work in protecting a network. Enterprise firewalls form the first line of defense in a security management plan. An enterprise firewall provides "perimeter security" because it sits on the outer boundary of the network and protects the entire network. Locating the enterprise firewall at the perimeter enables it to block viruses and infected e-mail messages from even entering the network, instead of allowing them to first come in and then "fight the battle." A single enterprise firewall is easier to manage than multiple distributed desktop firewalls. They also allow security managers to log the attacks that strike the network. Two of the most popular enterprise firewall products are the Linksys firewall/router and Microsoft Internet Security and Acceleration (ISA) Server.

Linksys

Linksys (*www.linksys.com*) offers a wide variety of routers, hubs, wireless access points, firewalls, and other hardware. Linksys is known for solid products that provide strong security while being easy to set up and use.

 In early 2003, Linksys was purchased by Cisco for one-half of a billion dollars. Linksys will remain a wholly owned subsidiary and will retain its name and product line.

Linksys firewalls come in a variety of configurations. One of the more popular models combines a firewall with a router, a four-port wired switch, and a VPN endpoint. This firewall/router is a good solution for connecting a small group of computers to a high-speed broadband Internet connection or to a 10/100 Ethernet backbone, while the VPN endpoint can create IPSec VPN tunnels. Either four computers can be directly connected to the wired ports or switches or hubs can connect multiple computers to the firewall/router. A single Linksys firewall/router can protect a maximum of 253 computers.

 Many Linksys firewall/routers provide a dedicated port for DMZ hosting that act as the only externally recognized Internet gateway on the local area network (LAN).

The Linksys firewall/router features an advanced stateful packet inspection firewall. However, it does not block transmissions based on the application as the software desktop firewalls can. The Linksys firewall/router can block incoming or outgoing traffic at scheduled times and can filter content based on the **Uniform Resource Locator (URL)**, also known as the Web address, or by keywords.

Some of the Linksys firewall/router features include:

- *Web filter*: Users can enable or disable filtering of Web material in any of four different methods. A Proxy filter allows local users who have access to WAN proxy servers to circumvent the firewall/router's content filters and access Internet sites normally blocked by the firewall/router. A Java filter prevents Java applets from being passed through while an ActiveX filter restricts ActiveX applications from running. The cookie filter prohibits data stored on a computer and then used by Internet sites.

- *Block WAN request*: Blocking a WAN request prevents a network from being detected (by "pinging") from outside users. It also hides the network ports.

- *Multicast pass through*: **IP Multicasting** occurs when a single data transmission is sent to multiple recipients simultaneously. Enabling this feature allows IP multicast traffic to be forwarded to the appropriate computers.

- *IPSec pass through*: This option allows Internet Protocol Security (IPSec) packets to pass through the firewall/router.

- *PPTP pass through*: VPN sessions used by a Windows NT 4.0 or Windows 2000 server use Point-to-Point Tunneling Protocol (PPTP). This option allows this data to pass through the firewall/router.

- *Remote management*: This feature allows the firewall/router to be managed from a remote location over the Internet.

 To remotely manage the Linksys firewall/router, the user enters the IP address and port of the device.

Linksys firewall/routers also support system traffic logging and event logging so it is possible to see what actions are taking place on the firewall/router. System logs can be grouped by system, access, firewall, or VPN entries. A separate "Logviewer" program makes logs easier to read. Customized rules can also be created for specific users or groups.

 Linksys does not support automatic alerts nor does it send e-mails when an alert occurs.

The wide variety of options on the Linksys firewall/router has made it a very popular device for small to medium networks that need strong protection. With the backing of its new parent company Cisco, Linksys will continue to grow in popularity as a product that can protect the entire network enterprise.

Microsoft Internet Security and Acceleration Server 2000

Microsoft (*www.microsoft.com*) Internet Security and Acceleration (ISA) Server 2000 is an enterprise firewall that integrates with the Microsoft Windows 2000 operating system for policy-based security and management. The list of features of ISA Server is very lengthy and provides a tremendous amount of flexibility. ISA Server builds on top of the features in Windows 2000 Server by providing control over security, directory, virtual private networking (VPN), and bandwidth. ISA Server is available in two product versions. ISA Server Standard Edition is a stand-alone server supporting a maximum of four processors. ISA Server Enterprise Edition is designed for larger-scale deployments, supporting server arrays, multilevel policy, and computers with any number of processors.

ISA Server provides two tightly integrated modes. The first mode is a multilayer firewall. This firewall filters data at the packet, circuit, and application layer as well as performs stateful inspection to examine all data crossing the firewall. The second mode of ISA is a Web **cache server**. A cache improves network performance by storing frequently requested Web content. ISA also contains sophisticated management tools that help with such tasks as policy definition, traffic routing, server publishing, and monitoring.

 The ISA firewall and cache can be deployed separately on dedicated servers or integrated on the same saver.

The ISA Server firewall software uses a **multihomed server**. A multihomed server means that it has more than one network connection. Typically one network interface card (NIC) is connected to the internal private network while another NIC connects to the outside public Internet. This is illustrated in Figure 10-18.

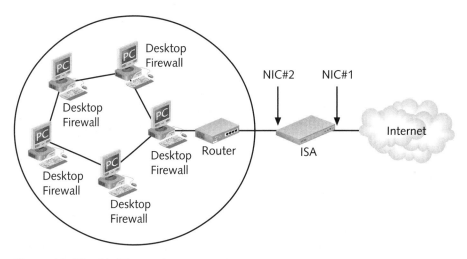

Figure 10-18 Multihomed server

ISA firewall protection is based on what are known as rules. Rules instruct the ISA Server to accept and process requests from internal and external Web clients in a specified manner. ISA Server's rules are processed in the following order.

Incoming requests:

1. Packet filters

2. Web publishing rules

3. Routing rules

4. Bandwidth rules

Outgoing requests:

1. Bandwidth rules

2. Protocol rules

3. Site and content rules

4. Routing rules

5. Packet filters

These rules include:

- *Packet filters*: Packet filters control the types of IP packets accepted on the external interface. When packet filters are enabled, all packets coming into the firewall are denied entrance unless a specific packet type has been configured to be accepted. For outgoing requests, ISA Server opens TCP ports dynamically as they are needed and then monitors the ports for responses.

- *Web publishing rules*: Web publishing rules are used to configure the ISA Server to forward requests from external users to internal network Web servers. Web publishing rules determine security restrictions for all incoming requests, how the requests are encrypted, and when they are forwarded to the internal server.

- *Routing rules*: Routing rules route requests to ISA Server computers or redirect requests to alternate destination servers. Routing rules specify which requests are routed, redirected, or retrieved directly from the destination server. Routing rules can also specify whether to serve objects from the cache or to cache the responses from the destination server.

- *Bandwidth rules*: Bandwidth rules are based on **Quality of Service (QoS)**. QoS can be used to control the amount of bandwidth available to a particular application or to a group of users. ISA Server uses bandwidth rules to determine what priority to request from the QoS service.

- *Protocol rules*: Protocol rules control access to specific protocols that are allowed to pass through the ISA Server. For example, in cache mode the only protocols that can pass are Hypertext Transport Protocol (HTTP), Secure Hypertext Transport Protocol (HTTPS), File Transfer Protocol (FTP), and a seldom-used protocol known as Gopher. In firewall mode any protocols can be defined using protocol definitions and allowed or denied using protocol rules.

- *Site and content rules*: Site and content rules control access to specific servers and their content types by internal users on the network. The destinations are created using destination sets. A destination set can be an entire domain, a specific server, or a specific URL.

The order in which ISA Server rules are processed is important. ISA Server rules can be grouped into two types of rule sets and the ISA Server then processes the rules differently based on the type of rule set. An ordered rule set includes Web publishing rules,

10

bandwidth rules, and routing rules. ISA Server processes these rule sets in the order they appear in the list. The last rule in an ordered rule set is the default rule and cannot be deleted. The default rule functions in different ways depending on the rule set. When a request arrives related to one of these rule sets, ISA Server will use the first rule in the list that matches the request. Unordered rule sets include packet filters, protocol rules, and site and content rules. For these rule sets, ISA Server processes "deny" rules first and then processes "accept" rules. The default for unordered rule sets is to deny everything. With unordered rule sets, if no rules exist in a rule set, ISA Server will deny all requests for that rule set.

Microsoft ISA Server uses what is known as policy elements that are applied to groups of objects. For example, all of the computers in the Accounting Department can be grouped in a single client address set called "Accounting Computers." Policies can then be applied to this group. Some of the following policy elements available are:

- *Schedules*: A rule can be created that is only in effect at certain times. For example, a schedule can be created for access on weekends. Sets define time periods during the day and the days during the week. A schedule can restrict access to specific resources during specified times while allowing access at others.

- *Bandwidth priorities*: Bandwidth priorities are assigned a number between 1 and 200: the higher the number, the higher the priority that is assigned to that communication. Bandwidth priority can be used to provide more or less bandwidth for a group of users.

- *Destination sets*: Destinations sets define locations on the Internet. This can be done by hostname, IP address or a range of IP addresses. Destination sets can be created for a specific destination or a group of destinations using wildcards or IP address ranges. Destination sets can also be used to apply a rule to a specific URL.

- *Client address sets*: Client address sets allow security managers to specify clients by a range of IP addresses. Client address sets can represent internal clients on the network with access to Internet resources or external clients that access internal servers.

- *Content groups*: Content groups restrict or grant access to resources based upon the content type. For example, a content group can restrict access based on the file extensions of an attachment.

These features represent only the basics of what is available in ISA Server. Microsoft's ISA product is well-known as an extremely powerful and versatile enterprise firewall.

Chapter Summary

- Although there are a variety of different ways in which firewalls can be categorized, today firewalls are often classified as either enterprise or as desktop firewalls. An enterprise firewall is one that protects the entire network or a network segment and can be either a separate hardware appliance or a software-only firewall. A desktop firewall is a software-only firewall that is intended to be installed on one client computer on the network and provide protection only to that device. Software-only firewalls today have generally replaced separate hardware firewalls for protection of a single device. A desktop firewall can help protect the network by providing additional security at each network device.

- Tiny Personal Firewall is unique among most desktop firewalls for the advanced security features that it includes. Tiny Personal Firewall is based on a technology that has been certified by the ICSA, an independent group that tests and certifies firewalls. Tiny Personal Firewall is made up of several different components called "engines." The Firewall Engine performs stateful packet inspection. The Firewall Engine uses a method to ensure that the application program on the computer is the real program and not a Trojan horse. It accomplishes this by creating and checking MD5 signatures of application programs. Tiny Personal Firewall also uses sandbox technology to create a closed environment around an application and restricts its access to resources.

- Sygate Technologies offers several desktop firewall products that range in design from enterprise-based security systems to personal firewall systems. The Sygate Secure Enterprise is the top-of-the-line product that combines protection with centralized management. Security managers can create a global security policy that applies to all users and groups, and subgroups can be created within the global group. The Personal Firewall Pro contains additional features that are not commonly found on most desktop firewall products, such as testing the connection. In addition, Personal Firewall Pro protects against MAC and IP spoofing.

- Some of the best-known software desktop firewalls are products known as ZoneAlarm. These firewalls are bi-directional and provide protection from both incoming and outgoing traffic. If an unknown outside source attempts to connect to a computer, a pop-up window alerts the user to the intrusion attempt and prompts whether to grant or deny access. The ZoneAlarm firewall uses fingerprints to identify all components of a program as well as the program itself. ZoneAlarm's Internet Lock blocks all Internet traffic while the computer is unattended or while the Internet is not being used.

- Linksys firewalls/routers come in a variety of configurations. They are good solutions for connecting a group of computers to a high-speed broadband Internet connection or to a 10/100 Ethernet backbone and also support VPN. The Linksys firewall/router features an advanced stateful packet inspection firewall. However, it does not block transmissions based on the application as the software desktop firewalls can. Linksys

10

firewall/routers also support system traffic logging and event logging so it is possible to see what actions are taking place on the firewall/router.

❏ Linksys is a company that offers a wide variety of routers, hubs, wireless access points, firewalls, and other types of networking hardware. Designed for the small office/home office (SOHO) user, Linksys has a reputation for producing solid products that provide strong security while being easy to set up and use.

❏ Microsoft Internet Security and Acceleration (ISA) Server 2000 is an enterprise firewall that integrates with the Microsoft Windows 2000 operating system for policy-based security and management. ISA Server builds on top of the features in Windows 2000 Server by providing control over security, directory, virtual private networking (VPN), and bandwidth. ISA Server provides two tightly integrated modes. The first mode is a multilayer firewall. This firewall filters data at the packet, circuit, and application layer as well as performs stateful inspection to examine all data crossing the firewall. The second mode of ISA is a Web cache server.

KEY TERMS

active content — Special programming tools that provide enhanced functions to static Web pages.

cache server — A server that stores frequently requested Web content.

checksum — A unique number that is generated based on the contents of application programs.

fingerprinting system — A system that creates and checks the signatures of application programs.

IP Multicasting — A single data transmission that is sent to multiple recipients simultaneously.

MD5 signature — A unique number that is generated based on the contents of application programs.

multihomed server — A server that has more than one network connection.

Quality of Service (QoS) — A service that controls the amount of bandwidth available to a particular application or to a group of users.

rogue access point — An unauthorized access point that can compromise security.

sandbox — A technology that creates a closed environment around an application and restricts its access to resources.

Uniform Resource Locator (URL) — The address of a Web site.

wireless access point — A device used to connect wireless computers to a wired network, and connect it to the wired network in his or her office.

REVIEW QUESTIONS

1. The best firewall is
   a. an enterprise firewall
   b. a software-only firewall
   c. a proxy firewall
   d. a firewall that supports the security policy

2. Firewalls are classified as either enterprise or
   a. desktop firewalls
   b. management servers
   c. proxy logs
   d. policy firewalls

3. An unauthorized access point is called a(n)
   a. DMZ point
   b. peer-to-peer point
   c. rogue access point
   d. private configurated server (PCS)

4. The ICSA is an independent group that that tests and certifies
   a. log viewers
   b. proxy managers
   c. servers
   d. firewalls

5. A program that pretends to be a regular and known program but it has a malicious intent is known as a(n)
   a. Trojan horse
   b. proxy manager
   c. DMZ
   d. viral supplicant

6. An MD5 signature is also known as a(n)
   a. print scan
   b. checkpoint signature
   c. URL
   d. checksum

7. The technology that creates a closed environment around an application and restricts its access to resources is known as a(n)

   a. loop

   b. curtain

   c. container

   d. sandbox

8. Each of the following is an example of active content except

   a. ActiveX

   b. VisualBASIC script

   c. Javascript

   d. ActiveY

9. Each of the following is a Tiny Personal Firewall sandbox object except

   a. cache

   b. registry

   c. OLE

   d. services

10. Changes to a parent group using Sygate Management Server (SMS) results in those same changes being inherited by all

    a. trees

    b. subgroups

    c. forests

    d. locations

11. The most flexible firewalls restrict packets based on either TCP port or

    a. server code

    b. DNS action

    c. connection

    d. application

12. A _____ system creates and checks the signatures of application programs.

    a. cache

    b. MI5

    c. fingerprinting

    d. sandtree

13. ZoneAlarm's Internet Lock blocks all Internet traffic while the computer is

    a. off

    b. unattended

    c. on

    d. booting

14. The maximum number of devices that a single Linksys firewall/router can protect is

    a. 2

    b. 25

    c. 253

    d. 2534

15. Another name for a Web address is the

    a. Uniform Resource Locator (URL)

    b. Hypertext Transport Protocol (HTTP)

    c. Extensible Web Address (EWA)

    d. TCP Tag Line

16. Sending a single data transmission to multiple recipients simultaneously is known as

    a. TCP transmitting

    b. Internet Protocol scripting

    c. Host spawning

    d. IP multicasting

10

17. The firewall Internet Security and Acceleration (ISA) Server 2000 was developed by

    a. Sygate

    b. Microsoft

    c. Zone Labs

    d. Linksys

18. A server that it has more than one network connection is known as a(n)

    a. multihomed server

    b. dual WNIC device

    c. autosensing server

    d. DMZ appliance

19. Each of the following is an Internet Security and Acceleration (ISA) rule for processing incoming requests *except*

    a. packet filters

    b. user name

    c. Web publishing rules

    d. bandwidth rules

20. Quality of Service (QoS) can be used to control the amount of _____ available to a particular application or to a group of users

    a. bandwidth

    b. time

    c. hard drive space

    d. protocol

HANDS-ON PROJECTS

Project 10-1: Download ZoneAlarm Pro

ZoneAlarm Pro is a software-only desktop firewall that has a strong reputation for being a solid firewall product. ZoneAlarm Pro can be downloaded from Zone Labs for free from the Internet for a 30-day evaluation period. Zone Labs also offers another product entitled ZoneAlarm that can also be downloaded for free but has no limitation on how long it can be used. However, ZoneAlarm Pro has additional features not found in ZoneAlarm.

In this project you will download and install ZoneAlarm Pro. Note that Zone Labs may change the location on their Web site of where the 30-day trial of ZoneAlarm Pro is found. If changes to their Web site are made it may be necessary for you to search their Web site in order to locate it.

1. Open your Web browser. In the Address bar, type **http://www.zonelabs.com** and press **Enter**.

2. Click **Download & Buy** in the list on the left side of the page.

3. Scroll down the page and locate the information about ZoneAlarm (not ZoneAlarm Pro). Click **Free Download**.

4. The "What Are Your Security Needs?" page appears. Under Step #1, click **Personal Purposes** under I Use My For (Check One). Under Step #2, uncheck all choices except for the first choice, A Strong Firewall for My PC. Under Step #3, click the **Submit** button.

5. Zone Lab's products are listed. Under the ZoneAlarm (not ZoneAlarm Pro), click **Download Now**. A pop-up dialog box appears asking if you would like to download a free 30-day preview of ZoneAlarm Pro. Click **Click Here To Download**.

6. On the next screen click **Download Now! ZoneAlarm Pro Free Trial**.

7. A File Download dialog box opens. Click **Open** to download the file and automatically begin installing it.

8. When the Installer Program opens, follow the steps indicated to installed ZoneAlarm Pro desktop firewall on your computer. When the License Wizard dialog box appears, click **Try**. The steps for configuring ZoneAlarm Pro are found in Project 10-2.

Project 10-2: Configure ZoneAlarm Pro

After you have installed ZoneAlarm Pro, you will need to configure it to provide the security that you need.

1. After the ZoneAlarm Pro Welcome Screen appears, click **Next**.

2. The configuration wizard starts. When asked "Would you like to enable ZoneAlarm Pro privacy control?" click **Leave Privacy Control Off For Now**. Click **Next**.

3. The next screen is a review of the alert settings. When asked "What kind of blocked traffic do you want to be alerted to?" click **Alert Me Whenever ZoneAlarm Pro blocks traffic**. This will enable you to see all of the traffic that your computer is sending and receiving. Click **Next**.

4. You will then be asked on the next screen to create a password. Click **I do not want to create a password** unless your instructor or lab supervisor gives you different instructions. Click **Finish**.

5. The program wizard now starts. The first screen is about preconfiguring your browser and its components. This allows ZoneAlarm Pro to automatically set up the necessary permissions for you to surf the Internet with your browser. When asked "Do you want ZoneAlarm Pro to preconfigure access permission?" click **Next**. Then click **Finish**.

6. The network security wizard now starts. The first screen will indicate that "New Network Detected: IP Address xxx.xxx.xxx.xxx" where the x's indicate the IP address of the network device. This is the network to which your computer is connected. Click **Next**.

7. You will next be asked about the connection of this computer. Click **Single computer connected directly to the Internet.** Click **Next**.

8. ZoneAlarm Pro will then ask you to name this network. This becomes a trusted network. Enter the name **Project 10**. Click **Finish**.

Project 10-3: Test Configuration and View Log

After a firewall is configured it should be properly tested. This involves taking steps that could result in denied access and then viewing the log files. While you are performing these tests, ZoneAlarm Pro may pop up a Program Alert, which means that a program is attempting to access the Internet. Read carefully what the program is and either grant or deny permission by clicking Yes or No. ZoneAlarm Pro may also display Firewall Alerts, which show that traffic was automatically blocked for you. If these appear, click OK.

10

1. Open a command window by clicking **Start** and **Programs** and enter **CMD** and press **Enter**.

2. The FTP site mirrors.kernel.org contains free Linux software. The TCP/IP Ping command sends a signal to a site and expects an answer back to see if that remote site exists and is functioning. In the command window, type **ping mirrors.kernel.org**.

3. Notice that a ZoneAlarm Pro New Program dialog box opens. It asks, "Do you want to allow TCP/IP Ping command to access the Internet?" Click **Yes**. However, by this time the ping request has probably "timed out."

4. In the command window, type **ping mirrors.kernel.org**. When then ZoneAlarm Pro New Program dialog box again asks if you want to allow ping to access the Internet, check the **Remember the answer the next time I use this program** check box. Then, click **Yes**. If the ping request has timed out again, type **ping mirrors.kernel.org**. ZoneAlarm Pro now allows the ping request to go through. Type **Exit** to close the command window.

5. View the log file that ZoneAlarm Pro is creating regarding your computer. Click **Alert and Logs** in the left pane of the ZoneAlarm Pro command center. Maximize the window and click the **Log Viewer** tab. Scroll both down and across to view the log file. Locate the failed attempts to use ping and then the successful attempts.

Project 10-4: Connecting and Configuring Your PCs and Linksys BEFSX41 Firewall Router

Unlike a hub or a switch, a router/firewall setup consists of more than simply plugging hardware together. You will have to configure your networked PCs to accept the IP addresses that the Router assigns them (if applicable), and you will also have to configure the Router with setting(s) provided by your Internet Service Provider (ISP). This project will walk you through connecting and configuring your firewall router.

For the purpose of this project, we are utilizing a Linksys BEFSX41 router connected to a broadband cable modem. Our network consists of two PCs running Windows 2000 Professional. If you are utilizing different hardware the setup will basically be the same, consult the documentation that came with your router for specific settings for your hardware.

Connecting the router:

1. Before you begin, make sure that all of your hardware is powered off, including the router, PCs, and cable or DSL modem.

2. Connect one end of an Ethernet cable to one of the LAN ports (labeled 1, 2, 3, or 4/DMZ) on the back of the router, and the other end to your PCs Ethernet adapter. For ease of installation, start with the LAN port labeled 4/DMZ, then port 3, 2, 1.

3. Connect the Ethernet cable from your cable or DSL modem to the WAN port on the router's back panel. This is the only port that will work for your modem connection.

4. Connect the power adapter to the power port on the back panel of the router, and then plug the power adapter into a power outlet.

5. Turn on the cable or DSL modem and PCs.

Configuring the PCs

The instructions in this section will help you configure each of your computers to be able to communicate with the router. To do this, you need to configure your PC's network settings to obtain an IP (or TCP/IP) address automatically (called DHCP).

1. Find out which operating system your computer is running, such as Windows 95, 98, Millennium, NT 4.0, 2000, or XP. You can find out by clicking the **Start** button and then going to the **Settings** option.

2. Click **Control Panel**, and then double-click the **System** icon. If your Start menu doesn't have a Settings option, you're running Windows XP. Click the **Cancel** button when done. You may need to do this for each computer you are connecting to the router.

 For this project purposes we will assume all computers are Windows 2000. If you are using a different operating system, please consult the documentation that came with your O/S or router.

3. Go to the Network screen by clicking the **Start** button. Click **Settings** and then **Control Panel**. From there, double-click the **Network and Dial-up Connections** icon.

4. Select the **Local Area Connection** icon for the applicable Ethernet adapter (usually it is the first Local Area Connection listed). Double-click **Local Area Connection**. Click the **Properties** button.

5. Select **Internet Protocol (TCP/IP)**, and click the **Properties** button.

6. Select **Obtain an IP address automatically**. Once the new window appears, click the **OK** button. Click the **OK** button again to complete the PC configuration.

7. Restart your computer.

Configuring the Router

This section will show you how to configure the Router to function in your network and gain access to the Internet through your Internet Service Provider (ISP). Detailed description of the Router's Web-based configuration utility can be found in "Chapter 7: The Cable/DSL Firewall Router's Web-based Utility" of your Linksys user guide.

Your ISP may require the use of a host name and domain name. In addition, you will set the WAN connection type on the router's Setup tab based on the information provided by your ISP. You will need the setup information from your ISP. If you do not have this information, please contact your ISP before proceeding.

The instructions from your ISP will tell you how to set up your PC for Internet access. Because you are now using the router to share Internet access among several computers, you will use the setup information to configure the router instead of your PC. You only need to configure the router once using the computer you connected into port 4 of the router/firewall.

1. Open your Web browser. (It is all right if you get an error message at this point. Continue following these directions.) Enter **http://192.168.1.1** in the Web browser's Address field. Press the **Enter** key.

2. An Enter Network Password window will appear (Windows XP users will see a Connect to 192.168.1.1 window). Leave the User Name field empty, and enter **admin** in lowercase letters in the Password field (**admin** is the default password). Then, click the **OK** button.

3. The Router configuration screen will appear with the Setup tab selected. Based on the setup instructions from your ISP, you may need to provide the following information:

   ❑ Host Name and Domain Name: These fields allow you to provide a host name and domain name for the Router. These fields are usually left blank. If requested by your ISP (usually cable ISPs), complete these two fields.

   ❑ Device IP Address and Subnet Mask: The values for the Router's IP Address and Subnet Mask are shown on the Setup screen. The default value is 192.168.1.1 for the IP Address and 255.255.255.0 for the Subnet Mask.

4. The Router supports six connection types: DHCP (obtain an IP automatically), PPPoE, Static IP Address, RAS, PPTP, and HBS. These types are listed in the drop-down menu for the WAN Connection Type setting. Each Setup screen and available features will differ depending on what kind of connection type you select. Proceed to the instructions for the connection type you are using, then continue with this step sequence.

 For the purposes of this project, we are assuming your ISO stated you are connecting through DHCP or a dynamic IP address from your ISP and that you should perform the following steps. If your ISP stated you are connecting via another connection type, consult the setup documentation received with your router.

5. **Select Obtain an Automatically** as the WAN Connection Type.

6. Click the **Apply** and **Continue** buttons to save the setting.

7. Close the Web browser.

8. Reset the power on your cable or DSL modem.

9. Restart your computers so that they can obtain the router's new settings.

Project 10-5: Hardening the Linksys Router (BEFSX41)

After the Linksys BEFSX41 router is configured using the instructions in Project 10-4 or provided by Linksys, it is recommended that users "harden" or properly secure their router/firewall settings. This project describes how to harden the Linksys BEFSX41 router to prevent Internet based attackers from accessing your home-based network due to excessive ports, protocols, or functionality being enabled on your firewall.

The first step in hardening any operating system or device is to determine what services are absolutely required in my environment. Understanding what is required for your network to function as designed is essential in determining the steps to hardening the device. The recommendations made in this project assume that the user has a home network that consists of several computers with the main goal being to allow multiple users to utilize the broadband connection to access the Internet. Some of the recommendations below may not apply to users that have a more complex network environment that include Web, FTP, or other types of external facing servers.

1. Once you have completed the Linksys installation steps for BEFSX41, open your browser to 192.168.1.1.

2. Check the firmware version and make sure you have the most current version. Check *www.linksys.com* under support for the latest firmware. Read the updates on the latest release, as they document bug fixes for that device. If you need to upgrade, do it before configuring the router, as some upgrades reset the configuration to Linksys defaults.

3. In the Firewall Filter page, check the following:

   □ *Advanced Firewall Protection*: Enabled

   □ *Proxy*: Deny

   □ *Java*: Allow for Java acceptance

   □ *ActiveX*: Deny blocks hostile ActiveX attacks

   □ *Cookie*: Allow

   □ *Time Filter*: If you know that you will not be utilizing the system after a specific time, it is a good idea to utilize this feature.

4. On the VPN tab, verify the Tunnel is set to **Disable**.

5. On the Password tab, check the following:

   □ *Router Password*: Change your password!

   □ *SNMP Community*: Change these from PUBLIC and PRIVATE to something only you know; don't use any dictionary word or any easily guessed phrase.

   □ *Restore Factory Defaults*: No, unless your system is unusable. Then reconfigure with security parameters again.

   □ *UpnP Function*: Set to no.

   □ *UpnP Control*: Set to no.

6. Select the **Apply** button when finished selecting the correct settings.

10

7. On the DHCP tab the following settings are recommended for securing the router/ firewall:

   ❑ *DHCP Server*: Enable only if you want DHCP assigned TCPIP addresses on your home network.

   ❑ *DNS1-3*: Set to the TCPIP addresses of your broadband vendor.

   ❑ *WINS*: Do not set any WINS addresses from your broadband vendor, or any other external source.

8. On the Log tab, the following settings are recommended.

   ❑ *Log*: Enable

   ❑ *Send Log to*: If you want send log files to another system on your network, enter the TCPIP address of the workstation you want to record the logging files.

9. Select the Apply button after selecting your configuration choices.

10. On the **Advanced** tab, set the following settings for hardening your Linksys (BEFSX41) router:

    ❑ *Block WAN Request*: Enable

    ❑ *Multicast Pass Through*: Disable

    ❑ *IPSec Pass Through*: Disable

    ❑ *PPTP Pass Through*: Disable

    ❑ *Remote Management*: Disable

    ❑ *Remote Upgrade*: Disable

11. On the Dynamic Routing tab, set the following configuration settings:

    ❑ *Working Mode*: Select gateway mode if this is the firewall/router connecting to your broadband vendor.

    ❑ *Dynamic Routing TX,RX*: Disable

12. On the DMZ host tab, verify that DMZ Port is set to **Disable**.

13. On the DMZ host tab verify that User Defined WAN MAC Address is set to **Leave blank or un-activated**.

14. On the DDNS host tab, verify that DDNS Service is set to **Disable**.

Project 10-6: Installing the ISA Server

To install ISA Server 2000:

1. Insert the ISA Server Enterprise Edition CD in the CD drive, or double-click the **ISAAutorun.exe** file in the ISA Server directory. The Microsoft ISA Server Setup dialog box appears.

2. Click **Install ISA Server**. The Welcome window opens.

3. Click **Continue** in the Welcome window. The CD Key dialog box appears.

4. Enter **880-2897414** as the CD Key, and then click **OK**. Click **OK** in the Product ID dialog box that follows. The End User License Agreement appears.

5. Click **I Agree**. The installation selection dialog box appears.

6. Click **Custom Installation**. The Custom Installation dialog box appears.

7. Click **Select All** in the Custom Installation dialog box. All three check boxes should be selected. Click **Continue**. See Figure 10-19.

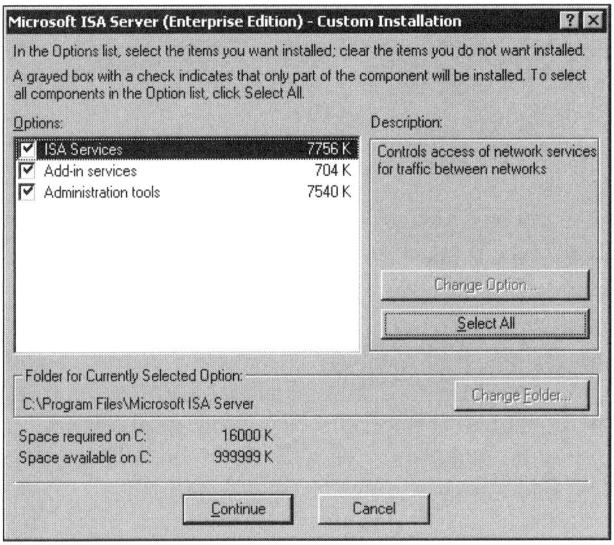

Figure 10-19   Custom Installation dialog box

8. When prompted to install the server as an array member, click **Yes**. Type **ISAArrayX** (where *X* is a unique number assigned by your instructor) in the Array name box, and click **OK**. The Configure enterprise policy settings dialog box appears, as shown in Figure 10-20.

9. Click **Use custom enterprise policy settings**, click **Use this enterprise policy**, and then click **Continue**. The Mode Selection dialog box appears.

10. Ensure that **Integrated mode** is selected, and then click **Continue**. When an informational dialog box appears, click **OK**. The cache selection window appears.

11. Ensure that the drive where the ISA Server is installed is selected, change the cache size to **10** MB, and then click **Set**. The Maximum Size column next to the C: drive should change to 10 MB. Click **OK**. The Local Address Table (LAT) dialog box appears.

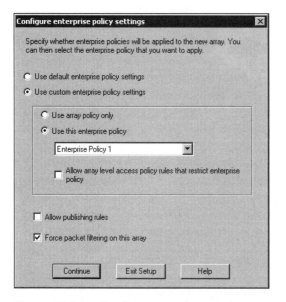

Figure 10-20   Configure enterprise policy settings dialog box

12. Click **Construct Table**. In the LAT window, deselect the **Add the following private ranges** check box, and then click **Add address ranges based on the Windows 2000 Routing Table**, if necessary. Select the network card that corresponds to your internal LAN, and then click **OK**. See Figure 10-21. A message notifies you that the LAT has been constructed. Click **OK**, then click **OK** in the original LAT window. Setup stops all necessary services, then copies the program files to your server. The Launch ISA Management Tool dialog box appears.

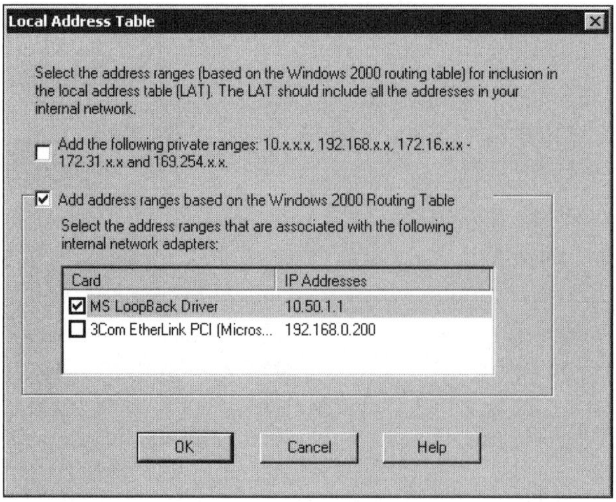

Figure 10-21   Local Address Table dialog box

13. Ensure that the **Start ISA Server Getting Started Wizard** check box is selected, and then click **OK**. Click **OK** in the completion window. ISA Server has been successfully installed.

CASE PROJECTS

Case 10-1: Test ZoneAlarm Pro

In addition to performing your own tests on the ZoneAlarm Pro software, there are a number of testers available on the Internet that will test your configuration and let you know the results. Two of the best testers are Shields Up!, which tests both the computer and the ports over the Internet, and Leak Test, which requires you to download software onto your computer to test the firewall, both freely available from Gibson Research (*www.grc.com*). Another tester is FireHole (*keir.net/firehole.html*). Test your ZoneAlarm Pro firewall with two of these three testers. What did they tell you?

Case 10-2: Remote Access Software and Firewalls

Remote Access Software allows users to access files on their computer or remotely control it through the Internet. Some of the most widely used are GoToMyPC, PC Anywhere, and TightVNC. Users find this software helpful in cases where a file was left on the office computer but was needed to work on at home in the evening. However, security administrators consider these to be a breach in security. Using the Internet and other resources, research these three products, how they work, and what is their focus on security. Do you feel that they are secure enough to recommend for a trusted network? Write a one-page paper on your findings.

10

Case 10-3: Which Firewall to Use

Assume that you are working as a consultant to a network security organization. They have asked you to prepare a presentation comparing the five firewalls discussed in this chapter. Using the Internet and other sources, create a PowerPoint presentation that gives the strengths and weaknesses of each product. Also, include a recommendation regarding where this product should generally be used. Your presentation should be a minimum of 20 slides.

Case 10-4: View Log File

Allow ZoneAlarm Pro to protect your computer for at least one hour and then view the log results. What conclusions can you draw regarding the types of applications that were trying to access the network and the attempts to breach network security? What would have happened if ZoneAlarm Pro was not installed? What recommendations do you have for your overall network security? Write a one-page paper on your recommendations.

11

ONGOING ADMINISTRATION

After reading this chapter and completing the exercises, you will be able to:

♦ Learn how to evolve a firewall to meet new needs and threats

♦ Adhere to proven security principles to help the firewall protect network resources

♦ Use a remote management interface

♦ Track log files for security

♦ Follow the basic initial steps in responding to security incidents

♦ Take advanced firewall functions into account when administering a firewall

Setting up a firewall is only the start of an effective perimeter security effort. Ongoing firewall administration ensures that the network is actually protected and that intrusions are detected and thwarted. Without routinely reviewing logs, evaluating firewall performance, and upgrading hardware and software as needed, the best firewall configuration in the world can quickly become useless.

In this chapter, you'll learn about the various administrative tasks that are required to keep a firewall running smoothly as the network it protects continues to grow and as new security threats arise. First, you'll discover how to expand a firewall to meet new needs. You'll learn about the importance of observing fundamental principles of network security when maintaining your firewall. You'll understand the importance of being able to manage the firewall remotely and having log files for review and how to respond to security incidents when they occur. Finally, you'll examine advanced firewall functions, some of which require the firewall to work in tandem with third-party products for added security.

MAKING YOUR FIREWALL MEET NEW NEEDS

You need to keep upgrading your firewall architecture and adding new components to keep your perimeter protected and traffic running smoothly. Overall, you need to gain and maintain the following:

- *Throughput:* Because the firewall is the point through which all traffic flows, you need to make sure traffic flows quickly through it and it is not slowing down the network.

- *Scalability:* Very few, if any, networks get smaller. It's almost inevitable that your network will grow, either in terms of the number of hosts that need to be protected or in the amount of traffic you receive from the external Internet. Your firewall and other security systems need to be able to grow along with your needs.

- *Security:* This is the effectiveness with which the firewall blocks traffic that has been identified as unacceptable based on its rule base and—if the firewall is also full-featured enough to provide some intrusion detection functions—the effectiveness with which it detects and provides notifications of intrusion attempts.

- *Recoverability:* The firewall is critical not only to the network's security but to the network's connection with outside networks. If the firewall crashes, you need to restart it, recover the original security configuration, and get back online quickly.

- *Manageability:* The firewall should be easy to manage, either from within the organization or from a remote location.

To achieve these goals, you might need to upgrade your security software, hardware, or even add new layers of security to your overall firewall perimeter. The process that you'll go through as you make these decisions is described in the following sections.

Verifying Resources Needed by the Firewall

You have to test how well the firewall is working and evaluate its performance so that you can make network traffic move more efficiently. One of the factors that can be easily evaluated for software-only firewalls is memory and CPU usage—You can check just how much memory you need in one of two ways. The first way is to use the following formula:

```
MemoryUsage = ((ConcurrentConnections)/(AverageLifetime))
*(AverageLifetime + 50 seconds)*120
```

This formula indicates that the memory needed by the firewall equals the result of the following steps:

1. The number of **concurrent connections**—the number of connections made to hosts in the internal network at any one time—is divided by the

average lifetime of a typical connection (how long a connection to a host lasts) as indicated by your log files.

2. The number resulting from Step 1 is multiplied by the average lifetime plus 50 seconds times 120.

For example, if there are 100 connections and the average lifetime of a connection is 10 minutes, the memory needed to run Check Point NG is (100/10) * 10+50 * 120 = 72000, or 72MB of RAM.

A second way to keep track of the memory and system resources being consumed is to use the software's own monitoring feature. For example, Figure 11-1 illustrates the Status Manager module in Check Point NG. If you open the module and select your own network, you get data that tells you how much memory is being consumed and how much of your available system resources are being used by the firewall. For a small network, the memory and system resources being used may be relatively small. But on a large enterprise in which hundreds or even thousands of users may send traffic through the firewall at any one time, such data can be invaluable to the network administrator attempting to track down network bottlenecks. CPU usage that climbs to a high level (perhaps as much as 60 percent, though this depends on the operating system being used) should be a warning to the administrator that some kind of load balancing is needed, possibly by adding another firewall to the network.

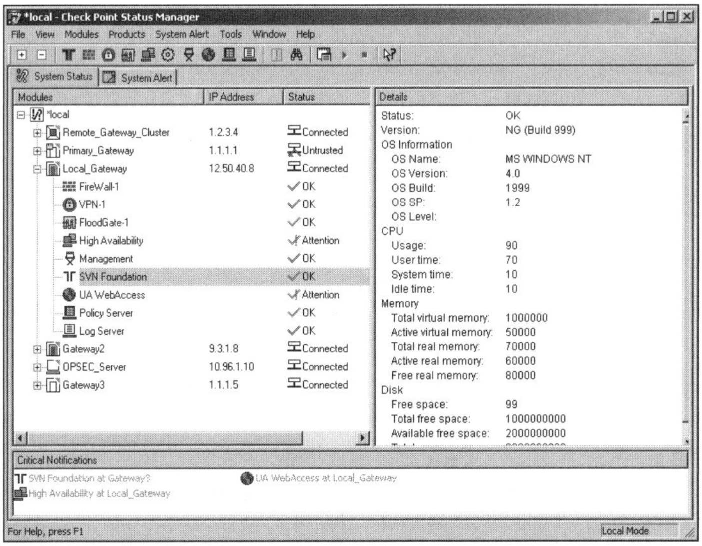

11

![The Check Point NG Status Manager screenshot]

Figure 11-1   The Check Point NG Status Manager

Hands-on Project 11-1 shows you how to use the Status Manager, while Project 11-2 shows how to allocate more memory if needed.

If you need more memory, you can use the Windows Registry Editor or, on Linux, you can dynamically reallocate memory using malloc(), calloc(), or realloc(). If you have a GUI program available like Check Point's Policy Editor, you can use that as well. If more memory is not available, you could reduce the hash file size or the maximum number of concurrent connections (see Figure 11-2).

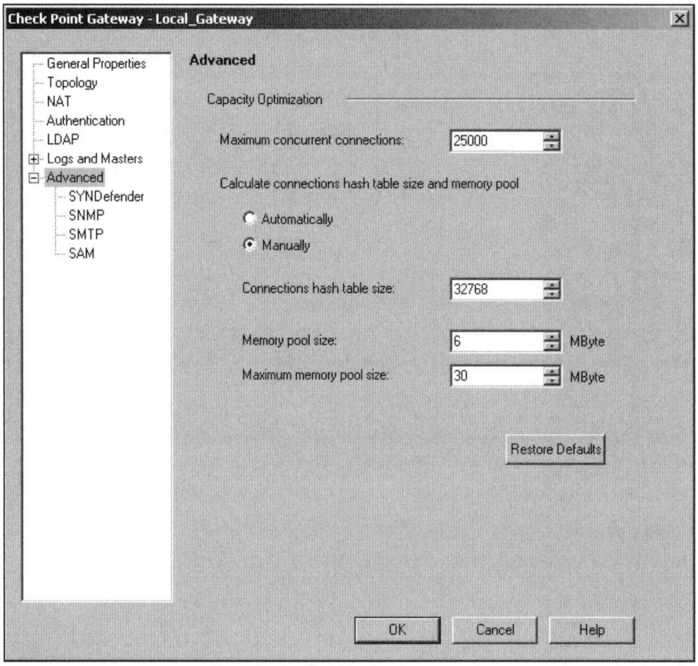

Figure 11-2   Changing memory in the Policy Editor

Identifying New Risks

A firewall needs regular care and attention to keep up with the new threats that are constantly appearing. It's a good idea, after you first get your firewall up and running, to monitor its activities for a month and store all the data that accumulates in the form of log files. Then go through the logs and analyze the traffic that passes through the firewall, paying particular attention to suspicious activity that may arise.

Every day, it seems, new viruses, hack attacks, and other threats are reported on Web sites that track such things. When you install and maintain a firewall, it's important to keep up with the new threats so the firewall can meet them. Visit the sites listed in Appendix A of this book to keep informed of the latest dangers, so you can install patches and updates as they become available.

Adding Software Updates and Patches

The best way to combat the constant stream of new viruses and security threats is to install updated software that is specifically designed to meet those threats. First, test updates and patches as soon as you install them. Make sure the new software does not slow down your system, crash applications, or cause other problems. Second, ask the vendors of your firewall, VPN appliance, routers, and other security-related hardware and software to notify you when security patches become available for their products. Also check the manufacturer's Web site for security patches and software updates.

 It's a good idea to participate in firewall-related mailing lists, not just to share ideas and ask questions of your colleagues, but to learn about new security threats as they occur and news about patches as they become available.

Sometimes, software manufacturers will remind *you* of patches or other software you need to install. If your firewall's manufacturer provides a newsletter or other notification service, sign up for it. These announcements inform users and potential customers of new products and software patches.

Some software-only firewalls provide a module that automatically handles the updating of the software you have installed. The module enables licensed users of the software to do remote installations and updates by connecting to the vendor's download center (see Figure 11-3 for an example of Check Point NG SecureUpdate). You are prompted to enter a username and password, which you obtain when you purchase a license to use the software.

11

Check Point Nodes	IP Address	OS	Vendor	Version	Service Pack
*local					
Remote_Gateway2	100.200.4.2	Linux 7.0			
SVN Foundation			Check Point	NG	
VPN-1 & FireWall-1			Check Point	NG	
Remote_Gateway	20.13.5.2	WinNT 4.0			
SVN Foundation			Check Point	NG	FP2
VPN-1 & FireWall-1			Check Point	NG	FP2
Primary_Gateway	1.1.1.1	WinNT 4.0			
SVN Foundation			Check Point	NG	FP2
Local_Gateway	12.50.40.8	WinNT 4.0			
Real-Time Monitoring			Check Point	NG	FP2
VPN-1 & FireWall-1			Check Point	NG	FP2
FloodGate-1			Check Point	NG	FP2
SVN Foundation			Check Point	NG	FP2
Policy Server			Check Point	NG	FP2
Gateway2	9.3.1.8	Solaris 2.6			
VPN-1 & FireWall-1			Check Point	4.1	SP3
OPSEC_Server	10.96.1.10	Solaris 8			
OPSEC Application			ABC Software	1.0	
SVN Foundation			Check Point	NG	FP2

Figure 11-3   Check Point NG SecureUpdate

You don't have to use the automated update feature or another GUI software program to obtain updated software, however. You can also go to the vendor's Web site to obtain updates (See Figure 11-4).

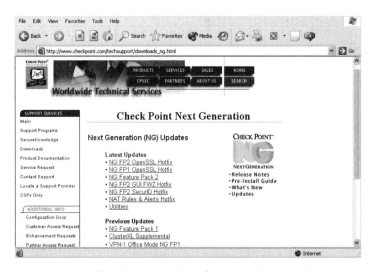

Figure 11-4   Check Point NG's software update Web page

 It can be difficult to remember to check a Web site for an update on a routine basis—that is, if you aren't facing an immediate problem. Configure a calendar or scheduling program to send you a monthly reminder. Develop a maintenance window—a period of two or three hours that is set aside every month for performing improvements such as software upgrades. It's a good way for organizations—even small ones—to manage changes to the network environment while minimizing the impact on production applications.

Adding Hardware

Whenever you add a piece of hardware to your network, you need to identify it in some way so your firewall can include it in its routing and protection services. Different firewalls require you to identify network hardware in different ways. With Microsoft Internet Security and Acceleration Server (ISA), which functions as a proxy server, you record the IP addresses of hosts or gateways on a Local Address Table. With Check Point FireWall-1, you "define" an object by giving it a name and recording its IP address and other information.

The need to list hardware as being part of your protected network applies not only to workstations that you add to the network, but also to the routers, VPN appliances, and other gateways you add as the network grows. This applies particularly to proxy servers such as ISA, which function as the default gateway for a network and need to know exactly how to route traffic through your different hardware devices.

Different types of hardware can be secured in different ways, but one of the most important is simply choosing good passwords that you guard closely. Some network hubs require the administrator to enter two separate passwords to manage or update those devices. One password gives the administrator read access, and the other gives the administrator write permission so he or she can change configuration files on the router if needed.

It's always a good idea, with routers and other hardware or software, to change the write password from the default value to a value of your own choosing for extra security. Switches and routers have their own passwords as well; some switches also have timeout periods that you can configure so they disconnect themselves from the network automatically from a management console if it is idle for a period of time.

Dealing with Complexity on the Network

Firewall configurations can take many forms, and they can grow in complexity as a network grows. One level of complexity you may need to manage comes from **distributed firewalls**, which are installed at all endpoints of the network, including the remote computers that connect to the network through VPNs. They add complexity because they require you to install and/or maintain a variety of firewalls that are located not only in your own corporate network but in remote locations; however, distributed firewalls also add security because they protect your network from viruses or other attacks that can originate from remote laptops or other machines that use VPNs to connect.

A firewall that is deployed on the desktop of a VPN client needs to adopt the security policy of the network to which it connects. It also needs to use Internet Protocol Security, (IPSec) which, as explained in Chapter 9, provides for encryption, encapsulation, and authentication.

If you need to configure remote users to access your network via a VPN, determine what level of firewall security (if any) they already have. If they don't have a firewall already (or if they already installed their own firewall software and you find it to be weak or improperly configured), install a more effective desktop firewall along with the VPN client software. For example, one of Check Point's two VPN clients, Secure Desktop, includes desktop firewall support along with its VPN client software (see Figure 11-5).

If you have a team of administrators involved in maintaining a security system, you need to keep strict records about any changes that are made to the system so that everyone on the team can be informed. You should hold regular meetings and report on any changes that have been made or problems that have been identified.

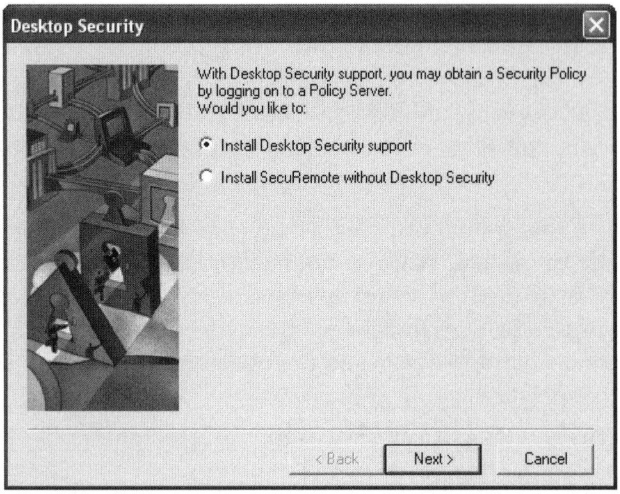

Desktop Security ☒

With Desktop Security support, you may obtain a Security Policy by logging on to a Policy Server.
Would you like to:

⦿ Install Desktop Security support

○ Install SecuRemote without Desktop Security

< Back | Next > | Cancel

Figure 11-5   Installing Secure Desktop enables you to install a distributed firewall

ADHERING TO PROVEN SECURITY PRINCIPLES

Part of firewall management—and network management in general—is adherence to principles that others have put forth by reputable organizations to ensure that you are maintaining your firewall and network security configuration correctly. The **Generally Accepted System Security Principles (GASSP)** is a set of security and information management practices put forth by the International Information Security Foundation (I2SF). The GASSP gives you some good guidelines to follow that help you to manage your firewall as well as the information that passes through it.

The following sections focus on the aspects of the GASSP that apply to ongoing firewall management: securing the physical environment in which the firewall-related equipment is housed and the importance of locking software so that unauthorized users cannot access it.

 The GASSP is published on the Web by the Massachusetts Institute of Technology (MIT) at *http://web.mit.edu/security/www/gassp1.html*.

Environmental Management

The GASSP recommends the **environmental management** of IT assets and resources: the measures taken to reduce risks to the physical environment where the resources are stored. At the most basic level, this means that you need to secure the building where your network resources are located to protect them from natural disasters such as earthquakes, floods, hurricanes, tornadoes, and other catastrophic events.

Such problems might seem unlikely, but many businesses have run up huge losses due to hurricanes and other weather-related problems. In the author's experience, computer systems have failed due to critical computers being placed on the top floor of buildings that were poorly air conditioned. Additional fans had to be provided and were pointed at the servers until the air conditioners could be upgraded.

On a much larger scale, after Hurricane Floyd hit in 1999, 26 companies had to declare a disaster due to computer-related losses. In 1997, the search service DejaNews was hit by a tornado at its Austin, Texas, office and was offline for eight hours. While 40 employees cowered in a stairwell during the storm, a customer called and asked when the service would be back online!

To prepare for environmental problems, an organization should consider installing the following:

- Back-up power systems to overcome power outages

- Back-up hardware and software to help recover network data and services in case of equipment failure

- Sprinkler and alarm systems to reduce damage from fire

- Locks to guard against theft

 The American Red Cross has published a guide called "Preparing Your Business for the Unthinkable" that presents a step-by-step checklist for preparing for natural disasters and other catastrophic events. View it online at *www.redcross.org/services/disaster/beprepared/busi_industry.html*.

BIOS, Boot, and Screen Locks

Laptop computers that are used to connect to the main network should be secured not only by desktop firewalls but also by more obvious, low-level types of security. Some of the most basic features you should look for in a laptop include BIOS boot-up and supervisor passwords, which protect the machine while it is booting up. A screen password should also be assigned.

The GASSP document related to this topic includes the suggestion that a public notice be included in the company's logon screen that advises anyone who uses the network of the existence of the organization's security policy. Such a notice might state the following: "Notice: Anyone who logs on to the *[Company Name]* network is hereby notified that the files and databases they are about to access are valued assets and that they include much proprietary information that is protected by copyright. Unauthorized access to such resources is prohibited and violators will be prosecuted."

BIOS and Boot-up Passwords

Most computers give you the chance to set a **boot-up password**, a password that must be entered to complete the process of starting up a computer. Boot-up passwords (which are often called BIOS passwords or CMOS passwords) aren't perfect: they won't work when your computer is already on and is left unattended, for instance. In addition, a thief who can't crack your BIOS password can remove the hard drive and attach it to a computer that does not have a BIOS password, or remove the lithium battery from the computer's motherboard, thus erasing the BIOS password from memory.

Nevertheless, forcing individuals to enter a BIOS password on startup does add another level of defense to a computer. The BIOS password alone may discourage many thieves from putting out the effort to crack it. In addition, having a BIOS password in place prevents someone from starting up your computer and accessing your hard disk files with a floppy disk called a boot disk.

Supervisor Passwords

Some systems only use a BIOS password to enable the computer to complete booting up. On others (such as Windows NT and 2000), a second, higher-level password called a **supervisor password** is also used. In a case where a supervisor password and a BIOS password are used, the supervisor password is used to gain access to the BIOS set-up program or to change the BIOS password.

 Take care when assigning a supervisor password. Because of its importance, it should only be assigned to an administrator. Make every effort not to lose this password: if you do, you'll have to replace the system motherboard to access the BIOS.

Screen Saver Passwords

A screen saver is an image or design that appears on a Windows computer monitor when the machine is idle. A screen saver password is a password you need to enter to make your screen saver vanish so you can return to your desktop and resume working. Configuring a screen saver password protects your computer while you're not working on it. It's thus a good counterpart to a BIOS password, which protects your computer during startup but not when the machine is running, but idle for a time. Whereas a screen saver password can be easily circumvented by rebooting the computer, a BIOS password will be needed during the reboot.

USING REMOTE MANAGEMENT INTERFACE

A Remote Management Interface is software that enables you to configure and monitor one or more firewalls that are located on different network locations. You use it to start and stop the firewall or change the rulebase from locations other than your primary computer. Without it, most administrators would find themselves spending hours moving from room to room or building to building making the same changes on each of a company's firewalls.

Why Remote Management Tools Are Important

A remote management system is important because it saves many hours of time and makes the security administrator's job much easier. For instance, the Global Enterprise Management System (GEMS) for the McAfee Gauntlet firewall enables the administrator to use the same Graphical User Interface (GUI) as a standalone firewall, but gives the administrator the ability to establish rules for as many as 500 separate firewalls. Although it's unlikely that any one administrator would actually have to manage that many firewalls, it's not uncommon for dozens of firewall devices to be involved in a large-scale network.

Besides reducing time for the administrator, such remote management tools reduce the chance of configuration errors that might result if the same changes have to be made manually for each firewall in the network. Many remote management programs come with a graphical interface in which network components are highlighted with colored icons to make it easier for the manager to evaluate their activities and determine the need for load balancing.

Security Concerns with Remote Management Tools

A Security Information Management (SIM) device is a GUI program that can be used to remotely manage a firewall. Because a SIM has access to all of the firewalls on your network, it needs to be as secure as possible to prevent unauthorized users from circumventing your security systems. To begin with, the SIM offers strong security controls such as multi-factor authentication and encryption. The SIM should also be equipped with auditing features that keep track of who uses the software and when. The best remote management tools will use tunneling to connect to the firewall or use certificates for authentication, rather than establishing a weak connection like a Telnet interface. Once the SIM software is installed and you begin to use it, be sure to evaluate the software to ensure that it does not introduce any new security vulnerabilities into the environment.

A remote management interface should provide the administrator with a consistent appearance and operation across multiple platforms. Both netForensics (*www.netforensics.com/*) and e-Security (*www.esecurityinc.com/main.asp*) make such devices. AltaVista Firewall 98 (*www.hallogram.com/avfirewall/*) is an example of a Remote Management Interface, and it uses an HTML-based interface that enables administrators to manage the firewall through a Web browser. The WatchGuard Central Policy Manager (CPM) tool, which is designed for use with WatchGuard's Firebox line of firewall appliances (*www.watchguard.com/products/firebox.asp*), enables administrators to monitor multiple appliances using a drag-and-drop interface.

Basic Features Required of Remote Management Tools

Any SIM or remote management program should enable you to monitor and configure firewalls from a single centralized location. They should also enable you to start and stop

11

firewalls as needed. Starting and stopping a firewall is a drastic step because it can affect network communications (unless you have a hot standby or load-sharing system set up as described in the section "Configuring Advanced Firewall Functions" later in this chapter), but it's one you need to have at your disposal in case you detect an intrusion.

Remote management tools should also help you perform such remote management tasks as the following:

- View and change firewall status
- View the firewall's current activity
- View any firewall event or alert messages
- Stop or start firewall services if needed

Be careful when giving out management accounts that enable others to administer the firewall. If unauthorized users steal account passwords or user-names, the consequences can be devastating for your network.

TRACKING THE CONTENTS OF LOG FILES FOR SECURITY

Log files are part of the responsibility of every firewall administrator. Although reviewing log files is tedious and time-consuming, it's an important activity that can help detect break-ins that have occurred and possibly help you track down the intruders (though this is, frankly, very difficult). The following sections give you some tips for managing your log files.

Log files always seem to expand to quickly to fill in as much available disk space as you have available. The sheer size of such files can make it difficult to detect individual events. Auditing software like Tripwire for Network Devices (*www.tripwire.com/products/network_devices/*) can alert you to new files that suddenly appear on your system.

Preparing Usage Reports

When you first start monitoring the firewall, you'll probably be called upon to prepare reports that indicate how the network is being used and what kinds of filtering activities the firewall is performing. To meet those requests, sort the logs by time of day and per hour. (Sorting the log files provides you with a way to approach them in an organized way that is less intimidating than simply reviewing them as they are produced by the server, firewall, or other device.) Also be sure to check the logs to learn when the peak traffic times are on your network, and try to identify the services that consume the largest part of your available bandwidth. Figure 11-6 illustrates a real-time monitor that can graphically display traffic as it passes through the firewall.

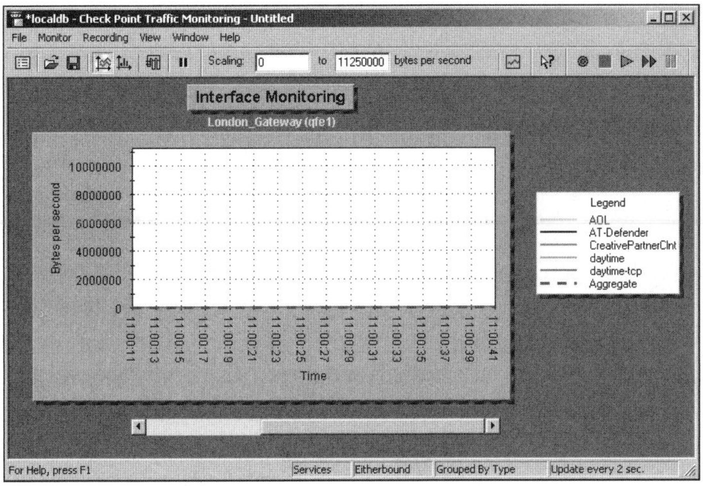

Figure 11-6   Real-time traffic monitoring on a firewall

Track the number of Web hits in a particular hour, as well as the number of e-mail messages received, FTP files transferred, and NTTP messages posted during that same hour. Reviewing logs can give you real-world evidence of how heavily your available network bandwidth is being used, and whether the computers that host your firewalls and other security software can hold up to the load. One way to determine whether your network has enough bandwidth and whether your bastion hosts have enough memory and processor speed is to add up the heaviest load displayed by all services—the total will give you a worst-case scenario for the heaviest load your network is likely to face.

> A log file analysis tool that is intended to perform intrusion detection can be invaluable in analyzing the often voluminous and monotonous data presented in log files. LANguard Security Event Log Monitor by GFI Software Ltd. can perform real-time event monitoring and provide an audit trail that goes far beyond what the Event Viewer and other logs in Windows 2000 and XP can provide. Find out more about this tool at *www.gfi.com/languard*.

Watching for Suspicious Events

To help you and your coworkers use log files more efficiently, develop a log file checklist, paying special attention to events such as:

- Rejected connection attempts
- Denied connections
- Error messages
- Dropped packets
- Successful logons to critical resources (this gives you the ability to track unauthorized successful logons to those resources)

If you see a suspicious event, you have the ability to block that connection immediately and prevent future connections. Most software firewalls give one of three options:

- *Block only this connection:* This option immediately terminates the selected connection and blocks all future attempts to establish a connection from the same source IP address to the same destination IP address and port.

- *Block access of this source:* The active connection is terminated, and all future attempts to make connections by this source IP address will be denied, no matter what the destination IP address and port.

- *Block access to this destination:* The selected connection is terminated, and all future attempts to establish a connection to the destination IP address will be denied no matter what the source IP address is.

If you take the time to block connections from IP addresses that send you unwanted e-mail, attempt to download files to which they do not have access, and attempt to access your network at predictable times because they are searching for open ports, you'll not only improve security, but network performance will improve as well. A rule base that calls for the blocking all but the most-essential traffic, using one of the three scopes previously listed, will cause the network to perform more quickly.

The following sections give you some ideas of other ways to respond if you actually detect break-in attempts: you can track the attacks, and you can take steps to locate and prosecute the offenders.

Tracking Attacks

It can be very difficult to catch network intruders, but it is not impossible either. Expect and watch for attacks at odd hours, especially overnight on weekends and holidays. When you do detect an intrusion, you should make use of a tool that helps you do some investigating, such as the following:

- *Sam Spade (www.samspade.org):* This program can find a good deal of public information associated with an IP address or DNS address.

- *Netstat:* This tool, which comes built-in with most versions of Windows and UNIX, has been mentioned in previous chapters, and it can tell you which ports are in use on your computer so you can see if there are any that are being used that should *not* be in operation.

- *NetCat (www.atstake.com/research/tools/index.html):* NetCat is a powerful network diagnostics tool available for both Windows and UNIX. It can be used to send packets as well as capture network packets so you can analyze them. NetCat was developed by the well-known hacker group L0pht, which recently changed its focus and became affiliated with the security organization @stake in order to help prevent security breaches. The new alliance is putting into practice the approach that using a hacker's own tool is often a good way to defeat them.

Compiling Legal Evidence

Computer security law is a constantly evolving field, but the recent urgency to track down and deter terrorists has thrown a spotlight on the field. In order to prosecute, you have to compile evidence showing that an actual prosecutable offense has taken place.

Examples of such offenses include:

- Defamation

- Fraud and abuse

- Threats to injure, extort, or murder someone

The field of **computer forensics** covers the use of computer resources to track down criminal activity. Computer forensics is a complex and evolving area, and it's not possible to give a detailed rundown of all the strategies and tools you can use to track down network intruders. However, the following is a brief step-by-step overview of ways to compile legal evidence that you can use against a hacker.

1. Begin by identifying which computer or computer media (such as tape drives or hard disks) may contain evidence.

2. Shut down the computer and isolate the work area until the person designated to perform the computer forensics (if this is someone other than you) arrives.

3. Any removable media should be write protected so new information cannot be written to it. On cassette back-up tapes, the record tab should be removed. On floppy disks, the write-protect tab should be placed in the "open" position. On removable hard disks, tape should be placed over the notch that enables the drive to write data to the disk.

4. Take steps to preserve that evidence so it is not manipulated, either accidentally or on purpose, by making a mirror image of the media (See Chapter 8 for suggestions on making images of disk drives.)

5. Once you have made an image of the media, either examine the mirror image, or make a second copy that you can examine. Do not examine the original media.

6. After reviewing the log files or other data on the media, report your findings to the management of your organization.

7. Preserve the evidence by making a "forensically sound" copy of every bitstream on it. Special tools are available for this sort of copying, including the

11

Linux "dd" (Driver Disk) tool (*www.redhat.com/docs/manuals/linux/ RHL-7.2-Manual/install-guide/ch-driverdisk.html*) and SnapBack DatArrest (*www.snapback.com*).

When you locate your findings, record them in an evidence log that you can take to court. The evidence log provides you with a summary of your findings that you can read in response to questions. The log should also provide documentation about the chain of custody: who had possession of the evidence from the time it was identified to the time of the court appearance.

Extreme care must be taken when reviewing computer media because the ultimate goal is to assemble a case that will stand up in court. You should observe the **"three As" of computer forensics**: *acquire* the evidence without damaging or changing it in any way; be able to *authenticate* that the evidence is the same as the original seized data; *analyze* the data without modifying it. Be aware that you will be called on to testify as to how evidence was handled. If you want to find out more about how to handle evidence, review the procedures listed on the Web site of the Library Accreditation Board of the American Society of Crime Lab Directors (*www.ascld-lab.org*).

Take care when you collect evidence; be careful not to violate anyone's privacy rights. Acting on "probable cause" may be important where the safety or privacy of an entire organization is concerned, but be sure you follow clearly stated rules and procedures when you do so. Not only is the violation of individual privacy rights wrong in and of itself, but it also could cause your case to fail if a court finds you acted improperly in investigating security breaches. If you believe a crime has been committed, you should establish a rapport with local, state, and federal authorities and consult with them if they believe activities constitutes a crime. Also, become familiar with the laws governing the use and abuse of IT systems in your state.

Automating Security Checks

You can hire a service to do the ongoing checking and administration of a firewall for you. This is not simply passing the buck: if your time as a network administrator is taken up with making sure the network is up and running and adding or removing users as needed, it's more efficient to consider outsourcing the firewall administration. Be aware, though, that if you outsource your firewall management, you have to put a high level of trust in the outsourcer to maintain your network security. You can't always expect outside companies to devote as high a level of attention to your log files as in-house employees would.

Presinet (*www.presinet.com/Main/Deadbolt.htm*) is just one of many companies that can remotely manage your firewall for you. The best way to find a company to which you can outsource your firewall management responsibilities is to ask network administrators in other organizations for their personal recommendations, or scan security-related sites such as SANS (*www.sans.org*) for recommendations.

SECURITY BREACHES WILL HAPPEN!

Don't expect that when you install a firewall configuration that you will never experience a break-in again. It's far safer—not to mention more realistic—to expect that an attack will definitely occur (and it probably will).

The following sections give a brief overview of how to adequately plan for an attack: use software designed to detect the attack and send you alert notifications, take countermeasures to minimize damage, and take steps to prevent future attacks.

Using an Intrusion Detection System

Perimeter security is only effective when attacks are anticipated, detected, and handled effectively. An **intrusion detection system (IDS)** is software or hardware that detects whether a network or server has experienced an unauthorized access attempt and that sends notification to the appropriate network administrators so that the intrusion attempt can be analyzed, damage can be assessed, and responses can be made, if necessary.

When choosing an intrusion detection system, you have several things to consider:

- *Where the IDS should be located:* You can choose a host-based IDS that is located on a single host or a network-based IDS that is located on the perimeter of a network.

- *What intrusion events should be gathered:* You can perform IDS in two ways: by analyzing patterns of attack called **signatures** or by doing **heuristic analysis** that looks for patterns of traffic that do not match what has been defined as "normal" network traffic.

The following two sections compare host-based versus network-based IDS systems and signature versus heuristic intrusion detection.

Network-Based Versus Host-Based IDS

A network-based IDS tracks traffic patterns on an entire subnet or other network segment. Network-based IDS systems collect raw network packets in much the same fashion as "packet sniffer" software. They can look at packet headers, determine if any known signatures are present that match common intrusion attempts, and then take action based on the contents.

Network-based IDS systems are excellent choices if your network has been subject to port scanning or if you have had malicious activity on particular ports such as HTTP Port 80. Such systems are usually operating system-independent, so if your network uses a variety of operating systems, a network-based system is a good choice. Finally, network-based systems don't have a dramatic impact on network performance, so if you lack bandwidth or have been having problems with heavy network traffic, network-based systems won't slow down traffic any further.

11

Host-based systems collect data from the individual computer on which they reside rather than an entire network segment. They review audit logs and system logs, looking for signatures—they do not monitor actual network packets. One big benefit of using a host-based system is that it can perform intrusion detection in a network where traffic is usually encrypted, such as a VPN; a network-based IDS looks at packets, and if those packets are encrypted, it can't check their contents. Another benefit of a host-based IDS is that you don't need additional hardware to use it; rather, you install host-based systems on your existing computers. On the downside, host-based systems cannot detect port scans or other intrusion attempts that target an entire network.

Signature-Based Versus Heuristic IDS

Many IDS systems make use of known signatures: patterns of behavior or technical values such as IP headers or flags that point to a particular type of attack. Some IDS devices maintain a database of such signatures; when a packet arrives at the IDS with one of the suspicious signatures, the packet is dropped and an alert is sent. The more-advanced IDS devices enable the administrator to customize signatures or write your own to match new types of threats. Signatures not only tell you when intrusion attempts occur, but they can help you prevent future attacks as well.

Of course, when an attack occurs, knowing the signature won't help you respond to it. The most dramatic countermeasure you can take is to shut down the server and completely break your connection to the Internet. You may also be able to shut down a particular server so you can keep the rest of the network communications intact.

A signature-based IDS provides far fewer false alarms than a heuristic system, so if your IT resources are low and you don't have the time to continually respond to intrusion alarms, signature-based systems are a good choice. In addition, because information about signatures is stored in the database, the network administrator is supplied with an extensive set of information about how to prevent or take corrective action against attacks.

Signature-based IDS systems can work with either host-based or network-based IDS. The obvious drawback with such systems is that they can't keep up with the very latest types of attacks unless you periodically update the database. Signature-based IDS tools are often closely tied to a specific hardware and operating system as well.

Heuristic intrusion detection looks at traffic patterns and compares them against a traffic pattern that has previously been identified as "normal activity." Once the traffic pattern deviates from what has been defined as normal, an alarm is set off. Such IDS systems can identify any possible attack, including new types that signature-based IDS systems won't be able to track. On the other hand, heuristic systems generate a high rate of false alarms and require the network administrator to do analysis to determine exactly what set off the alert. In addition, an organization's concept of what constitutes "normal" traffic can change over time, so if your network is rapidly growing and evolving, this may not be a good choice.

It's also important to note that, whatever type of configuration you install, an effective intrusion detection system does not operate in isolation but implements an organization's approach to security and works in a coordinated way with other security tools such as firewalls and VPNs. Many firewalls have intrusion detection systems built into them; IDS systems can also be added to an existing firewall configuration as software or hardware.

Receiving Security Alerts

A good IDS system is more than just a "house alarm" that goes off when someone tries to break in. A good system also notifies the appropriate individuals and provides information about what type of event occurred and where in your network the intrusion attempt actually took place. Usually, you can tell your firewall or IDS system to notify you in one of several different ways:

- *E-mail:* You can have the system send you an e-mail message.

- *Alert:* The firewall or IDS system can display a pop-up message.

- *Pager:* If your pager can accept e-mail, some IDS systems can communicate with it.

- *Log:* You can have the IDS system send an alert message to the log files.

An IDS can even point to the source of the intrusion if genuine (rather than "spoofed") source IP information has been provided. Some systems can provide an immediate response to an attack attempt, such as dropping the connection, or blocking it for a predefined period of time.

When an Intrusion Occurs

When an intrusion is detected, it's important not to panic. Instead, react rationally. Use the alerts to begin to assess the situation. Ask yourself: first, did the hacker actually succeed in breaking in? Is the hacker still present on your site? Analyze what resources were hit and what damage occurred, if any. You would do this by performing real-time analysis of network traffic to see if any unusual patterns are present. Also check the ports on the machine that was attacked to see if any ports that are normally unused have been accessed. A network auditing tool like Tripwire (*www.tripwire.com*) is invaluable in this instance because it reports on any new programs or files that were added to a system at a particular point in time. You can scan the list of files to see if any suspicious executable programs were added.

During and After an Intrusion

Your next step is to document the existence of any of the following:

- Executables that were added to the system

- Any files that were placed on computers

11

- Any files that were deleted

- Files that were accessed by unauthorized users

- Web pages that were defaced

- E-mail messages that were sent as a result of the attack

You then need to document everything you do in response to the intrusion. Such documentation can prove invaluable in the event the hacker is located and prosecuted—or in case you have to recommend the purchase of new security equipment as a result of the attack.

 You shouldn't shut down your server if you plan to try to catch the hacker: an active connection can be used to trace the individual—though it's likely the hacker will be using a spoofed rather than genuine IP address.

CONFIGURING ADVANCED FIREWALL FUNCTIONS

Configuring and implementing a firewall is only the start. The ultimate goal for many organizations is the development of a high-performance firewall configuration that has **high availability** (in other words, it operates on a 24/7 basis or close to it) and that can be **scaled** (that can grow and maintain effectiveness) as the organization grows. This section briefly discusses some advanced firewall functions that can be implemented to keep the firewall running effectively on a day-to-day basis: data caching, redundancy, load balancing, and content filtering.

Data Caching

Caching—the practice of storing data in a part of disk storage space so it can be retrieved as needed—is one of the primary functions of proxy servers. Firewalls can be configured to work with external servers to cache data, too. Caching of frequently accessed resources such as Web page text and image files can dramatically speed up the performance of your network because it reduces the load on your Web servers. The load on the servers is reduced when end users are able to call pages from disk cache rather than having to send a request to the Web server itself.

Usually, firewalls give you a variety of options for how data is cached. First, you need to set up a server that will receive requests for URLs and that will filter those requests against different criteria you set up. Those criteria include whether the Web page requested can be viewed by the public as part of the organization's security policy; whether the Web page requested is part of a site that has been identified as containing harmful or inappropriate content and that should not be viewed by employees; and whether the site already exists in disk cache because it has been previously viewed and its contents have not changed since the last time it was viewed. The server returns the URL to the requesting host only if a set of caching criteria is met.

Typically you choose one of four options for how data is to be cached:

- *No caching:* Caching is turned off in this instance, and every request has to go to the originating Web server. This produces a heavier load on Web servers, but you might still choose this option if your server configuration changes frequently and you want to filter each request using the most up-to-date criteria.

- *UFP server:* This option specifies the use of a **URI Filtering Protocol server**—a server that filters and processes requests for URIs and that can work in conjunction with firewalls—to call up Web pages from cache if needed. The UFP server reviews the requests, checks the URI against the contents of disk cache, and returns documents from cache if they are present.

- *VPN & Firewall (one request):* The VPN and firewall servers rather than the UFP server, control caching. When a Web page is requested by an end user for the first time, it is immediately sent to the UFP server after that one request and added to disk cache, which considerably improves network performance.

- *VPN & Firewall (two requests):* URIs are sent to the UFP server two times before they are added to disk cache. Performance isn't as good as with a one-request system, but security is improved because each URI is checked by the firewall twice before being sent to cache.

Hot Standby Redundancy

One way to balance the load placed on a firewall is to set up a **hot standby** system in which one or more auxiliary or failover firewalls are configured to take over all traffic if the primary firewall fails. Usually, hot standby only involves two firewalls, the primary and the secondary systems. Only one firewall operates at any given time. The two firewalls need to be connected in what is sometimes called a **heartbeat network**: a network that monitors the operation of the primary firewall and synchronizes the state table connections so the two firewalls have the same information at any given time. This setup is shown in Figure 11-7.

Figure 11-7 shows a simplified diagram of a hot standby setup (simplified because in reality there would be more routers joining the various networks and probably more servers in the DMZs). The heartbeat network is made up of the two firewalls. The dashed line indicates the paths through which network traffic would flow if the primary firewall fails. The advantage of a hot standby system is the ease and economy with which it can be set up and the quick back-up system it provides for the network. Another advantage is that one firewall can be stopped for maintenance purposes without stopping traffic to and from the network. On the downside, hot standby by itself doesn't improve network performance, and VPN connections may or may not be included in the failover system, depending on whether the firewall supports failover for VPN connections.

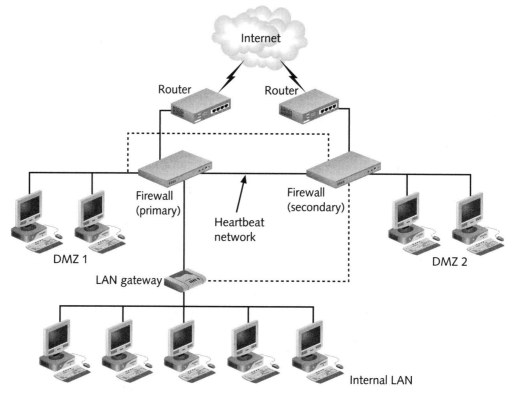

Figure 11-7 A hot standby redundancy setup

 Hot standby systems are just one aspect of disaster recovery management (DRM), a field growing in importance due to terrorist attacks and increased threats of cyberterrorism. See "Securing the Machine Itself" in Chapter 8 for a more detailed discussion of how to secure all types of hardware in case of disaster.

Load Balancing

As discussed in the early chapters of this book, the simplest firewalls function as gateways, monitoring all traffic as it passes into and out of a network. As organizations grow and Web, e-mail, and e-commerce services grow, it can be a liability to have a single firewall gateway that can become a single point of failure. When the firewall becomes **mission-critical**—an integral, key part of the company's core operations—everything possible must be done to maximize the firewall's uptime and smooth operation. One way to accomplish this goal is **load balancing**: the practice of balancing the load placed on the firewall so that it is handled by two or more firewall systems.

Another type of load balancing is **load sharing**: the practice of configuring two or more firewalls to share the total traffic load. Each firewall in a load-sharing setup is active at the same time. Traffic between the firewalls is distributed by routers using special routing protocols such as:

- *Open Shortest Path First (OSPF):* This protocol can route traffic based on its IP type. It can also divide traffic equally between two routers that are equally far apart or that have an equal load already.

- *Border Gateway Protocol (BGP):* This protocol uses TCP as its transport protocol to divide traffic among available routers.

A load-sharing setup has many advantages: total network performance is improved because the load is balanced among multiple firewalls, and the routing protocols needed to distribute traffic are present in virtually all routers. A big advantage is that maintenance can be performed on one firewall without disrupting total network traffic to the other firewall(s). On the downside, the load is usually distributed unevenly, and the configuration can be complex to administer. The connections between load sharing firewalls may or may not include failover functions. This depends on whether the firewalls involved support failover connections. A load-balancing setup is illustrated in Figure 11-8.

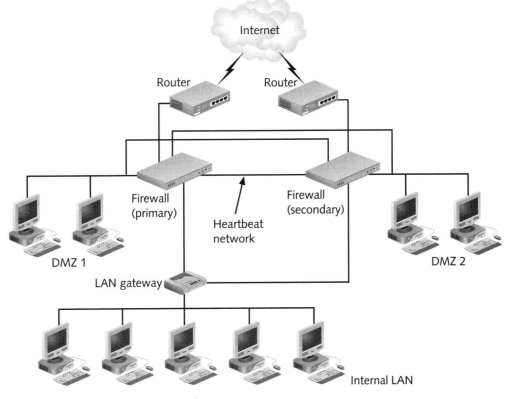

Figure 11-8   A load-sharing configuration

The even distribution of traffic among two or more load-sharing firewalls can be achieved through the use of **layer four switches**: network devices with the intelligence to make routing decisions based on source and destination IP address or port numbers as specified in layer four of the OSI reference model.

Filtering Content

One of the most malicious and difficult to filter type of attacks on a network is the inclusion of harmful code in e-mail messages. Firewalls, by themselves, don't do virus scanning, but their manufacturers enable them to work with third-party applications to scan for viruses or other functions. Zone Alarm and Check Point NG, for instance, have an **Open Platform for Security (OPSEC) model** that lets you extend its functionality and integrate virus scanning into its set of abilities.

Many advanced firewalls support the **Content Vectoring Protocol (CVP)**, a protocol that enables firewalls to work with virus-scanning applications so such content can be filtered out. For instance, you can define a network object such as a server that contains anti-virus software and then have the firewall send SMTP traffic to that server using CVP. Once you define the server as a network object, you set the application properties for that server (see Figure 11-9).

In Figure 11-9, the antivirus server is identified as an OPSEC_Server in the Host list. CVP is being identified as a server entity, and an OPSEC-compliant vendor intended for use on the anti-virus server is being chosen from the Vendor list. You then set options in the CVP Options tab to identify the server as a CVP object and identify the types of data you want to send to that server. CVP and OPSEC are two important tools you can use to help your firewall grow along with your organization's security needs.

Anti-virus protection is fast becoming one of the most important aspects of network security due to the proliferation of viruses borne by e-mail messages. For this reason, consider installing an anti-virus software on your SMTP gateway in addition to providing desktop anti-virus protection for each of your computers. Be sure to choose an anti-virus gateway product that provides for content filtering, can be updated regularly to account for recent viruses, can scan the system in real time, and has detailed logging capabilities.

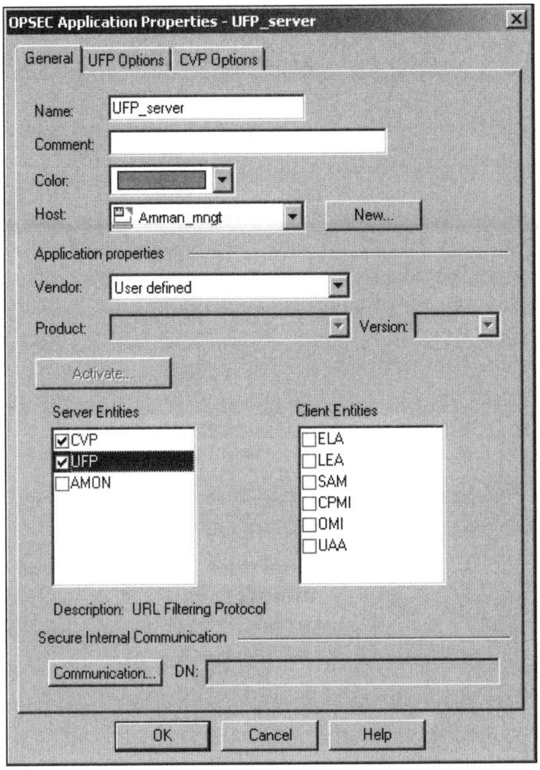

Figure 11-9   Configuring a server to communicate with Check Point NG through CVP

CHAPTER SUMMARY

This chapter examined issues involved in administering a firewall after it is installed in order to meet evolving network needs and defeat new security threats as they arise. You need to perform many different administrative tasks to achieve adequate throughput, effective security, and recoverability of the firewall in case it crashes. Consider the following points covered in this chapter:

▫ You need to test the firewall periodically to make sure it is moving traffic efficiently. The efficiency of a firewall depends in part on the amount of memory and CPU resources it is consuming. If the firewall is consuming more memory than is allocated to it, you can allocate more memory to the program or reduce CPU usage by adding another firewall to the network to balance the load. Over time, you may be called upon to add new software or hardware to the network, and each resource you add should be defined as an object so the firewall can protect it.

▫ Adhering to basic security principles can augment the firewall and improve your overall network security. You need to maintain a secure physical environment for your network equipment, and make sure laptops and other computers have adequate password protection. Laptops that connect to the network through a VPN should have their own distributed firewall protection, too.

❑ A remote management interface is a key element in any firewall management program. A remote management interface that is easy to use and that has a consistent interface from platform to platform is a good choice. Any remote management program should let you view the firewall's current activity, read its alert messages, and let you start or stop the firewall as well.

❑ Reviewing and analyzing log files regularly is another key aspect of ongoing firewall administration. Review your log files each week or each month, and pay particular attention to heavy-use periods and frequently used services. Also pay attention to unusual patterns regarding dropped packets, denied connections, and other signs of possible break-in attempts—for example, denied connection attempts that occur at the same time at 10 p.m., which might indicate that someone is scanning your network each evening at the same time. Consider hiring an automated management service to review your logs, test your network, and administer the firewall for you if you don't have time to perform the task yourself.

❑ An intrusion detection system (IDS) is an essential part of any network security configuration. An IDS should send you an alert message as soon as a possible attack is detected, so you can respond quickly. Although an IDS can tell you when an intrusion attempt occurred, it is up to you to determine whether the hacker actually gained access to your network and whether any damage occurred. Keep track of intrusion signatures and add new ones to the IDS as they become available.

❑ As time go on, you may be called upon to configure advanced firewall functions that ensure high availability as well as scalability. These include data caching to improve network performance, load balancing to provide failover or "hot standby" systems, load sharing to divide the load among multiple firewalls, and content filtering to screen out executable e-mail attachments and other potentially harmful software. You may need to use third-party software such as virus scanners in conjunction with the firewall to perform some of these tasks.

KEY TERMS

average lifetime — The length of a typical connection to a host as indicated by your log files.

boot-up password — A password that must be entered to complete the process of starting up the computer.

computer forensics — A field of activity that focuses on the use of computer resources to track down criminal activity.

concurrent connections — The number of connections made to hosts in the internal network at any one time.

Content Vectoring Protocol (CVP) — A protocol that enables firewalls to work with virus-scanning applications so that malicious code or other harmful content can be filtered out of e-mail messages or other communications.

distributed firewalls — Firewalls that are installed at all endpoints of the network, including the remote computers that connect to the network through VPNs.

environmental management — Measures taken to reduce the risk to the physical environment where hardware and software are stored to protect them from storms, theft, or other disasters.

Generally Accepted System Security Principles (GASSP) — A set of security and information management practices put forth by the International Information Security Foundation (I2SF).

heartbeat network — A network that monitors the operation of the primary firewall and synchronizes the state table connections so the two firewalls have the same information at any given time.

heuristic analysis — A type of intrusion detection that looks for patterns of traffic that do not match what has been defined as "normal" network traffic.

high availability — The fact that a firewall or other system is up and running on a 24/7 basis or as close to this as possible.

hot standby — An approach to load balancing in which a secondary or failover firewall is configured to take over traffic duties in case the primary firewall fails.

intrusion detection system (IDS) — Software or hardware that detects whether a network or server has experienced an unauthorized access attempt and that sends notification to the appropriate network administrators.

layer four switches — Network devices with the intelligence to make routing decisions based on source and destination IP address or port numbers as specified in layer four of the OSI Reference Model.

load balancing — The practice of balancing the load placed on the firewall so that it is handled by two or more firewall systems.

load sharing — The practice of configuring two or more firewalls to share the total traffic load.

mission-critical — The quality of being an integral, central part of an organization's core operations.

Open Platform for Security (OPSEC) model — An application standard that is present in Check Point NG and that lets third-party vendors design their applications to work with Check Point NG. OPSEC lets you extend firewall's functionality and integrate virus scanning into its set of abilities.

scale — The practice of expanding a system to meet a growing need.

signatures — Patterns of behavior or technical values such as IP headers or flags that are used by IDS hardware or software to point to a particular type of attack.

supervisor password — A password that is used to gain access to the BIOS set-up program, or to change the BIOS password.

11

"three As" of computer forensics — *Acquire* the evidence without damaging or changing it in any way; be able to *authenticate* that the evidence is the same as the original seized data; and *analyze* the data without modifying it.

URI Filtering Protocol server — a server that filters and processes requests for URIs and that can work in conjunction with a firewall to do content filtering.

REVIEW QUESTIONS

1. What are the three primary goals you need to keep in mind when you consider upgrading your firewall architecture?

   a. authentication, encryption, and encapsulation

   b. throughput, security, and recoverability

   c. privacy, authenticity, and reliability

   d. none of the above

2. A network administrator should be concerned when a firewall's CPU consumption climbs above what percentage of total CPU usage?

   a. 40

   b. 50

   c. 60

   d. 75

3. What should you do first if you discover that your firewall is in danger of consuming all of the memory that is allocated to it?

   a. cut down on concurrent connections

   b. allocate more memory to the firewall

   c. reduce the hash size

   d. remove the firewall

4. In a Windows environment, what are two possible ways to allocate more memory to a firewall? (Choose all that apply.)

   a. the Registry Editor

   b. Administrative Tools

   c. the Microsoft Management Console

   d. a GUI tool

5. When you add a new piece of hardware to a network, for it to be protected by the firewall, you need to _____.

   a. encrypt it

   b. assign it an IP address

   c. define it

   d. install IPSec on it

6. Distributed firewalls are positioned at the _____ of a network.

   a. perimeter

   b. DMZ

   c. gateways

   d. endpoints

7. What does load sharing fail to accomplish without the use of switches or routers?

   a. load balancing

   b. redundancy

   c. IP forwarding

   d. URI filtering

8. When should you consider turning off data caching?

   a. to ensure that viewers get the most up-to-date content

   b. to give the most up-to-date-criteria for filtering

   c. to use Web server resources more efficiently

   d. to speed up communications

9. Why would you consider recommending that your company hire an outside firm to handle the ongoing administration of a firewall? (Choose all that apply.)

   a. It frees you up for other network administration tasks.

   b. It saves the company money.

   c. It increases security.

   d. It's good to have another pair of eyes to review log files.

10. What should you do with old firewall logs? (Choose all that apply.)

    a. publish them online

    b. rotate them

    c. save them for at least a year

    d. store them on CD

11

11. Which of the following should you pay special attention to when reviewing log files?

    a. file transfers

    b. heavy NNTP usage

    c. dropped packets

    d. big e-mail attachments

12. You are fortunate enough to discover that a hacker has broken into your Web server and is currently looking through the files on that server. You are ordered to shut down the Web server immediately. You hesitate. How would you explain your hesitation to your superiors?

13. Why use a network-auditing program when you have plenty of log files available for review? (Choose all that apply.)

    a. The auditing program sorts and uses log files.

    b. The auditing program can alert you more quickly.

    c. The auditing program is cross-platform.

    d. The auditing program can identify new files that have appeared in directories.

14. Which of the following is a quality you should look for in a remote management program?

    a. portability due to being written in the Java language

    b. consistent interface

    c. cross-platform support

    d. the ability to start and stop the firewall

15. Which of the following are functions for which a firewall might need to use an external application or server as a network grows? (Choose all that apply.)

    a. Network Address Translation (NAT)

    b. content filtering

    c. load balancing

    d. data caching

16. What protocol enables firewalls to work with virus-scanning software?

    a. IPv6

    b. IPSec

    c. CVP

    d. SMTP

17. What aspect of the seven-layer OSI reference model of network communications gives layer four switches the ability to distribute traffic?

    a. They make use of TCP/IP, which is provided for in Transport layer.

    b. They can use IP source and destination header information.

    c. They transport data from one network location to another.

    d. They reassemble messages and add their own header information to packets.

18. What is the primary advantage of using a hot standby setup to achieve load balancing?

    a. economy and ease of setup

    b. security

    c. the ability to stop firewalls for maintenance

    d. improved network performance

19. What approach can reduce the risk posed by a single-firewall system?

    a. high availability

    b. content filtering

    c. data caching

    d. load balancing

20. When does the expense of setting up a load-sharing configuration make sense?

    a. when you need to maximize network uptime

    b. when you need to improve network performance

    c. when you need to evenly distribute traffic among firewalls

    d. when you need to stop firewalls for maintenance

11

HANDS-ON PROJECTS

Project 11-1: Using Status Manager

One of the most important factors in determining how well FireWall-1 performs is memory. Once you have a firewall up and running, you need to monitor it periodically to see how much memory it is consuming and how much memory is available to it. Check Point NG includes a tool for checking the firewall's performance called Status Manager NGFP2. If you have installed Check Point NG on a standalone workstation in your lab, you aren't likely to see much detail as far as memory usage. In this case, it's more revealing to run the program in Demo mode to see a sampling of statistics that indicate how the firewall would run in a real-world environment.

1. Click **Start**, point to **Programs** (**All Programs** on Windows XP), point to **Check Point Management Clients**, and click **Status Manager NGFP2**.

2. When the Welcome to Check Point Status Manager dialog box opens, check **Demo mode**, and then click **OK**.

3. The left side of the Status Manager window, labeled Modules, displays the modules that are currently deployed in the sample enterprise configuration included with the program. Click the plus sign next to **Local_Gateway** to expand it.

4. Click **FireWall-1** to select it.

5. Review the memory usage information displayed in the Details pane on the right side of the Status Manager window. How much memory is being used by the firewall?

6. Click **SVN Foundation** in the Modules pane of the Status Manager.

7. Review the new set of performance information in the Details pane. The CPU figures indicate the percentage of Central Processing Unit (CPU) resources that are being consumed by the firewall. How much CPU is being used? Do you think this figure is something you should be concerned about? How could you reduce the amount of CPU resources being used by the firewall?

8. Leave the Status Manager open if you want to proceed immediately to the next project. Otherwise, click **File** and click **Exit** to close Status Manager and return to the desktop.

Project 11-2: Configure a System Alert

High CPU or memory usage is a warning sign that the bastion host on which the firewall resides may become overloaded and cease to function. You can use Check Point NG's Status Manager to define the conditions under which you want to get a system alert. This is not a security alert as such; it is an alert that tells you free disk space is low or that CPU usage is low. (Such a situation, though, can result from a SYN flood or other attack in which a hacker tries to overload the gateway and gain access to the internal network.)

1. Click **Start**, point to **Programs** (**All Programs** on Windows XP), point to **Check Point Management Clients**, and click **Status Manager NGFP2**.

2. When the Welcome to Check Point Status Manager dialog box opens, check **Demo mode**, and then click **OK**.

3. Once Status Manager is up and running in Demo mode, drag the horizontal divider up from the bottom of the window just above the heading Critical Notifications. This is the Critical Notifications pane, which displays any firewall modules that are experiencing troubles. For instance, double-click **SVN Foundation**. What kind of problem is being reported?

4. Click the **System Alert** tab to bring it to the front. Notice that the right-hand pane's name changes to Network Object System Alert Definition.

5. Click **Local_Gateway** in the Modules pane to select it.

6. Click **Custom**.

7. Click the **SVN Foundation** tab.

8. In the box next to "CPU usage more than," change the default value 95% to **90%**.

9. Make any other changes you want to make in this tab. For instance, click the **CPU usage more than** list arrow and click **Mail** to select another notification method than the default Alert.

10. Click **Apply**.

11. Click **File** and click **Exit** to exit the Status Manager.

Project 11-3: Allocate More Memory to the FireWall-1 Kernel

In Project 11-1, you learned how to check the memory being consumed by Check Point FireWall-1. If you find that the computer is consuming more memory and system resources than you have available, you can change the firewall settings using the Policy Editor.

1. Click **Start**, point to **Programs** (**All Programs** on Windows XP), point to **Check Point Management Clients**, and click **Policy Editor NGFP2**.

2. When the Welcome to Check Point Policy Manager dialog box opens, type your password in the Password text box, and then click **OK**.

3. When the Policy Editor window opens, click **Manage** and click **Network Objects**.

4. In the Network Objects dialog box, click **Local_Gateway**, and then click **Edit**.

5. In the Check Point Gateway – Local_Gateway dialog box, click **Advanced** in the list of categories on the left.

6. Click the **Memory pool size** up scroll arrow and the **Maximum memory pool size** up scroll arrow to increase the amount of memory allocated to the program.

7. Optionally, you can click the **Maximum concurrent connections** down scroll arrow to reduce the number of connections FireWall-1 can handle at one time, but be very careful lest you keep the firewall from functioning smoothly.

8. Click **OK**, and then click **Close** to close the Network Objects dialog box.

9. Click **File** and click **Exit** to close Policy Editor and return to the desktop.

11

Project 11-4: Perform Real-Time Monitoring

FireWall-1 NG's Traffic Monitoring tool enables you to manage bandwidth and check traffic on a real-time basis. At any time, you can use Traffic Monitor to see how the firewall is performing.

1. Click **Start**, point to **Programs** (**All Programs** on Windows XP), point to **Check Point Management Clients**, and click **Traffic Monitoring NGFP2**.

2. When the Welcome to Check Point Traffic Monitoring dialog box opens, type your password and click **OK**.

3. When the Session Properties dialog box opens, scroll down the list of resources and click on the name of your workstation, which should appear beneath **Local_Gateway**.

4. Click the **Interface Monitoring** tab. Click **Services**, if necessary, and click the service you want to monitor. For this example, click **http, daytime-tcp, daytime-udp, domain-tcp, domain-udp, smtp**, and **pop-3** from the Available list box while holding down the Ctrl key. Then click **Add>** to move the items to the Selected box on the right.

5. In the Data Direction section, click **Eitherbound**, if necessary.

6. Click **OK**.

7. The Interface Monitoring chart opens in the Check Point Traffic Monitoring window. Because you are only a single workstation, it's unlikely you'll see a chart reporting multiple-megabytes worth of data transfers, so you may not actually see a chart. Click **Monitor**, point to **Measurement**, and click **Line Utilization** to see a real-time display of how much of your bandwidth you are currently using. The display is refreshed every two seconds by default.

8. Click **Monitor**, point to **ChartType**, and click **Bar Graph** for a different display showing how much of your resources are being used by the various services you selected.

9. Click **File** and click **Save**.

10. In the **Configuration Name** text box in the Save As dialog box, type **Daytime_Activity**, and then click **OK**.

11. Click **File** and click **Exit** to exit Traffic Monitoring and return to your desktop.

Project 11-5: Create a Report

Network administrators and security professionals alike are frequently called upon to report on the performance of firewalls, servers, and other network components. Check Point NG streamlines the process of reporting with its Reporting Tool. Most of the reports you can prepare with the Reporting Tool are designed for use on a network, and you have probably installed Check Point NG on a standalone workstation. However, in this project, you can still view some sample reports that come with the software. Then you'll create your own intrusion detection report.

1. Click **Start**, point to **Programs** (**All Programs** on Windows XP), point to **Check Point Management Clients**, and click **Reporting Tool NGFP2**.

2. When the Welcome to Check Point Reporting Tool dialog box opens, type **Administrator** in the User Name text box, your password in the Password text box, and ***local** in the Reporting Server text box, and then click **OK**.

3. Click the plus sign next to **Sample** to expand it.

4. Click **Sample-Alerts_details**, and then click **OK**. The Run Time Parameters dialog box opens, displaying parameters for this report.

5. In the Available Attributes List box, click **Source**.

6. Click **OK** to generate a sample report listing security alerts for each host on the sample network. Which connection generated the most security alerts?

7. See how often this report is scheduled to run by clicking **View** and clicking **Schedules Per Report** on the Check Point Reporting Client menu bar.

8. In the View Schedules dialog box, click the first report displayed and click **Edit Schedule** to change how often the report is to be run.

9. View the details in the Scheduler dialog box, and then click **OK**. Click **OK**.

10. Click **Close** to close View Schedules.

11. Click **File** and click **Exit** to close the Check Point Reporting Tool and return to the desktop.

11

CASE PROJECTS

Case 11-1: Monitoring Traffic

You need to monitor different types of traffic at different times of day using your firewall-protected network. You primarily want to monitor e-mail, Web, and videoconferencing activity during the day, but in the overnight offices, branch offices around the world might connect to your network for FTP, TCP, and UDP traffic. How would you specify different monitoring parameters for different times of the day?

Case 11-2: Improving Load Balancing Among Firewalls

You have set up a load-sharing configuration in which three firewalls provide separate gateways for an internal network. You are alarmed to discover that only a slight improvement in network traffic performance has resulted, despite the fact that you purchased and configured two new bastion hosts and firewall products. What might be the cause of the continued poor network performance? What could you do to improve the situation?

Case 11-3: Extending the Firewall To Handle Content Filtering

Despite the fact that you have installed an enterprise-class firewall, your company's employees have reported receiving e-mail messages that contain potentially harmful executable code attachments. Such attachments have been identified and isolated by the virus protection software installed on each workstation. You know, however, that the number of such harmful attachments is growing all the time, and you are worried that one will slip through that the virus protection software isn't yet configured to handle. What can you do to block such harmful e-mail messages from entering the protected network in the first place?

Case 11-4: Responding to an Intrusion

You congratulate yourself on configuring your firewall. The next morning, you check the log files. You discover a number of unsuccessful attempts to log on to the FTP server. You turn on your firewall's real-time monitoring program and you immediately notice that 15MB worth of files is in the process of being transferred to an external user. You realize an attack is probably in progress. What should you do?

A

SECURITY RESOURCES

Firewalls, intrusion detection, and network security are all constantly evolving fields. To keep up with the latest developments in the field, you should visit the Web sites mentioned in this appendix. Many of the sites contain information about firewalls, and present white papers, research papers, and other background information on topics such as packet filtering, authentication, and encryption. In addition, these sites contain information about the latest threats against which your firewall needs to defend. Bugs, security holes, and the patches to repair them will be available online before you read about them in a book.

SECURITY-RELATED WEB SITES

The following Web sites are important resources you can turn to if you need general information about Internet and network security.

The Center for Internet Security (*www.cisecurity.org/*)

The Center for Internet Security is a nonprofit organization devoted to the development of security standards it calls "benchmarks." For instance, the group recently published a set of benchmarks establishing the secure operation of a Windows 2000 computer. Benchmarks are available for Linux, HP-UX, and other operating systems as well.

SANS Institute (*www.sans.org*)

The SystemAdmin, Audit, Network, and Security (SANS) Institute is a research and education organization that focuses on network security. SANS conducts seminars and workshops on security around the country and offers tests to prepare for important certifications such as the Global Information Assurance Certification (GIAC) Security Essentials and the CISSP certification offered by ISC2. The SANS Web site includes links to important resources such as a list of the Twenty Most Critical Internet Security Vulnerabilities (*www.sans.org/top20.htm*) and the SANS Security Policy Project (*www.sans.org/newlook/ resources/policies/policies.htm*), the latter of which contains sample security policies and guidelines for producing your own.

The Cert Coordination Center (*www.cert.org*)

The Cert Coordination Center, a group affiliated with the Carnegie-Mellon Institute, contains lists of security alerts, incident notes, and vulnerabilities on its home page. CERT also offers tips and articles about aspects of network security plus training courses. Contents are oriented not only toward corporate and educational users, but also to home users who need to know about security.

W3C Security Resources (*www.w3.org/security*)

This page, which is provided by the World Wide Web Consortium, provides an overview of Web security issues, security hole alerts, and practical advice for avoiding unpleasant surprises. It serves as an excellent starting point for exploration into issues affecting security on the Internet and World Wide Web.

Microsoft Security and Privacy (*www.microsoft.com/security*)

You'll find general security information on this site, but more importantly, you'll find Microsoft's own news about, and patches to, vulnerabilities affecting its own software. Start here to search for bulletins and patches; you can also submit your own reports of security vulnerabilities you detect yourself.

ANTI-VIRUS SITES

The Web sites in this section keep close watch on the latest virus outbreaks, publish instructions on how to detect and remove viruses, and provide software to remove viruses, worms, and Trojan horses.

Symantec Security Response (*http://securityresponse.symantec.com*)

The virus alert page provided by software manufacturer Symantec Corporation, which produces Norton Anti-Virus, contains security alerts about the most urgent viruses that have emerged on the Internet and software to delete them if your equipment is infected.

McAfee.com—Anti-Virus (*www.mcafee.com*)

Like Symantec, McAfee produces anti-virus software, and it maintains its anti-virus page to keep users informed of the latest security threats. The McAfee.com—AntiVirus page provides some different perspectives on virus attacks, too. A virus map gives you a look at virus attack patterns worldwide. A virus glossary helps you discover the differences between various types of malicious programs.

FREE ONLINE SECURITY SCANNERS

After you have configured firewalls and intrusion detection devices to protect your network, you can test them by connecting to a Web site that will scan your system for open ports or other vulnerabilities. Be sure you trust the Web site before you do this. Fortunately, the sites mentioned below are reputable and will give you extensive information about any vulnerabilities you need to correct.

Shields UP! Port Scanner (*https://grc.com/x/ne.dll?bh0bkyd2*)

This site tests your computer or network defenses to see what kind of information, if any, is visible to users on the Internet. By going to the Shields UP! Web site and clicking Test My Shields!, you can let the site determine if any ports are open based on your IP address. By clicking Probe My Ports!, you learn whether any ports are currently open and listening. Intruders might attempt to attack these ports. This is also a useful site to visit if you want to test your computer's firewall and intrusion detection systems. When you are "probed" by the site, your firewall or IDS should present you with alert messages. If they don't, you need to reconfigure them.

broadbandreports.com

This site, which provides information about Dynamic Subscriber Line (DSL) connections, conducts a more extensive set of port scans so that you can test your defenses. SYN packets are sent to TCP ports; echo requests are sent to UDP ports, and more.

INCIDENT RESPONSE SITES

The following Web sites specialize in information about intrusion detection and how to respond to security incidents if they occur.

Incidents.org (*www.incidents.org*)

This site, which is also affiliated with SANS, specializes in various aspects of network security: intrusions, incidents, security alerts, and how to respond to all of the them. The organization's Web site is called the "Internet Storm Center," among other things, and, as the name indicates, you can find an up-to-date list of recently reported security breaches, as well as papers on how to respond to specific kinds of threats.

FIRST (*www.first.org*)

The Forum of Incident Response and Security Teams (FIRST) is a coalition of security incident response teams working in government, commercial, and academic organizations that seeks to promote rapid reaction to security incidents by coordinating communication and sharing information among its members. If you're a member of an incident response team, you should strongly consider joining FIRST.

Internet Fraud Complaint Center (*http://www1.ifccfbi.gov/index.asp*)

The Internet Fraud Complaint Center (IFCC) publishes security warnings on its Web site, and the warnings tend to be related to terrorist threats. This isn't surprising because the IFCC is the result of a partnership between the Federal Bureau of Investigation (FBI) and the National White Collar Crime Center (NW3C). The main purpose of the site is to give you a place to report fraud if you encounter it.

SECURITY CERTIFICATION SITES

The following sites offer certification through study program and exams. Having these certifications can be invaluable for obtaining employment in the field of network security.

CompTIA Certification Home Page (*www.comptia.org/certification/index.htm*)

Best known for its A+ certification, CompTIA also offers a Security+ certification that focuses on five areas: general security concepts, communications security, infrastructure security, cryptography, and operational/organizational security.

Global Information Assurance Certification (GIAC) (*www.giac.org*)

The GIAC Web site provides information about the certification exams and deadlines offered by the SANS Institute. Programs range from the entry-level Basic Information Security Officer to more specialized certifications, such as the GIAC Certified Firewall Analyst (GCFW).

(ISC)^2 (*www.isc2.org*)

The International Information Systems Security Certification Consortium (ISC)^2 is an international nonprofit organization dedicated to maintaining a common body of knowledge that is pertinent to information security and to certifying industrials. (ISC)^2 prepares and administers two of the most highly prized certifications in the field of network security: the Certified Information Systems Security Professional (CISSP) and the System Security Certified Practitioner (SSCP).

BACKGROUND INFORMATION ON SECURITY TOPICS

If you're doing research on, say, virtual private networking (VPN) or authentication and you want some background information on the topic, you should turn to the book you have in your hand first...but after that, you can find some useful information at the following Web sites.

SANS Reading Room (*http://rr.sans.org*)

Students who take one of the GIAC certifications and who are required to submit papers on various security-related topics have those papers published in the Reading Room. The result is an invaluable storehouse of research information about firewalls and all aspects of network security. You need to register to access the reading room articles, but registration is free and you only have to do it once. I highly recommend this site.

searchSecurity.com (*http://searchsecurity.techtarget.com/*)

searchSecurity.com is a search engine that focuses solely on terms and topics of interest to security professionals. This is a great place to go if you need the definition of a term or an explanation of how a particular process works.

Internet Firewalls FAQ (*www.interhack.net/pubs/fwfaq/*)

This detailed and comprehensive FAQ was prepared by two experienced firewall administrators and covers many practical techniques. Although it's not primarily intended for beginners to network security and it does assume some knowledge of computer networking, you can still learn a great deal about firewall basics, DMZs, packet filtering, and IPSec. There's a good section on how to make RealAudio, SSL, and other technologies work with a firewall.

NEWSLETTERS, NEWSGROUPS, AND MAILING LISTS

It can be difficult to remember to visit sites like Incidents.org to find out about the latest security alerts. Sometimes, it's easier to absorb current information if it's sent to your e-mail inbox. Here are a couple of suggested mailing lists and newsletters you can subscribe to keep up with the threats you need to combat.

The Newsgroup (*comp.security.firewalls*)

Despite the fact that many experienced security administrators frequent this newsgroup and the discussion tends to be highly technical, beginners can and do participate and ask questions. This group is a good place to turn to if you need recommendations about which firewall to choose or if you're having problems with a particular program.

FIRST membership Mailing Lists (*www.first.org/docs/mail.html*)

If you are a member of FIRST, you can participate in a number of mailing lists the group puts out. Some of the lists on the site contain announcements for the seminars the group holds around North America.

SANS Newsletters (*http://server2.sans.org/sansnews*)

The set of newsletters published by the SANS Institute includes a weekly News Bites publication as well as a weekly Security Alert Consensus listing current security threats and their available countermeasures.

CNET Newsletters (*http://nl.com.com/general.jsp*)

CNET will send e-mail newsletters to your inbox every week, and you can choose from more than twenty publications on topics ranging from MP3s to downloadable software to online shopping. For students of network security, the Virus & Security Newsletter and CatchUp Security Alert should keep you abreast of the latest security threats.

Glossary

/etc/passwd — Contains the encrypted passwords on a Linux system.

AAA services — Cisco Systems' term for the three primary functions of a centralized authentication server: authentication, authorization, and auditing.

Access Control Lists (ACLs) — Lists of individual users or computers that can access a set of networked resources.

Access Control Server (ACS) — A server that hosts centralized authentication software, such as RADIUS, and that performs authentication, authorization, and auditing functions.

ACK (Acknowledgement) flag — A part of a TCP header that tells a computer that sent a packet that the packet reached its destination.

active content — Special programming tools that provide enhanced functions to static Web pages.

alerting — A feature of some proxy servers that enables them to notify a network administrator if an unauthorized access attempt is in progress.

application layer gateway — A fundamental activity of firewalls. Proxy services are provided to hosts inside the network to shield them from the outside. The proxy receives requests from a host and forwards them to their destination on behalf of the host.

application proxy — *See* proxy server.

application-level gateway — *See* proxy server.

asymmetric key encryption — Encryption that involves the use of public and private keys (also called public key encryption).

audit — To test a system for performance qualities or vulnerabilities.

auditing — The process of keeping records of who is or is not authenticated and what level of authorization those individual users are given.

authentication — The process of identifying that individuals are who they claim to be. This is usually accomplished using a username and password.

Authentication Header (AH) — An IPSec protocol that adds a digital signature to packets to protect against repeat attacks, spoofing, or other tampering.

average lifetime — The length of a typical connection to a host as indicated by your log files.

back door — A way into a system (or network) that is not the usual or typical way. A "back door" is usually a secret or hidden way leading into the system (or network).

bandwidth — The amount of data that can be transmitted over a network in a fixed amount of time. Bandwidth for digital transmission is usually expressed in bits per second (bps) or bytes per second. Bandwidth for analog transmission is usually expressed in cycles per second or Hertz (Hz).

baseline — The minimum level of service or performance that is determined to be acceptable and that is used for comparison in future tests of a system.

basic authentication — A server maintains a local file of usernames and passwords that it refers to for matching the username-password pair being supplied by a client.

bastion host — A gateway between an internal (private) network and an external (public) network. Bastion hosts typically have all unnecessary services disabled to reduce the chance of exploitation.

benchmark — A level of performance that you consider acceptable and against which the system can be compared.

binary drive image — A copy of a floppy or hard disk that includes all information on it, including the operating system, applications, and individual files.

biometrics — The use of unique physical characteristics such as fingerprints and retinal patterns to identify someone.

boot-up password — A password that must be entered to complete the process of starting up the computer.

brute force attack — A way of breaching a firewall-protected network by flooding it with so much traffic that the firewalls crash and cease to function, thus letting traffic pass through.

buffer overflow — A situation where a program or process attempts to store more data than can be held in a temporary disk storage area called a buffer. This can result from a common type of attack called a buffer overflow attack.

cache — A section of disk space set aside for storage, usually to help speed up performance of applications that need the resources stored there.

cache server — A server that stores frequently requested Web content.

caching — The process of storing data in a part of a hard disk called a cache so that it can be retrieved later on. Files that are requested repeatedly can be called up from the disk cache, thus relieving the load on a Web server.

centralized authentication service — A centralized server handles three separate and essential authentication practices: authentication, authorization, and auditing.

Certification Authority (CA) — An entity that grants digital certificates and verifies the identity of their owners.

challenge-response — A type of authentication in which the authentication server sends the user a challenge, usually a numeric code. To authenticate, the user needs to respond by resubmitting the code and a secret PIN or password.

challenge-response authentication — The authenticating computer or firewall generates a random code or number (the challenge) and sends it to the user who wishes to be authenticated.

checksum — A unique number that is generated based on the contents of application programs.

chkconfig — A UNIX utility that reports on the services that are currently started so that you can verify whether all of them are absolutely necessary.

ciphertext — Ordinary text that has been rendered unreadable as a result of encryption.

circuit-level gateway — A protocol that works at the Session layer to monitor internal traffic leaving a protected network.

cleartext — Plain, unencrypted text.

client authentication — Same as user authentication but with additional time limit or usage limit restrictions.

client-based digital certificates — Digital certificates that a user obtains from a CA, which issues them and vouches for the owner's identity.

client-to-site VPN — A VPN that makes a network accessible to remote users who need dial-in access.

co-locate — To host a Web server at an ISP or Web-hosting service's facility for greater security.

computer forensics — A field of activity that focuses on the use of computer resources to track down criminal activity.

concurrent connections — The number of connections made to hosts in the internal network at any one time.

configuration file — A file that contains configuration information for an application.

Content Vectoring Protocol (CVP) — A protocol that enables firewalls to work with virus-scanning applications so that malicious code or other harmful content can be filtered out of e-mail messages or other communications.

crack — The act by an unauthorized individual of determining—by guessing, brute force, or deception—someone else's supposedly secret password.

critical resource — A software- or hardware-related item that is indispensable to the operation of a device or program.

Cyclical Redundancy Check (CRC) — An error-checking procedure performed in the trailer section of an IP packet.

data — The part of a packet that contains the information it is intending to send (such as the body of an e-mail message) and that is visible to the recipient—in contrast to the header of a packet, which is not visible to an end user.

datagram — Another term for a packet of digital information.

Defense in Depth (DiD) — A term used to describe a multilayered approach to network security. Rather than relying on a single security mechanism, DiD makes use of several security components that work together.

Demilitarized Zone (DMZ) — A network of publicly accessible servers, such as Web and FTP servers, that is connected to the firewall but that is isolated from the internal network to protect internal users from intrusions and attacks.

dependency services — Services that an operating system or application needs to function properly.

dictionary attack — An attack in which a hacker compiles a database of commonly used words and passwords that can be encrypted using all 4096 possible salts and compares its database of encrypted terms against the encrypted passwords found in the /etc/passwd directory on Linux. If a match is found, the actual password is known and access is gained.

Diffie-Hellman encryption — Stronger than RSA; it uses two large numbers that are processed by an algorithm.

digital certificate — An electronic document issued by a CA that contains a digital signature and other information, and that verifies the identity of the possessor.

digital signature — A series of numerals and characters generated by an encryption process that is easily transportable, can be time-stamped, and is commonly used to authenticate the identity of the person who possesses it.

Distributed Denial of Service (DDoS) attacks — Many compromised systems attack a single target. This causes a denial of service to users who would regularly use the targeted system. DDoS attacks flood the target system with incoming messages and essentially force it to shut down, thereby denying service to the system to legitimate users.

distributed firewalls — Firewalls that are installed at all endpoints of the network, including the remote computers that connect to the network through VPNs.

Domain Name System (DNS) — The system that enables Internet domain names to stand as aliases for IP addresses. The lists of DNS addresses are maintained by official registrars and mapped by DNS servers that are used by ISPs.

dual-homed host — A workstation that has both an internal interface and an external interface to the Internet.

encapsulation — The act of enclosing one data structure within another structure; an IP packet is enclosed within another IP packet.

Encapsulation Security Payload (ESP) — One of two protocols available for use with IPSec. It is considered more robust than the other IPSec protocol, AH, because it encrypts the data part of packets as well as the headers.

encryption — The process of encoding and decoding information to preserve its integrity, maintain privacy, and ensure the identity of the users participating in the encrypted data session.

encryption domain — The computers, routers, and other devices in a network that is protected by a gateway that performs encryption.

endpoint — One end of a VPN. The endpoint is provided by a router, VPN appliance, or firewall that sits at the perimeter of a network and does authentication, encapsulation, and encryption.

environmental management — Measures taken to reduce the risk to the physical environment where hardware and software are stored to protect them from storms, theft, or other disasters.

event — A specific request or response associated with an attempt to access a networked resource such as a dropped packet, a hangup, a response, and so on.

external interface — The interface that connects a router to an external network such as the Internet.

extranet — An extension of your corporate network to a new location.

failover firewall — A firewall that is designed to maintain connections in case a primary firewall stops working.

fingerprinting system — A system that creates and checks the signatures of application programs.

firewall — Hardware or software that monitors and records the transmission of data into and out of a network and that permits packets to pass based on rules.

firewall sandwich — A combination of two firewalls enclosed by two load balancing switches.

footer — A short section that tells a machine that the end of a packet has been reached.

fragment — An incomplete part of a packet that needs to be reassembled so that the packet can be processed.

frame relay — A telecommunications service that enables data to be transmitted in units called frames between endpoints in a wide area network or two points in a local area network.

fully qualified domain name (FQDN) — The complete DNS name of a computer, including the computer name, domain name, and domain name extension; example is *www.course.com*.

gateway — A point in a network through which data is allowed to pass.

Generally Accepted System Security Principles (GASSP) — A set of security and information management practices put forth by the International Information Security Foundation (I2SF).

hardened — A term used to describe a computer that has been secured by removing all unnecessary applications, file shares, permissions, and services and installing security software.

hash — An encrypted password created by an algorithm called a hash function that is used to protect information. A hash is also called a fingerprint or digest and can be used as part of a digital certificate.

hashed — Encryption using a complex formula called an algorithm.

header — The part of a packet that contains general information, such as the protocol and the source and destination IP addresses.

heartbeat network — A network that monitors the operation of the primary firewall and synchronizes the state table connections so the two firewalls have the same information at any given time.

heuristic analysis — A type of intrusion detection that looks for patterns of traffic that do not match what has been defined as "normal" network traffic.

high availability — The fact that a firewall or other system is up and running on a 24/7 basis or as close to this as possible.

holes — Vulnerable points in a network through which unauthorized users might be able to access supposedly protected resources.

honey pot — Something (a server or an Administrator account, for example) that is configured to intentionally attract hackers so that they can be identified and caught without causing any harm to your system.

host — Any hardware device (not just a desktop computer) that can access the Internet and communicate via a network; it also has an IP address.

hot standby — An approach to load balancing in which a secondary or failover firewall is configured to take over traffic duties in case the primary firewall fails.

hub-and-spoke configuration — A VPN configuration in which a single VPN router maintains records of all SAs; any device that wishes to participate in the VPN need only connect to the central router.

hybrid — A security method (for example, PGP) that uses both symmetric and asymmetric cryptography to obtain the advantages of both approaches.

hybrid firewall — A firewall that combines several different security methods, such as packet filtering, application-level gateways, and VPNs.

Hypertext Transport Protocol (HTTP) — The set of standards used to transmit data on the World Wide Web.

internal interface — The interface that connects a router to an internal network, such as a LAN, that it is protecting either on its own or with a firewall or other devices.

Internet Control Message Protocol (ICMP) — A protocol that handles error reporting and provides status information and limited control for Internet Protocol (IP).

Internet Engineering Task Force (IETF) — A group of individuals and organizations that seeks to keep the Internet running smoothly and safely.

Internet Key Exchange (IKE) — A protocol that generates security keys for IPSec and other protocols.

Internet Protocol Security (IPSec) — An IETF-standardized encryption protocol based on the IP protocol that encrypts IP header information and is used to authenticate computers.

Internet Security Association Key Management Protocol (ISAKMP) — An IPSec protocol that enables two computers to reach agreed-upon security settings and securely exchange security keys so they can communicate with encryption.

intranet — An internal network that uses Web servers, Web browsers, and other Internet-based software to enable communication and allow information to be shared.

intrusion detection system (IDS) — Software or hardware that detects whether a network or server has experienced an unauthorized access attempt and that sends notification to the appropriate network administrators.

IP address — A number that identifies a machine that is connected to the Internet and sends or receives information in the form of packets. The newest version of Internet Protocol, IPv6, provides for 128-bit IP addresses.

IP forwarding — A function that allows packets to be sent from one network interface to another. Many operating systems perform IP forwarding, as do routers.

IP Multicasting — A single data transmission that is sent to multiple recipients simultaneously.

IP Security (IPSec) — A set of security standards developed by the IETF and for the next version of IP—IPv6—as an optional extension to IP4. It is included in Windows 2000 and XP as well as many routers sold by Cisco Systems Inc. IPSec enables devices to connect in a secure manner. First, host and destination computers authenticate one another. Then data is transmitted using encryption.

IP spoofing — An attempt by a hacker to put a false IP source address into a packet header to make it seem legitimate and sneak it past the firewall.

IPSec Concentrator — A device that terminates VPN connections.

IPSec driver — Software that performs protocol-level tasks needed to encrypt, decrypt, authenticate, and verify packets.

IPSec Policy Agent — A Windows 2000 service that retrieves IPSec policy settings from Active Directory and applies them upon system start-up.

JavaScript — A low-level programming language that is primarily used to add functionality to Web pages.

Kerberos — A simple authentication method that uses a Key Distribution Center (KDC) to issue tickets to those who want to gain access to resources.

key — A value that can be processed by an algorithm to encrypt text or to decrypt text that has already been encrypted.

key server — A program that holds and distributes keys on a network.

Layer 2 Tunneling Protocol (L2TP) — An extension to Point-to-Point Protocol (PPP) that enables dial-up users to establish a VPN connection to a remote access server.

layer four switches — Network devices with the intelligence to make routing decisions based on source and destination IP address or port numbers as specified in layer four of the OSI Reference Model.

leased line — A connection used for network communications, such as a frame relay setup, that is leased from the telecommunications company that owns and operates it.

least privilege — The practice of designing operational aspects of a system to work with a minimal amount of system privilege.

Lightweight Directory Access Protocol (LDAP) — A database that holds names of users and digital certificates and is publicly available. Any client can connect to the database using LDAP to verify someone or something's identity.

listening — In computer systems, this generally is a term used for TCP or UDP ports. The ports on a system have the ability to listen to the network to see if traffic coming into the system is intended for that particular port.

load balancing — The practice of balancing the load placed on the firewall so that it is handled by two or more firewall systems.

load balancing switch — A hardware device that routes requests for information to the best Web server or cache available on a network, based on best response time and lightest load for the requested content.

load sharing — The practice of configuring two or more firewalls to share the total traffic load.

Local Area Network (LAN) — Two or more computers that are connected (either physically or by wireless communications) so that they can share files and communicate. Networked computers that are part of a LAN are usually in the same building or in physical proximity to one another.

log file — A file that contains information about accesses and events that have occurred on a server, operating system, or individual application.

man-in-the-middle attack — An attack in which a hacker intercepts the public key being exchanged by two individuals using encryption. The hacker substitutes his or her own public key to impersonate the recipient.

MD5 — An algorithm used to provide a 128-bit encrypted output called a message digest that is considered very secure.

MD5 signature — A unique number that is generated based on the contents of application programs.

Memorandum of Understanding (MOU) — An agreement in which various parties agree to observe rules of behavior governing network use and passwords.

mesh configuration — A VPN configuration that is used to connect multiple computers that each have a security association (SA) with all other machines in the VPN.

message digest — The encrypted data file that results from processing a message through an algorithm such as MD5.

mission-critical — The quality of being an integral, central part of an organization's core operations.

multifactor authentication — The use of two or more authentication tools (something the user knows, such as a password; something the user has, such as a smart card; and something physically associated with the user, such as a fingerprint) to identify remote users.

multihomed server — A server that has more than one network connection.

network — One or more computers connected and able to share information.

Network Access Point — A network exchange facility where Internet Service Providers (ISPs) can connect to one another and to a high-speed part of the Internet called the "Internet backbone."

Network Address Translation (NAT) — Offers a form of protection to internal (private) networks. An internal network can be configured with an IP address range that is not routable on the external (public) network. For internal users to communicate on the external network, a NAT device translates the user's private IP address to a public IP address.

network boundary — The point at which one network stops and another network begins.

network topology — The structure of how the computers and other devices within them are connected to one another. For instance, in a network with a star topology, the computers, printers, and other hardware are connected in a star pattern to a central server. In a bus topology the computers and other devices are connected in a line.

nonrepudiation — The use of encryption to prevent one participant in an electronic transaction

from denying that it performed an action. Nonrepudiation uses digital signatures to ensure that an electronic transaction occurred, that an action was performed by the legitimate originating party, and that the party that was supposed to receive something as a result of the transaction actually received that result.

Oakley — A protocol that uses the Diffie-Hellman algorithm to generate a master key as well as session-specific keys that can be used for IPSec communications.

one-time password — A password that is generated using a secret key and that is used only once, when the user authenticates. Different passwords are used for each authentication session.

Open Platform for Security (OPSEC) model — An application standard that is present in Check Point NG and that lets third-party vendors design their applications to work with Check Point NG. OPSEC lets you extend a firewall's functionality and integrate virus scanning into its set of abilities.

packet — Discrete chunks of digital information that are transmitted over the network.

packet filtering — A basic firewall function in which IP packet header information is screened, and decisions to allow or drop the packet are based on rules in the firewall's rule base.

packet filters — Block or allow transmission of packets of information based on criteria such as port, IP address, and protocol.

page file — An area of disk memory that is allocated for applications or data when RAM or other memory resources are running low.

parameters — Aspects of a filtering rule that enable an application (such as a proxy server) to determine how the rule is to be enforced; aspects might include length of time, the IP address of a host, and so on.

perimeter network — A screened subnet that connects to a firewall positioned at the perimeter of a protected network; same as screened subnet or DMZ.

Point-to-Point Protocol (PPP) — A protocol that enables computer users to establish a dial-up modem connection with a remote access server. PPP is still used to give many individuals dial-up access to the Internet.

Point-to-Point Protocol (PPP) over Secure Shell (SSH) — A protocol used to give UNIX users VPN access to a remote network by means of the UNIX secure shell, which uses secret key encryption to authenticate participants.

Point-to-Point Protocol (PPP) over Secure Sockets Layer (SSL) — A protocol used to give UNIX users VPN access to a remote network using SSL to encrypt data sent between client and server.

Point-to-Point Tunneling Protocol (PPTP) — A protocol developed by Microsoft for granting VPN access to remote users over dial-up connections; it has since been replaced by L2TP.

port — A virtual pathway through which data can pass. Each TCP/IP protocol is assigned its own port so that it won't interfere with other types of information.

Post Office Protocol, version 3 (POP3) — Protocol used to retrieve and organize mail from an e-mail server.

pre-shared key — A secret key that both parties must have beforehand to establish a secure VPN connection.

Pretty Good Privacy (PGP) — A personal encryption system developed by Phil Zimmerman that uses both symmetric and asymmetric encryption; it relies on a "Web of Trust" in which users authenticate one another by exchanging public keys.

private key — One of two keys used in public key cryptography. The private key is never exchanged but is used to generate a public key that can be exchanged freely on the Internet.

proprietary — A term used to describe something that is owned by a company and that can only be used in that company's products.

proxy server — A server that sits between a client and a server (usually between a client and a Web server). It intercepts all requests from the client to the Web server to see if it can fulfill the requests itself. If not, it forwards the request to the real server.

proxy service — *See* proxy server.

public key — One of two keys used in public key cryptography. Individuals who want to encrypt communications exchange their public keys and then use those keys to perform the encryption.

Public-Key Infrastructure (PKI) — A system used to store, distribute, and manage public and private keys within an organization.

Quality of Service (QoS) — A service that controls the amount of bandwidth available to a particular application or to a group of users.

Registration Authority (RA) — A networked resource that individuals can use to apply for digital certificates.

Remote Authentication Dial-In User Service (RADIUS) — A centralized dial-in authentication service that uses UDP. RADIUS is thought to provide a lower level of security than TACACS+, even though it's more widely supported.

reverse firewall — A firewall that has the primary responsibility of inspecting and monitoring traffic that leaves a local network rather than blocking incoming traffic. Such a firewall helps block Distributed Denial of Service (DDoS) attacks.

reverse proxy — A proxy server that is configured to monitor inbound rather than outbound traffic.

Rivest-Shamir-Adleman (RSA) encryption — Used for older versions of PGP.

rogue access point — An unauthorized access point that can compromise security.

rotate — Delete old log file entries and replace them with fresh entries.

router — A device that connects and directs traffic between networks.

routing table — A list of network addresses and corresponding gateway IP addresses that a router uses to direct traffic.

rules — Statements that tell a firewall which packets to allow and which to deny based on the packet's source IP address, protocol, or other characteristics.

SA table — A list of all the machines or individuals that have a security association (SA).

salt — A randomly generated value that is used to encrypt passwords in the Linux environment.

sandbox — A technology that creates a closed environment around an application and restricts its access to resources.

scale — The practice of expanding a system to meet a growing need.

screened subnet — A network that is exposed to an external network, such as the Internet, but that is partially protected by a firewall.

screening router — A router that filters traffic passing between one network and another.

Secure Shell (SSH) — A Unix-based protocol that enables secure access to a remote computer through a command interface.

security association (SA) — A relationship that enables two computers or individuals to trust one another and share information over a network.

security policy — A set of organization-level rules governing acceptable use of computing resources, security practices, and operational procedures.

security policy — The set of rules in a Check Point FireWall rule base. Also, a set of rules and procedures governing the use of network resources.

Security User Awareness program — A program that instructs employees on an organization's overall security policy.

security workstation — A machine dedicated to holding security policies, a firewall, and other security software for a corporation.

security_patch_check — A UNIX utility that automates the process of analyzing security patches that are already on the system and reporting on patches that should be added.

server-based digital certificates — Digital certificates issued by a CA to a company that issues them to individuals.

service network — A screened subnet that contains an organization's publicly accessible servers, such as its Web server or e-mail server.

Service-Level Agreement (SLA) — A document that defines an agreed-upon level of service that the host will provide.

session authentication — Authentication that is required any time the client establishes a session with a server or other networked resource. Authentication is done by software called a session authentication agent that resides on the client computer.

session hijacks — Attacks that involve a communication session that has already been established between a server and a client.

session keys — Symmetric keys that are used only for the duration of one communications session because of their efficiency.

shadow password system — A feature of the Linux operating system that enables the storage of passwords so they can't be discovered by unauthorized users who attempt to break into a system.

signatures — Patterns of behavior or technical values such as IP headers or flags that are used by IDS hardware or software to point to a particular type of attack.

Simple Mail Transport Protocol (SMTP) — Used to send mail between servers.

site-to-site VPN — A VPN that links two or more networks.

smart card — A card that contains embedded authentication information and that can be read by a card reader—for example, an ATM machine.

social engineering — A hacker obtains confidential information by contacting employees and deceiving them into giving up passwords, IP addresses, server names, and so on.

socket — A protocol used to establish TCP/IP network connections; a standard identifier that represents an established connection.

SOCKS — A protocol that applications can use for proxy servers when proxy servers don't exist for them.

source routing — A group of values in the Options field of an IP packet header that supply routing instructions. Gateways can use such instructions to send the packet to its destination. However, such instructions can easily be misused by a hacker and are often blocked by packet filters or firewalls.

specific sign-on — A type of client authentication in which the client is required to be authenticated each time the user wants to access a server or use a service.

split tunneling — The establishment of two connections over a single VPN line.

standard sign-on — A type of client authentication in which the client, after being authenticated, is given access to all network resources and the ability to perform all desired functions (copying, viewing Web pages, transferring files, and so on).

state table — A list of active connections maintained by a stateful packet filter. Such a filter allows only those packets that match the state table to pass through.

state update packets — Packets sent between primary and failover firewalls that contain information about the state of current network connections.

stateful failover — A situation in which a primary firewall stops functioning and a second firewall (the failover firewall) provides backup services by maintaining copies of the connection states that were in the primary firewall.

stateful inspection — The examination of the data contained in a packet; memory of the state of the connection between the client and the server is kept in disk cache.

stateful packet filtering — A type of packet filtering in which a firewall checks a state table to make sure a connection has actually been established before checking its rule base to decide whether to allow or block a packet.

stateless inspection — Occurs when a firewall inspects packet headers without paying attention to the state of the connection between the server and client computer.

stateless packet filtering — Packet filtering that determines whether to block or allow packets based on protocol type, IP address, port number, or other information, without regard to whether a connection has been established.

static IP address — An IP address that does not change, in contrast to a dynamic IP address that is generated by a server each time a computer connects to a network.

Static Network Address Port Translation (NAPT) — Makes use of static rather than dynamic IP addresses and conceals the source IP address and source port number when a packet leaves the public interface of a router or firewall.

static packet filter — When data arrives at an interface, static packet filters either allow or deny it based on information in the packet header only.

StuffIt — A popular application for the Macintosh that is used to compress and transport groups of files across a network or from one computer to another.

subnet — A collection of network devices that share a common network ID.

supervisor password — A password that is used to gain access to the BIOS set-up program, or to change the BIOS password.

symmetric key encryption — The use of only one key to encrypt information, rather than a public-private key system. The same key is used to encrypt and decrypt a message; both sender and recipient must have the same key.

syslog — A UNIX utility that records log messages to files.

Terminal Access Controller Access Control System (TACACS+) — TACACS+—commonly called "tac-plus"—is the latest and strongest version of a set of authentication protocols for dial-up access developed by Cisco Systems.

terminate — Drop or end a communication session.

terminator — A device that provides an endpoint for a VPN session, such as a router, a VPN appliance, or a firewall; *See* IPSec concentrator.

"three As" of computer forensics — *Acquire* the evidence without damaging or changing it in any way; be able to *authenticate* that the evidence is the same as the original seized data; and *analyze* the data without modifying it.

three-pronged firewall — A firewall that has three network interfaces connecting it to the external network, the DMZ, and the protected LAN.

Ticket-Granting Server (TGS) — An element in the Kerberos authentication system. The TGS accepts a TGT from a client and generates a session ticket, which gives the client access to requested services.

Ticket-Granting Ticket (TGT) — A part of the Kerberos authentication system; a random number is generated that is associated with the service being requested by a client. The session key serves as a TGT, which is presented to a TGS, which, in turn, grants a session ticket that permits access to the requested resources.

token — Any kind of physical object (a smart card, for example) that is used to identify someone on a network.

trailer — A short section that tells a machine that the end of a packet has been reached.

transport mode — One of two communications modes supported by IPSec. In transport mode, IPSec authenticates two computers that establish a connection. IPSec also encrypts communications in transport mode without using a tunnel.

tri-homed firewall — 1) A firewall that has interfaces with an internal protected network, a service network, and the Internet. 2) The use of two firewalls to set up three separate networks, the internal protected network; the external private network or service network, which includes Web and e-mail servers and other publicly accessible services; and the external network (the Internet or another branch network).

Trojan horse — A destructive program that acts as an innocent program until it is activated. Trojan horses have varying levels of destructive capabilities.

Trusted Computing Base (TCB) — A collection of software on UNIX, including the system kernel, that maintain relevant security information.

tunnel — A private network that uses a VPN client and VPN gateway to set up secure communications between two specific computers in different networks.

tunnel mode — One of two communications modes supported by IPSec. In tunnel mode, IPSec encapsulates IP packets and can optionally encrypt them.

tunnel server — A computer that enables VPN clients to connect to it based on their IP addresses.

two-factor authentication — A system that requires users to authenticate themselves by supplying two separate things—ideally, something they know (a password) and something they possess (an identification card).

Uniform Resource Locator (URL) — The address of a Web site.

up time — The time a server is online and available.

URI Filtering Protocol server — A server that filters and processes requests for URIs and that can work in conjunction with a firewall to do content filtering.

URL redirection — The ability of some proxy servers to key in on the host, file, or directory being requested, as listed in the HTTP header, and direct the request to a specific location.

user authentication — Basic authentication in which an individual user supplies a username and static password to access networked resources.

User Datagram Protocol (UDP) — A connectionless protocol, UDP is primarily used for broadcasting messages over a network.

virtual private network (VPN) — A system for point-to-point communications that encapsulates and encrypts data and uses authentication, and that uses the Internet to join users to a remote LAN.

viruses — A script or code that is placed on a machine without the knowledge of the machine's owner. The virus could be destructive, replicate itself, or perform any number of other malicious actions.

VPN appliance — A hardware device specially designed to terminate VPNs and join multiple LANs.

wipe — Remove all traces of a file from a disk permanently.

wireless access point — A device used to connect wireless computers to a wired network, and connect it to the wired network in an office.

worms — Programs or algorithms that replicate themselves over a computer network and that are usually malicious in action or intent. These actions can include using up the computer's resources or shutting down the system.

Zip archive — A compressed file that holds multiple files and that is created by the popular applications WinZip or Gzip.

Index